TIME
of the
MAGICIANS

TIME
of the
MAGICIANS

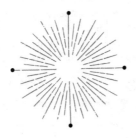

Wittgenstein, Benjamin, Cassirer, Heidegger,
AND THE **Decade That Reinvented Philosophy**

WOLFRAM
EILENBERGER

Translated by Shaun Whiteside

PENGUIN PRESS | NEW YORK | 2020

PENGUIN PRESS
An imprint of Penguin Random House LLC
penguinrandomhouse.com

Originally published in German as *Zeit der Zauberer* by Klett-Cotta, Stuttgart

Pages 397 and 399 constitute an extension of this copyright page.

LIBRARY OF CONGRESS CATALOGING-IN-PUBLICATION DATA

Names: Eilenberger, Wolfram, 1972– author. | Whiteside, Shaun, translator.
Title: Time of the magicians : Wittgenstein, Benjamin,
Cassirer, Heidegger, and the decade that reinvented philosophy /
Wolfram Eilenberger ; translated by Shaun Whiteside.
Other titles: Zeit der Zauberer. English
Description: New York : Penguin Press, 2020. | Translation of: Zeit der Zauberer.
Stuttgart : Klett-Cotta, c2018. | Includes bibliographical references and index.
Identifiers: LCCN 2019050893 (print) | LCCN 2019050894 (ebook) |
ISBN 9780525559665 (hardcover) | ISBN 9780525559672 (ebook)
Subjects: LCSH: Philosophy, German—History—20th century. |
Germany—History—1918–1933.
Classification: LCC B3181 .E5513 2020 (print) |
LCC B3181 (ebook) | DDC 193—dc23
LC record available at https://lccn.loc.gov/2019050893
LC ebook record available at https://lccn.loc.gov/2019050894

Printed in the United States of America
1 3 5 7 9 10 8 6 4 2

Designed by Alexis Farabaugh

The best that we have from history is
the enthusiasm that it stimulates.

Johann Wolfgang von Goethe,
Maxims and Reflections

CONTENTS

I.

PROLOGUE: THE MAGICIANS

1

The Arrival of God • High Fliers • Maintaining One's Composure
The Davos Myth • Human Questions • Without Foundation
Two Visions • At a Crossroads • Where Is Benjamin?
Fail Better • Does My Life Need a Goal? • The One-Man Republic

II.

LEAPS: 1919

29

What to Do? • A Refuge • Critical Days • Romantic Theses
New Self-Awareness • Flights • The Transformation • Ethical Acts
A Sorrow Beyond Dreams • An Interesting Condition
Exposed Flanks • A World Without a View • The Primal Scientist
No Alibi • The New Realm • Fidelity to the Event
German Virtues • Unloved • Electrified

III.

LANGUAGES: 1919–1920

61

Figuratively Speaking • Viennese Bridges • Poetic Precision
Against the World • Three Dots in The Hague
Pictures of Facts • The Barber • Russell on the Ladder
Why the World Does Not Exist • Under Pressure
The Obscured Gaze • Lonely Together • Two Oddballs
Worlds Ahead • The Breakthrough of Authenticity
Something in Media • Flappers • The Task
Radical Translation • Cult and Sound • Goethe in Hamburg
The Fundamental Phenomenon • The Will to Multiplicity
Onward • Does *the* Language Exist?

IV.

CULTURE: 1922–1923

115

A Hut of One's Own • Strange Callings • Existential Health Check
Stormy Weather • Wars of Attrition • Bad Neighbors
Good Neighbors • Utopia on the Bookshelf • The Outcome of Myth
The New Enlightenment • Across the River
In the Maelstrom • The Third Man • Goethe in Weimar
More Light • Freedom or Fate • Choice or Decision
The Divorced Republic • Leap of Salvation
Redeeming Transcendence • Ruthlessness
Three-Quarters Understood • In Therapy • Top Down

V.

YOU: 1923–1925

163

The Idiot • It's Complicated • Hospitality

From Hamburg to Bellevue • Snake Experiments

Tunnel and Light • Weimar Topples • Mighty Fortresses

Being an Event • You, Demon • In the Midst of Being

To Think the Hardest Thing • Amor Mundi • Hunger Cures

Goodbye Deutschland • Grapes and Almonds • New Beginnings

VI.

FREEDOM: 1925–1927

205

Red Stars • Critical Prologues • A Case for Adam

Grief Work • Remembered Perception • Tristes Tropiques

Critical Album • Palestine or Communism • Neighbors

To Work • Exposing the Question

The Time of Dasein

Philosophizing with a Hammer: The Study of Equipment

Sturm und Angst

That Certain Something: Running Ahead into Death

The Hamburg School • The Hidden Origin

Plurality of Outcome • Self-Fashioning Through Openness

The Fault in Our Stars • Out of the Mouths of Babes

Engineers of Speech • A Little List • The Responsibility Principle

A Fainting Fit

VII.

ARCADES: 1926–1928

263

Technical Talent • For Gods Alone

A Circle Without a Master • Much to Learn You Still Have

Instability • Moscow or Bust • The Hell of Other People

A Man Without a Framework • Party for One • High Seas

In the Eye of the Storm • An Emergency in Frankfurt

Individual and Republic • Building Work • Age of the Demon

After Being • Foundation and Abyss

Back to the Origin • Homecoming • Dizzy Heights

VIII.

TIME: 1929

317

Slaloming • Among People • On the Eve • Relax!

Verbal Storms: The Davos Debate • Licking Wounds

Spring Awakenings • The Three-Hundred-Penny Opera

The Doors • Breathless • Gaslight • The Self-Destructive Personality

Hot Dogs • The Hiker • A Day Off

Internal Difficulties • Back to the Everyday

Naples in Cambridge • Useful Reminders

The City of Words • Against the Wall

Epilogue   363

Acknowledgments   367

List of Works   369

Notes   373

Selected Bibliography   387

Photograph Credits   397

Index   401

I.

PROLOGUE
THE MAGICIANS

THE ARRIVAL OF GOD

D ON'T WORRY, I know you'll never understand it." This sentence concluded what was probably the most peculiar oral exam in the history of philosophy. Appearing for his doctoral examination at Cambridge on June 18, 1929, before a panel consisting of Bertrand Russell and G. E. Moore, was a forty-year-old former multimillionaire from Austria who had for the previous ten years been working chiefly as a primary school teacher.[1] His name was Ludwig Wittgenstein. Wittgenstein wasn't some obscure returning Cambridge student. On the contrary, from 1911 until just before the outbreak of the First World War, he had studied there with Russell and had quickly become a cult figure, known for both his obvious brilliance and his waywardness. "Well, God has arrived, I met him on the 5:15 train," John Maynard Keynes wrote in a letter dated January 18, 1929. Keynes, at the time probably the most important economist in the world, met Wittgenstein by chance the day after his return to England. It says a great deal about the intimate, rumor-filled atmosphere of university life at the time that Wittgenstein's old friend G. E. Moore was on the same train from London to Cambridge.

But it would be a mistake to think that the atmosphere in the compartment was entirely convivial. Wittgenstein at least was not given to small talk or other social niceties. The genius from Vienna was prone to sudden outbursts of fury, and could be extremely unforgiving. A single word out of place or jocular observation could lead to years of rancor, indeed to a break-down in relations—as had happened several times with Keynes and Moore. However: God was back! And accordingly, joy was unconfined.

The next day, a meeting of the "Apostles"—a highly elitist, unofficial students' club notorious at the university for the sexual proclivities of its members—was called in Keynes's house to welcome the prodigal son.[2] At a ceremonial dinner Wittgenstein was promoted to the rank of "Angel," an honorary senior member of the society. Most of the group's members hadn't met for more than a decade. A lot had happened in the meantime, but to the Apostles, Wittgenstein appeared almost unchanged. It wasn't just that he was wearing his typical outfit of an open-necked shirt, gray flannel trousers, and heavy, agricultural-looking boots. Physically, too, the years seemed to have passed without leaving a trace. At first sight, he looked like one of the gifted students who had also been invited, and who had previously known the strange man from Austria only from their pro-fessors' stories. And, of course, that he was the author of the *Tractatus logico-philosophicus*, the legendary work that had shaped, if not actually dominated, philosophical discussion in Cambridge for several years. None of those present would have claimed that they had even begun to under-stand the book, but this fact only boosted its fascination.

Wittgenstein had finished the book in 1918 as a prisoner of war in Italy, convinced that he had found the solution to philosophical questions *"on all essential points,"* and thus decided to turn his back on the discipline. Only a few months later, as the heir to one of the wealthiest industrial families in Europe, he transferred his entire inheritance to his siblings. As he told Russell in a letter at the time, from now on—plagued as he was by severe depression and thoughts of suicide—he would support himself "with hon-est toil." He would become a teacher at a provincial primary school.

Wittgenstein was back in Cambridge. Back, it was said, to philosophize. The genius, now forty years old, had no academic title and was utterly penniless. The little money that he had managed to save lasted only a few weeks in England. Cautious inquiries about the willingness of his siblings to help him out financially were intemperately dismissed. "Will you please accept my written declaration that not only I have a number of wealthy relations, but also that they would give me money if I asked them to. BUT THAT I WILL NOT ASK THEM FOR A PENNY," Wittgenstein wrote to Moore the day before his oral examination.[3]

What was to be done? No one in Cambridge doubted Wittgenstein's exceptional gifts. Everyone, including the most influential figures at the university, wanted to keep him there. But without an academic title, it proved institutionally impossible to find a research grant, let alone a regular teaching post, for the former dropout, even in the clubby atmosphere of Cambridge.

In the end they hatched a plan: Wittgenstein would submit the *Tractatus logico-philosophicus*, his first and so far his only book, as a doctoral thesis. Russell had personally advocated for its publication in 1921–1922, and had written a foreword to help the process along, since he considered the work of his former pupil far superior to his own groundbreaking studies in the philosophy of logic, mathematics, and language. No wonder, then, that upon entering the examination room Russell swore that he had "never known anything so absurd in my life."[4] Still: an exam is an exam, and after a few minutes of friendly inquiry Moore and Russell started asking some serious questions. These concerned one of the central riddles of the *Tractatus*, a book not exactly short on opaque aphorisms and mystical one-liners. Take, for example, the very first sentence of the work, strictly organized according to a decimal system: "1. The world is everything that is the case."

Take also entries like: "6:432. How the world is, is completely indifferent for what is higher. God does not reveal himself in the world." Or: "6:44. Not *how* the world is, is the mystical, but *that* it is."

The fundamental impulse behind the book is nonetheless clear: Wittgenstein's *Tractatus* stands in a long tradition of modern philosophy such as Spinoza's *Ethics*, Hume's *An Enquiry into Human Understanding*, and Kant's *Critique of Pure Reason*. All of these attempt to draw a boundary between the propositions in our language, which are truly meaningful and thus capable of truth, and those that only seem meaningful, and because of that very illusoriness lead our thought and culture astray. In other words, the *Tractatus* is a therapeutic contribution to the question of what one can meaningfully talk about as a human being and what one cannot. It is no coincidence that the book ends with the aphorism "7. Whereof one cannot speak, thereof one must remain silent." And just before that, under entry 6:54, Wittgenstein reveals his own therapeutic method: "My propositions are elucidatory in this way: he who understands me finally recognizes them as senseless, when he has climbed out through them, on them, over them. (He must so to speak throw away the ladder, after he has climbed up on it.) He must surmount these propositions, then he sees the world rightly."

In the oral examination, Russell now focused on this very point. How precisely was that to happen? How can someone be helped through a sequence of nonsense propositions to a—the—correct vision of the world? Had Wittgenstein not expressly said in the preface to his book that "the truth of the thoughts communicated here" seems to him to be "unassailable and definitive"? How could that be so if the work, by the author's own account, consisted almost entirely of nonsense propositions?

The question was not new to Wittgenstein. Certainly not from Russell's lips. Over the years and throughout their lengthy correspondence it had become almost a ritual in their tense friendship. Hence, once again, in Wittgenstein's oral exam, "for old times' sake," Russell asked his question.

Unfortunately, we don't know what Wittgenstein said in his defense. We can assume that he spoke with his usual slight stammer, his eyes glowing, and with an idiosyncratic intonation that sounded less like the English tongue in a foreign mouth than the speech of someone attuned to a different significance and musicality in human language. And eventually, after several minutes of halting monologue, always in search of an elucidatory formulation—that, too, was Wittgenstein's manner—he would have concluded that he had spoken and explained enough. It was simply impossible to make everything comprehensible to every human being. He had said as much in the preface to the *Tractatus*: "This book will perhaps be understood only by those who have already thought the thoughts which are expressed in it—or similar thoughts."

The only problem was (and Wittgenstein knew it) that there were very few people, perhaps not a single one, who had thought and thus formulated similar thoughts. Not Bertrand Russell, author of the *Principia Mathematica*, which, in the end, Wittgenstein considered philosophically limited. And certainly not G. E. Moore, regarded as one of the most brilliant thinkers and logicians of his time, who, according to Wittgenstein, "shows you how far a man can go who has absolutely no intelligence whatsoever."

How was he to explain the ladder of nonsense thoughts that one had first to climb and then push away in order to see the world as it really is? Hadn't the wise man from Plato's cave, once he had reached the light, failed to make his insights comprehensible to the others still trapped deep inside?

Enough for today. Enough explanations. Wittgenstein stands up, walks around the table, claps Moore and Russell cordially on the shoulder, and utters the sentence that all aspiring doctors of philosophy must dream about the night before their oral exams: "Don't worry, I know you'll never understand it."

That was the end of the performance. It was left to Moore to write the examination report: "In my opinion this is a work of genius; it is in any case up to the requirements of a degree from Cambridge."[5]

The research grant was authorized shortly afterward. Wittgenstein, God, had arrived back in philosophy.

HIGH FLIERS

ON MARCH 17 of the same year, Martin Heidegger must have felt that he, too, had arrived, in the grander sense of the word, when he stepped into the banqueting hall of the Grand Hôtel Belvédère in Davos. From his youth in the Black Forest, he had seen his ascent to these intellectual heights as a matter of destiny. Nothing was to be left to chance. Not his slim, almost athletic, suit, which set him apart from the dignitaries in their traditional tails, not the severely combed-back hair, not his rustic tan, not his late arrival in the hall, and certainly not his choice to mingle with the crowd of students and researchers in the belly of the hall rather than take the seat reserved for him in the front row. Adherence to convention was out of the question, because for Heidegger there could be no philosophizing in falsehood. And just about everything in this kind of learned assembly in a luxurious Swiss hotel must have seemed fake to him.

The previous year Albert Einstein had delivered the opening lecture at the Davos University Conferences. In 1929, at age thirty-nine, Heidegger was one of the main speakers. Over the coming days he would deliver three lectures and, by way of conclusion, engage in a public debate with Ernst Cassirer, the other heavyweight philosopher present. While the venue might have displeased him, the validation and recognition that came with it stirred Heidegger's deepest wishes.[6]

Only two years previously, in the spring of 1927, his *Being and Time* had been published, and it was acknowledged within a few months as a milestone in the annals of thought. With this the sexton's son from Messkirch in Baden had established a reputation, in the words of his then student (and lover) Hannah Arendt, as the "secret king" of German-language philosophy. Heidegger had written the book in 1926 under enormous time pressure—and in fact it was only half finished. With it he had set the stage for his return from unloved Marburg to his Freiburg alma mater, where, in 1928, Heidegger assumed the prestigious chair of his former teacher and patron, the phenomenologist Edmund Husserl.

If John Maynard Keynes had captured something of Wittgenstein's transcendent otherworldliness with the title of "God," Arendt's choice of the term "king" is also revealing. The will to power and social dominance that it implies were immediately apparent to all who met Heidegger. Wherever he appeared, wherever he turned up, Heidegger was never one among many. In the banqueting hall at Davos he staked out this claim once again with his refusal to take his assigned place among the other professors of philosophy. People whispered, muttered, and even turned around to look: there's Heidegger.

Now things could begin.

MAINTAINING
ONE'S COMPOSURE

ERNST CASSIRER WOULD HAVE EXCUSED himself from the general muttering and murmuring in the hall. Don't let anything show: keep up appearances—and above all maintain composure. That was his motto. It was also the core of his philosophy. And what, after all, did he have to fear? The bustle and ceremony of a large academic conference were hardly new. The fifty-four-year-old professor had held his chair at the University of Hamburg for the past ten years, and for the winter semester of 1929–1930 he would even hold the rectorate there—only the fourth Jew in the history of all German universities to do so. The son of an affluent Breslau business-man, he was similarly familiar from earliest childhood with the etiquette of Swiss luxury hotels. He spent the summer months, as members of his circle tended to do, in the Swiss Alps taking a spa cure with his wife, Toni. Above all, 1929 marked the height of Cassirer's fame, the zenith of his career. Over the previous ten years he had committed his *Philosophy of Symbolic Forms* to paper. The encyclopedic breadth and systematic originality of the work— the third and final volume of which had appeared only a few weeks before the meeting in Davos—established Cassirer as the undisputed head of neo-Kantian philosophy, then predominant in the German academy.

Unlike Heidegger's, Cassirer's rise to preeminence had not been meteoric. Instead his reputation had grown steadily over the decades he dedicated to editorial labor and the production of histories of modern philoso-phy. He was known not for any charismatic or linguistic boldness, but for his extraordinary erudition and almost superhuman memory: when called upon, he could quote by heart whole pages from the great classics of philos-ophy and literature. Cassirer was almost notorious for his balance and his commitment to mediation and moderation. In Davos he represented—and was aware of playing this role—precisely the form of philosophizing, and the academic establishment that practiced and endorsed it, that Heidegger was determined to shake up. The photograph of the opening celebration shows Cassirer—second row, on the left—sitting beside his wife, Toni. His full head of hair is dignified and white, his gaze concentrated on the speaker's lectern. The chair in front of him is empty. A piece of paper stuck to the back of the chair identifies it as *"réservé"*: Heidegger's seat.

THE DAVOS MYTH

HEIDEGGER'S INFRINGEMENTS OF DAVOS ETIQUETTE were not entirely without effect. Toni Cassirer was so disturbed by the meeting that in her memoirs, written in 1948 when she was in exile in New York, she misdates it by a full two years.[7] In her memoirs she describes a "short man, entirely unremarkable, black hair and piercing dark eyes," who immediately reminded her—a businessman's daughter from the upper tiers of Viennese society—"of a craftsman, perhaps from southern Austria or Bavaria," an impression that was "further supported by his accent" at the subsequent gala dinner. Even then she saw clearly the force that her husband would soon be dealing with: "Heidegger's tendency toward anti-Semitism," she concluded, "was not unfamiliar to us."

Today the debate between Ernst Cassirer and Martin Heidegger at Davos is understood as a crucial event in the history of thought, even a "parting of the ways for twentieth-century philosophy," in the words of the American philosopher Michael Friedman.[8] Seemingly all present were aware of witnessing a profound shift in philosophy, the close of one era and the ushering in of another. Otto F. Bollnow, Heidegger's student and later an avowed Nazi, for example, described in his diary the "elevating feeling . . . of having witnessed a historical moment, just as Goethe said in his *Campaign in France*: 'A new era in world history begins here today'—in this case philosophical history—and you can say you were there."[9]

This rings true. If Davos had not happened, future historians of ideas would have had to invent it. Even in its smallest details, this historic summit captures the trajectory and most formative events of a whole decade. The son of a Jewish industrialist, originally from Breslau, now from Berlin, faced the Catholic sexton's son from the provinces of Baden. Hanseatic composure and restraint encountered forthright peasant manners and directness. Cassirer was the hotel; Heidegger the hut. When they met under the bright midday sun, the worlds for which they each stood were superimposed in a way that seemed unreal.

It was the insular, dreamlike atmosphere of a sanatorium at Davos that had inspired Thomas Mann to write *The Magic Mountain*, which was deemed to express the spirit of an era when it was published in 1924. The Davos debate four years later might therefore even have seemed to the participants like a realization of a fiction, and indeed Cassirer and Heidegger mirror with an almost uncanny precision the ideological struggle between Lodovico Settembrini and Leo Naphta.

HUMAN QUESTIONS

THE THEME CHOSEN by the organizers of the Davos meeting sounded appropriately revolutionary: "What is a human being?" The question was a leitmotif in the philosophy of Immanuel Kant. Kant's entire corpus of thought proceeds from an observation as simple as it is irrefutable: Humans are beings who ask themselves questions that they are ultimately unable to answer. In particular, these questions often address the existence of God, the conundrum of human freedom, and the immortality of the soul. According to a first approximation of a definition, then, a human is for Kant a *metaphysical being*.

What conclusions can be drawn from this? For Kant, these metaphysical riddles, precisely because they cannot be conclusively answered, open up a horizon of potential perfection. They guide us in our efforts to bring as much as possible into experience (cognition), to act with as much free-dom and self-determination as possible (ethics), to prove as worthy as pos-sible of possible immortality (religion). In this context Kant speaks of a *regulative* or a leading function of metaphysical inquiry.

Until the 1920s, Kant's premises remained crucial to German-language philosophy—indeed to modern philosophy as a whole. Philosophizing meant, not least for Cassirer and Heidegger, thinking in the wake of these questions. And the same went for the aforementioned attempts, with their logical orientation, by Ludwig Wittgenstein to draw a firm boundary between that of which one can and cannot speak. Crucially, however, Wittgenstein in the *Tractatus* forayed beyond Kant in considering the fun-damental human impulse to ask metaphysical questions—and hence to philosophize—as amenable to treatment, and in using experimentally the methods of philosophy as a kind of therapy. So, for example, he writes in the *Tractatus*:

6:5 When the answer cannot be put into words, neither can the ques-tion be put into words. The riddle does not exist. If a question can be framed at all, it is also possible to answer it.

6:51 Doubt can exist only where a question exists, a question only where an answer exists, and an answer only where something can be said.

6:53 The correct method of philosophy would really be the following: to say nothing except what can be said, i.e. propositions of natural science—i.e. something that has nothing to do with philosophy—and then, whenever someone else wanted to say something metaphysical, to demonstrate to him that he had failed to give a meaning to certain signs in his propositions.

It was typically hoped at the time that metaphysical questions could finally be left behind, that they had been superseded by the spirit of logic and natural science, which appeared ascendant. These aspirations were on display in the work of many participants at the Davos conference, including the Privatdozent (unsalaried lecturer at a German university) Rudolf Carnap, then thirty-eight years old and the author of books with such programmatic titles as *The Logical Construction of the World* and *Pseudo-Problems in Philosophy* (both 1928). After immigrating to the United States in 1937, Carnap became one of the leading lights in the "analytic philosophy" movement that sprang from Wittgenstein's works.

WITHOUT FOUNDATION

REGARDLESS OF THE TENDENCY or school with which the philosophers at Davos aligned themselves—idealism, humanism, *Lebensphilosophie*, phenomenology, or logicism—they were in agreement on one essential point: The view of the world and above all the scientific foundation on which Kant had once erected his impressive philosophical system had been undermined, or at least were in need of significant reform. Kant's *Critique of Pure Reason* was clearly based, not least in its understanding of space and time, on the physics of the eighteenth century. But Einstein's theory of relativity (1905) had displaced the Newtonian model. Space and time could no longer be considered independent of each other, nor were they in an identifiable sense a priori, based on theoretical deduction rather than experience. Darwin's theory of evolution had already swept away the idea of human nature as eternally unchanging, as something that did not develop over time. With Darwin's theory of natural selection, which would be influentially translated by Nietzsche from nature into the field of culture, the prospect of a teleological, reason-based account of history was rendered implausible. The complete transparency of human consciousness to itself—a starting point of Kant's transcendental method of investigation— was no longer self-evident by the time of Freud. More than anything else, however, the horrors of anonymized killing on an industrial scale in the First World War stripped all credibility from Enlightenment rhetoric about the civilizing progress of humanity, and the power of culture, science, and technology to realize this process. The political and economic crises that followed the war made the question "What is a human being?" more urgent than ever, even as the foundations of the accepted answer were deemed structurally unsound.

The philosopher Max Scheler—the author of *The Human Place in the Cosmos* (1928)—captured this sense of crisis in one of his last lectures: "In the roughly ten thousand years of history, ours is the first period when man has become completely and totally problematical to himself, when he no longer knows what he is, but at the same time knows that he knows nothing."[10]

This was the backdrop to Cassirer and Heidegger's meeting on the mountain at Davos. Over the previous decade that backdrop had inspired both thinkers to create their most significant works. Bur rather than attempt to directly answer Kant's question "What is a human being?" Cassirer and Heidegger concentrated on the tacit question that lay behind it, and it is there that their originality is to be found.

Humans are beings who must ask themselves questions that they are unable to answer. Fine. But what conditions must in fact exist so that they can actually ask themselves these questions? How is that asking possible? What is the source of this capacity to ask questions about questions? Cassirer's and

Heidegger's answers are to be found in the titles of their main works, *The Philosophy of Symbolic Forms* and *Being and Time*, respectively.

TWO VISIONS

ACCORDING TO CASSIRER, the human being is above all a sign-using and sign-making creature—an *animal symbolicum*. In other words, we give ourselves and our world meaning, support, and orientation through the use of signs. Our most important sign system is our mother tongue. But there are many other sign systems—*symbolic forms* in Cassirer's terminology—those of myth, art, mathematics, or music. These symbols, be they linguistic, pictorial, acoustic, or gestural, are never self-explanatory; they need interpretation by other human beings. The process by which signs are placed into the world, interpreted, and augmented by others is the process of culture, and it is the ability to use signs that enables human beings to ask metaphysical questions, indeed any questions, about themselves and the world. For Cassirer, Kant's *Critique of Pure Reason* becomes an investigation of the formal symbolic systems with which we give meaning to ourselves and our world and thus is really a *Critique of Culture* in all its inevitably contradictory breadth and diversity.

Heidegger, too, stresses the importance of the medium of language in human existence. He sees the actual foundation for humanity's metaphysical essence as lying not in a distributed system of signs, however, but in a distinctly individual feeling—anxiety. More precisely, the anxiety that grips individuals when they become fully aware that their existence is essentially finite. Knowledge of one's own finitude, which defines human beings as "existence (Dasein) thrown into the world," inaugurates the task of grasping and realizing one's own possibilities of being, of working toward a goal that Heidegger calls *authenticity*. Humanity's form of being is further distinguished by its ineluctable subjection to time. On the one hand because of the unique historical situation into which its existence has been thrown unasked, and on the other because of the knowledge that that existence has of its finitude.

For that reason, in Heidegger's view, the sphere of culture and the use of sign systems identified by Cassirer distracts human beings from their finitude and hence from the goal of authenticity, and it is the role of philosophy to keep human beings open to the true abysses of their anxiety and thus, in an authentic sense, to liberate them.

AT A CROSSROADS

KANT'S OLD QUESTION of what a human being is leads to one of two fundamentally contradictory ideals of cultural and indeed of political development, depending on whether we attempt to answer it in terms of Cassirer's or Heidegger's thought. It is the declaration of a belief in the equal humanity of all sign-using beings as against the elitist courage of authenticity; the hope that our deepest anxieties can be tamed by the civilizing process as against the demand for as radical as possible a struggle to defeat those anxieties; a belief in the pluralism of cultural forms and diversity as against the sense of the necessary loss of self in a sphere of superabundance; the idea of a moderating continuity as against a total break with the past and a new beginning.

When Cassirer and Heidegger met at ten o'clock in the morning on March 26, 1929, each of them was able to claim that, with their respective philosophies, they embodied whole world-images. What was at stake in

Davos, then, was the contest between two fundamentally opposed visions of the development of modern human beings, visions whose force and appeal continue to shape and determine our culture from within even today.

The students and researchers present at Davos had for the most part delivered their judgment even before the debate took place ten days into the conference. Predictably, the conflict had a generational dimension and the junior philosophers strongly favored the young Heidegger. It couldn't have helped that Cassirer, as if acting out the obsolescence of his bourgeois conception of culture, spent most of the conference convalescing in his hotel room, while Heidegger spent every spare minute on his skis, dashing down the *pistes noires* of the Grison Alps with the Young Turks of the student body.

WHERE IS BENJAMIN?

IN THE SPRING of the miraculous year when Cassirer and Heidegger met to set out the future of humanity on the peak of Davos, in the metropolis of Berlin the independent journalist and author Walter Benjamin was troubled by concerns of a quite different order. Benjamin's lover, the Latvian theater director Asja Lacis, had just evicted him from the love nest they had rented on Düsseldorfer Strasse, and he was—once again—forced to return to his parental home on Delbrückstrasse, where his mother lay on her deathbed, and his wife, Dora, and their eleven-year-old son, Stefan, were waiting for him. The sordid sequence—of rapturous love followed by financial imprudence and, all too swiftly, the end of the liaison—was by now familiar to all involved. This time, however, Benjamin exacerbated matters by informing Dora of his irrevocable decision to request a divorce, with a view to marrying the Latvian lover who had just left him.

One might be tempted to pluck Benjamin from this predicament and place him instead at the Davos conference. It's not implausible: he might have attended as a correspondent for the *Frankfurter Zeitung* or the *Literarische Welt*, for which he regularly reviewed. We might now imagine him, a chronic wallflower, clutching his black notepad in the hindmost corner of the ballroom (*"Keep your notebook as strictly as the authorities keep their register of aliens"*), straightening his metal-rimmed glasses with their jam-jar-thick lenses and recording in tiny spidery handwriting his observations. His pen could have glossed the pattern of the carpets or the sofa covers, say, and then, with a swift stab at the cut of Heidegger's suit, lamented the fundamental poverty of the spirit of the age—a time in which philosophers celebrated the *"simple life"* and, Heidegger chief among them, cultivated a *"rustic style of language"* characterized by a *"delight in the most violent archaisms"* and thus seemed to *"appropriate for himself the sources of linguistic life."* Perhaps he would then have turned his attention to the armchair in the drawing room, in which the *"comfortable man"* Cassirer would later make himself cozy, and allow it to represent the dusty staleness of an entire intellectual enterprise, the respectable bourgeois philosophy that still believed in forcing the diversity of the modern world into the corset of a unified system. Outwardly, Benjamin resembled a perfect hybrid of Heidegger and Cassirer. He was, like Cassirer, inclined to sudden fevers, and almost ludicrously unathletic. Though he was short in stature, Benjamin's presence was unmistakable, and he had a worldly air that people immediately found attractive.

The primary subjects of discussion at Davos were in fact central to his work: the transformation of Kantian philosophy against the backdrop of a new technological age, the metaphysical nature of ordinary language, the crisis in academic philosophy, the internal conflict within modern consciousness and perception of time, the increasing commercialization of urban existence, the search for salvation in times of total social collapse . . . Who had written about these subjects over the previous years, if not Benjamin? Why had no one sent him to Davos? Or to be blunt: Why had he not been invited as a speaker?

The answer is simply that in 1929, from the point of view of any academic philosopher, Walter Benjamin was a nonentity. He had tried to find employment at many different universities (Bern, Heidelberg, Frankfurt, Cologne, Göttingen, Hamburg, and Jerusalem) over the years and had failed each and every time, sometimes because of adverse circumstances, sometimes because of anti-Semitic prejudices, but mostly because of his own chronic indecisiveness.

In 1919, when he graduated summa cum laude from Bern University with a dissertation on the "Concept of Art Criticism in German Romanticism," all doors seemed open to him. His doctoral supervisor, Richard Herbertz, professor of German, told him a paid teaching post was within his grasp. But Benjamin hesitated, argued with his own father, and squandered his chance; eventually he opted to live as an independent critic. Over the next ten years he repeatedly attempted to divert back to the path not taken and establish a career within the academy, not least because of the realization of how difficult it would be for someone who lived as he did to continue on his present course. In those years, being Benjamin was a costly business. Along with his insatiable appetite for restaurants, nightclubs, casinos, and houses of pleasure, he developed a passion for collecting curiosities, such as antique children's books, which he tracked down all over Europe and bought almost compulsively.

Without his family home, the life of a journalist, even one who was hardly underemployed—the newspaper market in Germany exploded in the 1920s, and with it the demand for reviews—was for Benjamin therefore characterized by permanent financial insecurity. Whenever things began to get tight, the allure of the university grew: an academic office would supply him with the necessities of life and enable him to support his young, much-traveled family—the two things this profoundly conflicted thinker both longed for and feared.

FAIL BETTER

IN 1925, BENJAMIN'S ACADEMIC AMBITIONS reached their nadir with his postdoctoral dissertation (*Habilitation* in German) at Frankfurt University. At the suggestion of Benjamin's only advocate at the institution, the sociologist Gottfried Salomon (one of the future main organizers of the Davos conferences), Benjamin handed in a work titled *The Origin of German Tragic Drama*. At first glance it was an attempt to incorporate the tradition of the Baroque tragedy into the canon of German literature. For its "Epistemo-Critical Prologue," the work is recognized today as a milestone of twentieth-century philosophy and literary theory. At the time, however, the expert assessors appointed by the university were completely overwhelmed by its weight and impenetrability. After an initial review, they urgently requested that its author voluntarily withdraw; the alternative was formal failure at the hands of the examination committee.

Even this humiliating ultimatum did not lead Benjamin to abandon the idea of university completely. In the winter of 1927–1928, with the assistance of his friend and patron the author Hugo von Hofmannsthal, he sought to join the so-called Warburg School around Erwin Panofsky and Ernst Cassirer, with disastrous results. Panofsky's response to Hofmannsthal's overture was so crushingly negative that Benjamin had to apologize to his advocate for having involved him in the first place. Particularly galling for Benjamin would have been the knowledge that Cassirer must have been aware of the fiasco; as a student in Berlin in 1912–1913, he had eagerly attended the lectures of the then Privatdozent. These circles were tight and advocates were everything, but Benjamin was generally seen as a hopeless case: his approach was too independent, his style too unconventional, his day job too journalistic, and his theories so original as to be indecipherable.

In fact, the ballroom in Davos—and this would certainly not have escaped Benjamin as a correspondent—formed a sort of gallery of all his academic humiliations, crowned by the presence of Martin Heidegger, whom Benjamin profoundly hated. In 1913 and 1914 they had both attended the Freiburg seminars of the neo-Kantian Heinrich Rickert (later Heidegger's thesis supervisor). Since then Benjamin had attentively followed Heidegger's rise with no small amount of envy. In 1929 he planned, not for the first time, to set up a magazine (working title: *Krise und Kritik*, or "Crisis and Criticism"), whose mission, as he confided to Bertolt Brecht, his friend and prospective cofounder of the journal, was the "demolition of Heidegger." But in the end nothing came of that, either. Another experiment, another plan nipped in the bud.

By the age of thirty-seven, Benjamin could look back on dozens of large-scale failures. Over the previous decade spent juggling different roles—freelance philosopher, journalist, and critic—he had above all been an inexhaustible source of abortive projects. Whether attempts to found journals for publishing companies, academic papers or monumental translation commissions (the complete works of Proust and Baudelaire), series of thrillers or ambitious stage plays, they went no further than initial announcements and first outlines. In very few instances did pen meet paper. That is not to say that Benjamin was struck dumb by the *Habilitation* fiasco—he earned his living primarily through the daily tasks of writing commentaries, columns, and reviews. By the spring of 1929 he had published over a hundred of these in national newspapers. His subjects ranged from Jewish numerology to "Lenin as letter-writer" to children's toys; brisk reports on food fairs or haberdashery joined long essays about Surrealism or the châteaux of the Loire Valley.

And why not? Those who can write can write about anything. Especially when the author's approach lies in interpreting the object of his attention as a kind of monad, something whose very existence reveals nothing less than the entire state of the world—present, past, and future. Therein lies Benjamin's method and magic. His worldview is profoundly symbolic: for him each person, each artwork, each object is a sign to be deciphered. And each sign exists in dynamic interrelation with every other sign. And the truth-oriented interpretation of such a sign is directed precisely at demonstrating and intellectually elaborating its integration within the great, constantly changing ensemble of signs: philosophy.

DOES MY LIFE NEED A GOAL?

BENJAMIN'S SEEMINGLY IDIOTIC ARRAY of themes and interests in fact pursued a cognitive method of its own. This approach was given focus by a growing conviction that the most deviant statements, objects, and individuals, which were for that reason often ignored, contained the whole of society in microcosm. Benjamin's *Denkbilder* (thought-pictures) in *One-Way Street* (1928) or *Berlin Childhood around Nineteen Hundred* are just as clearly inspired by the poems of the flâneur Baudelaire as they are by a love of outsiders in the novels of Dostoyevsky or by Proust's struggle for memory. They have a Romantic penchant for the ephemeral and labyrinthine as much as for the esoteric interpretative techniques of the Jewish Kabbalah, all underpinned, as applicable, by Marxist materialism or the idealism of Fichte's and Schelling's natural philosophies. Benjamin's writing tests out the birth of a new mode of thinking with an ideological disorientation typical of its time. The first lines of his autobiographical *Berlin Childhood around Nineteen Hundred* (published posthumously) sound like a playful introduction to his method.

> Being unable to find one's way in a city doesn't mean much. But getting lost in a city as one gets lost in a forest takes training. Street names must speak to the wanderer like the cracking of dry twigs, and small streets in the inner city must reflect the times of day as clearly as a mountain valley. I learned this art late; it fulfilled the dream, of which the first traces were labyrinths on the blotting paper in my notebooks.[11]

The chronic irresolution, extreme variety, and reality-saturated contradiction of Benjamin's writing was, he recognized, the only way to achieve knowledge of the world and therefore of himself. In the convoluted words of the preface to *The Origin of German Tragic Drama*: Anyone who philosophizes must be concerned with allowing "the configurations of the idea to emerge—the sum total of all juxtapositions of such opposites—from the remotest extremes, the apparent excesses of the process of development." But for Benjamin the representation of an idea "cannot under any circumstances be considered successful unless the full range of extremes that it contains has been virtually explored."[12]

It is obviously much more than just a wayward epistemological theory. It is an outline of existence that transforms the Kantian question "What is a human being?" into another—namely, "How am I to live?"—because for

Benjamin what applies to the representation of an idea in the art of philosophy applies no less to the art of living. Free human beings who thirst for knowledge must with every fiber of their being *"open themselves up to remote extremes"* and cannot *"consider themselves successful"* in their lives until they have examined, walked, or at least tried out all extremes of possibility.

Benjamin's journey toward knowledge, like his design for life, exhibits in dramatic form the tension, typical of the age, that also impelled and inspired Wittgenstein, Cassirer, and Heidegger in the 1920s. His way of thinking, however, is based not on the ideal of a construction of the world that could be explained with logic but on the exploration of contradictory simultaneity. Where Cassirer strives for the unity of a polyphonic system that has as its basis a scientific understanding of the concept of the symbol, Benjamin is drawn to contrasting, eternally dynamic arrangements of knowledge. And he replaces Heidegger's fear of death with the ideal of a euphoria and excess that celebrate the lived moment as the medium of genuine sensation. Underlying all of this is a religiously charged philosophy of history that holds out the possibility of salvation, though the individual cannot bring it about or even predict when it will occur in the vulgar Marxist sense.

THE ONE-MAN REPUBLIC

DURING THE 1920S, attempting to find harmony between action and thought, Benjamin commuted both intellectually and physically back and forth among Paris, Berlin, and Moscow, invariably convinced of his imminent and complete breakdown. On occasion his consistent tendency toward self-destruction—the prostitutes, casinos, and drugs—was accompanied by fleeting phases of immense productivity and explosions of brilliance. Like the Weimar Republic itself, Benjamin never sought balance; for him the truth that was worth seeking—not least his own—always lay on the exciting margins of life and thought.

In this sense, the events of spring 1929 represent the heightening of an arrangement that had already defined Benjamin's life for the previous ten years.[13] He was torn between at least two women (Dora and Asja), two cities (Berlin and Moscow), two professions (journalist and philosopher), two intimate friends (the Judaic scholar Gershom Scholem and Bertolt Brecht), two major endeavors (the founding of the magazine and the start of a new major work of his own, which would later become *The Arcades Project*), as well as working off debts of all kinds. There can be few intellectuals whose biographies exemplify and encapsulate the tensions of the countries of their birth more than Walter Benjamin in the spring of 1929. He was a one-man Weimar, by his own account incapable of "making a cup of tea" (for which he naturally blamed his mother).

Benjamin's decision to traduce and abandon the only person he had truly been able to count on signals a turning point in his life, as the woman in question, incidentally, saw much more clearly than the philosopher himself. In May 1929 a concerned Dora Benjamin wrote to Gershom (Gerhard) Scholem:

....

Walter is in a very bad way, dear Gerhard, I can't tell you more than that because it is crushing my heart. He is entirely under Asja's influence and doing things that the pen resists writing, and which prevent me from exchanging even a word with him. He now exists only as a head and genitals, and as you know, or can imagine, in such cases the head is quickly overcome. It was always a great danger, and who can say what will happen. . . . Walter has sued me for my debt, as the first divorce proceedings failed to resolve this question—he wants neither to return the money borrowed from his inheritance (120,000 marks; my mother is seriously ill) nor to pay anything for Stefan. . . . I gave him all the books, and the next day he also demanded the collection of children's books. In the winter he lived with me for months without paying. . . . After we gave each other every freedom for eight years . . . he is suing me; now the German laws he despised are suddenly good enough for him.[14]

Dora was a sound judge of character. In autumn 1929, only five months later, almost as the markets on Wall Street tumbled, Benjamin had a breakdown. Unable to read or speak, let alone write, he booked himself into a sanatorium. With the great Crash, humanity crossed a threshold, entering a new age, darker and more deadly than even he had imagined.

II.

LEAPS

1919

Dr. Benjamin flees his father, Lieutenant Wittgenstein commits financial suicide, Privatdozent Heidegger loses his faith, and Monsieur Cassirer works on his enlightenment in the streetcar.

WHAT TO DO?

I F ON THE ONE HAND the character of a person, the way he reacts, were known in all its details, and if, on the other, all the events in the areas entered by that character were known, both what would happen to him and what he would accomplish could be exactly predicted. That is, his fate would be known."[1] Is that so? Is a life's journey really conditioned, determined, predictable in this way? Even one's own biography? How much leeway do we have to shape our own destinies? Walter Benjamin addressed these questions in September 1919 at the age of twenty-seven, in an essay titled "Fate and Character." Today it stands for a whole generation of young European intellectuals who, after the Great War, faced the challenge of reexamining their own culture and their lives, but as its first sentence suggests, what follows is really an attempt by Benjamin to read his own fortunes. This is writing as a means of self-illumination.

In the first summer after the war, Benjamin's future, for quite personal reasons, was profoundly uncertain. Many of the milestones of so-called adult life were behind him. He had married (1917), become a father (1918), and attained a doctorate (June 1919). He had managed to keep the apocalyptic horrors at arm's length. He first escaped the draft by staying up the night before the physical examination with his close friend Gerhard Scholem and drinking countless cups of coffee, so that when his pulse was tested it was irregular enough for him to be declared unfit. It was a popular trick at the time. His second maneuver was much more elaborate and imaginative. This time—highly successfully, in terms of outcome!—he had Dora convince him, through several weeks of hypnosis, that he suffered from severe sciatica. The military doctors found his symptoms pronounced and he was granted official permission to have his case examined more closely at a specialist clinic in Switzerland. Once there, he was safe from conscription. All he had to do was stay, which in the autumn of 1917 he and Dora decided to do.

A REFUGE

THEY FIRST TOOK UP lodgings in Zurich, which during the war had become a kind of collecting tank for young Germans, indeed for the whole of the European intelligentsia. It was there, for example, that Hugo Ball and Tristan Tzara proclaimed the beginning of Dadaism. Only a few meters away from the Cabaret Voltaire, a certain Vladimir Ilyich Ulyanov had, under the pseudonym Lenin, planned the Russian Revolution. These circles passed the young newlyweds by, however, and their mutual friend Scholem soon moved to Bern in central Switzerland, where Walter enrolled at the university as a doctoral student in philosophy.

This trio of Berlin exiles largely set themselves apart from the cultural life of the city, known even today for its leisurely pace. Benjamin and Scholem found the teaching at the university so stultifying that they invented an alternative institution called "Muri," complete with absurd courses such as "The Easter Egg—Threats and Advantages" (theology), "Theory and Practice of Insults" (jurisprudence), and "Theory of Free Fall Followed by Exercises" (philosophy).[2] They preferred to read and study together, perusing the works of the neo-Kantian Hermann Cohen, for example, sentence by sentence in sessions that lasted through the night.[3]

The ambiguity of his position suited Benjamin perfectly. By the time of his son Stefan's birth in April 1918, he had become enormously productive, finishing his doctoral thesis in less than a year. The impending end of the war, however, meant that he would need to decide what to do next. His father—whose finances had been badly affected by the conflict—was urging him to stand on his own two feet at last.

CRITICAL DAYS

WHEN THE YOUNG FAMILY withdrew to a pension on Lake Brienz for a spa cure in the summer of 1919, they had several labor-intensive months behind them. "Dora and I are quite exhausted," Benjamin wrote to Scholem on July 8, not least because of the state of health of little Stefan, who for months had had "a constant fever," so that they "never had peace."[4] Dora suffered from "the most serious exertions accumulated over months," which had led to anemia and "serious weight loss," while Benjamin was engaged in a painful struggle with his hypnotically induced sciatica. He mentioned that he had also "become sensitive to noise over the last six months," and he seems to have been close to what we would call burnout.

This summer vacation at the wonderfully named Mon Repos pension was exactly what the family needed. With a lake view, full board, and the support of the nanny they had brought with them (yes, their financial predicament might have been serious, but they were never truly penniless), they could eat well, sleep a lot, and read a little. Walter might even translate a poem by his beloved Baudelaire into German every now and again. It could have been so nice.

But as with virtually all of Benjamin's plans, nothing came of it. To avoid jeopardizing his father's financial contributions, he hadn't told his family back in Berlin about his successful doctoral examination. Meanwhile his father, who barely trusted him to cross the road unaccompanied, decided to pay a surprise visit to Switzerland, arriving at the resort with his wife on July 31, 1919.

No one familiar with the personalities involved, let alone the specific circumstances of their coming together, would have needed a crystal ball to predict how the meeting would go. On August 14, Benjamin described to Scholem the "*bad* days that now lie behind us," adding in passing: "It is now permitted to speak openly about my doctorate."

His father, finally up to speed, gave Benjamin an ultimatum: Find fixed and, most important, paid employment as soon as possible. This was easier said than done. In response to the urgent question of what he planned to do with his life, he could only give one truthful answer: A critic, Father. I want to be a critic.

What that self-description meant in practical terms had been the subject of Benjamin's three-hundred-page doctoral thesis, *The Concept of Art Criticism in German Romanticism,*[5] though the task of explaining it to a largely uncultured (and, like his son, chronically depressive) businessman must have been daunting, even before addressing how this might translate into gainful employment.

But it was worth a try. Particularly when behind the dry title of this academic dissertation lay an idea of singular originality: that openness was fundamental both to his own development as an individual and to the development of all culture on a new theoretical basis. The central activity that this openness made possible and endlessly renewed was what Benjamin in his doctoral thesis called simply "criticism." He was convinced that a specific form of intellectual activity was present in thinkers like Fichte, Novalis, and Schelling, which followed on from Kant, whose actual relevance to his own life and his own culture had hitherto remained undiscovered.

ROMANTIC THESES

FOR BENJAMIN the crucial impulse of these early Romantic thinkers lay in the fact that the activity of criticism—if understood correctly—leaves neither the criticizing subject (the art critic) nor the criticized object (the work of art) unaffected. Both are transformed in the process—ideally toward truth. The thesis of the constant enrichment of the work of art through criticism was based, in Benjamin's view, on two fundamental concepts in German Romanticism.

1. Everything that exists is in a dynamic relationship not only with other things but also with itself (the thesis of the self-referentiality of all things).

2. The subject, by criticizing an object, activates and mobilizes this dynamic relationship between the two by mobilizing their references both to each other and to other things (the thesis of the activation of all references through criticism).

From these propositions Benjamin derived conclusions in his dissertation that would revolutionize not only his image of himself as a critic but also the way art criticism has understood itself since. First and foremost among these is the conclusion that the function of art criticism lies *"not in judgment, but on the one hand [in] completion, consummation, systematization."*[6] Second is the elevation of the art critic to the status of partial creator of the work of art. Third is the recognition that an artwork is fundamentally unstable, and changes and rejuvenates its nature and possible significance across history. Fourth, following from the thesis of the self-reference of all things, is the understanding that any criticism of a work of art can also be seen as the artwork's criticism of itself.

Critics and artists, correctly understood, thus exist on the same creative plane. The essence of the work is not fixed, but constantly changing, and in fact works of art constantly criticize themselves. Imagine the bafflement and incomprehension that Benjamin's theses would have prompted in a person such as his father.

NEW SELF-AWARENESS

THE PLAUSIBILITY OF BENJAMIN'S SCHEME rests on our acceptance of the twin fundamental Romantic concepts—self-reference and hetero-reference—that underpin it. These may not be as far-fetched as they first seem. Benjamin could in their support have referred his father to one basic human experience, so self-evidently true and immediately verifiable that it is beyond dispute: self-consciousness. We all have this special ability. It consists of referring to one's own thoughts with one's own thoughts. We are all capable, each in our own way, of "thinking about our thinking." Each of us has experienced a process of cognition, in which both the object of criticism (the thought we think about) and the subject (the thinking about the thought) are altered, all the while experiencing themselves factually as single entities. For the Romantics this reflexive self-awareness is the textbook example of critical object-reference. More broadly, it is what happens when *the being-known of one being by another coincides with the self-knowledge of that being which is being known.*[7]

In fact, Benjamin could have explained to his father, this miraculous fluctuating self-reference is always ongoing, but it becomes particularly visible and efficacious when we think about the foundations of our relationship to ourselves and to the world. Great works of art are in fact nothing but the manifestation or product of such a process of reflection. For that reason these works, in the references they hold out, are rich, diverse, stimulating, unique, and hence promoting of knowledge:

> Thus, criticism is, as it were, an experiment on the artwork, one through which the latter's own reflection is awakened, through which it is brought to consciousness and to knowledge of itself. . . . Insofar as criticism is knowledge of the work of art, it is as its self-knowledge; insofar as it judges the artwork, this occurs in the latter's self-judgment.[8]

Herein lies, for Benjamin, the philosophical core of art criticism in Romanticism, even if the Romantics were not able to appreciate it. That clarity would not be achieved for 150 years, and the application of much interpretative labor—criticism, in other words. Precisely the task he wished to devote the rest of his life to. Not least because by it he would accomplish something outside and within himself, the constantly evolving "work" that he had recognized himself to be. Each of us can, to some degree, accompany and shape our own evolution and thereby become the person who we really are. We can call this process criticism. Or also simply: philosophy.

FLIGHTS

IN SUCH TERMS, Benjamin could have explained to his father during those two weeks on Lake Brienz the idea behind his proposed career as an independent critic. Presumably he did so. But as we might expect, he was unable to convince his father. This failure was due in part to an inability to answer the most important question: Where would the money for this life come from?

How could he define himself, without complying at some level with the "fate" set out for him by his parents? What was to be done?

Benjamin did what he always did when no solution was in sight: he fled, flitting from one location to the next, and threw himself into several new large-scale projects at once.

His journey that autumn led him through the Swiss villages of Klosters and Lugano to Breitenstein in Austria, where the young family, having run out of energy and money, eventually settled in a rest home run by Dora's Austrian aunt. "We are completely penniless here," Benjamin wrote to Scholem on November 16. Still, there was good news from his thesis supervisor in Bern: "Herbertz welcomed me very warmly, and suggested the possibility of a postdoctoral thesis, even perhaps an extraordinary teaching position. My parents are of course very pleased and have no objection to a postdoctoral thesis, but cannot yet commit themselves financially."[9]

So all was not lost. Only the question of money remained unanswered. During those same weeks and months, Wittgenstein was also preoccupied with his finances, albeit in a different way.

THE TRANSFORMATION

WAS HE TRULY AWARE of the scope of his decision? Had he spoken to his siblings about it? Might he not reconsider? No, he didn't want to. "Fine," the family lawyer sighed, "you are firmly determined to commit financial suicide."[10] Wittgenstein insisted. Rather than hesitate—still in his white lieutenant's uniform—he asked the lawyer to confirm that there was really no loophole, no special clause, no going back, and that with his signature he would absolutely and irrevocably rid himself of his entire fortune. Financial suicide was a good way of putting it.

Wittgenstein had been back in Vienna for less than a week, as one of the last officers released from an Italian prisoner-of-war camp. Now, on August 31, 1919, he sat in an elegant legal office and signed his entire inheritance—hundreds of millions of euros today—over to his older siblings Hermine, Helene, and Paul. Vienna, once the proud imperial capital, was now the seat of a small, bankrupt alpine republic that, in this first postwar summer, was headed toward complete collapse. A majority of Austrians had, in the face of catastrophe, voted to join with Germany, which was also in the process of self-dissolution, only for the victorious powers to veto the move. Inflation was sending food prices soaring. The currency was in free fall—and with it morale. The old hierarchies of the Habsburg Empire had disintegrated, and the new institutions were not yet in working order. Nothing was as it had been. Even Ludwig Wittgenstein, by now thirty years old, was a different person.

In the summer of 1914, only a few days after the outbreak of war, Wittgenstein volunteered to serve as a corporal, hoping for a fundamental change in his life. The scion of one of the biggest industrial families in Europe, from the lofty heights of Viennese society, the Cambridge student was even then recognized for his immense philosophical gifts. His patrons Bertrand Russell and Gottlob Frege urged him to take the "next big step" in thought. The war did in a sense entirely fulfill Wittgenstein's personal aspirations: he had shown courage at the front in Galicia, Russia, and Italy, looking death in the eye more than once. He had shot to kill, had—through his reading of Tolstoy—found his way to the Christian faith; and, during the long nights at the front, he had written his book, which he was convinced would be not only the next great step in philosophy, but its final and definitive one.

But what had he really achieved? Basically nothing. Nothing as he saw it. Nothing to stem the attacks of meaninglessness that still tormented him daily. As he wrote in the summer of 1918, while on leave from his last deployment at the front, in the foreword to his *Tractatus logico-philosophicus*, its final flourish:

> I am therefore of the opinion that the problems have in essentials been finally solved. And if I am not mistaken in this, then the value of this work secondly consists in showing how little has been done when this problem has been solved.

In other words: Philosophy has nothing to say and no judgment to make about what conditions a human life, what gives it meaning, value, and daily hope. But why it is fundamentally unable to do so—why no logical conclusion, argument, or theory of meaning has even been able to touch the actual questions of life—that was what Wittgenstein believed he had shown with his work once and for all.

ETHICAL ACTS

IN FACT, as Wittgenstein explained to the publisher Ludwig von Ficker two months after his return from the war, the "meaning of the book is an ethical one," since his work consisted of two parts: "the present one, and everything that I have *not* written. And that second part is the important one. The ethical is delimited by my book, so to speak."[11]

The realm of the sayable, which Wittgenstein's work delineates "from within" through logical linguistic analysis, applies only to the world of facts; this is therefore the only realm about which anything can be meaningfully said.

But to grasp this world of facts with all its qualities as precisely as possible is ultimately the task of the natural sciences. For Wittgenstein, it is "something that has nothing to do with philosophy" (T 6:53). Against this backdrop, then, the problem, or rather the actual philosophical solution, consists in the following conviction, or more precisely the following *feeling*:

> 6:52 We feel that even if all possible scientific questions be answered,
> the problems of life have still not been touched at all. Of course there
> is then no question left, and just this is the answer.

The largely positivistic spirit of the age assumed that only things about which we could meaningfully speak could be significant for our own lives. These were things that could be proved to exist using the methodical foundation of this essentially scientific vision of the world—logical analysis. That is, so-called facts. But Wittgenstein was able to show that the truth was in fact precisely the reverse. Everything that gives *meaning* to life, and the world in which we live, already lies within the boundaries of what can be directly said. Wittgenstein's philosophical approach was a severely scientific one, but his morality was existential. A good life is based not on objective grounds but on radically subjective decisions. It cannot be meaningfully said what a good life consists of; it must *show* itself in real, everyday execution. That was what Wittgenstein had decided to do in 1919.

A return to the old world of Vienna would have been unthinkable for him even had that world still existed. Neither war nor philosophy had freed him from the riddle and the misfortune that he was to himself. He returned from the war transformed but by no means clarified. In order to combat the remaining chaos within him, he spent long months in the Italian POW camp at Campo Cassino drawing up the most radical plan imaginable.

First of all: signing over his entire fortune to his siblings. Second: never again philosophy. Third: a life of honest toil—and lasting poverty.

A SORROW
BEYOND DREAMS

THE TENACITY WITH WHICH WITTGENSTEIN devoted himself to this plan on his return was a source of great concern to his siblings, particularly his eldest sister, Hermine. During those late August days she feared she would lose a fourth brother to suicide, after Johannes (d. 1902), Rudolf (d. 1904), and Kurt (d. 1918).

Johannes, the eldest brother, had fled their dominating father to America and "drowned" in a boating accident in Florida, never satisfactorily explained; the third son, Rudolf, born in 1888, took cyanide in a Berlin restaurant at the age of twenty-two. In his suicide note Rudolf attributed the act to grief over the death of a friend, though some believe he had been unmasked through an anonymous case study by the sexologist Magnus Hirschfeld about a "homosexual student" and feared exposure.[12] Heroically tragic, finally, was the suicide of Konrad (known as Kurt) who put a bullet into his brain while retreating from Italy during the last days of the war in October 1918—probably to escape being taken prisoner.

By this standard, the fourth of the five Wittgenstein brothers, Paul, was a remarkable success. Prodigiously musical, like all the family's offspring, he had established a career as a concert pianist before the onset of war. Young Paul was generally seen as exceptionally talented, and the musical soirees that his father organized at the family mansion were among the highlights of the Viennese social calendar around the turn of the century. In the first few months of the war, however, he was so badly wounded that his right arm had to be amputated. He ended up in a Russian camp, and wasn't released until 1916. He, too, seriously considered suicide after returning home, but then found new meaning in life by teaching himself, over countless hours of practice, to play the piano one-handed to an extremely high level using a special pedaling technique he developed. He was thus able to continue his career as a concert pianist and went on to become an international star.

The youngest of the brothers, "Luki" (as Ludwig was known in the family), likewise teetered on the edge upon his return. Given what he had been through, his family felt it sensible to grant him free rein. Perhaps all the more so because Ludwig's entire military career looked in retrospect like one long suicide attempt. As he rose swiftly through the ranks, Wittgenstein insisted to his superiors that he wanted to be sent to the front, not in spite of the danger but because of it.

In his war diaries Wittgenstein obsessively returned to the notion that it was only in a near-death situation, with his own life hanging in the balance, that he would truly see himself, above all his faith in God—and thus his capacity for happiness. In entries from the summer of 1916 on the Galician front, we can see the dovetailing of Wittgenstein's program of logical linguistic analysis with a Christian-existentialist ethic along the lines of Kierkegaard and Tolstoy:

In order to live happily, I must be in agreement with the world. And that is what "being happy" means.

I am then, so to speak in agreement with that alien will on which I appear dependent. That is to say: "I am doing the will of God."[13]

The fear of death is the best sign of a false, i.e. a bad life.[14]

Good and evil enter only through the *subject*. And the subject is not part of the world, but a limit of the world. . . .

What is good and evil is essentially the I, not the world. The I, the I is what is deeply mysterious.[15]

By August 1919, Wittgenstein had certainly lost any fear of death. But often it came to the critical question of whether a good, meaningful, and indeed happy life lay within reach for someone like him; he was plagued by doubts. It was these that led him, on September 5, 1919, to take the second step in his survival program and, now penniless, begin a one-year course at a training institute in Vienna to become a primary school teacher. No more philosophy, then. Never again.

Martin Heidegger knew nothing of Wittgenstein's life plan at the time. It might have shaken his own foundations. Because Heidegger, too, had just returned from the war—and there was only one thing he wanted to do: philosophy.

AN INTERESTING
CONDITION

"IT'S HARD TO LIVE the life of a philosopher," Martin Heidegger wrote on January 9, 1919, to his patron Engelbert Krebs. Because "inner truthfulness towards oneself and those for whom one is supposed to be a teacher demands sacrifices and struggles that the academic toiler can never know."[16] No doubt. This was someone being very serious. About himself, his thought, his journey. "I believe," Heidegger continued, "that I have an inner calling to philosophy."[17]

Held back for the first few years by a heart condition (self-diagnosis: "too much sport in my youth"), Heidegger had served as a meteorologist with the frontline weather service number 414 from August until November 1918. At Marne-Champagne, he provided forecasts to the German army from an observation post elevated a little above the battlefield to enable deployment of poison gas. Heidegger did not take part in any actual fighting, but through his binoculars he would have seen many thousands of German soldiers emerging from their trenches and running toward certain death. In his personal notebooks and letters, however, the horrors of the war go unmentioned. When Heidegger speaks of "sacrifice," "renunciation," and "struggles," he means first and foremost himself and his academic and personal situation.

For Heidegger, since the winter of 1917, the actual front had run not through the Ardennes but through his own four walls. This line was not national or geopolitical but denominational. In the end, it was actually difficult "to live—to forge a career within institutions"—as a Catholic philosopher sponsored by the Church, if, like Martin Heidegger, you secretly married a Protestant. All the more so if your wife, contrary to earlier statements of intent, did not convert to Catholicism, or have your child baptized as a Catholic.

EXPOSED FLANKS

IT IS DIFFICULT TODAY to grasp what a scandal a mixed-denominational marriage was in 1919 in Heidegger's personal and professional circles, not least for his strictly devout parents, whom he reassured again and again in touching letters that their son's soul and also that of their grandchild were not beyond salvation.

His marriage was very much a problem, and the problem would soon become even more acute. At the same time, everyone recognized that Thea

Elfride Petri was an excellent match for the sexton's son in purely fiscal terms. His bride, who had come to Freiburg in 1915 to study economics, came from money—the upper ranks of the Prussian military—and her family supported the young couple financially in the last years of the war. But the conclusion of the war saw the Petris, who like millions of other Germans had invested their fortune in war bonds, suffer severe losses, and that lifeline had been cut off.[18]

So when he returned to Freiburg from the front in November 1918, Heidegger found himself gazing into a financial abyss. If he wanted to live as a philosopher, he urgently needed a regular income, which meant getting a job, which meant finding a new patron. Though the Privatdozent had achieved that qualification with the help of a Church grant, he could not expect any more funding from the theology faculty of Freiburg University. As early as 1916, he was deemed in Church circles immature and liable to be conscripted, and he had been ostentatiously passed over, in spite of intense advocacy from Dean Engelbert Krebs. Now that last connection was severed, too.

Heidegger placed all of his academic hopes on the holder of the first chair of philosophy in Freiburg, the founder and head of the school of phenomenology: Edmund Husserl. Husserl, who declared himself entirely scientifically oriented, was highly suspicious of thinkers with strong religious associations. Heidegger initially found him difficult to win over. In 1916 and 1917 the old master took no notice whatsoever of the young sorcerer's apprentice. It was not until the winter of 1917 that Husserl got to know him better and offered him his personal support. A year later, in a letter of January 9, 1919, to Krebs, Heidegger revealed, with considerable pathos, a remarkable transformation: that "insights from epistemological theory . . . had rendered the *system* of Catholicism problematic and disagreeable to [him]." We might, at this distance, see this as the impeccably timed maneuver of a career philosopher who had, after taking in the new prevailing weather conditions, concluded that an overt disavowal of Catholicism represented his last chance at academia. Only two days before, Edmund Husserl had personally approached the Ministry of Education and Cultural Affairs in Karlsruhe to request the creation of a new assistantship for Heidegger, since there was otherwise a danger this extraordinary talent would be lost to "an ordinary job outside academia."[19]

In terms of Benjamin's biographical straitjacket of "character" and "fate," "inner disposition" and "external circumstances," Heidegger's renunciation of the "*system* of Catholicism" appears to be all too consistent with his career plans.

As hoped, Husserl's request did not go unheeded. The ministry was reluctant to assign a full assistantship (which was granted only in 1920), but it did authorize a paid teaching post. Heidegger's philosophical vocation was safe for now. Henceforth he would be able to think outside the constraints of the Catholic Church. A "war emergency semester" started on January 25, 1919, in Freiburg. Heidegger had exactly three weeks to prepare for his new role. Only four days before the start of lectures, his first son, Jörg, was born.

A WORLD
WITHOUT A VIEW

COMPARED WITH MAJOR CITIES such as Munich and Berlin, Freiburg had avoided the worst consequences of the war and its cessation. Its agricultural setting meant that food shortages were not quite as severe as they were elsewhere, and the city was spared civil revolts and fighting in the streets. And yet Heidegger's view from the lectern at his first lecture in 1919 must have been less than inspiring. Before him sat a scattered crowd of mostly defeated men, many already beyond student age, who now had to pretend that they saw themselves as having a future. How to reach them? Talk to them? Wake them up? By fleeing to the ivory tower of the most abstract and remote questions? Or rather by interpreting the here and now in a manner close to their experience? The young lecturer decided to do both at once. And by so doing he gave philosophy one of its finest hours.[20]

According to the prospectus, Heidegger was supposed to be delivering a talk on Kant, but at the last second he confidently opted for a change of subject. The new title was: "The Idea of Philosophy and the Worldview Problem."[21] In other words, it was about philosophy's understanding of itself as an autonomous discipline of knowledge; beyond the methods and declarations of the empirical natural sciences and, above all, beyond the genre of books based on an all-encompassing worldview, which were particularly dominant at the time—such as Oswald Spengler's sprawling interpretation of civilization, *The Decline of the West*. It seemed clear enough that the aims and methods of philosophy are not identical with those of the natural sciences. But how does it differ from the business of constructing a value-based worldview? Is there really a significant difference between the two?

If we follow Husserl's phenomenological approach, the answer is an unambiguous yes. Because what distinguishes phenomenology is a methodically rigorous method of discovering the world. But this differs from the natural sciences in that it does not strive to explain or predict the course of phenomena, but rather seeks to grasp those phenomena in their factual reality for human consciousness in as objective and value-free a way as possible. Under the battle cry "Back to the facts!" phenomenology attempted to establish itself as what Heidegger called a *"pre-theoretical primordial science"*: as a precise foundation of experience prior to any natural sciences and also, primarily, prior to all worldviews and ideologies distorted by prejudice.

THE PRIMAL SCIENTIST

THIS WAS PRECISELY the track that Heidegger, as Husserl's new assistant in Freiburg, took in his first lecture. In its simplest form, according to Heidegger's approach, the fundamental question of phenomenology was: *Gibt es etwas?* (Is there something? or Is there something given?) And if so, how does that *"es"* reveal our consciousness? How does it show itself? Let's listen for ourselves:

§13 THE EXPERIENCE-OF-THE-QUESTION: IS THERE SOMETHING (GIVEN)?

In the very question *"Gibt es . . . ?"* something is given. Our *entire* set of problems has reached a crucial point which, however, appears so meager as to be insignificant. Everything depends on . . . our understanding and following the meaning of this meagerness and persisting with it. . . . We stand at a methodical crossroads where the life and death of philosophy will be decided; we stand before an abyss: either an abyss of nothingness, i.e. of absolute objectivity, or a leap into *another world*, or more precisely: into the world itself for the first time. . . . Let us assume that *we* did not exist. Then that question [*gibt es*] would not arise.[22]

Just to examine once more, a few sentences later, this crucial questioning impulse in greater depth:

What is the meaning of: *"es gibt"*?

Es gibt numbers, *es gibt* triangles, *es gibt* paintings by Rembrandt, *es gibt* U-boats; I say *es gibt* rain today, *es gibt* roast veal tomorrow. A great variety of *es gibt*, and each time it has a different meaning and yet in each one it has an identical element of significance. . . . Again: the question asks whether *es gibt* something. The question is not whether *es gibt* chairs or tables, or houses or trees, or sonatas by Mozart or religious powers, but whether *es gibt* anything whatsoever. What does anything whatsoever mean? Something universal, indeed, one might say, the most universal, that applies to every possible object. To say of something that it is something is the smallest assertion I can make of it. I face it without presupposition.[23]

Here was a twenty-nine-year-old academic, in his very first lecture, challenging his audience, his voice quivering with resolution, to recognize the crucial question of philosophy itself in its most meager formulations. Who was he? A clown? A magician? A prophet?

It is worth lingering a little longer over this key passage of Heidegger's first postwar lecture, since it forms the nucleus of his whole philosophy of Dasein. If we follow Heidegger's exhortation to dwell on the formulation of *"es gibt"*—immersing ourselves meditatively, so to speak, in its possible meanings and applications—a profound riddle appears: What does this *es gibt* actually mean? Where does its true meaning lie? After all, in its most universal form it applies to everything and all things. To everything that *is*.

Precisely ten years later Heidegger would claim, in the same spot, that his entire philosophy revolved around nothing less than the meaning of the word *Sein* (be). And at that same lectern in Freiburg he would pronounce himself the first person in twenty-five hundred years to rediscover and revive the question of its meaning, and above all its significance for the life and thought of all human beings. This grand drama had already been previewed in 1919 when he discussed the question of *es gibt* as the "very crossroads" at which the "life and death of philosophy" will be decided.

If we plump for the path of "absolute objectivity" and thus leave the question of *es gibt* to the natural sciences, philosophy is threatened by the same fate also diagnosed by Wittgenstein: it becomes superfluous, at best the handmaid of the natural sciences. At worst it degenerates into precisely that kind of uninhibited generalization built upon false and prejudice-based foundations that Heidegger associates with worldview philosophy (*Weltanschauungsphilosophie*). Thus everything depends upon whether it is possible to make that "leap" into another world, another way of philosophizing and thus a different understanding of *Sein*. Into a third way.

NO ALIBI

BUT HEIDEGGER'S IDEA OF THE *LEAP*—a core concept in the religious philosophy of Søren Kierkegaard—already suggests that this redemptive alternative is not a purely logical, argumentative, or even only rationally motivated choice. Instead it is more a *decision*, and thus demands something more and something different. Something that is in fact based primarily not on reasons, but on will and courage, and above all on concrete personal experience, comparable to that of religious transformation: a vocation.

Another concept absolutely crucial to Heidegger's later thought appears in this passage. It is concealed behind the speculation about "us"—as human beings—not even being *da* (there). And hence not in the world. What then?

Heidegger maintains that the question of "*Gibt es* something?" would not otherwise exist. In other words, human beings are the only ones who can ask the question of "*Gibt es*" and thus what the meaning of *Sein* is. It is only for us that everything that exists is therefore *da*—and in terms of that given, everything is in fact questionable. "*Es gibt*" a world only for us. Soon Heidegger would replace the concept of "humanity" with that of "Dasein."

THE NEW REALM

IN HIS VERY FIRST LECTURE, Heidegger announced to an auditorium traumatized by the horrors of war the possibility of "another world"—the world *and* life-form of *genuinely* philosophical inquiry. Not least because this is necessarily implied by his speaking of the *leap*. The conquest of this new realm must be undertaken by each of us individually. On the road to philosophy there can be no alibis. Whatever precedes the leap and makes it possible cannot ultimately be conveyed abstractly or simply proclaimed from behind a lectern; it must be experienced and grasped personally from within, and then manifested in day-to-day life.

The "pre-theoretical primordial science" for which Heidegger's "experience-of-the-question" sought to blaze a trail was thus no longer a science in the classic sense of the word. It was aimed at something more and something other than the mere description of the given, namely a fundamentally different way of understanding the manner of its givenness. Even in the spring of 1919, it was apparent how much of Heidegger's thought was shaped by a ceaseless interweaving of "*Sein* questions" (ontology) and "Dasein questions" (existential questions). In the closing words of his lecture:

> But *philosophy* only manages to advance by immersing itself thoroughly in life as such. . . . It has no illusions, it is the science of absolute honesty. There is no chattering, only *insightful steps*; no theories clash within it, only authentic insights with inauthentic ones. But the authentic insights can only be achieved through honest and wholehearted immersion in the authenticity of life as such, ultimately only through the authenticity of the *personal* life itself.[24]

FIDELITY TO THE EVENT

THE IMMEDIATE CHALLENGE that young philosophers faced in 1919 can be summed up as follows: Draw up a plan for one's own life and generation, which moves beyond the determining "structure" of "fate and character." First, in literal biographical terms this meant daring to break away from the old frameworks (family, religion, nation, capitalism). And second, it meant finding a model of existence that made it possible to process the intensity of the experience of war, transferring it to the realm of thought and everyday existence.

Benjamin wanted to undertake that renewal with a Romantic notion of a criticism that was a universally energizing criticism. Wittgenstein pursued the goal of giving everyday permanence to the overwhelming mystical tranquillity and sense of reconciliation with the world that he experienced at moments of mortal peril. Meanwhile Heidegger, who already saw himself as a "wild thinker," attempted to reconcile the intensity of the experience of war—which he saw as having fundamental similarities with the intensity of thought—with a desire for "everydayness." A life in the storm of thought on the one hand, a reconciliation with the everyday on the other; it was a task that required him to straddle both extremes. As he wrote to Elisabeth Blochmann (his wife's best friend since her youth) on May 1, 1919:

> We must be able to wait for high-tension intensities of meaningful life—and we must live continuously with those moments—not so much enjoy them as incorporate them into our lives—carry them into life's advance and involve them in the rhythm of the life to come.[25]

Seldom can a married man have declared more philosophically his commitment to continue in an affair limited to some encounters of "high-tension intensity." But what applies to Heidegger as an erotic lover also applies to the Eros of his thought: he wanted to remain open to the great moments of significance, events that provided great insight, while experiencing the rest of his existence in fidelity, so to speak, to those great events. For that fidelity—the only one that interested him—he had to be one thing above all: free. In thought. In action. In love. So in the spring of 1919 he began at last to burst his chains: the chains of Catholicism, the parental home, his marriage, and, if we look closely, Husserl's phenomenology.

GERMAN VIRTUES

THE FIRST POSTWAR SEMESTER at Friedrich-Wilhelm University (today Humboldt University) also saw Ernst Cassirer—in the fourteenth year of teaching as a Privatdozent—face some substantial challenges. In the first weeks of January 1919, as his wife recalled, "there was a lot of shooting in the streets of Berlin, and Ernst often drove through machine-gun fire to the university to deliver his lectures. Once, during one such street battle, the cables that supplied the university building with electricity were shot through while Ernst was lecturing. He liked to relate afterward how he asked his students whether he should stop or go on speaking, and how they unanimously voted for 'go on speaking.' . . . So Ernst finished that lecture in a pitch-dark auditorium, while machine-gun fire continued uninterruptedly outside."[26]

Surely someone in a situation of such extremity embodies precisely what Heidegger and Wittgenstein held to be the ideal result of their thought—a deeply internalized belief in the value of one's own actions and the value of self-determination, coupled with an attitude of incontestability. In short, a genuine and authentic character capable of responding to personal destiny. Cassirer, however, would never have described his behavior in those terms. Partly for political reasons, he wanted to have as little as possible to do with the concept of "character," which was of prime importance to the conservative circles around popular philosophers such as Oswald Spengler, Otto Weininger, and Ludwig Klages. In Cassirer's view the philosophical potency of the concept of character—particularly in the form of national character—played into a rhetoric of national chauvinism as well as a cult of "authenticity" and the "true essential core" that was opposed to freedom. And it thus encouraged precisely those intellectual and political forces in Europe that had made the First World War seem like an inevitable, fateful struggle for survival between the different European civilizations. For Cassirer, those who saw the "true character of a person" or the "true core of a people" as an indelible, innate determinant of all of their actions—or, on the other hand, a redemptive resource for times of hardship—were above all supremely unenlightened. And in Cassirer's world that meant: eminently un-German.

In 1916, as the war reached its bloody peak, he had dealt with character by writing a book titled *Freedom and Form: Studies in German Intellectual History*. Here it says in a central passage:

> Because of course we should be clear that as soon as one asks the question of the uniqueness of the spiritual "essence" of a people, one touches upon the deepest and most dangerous problems of metaphysics and general critical epistemology (*Erkenntniskritik*). . . . "Because in fact," as Goethe writes in the preface to his *Theory of Color*, "we seek in vain to express the essence of a thing." We become aware of effects, and a complete history of those effects would probably incorporate the essence of the thing. We struggle in vain to describe a person's character; but if we assemble his actions, his deeds, we will encounter a picture of his character.[27]

Subjective investigations into the "true character" and "interior" of human beings are based in the end on fateful metaphysical premises. But Cassirer's thought—and here as always he follows his two philosophical lodestars, Kant and Goethe—prefers to get by without the assumption of a given inner core or essence. As sensory, finite, rational creatures, he temperately suggests, we should cleave in our judgments to what is openly revealed: what a thing is, who a person is. This is apparent in the totality of their actions and the effects they have on other things and people. Essence, in other words, cannot be abstractly defined, definitively decreed, or magically invoked but will repeatedly show and prove itself in any given setting.

In Cassirer's view, therefore, the catastrophe of the Great War had been caused partly by bad metaphysics and a false, entirely "un-German" answer to the question of man's essence. So it is easy to imagine the appeal of that story of the postwar period in the auditorium. Cassirer valued the remarkable human ability to remain faithful to one's own philosophical ideals even in dire situations, and to embody them as visibly as possible for others. And for Cassirer that ideal was simply to be as autonomous as possible. To cultivate for ourselves and others forms and abilities that allow us to actively shape our own lives rather than be purely passive companions to them. Self-formation rather than definition by others. Objective grounds rather than internal actuality. That was, he was convinced, the actual contribution of German culture to the universal idea of man, radiantly embodied by the twin pillars of Cassirer's philosophy: Kant and Goethe.

UNLOVED

BUT IN THE WINTER OF 1919 it would be hard to claim that this German culture had been particularly kind to him. In his fourteenth year as Dozent at Berlin University, Cassirer was an internationally recognized scholar, though only with the misleading title of "extraordinary professor," which meant that he still lacked an official post, and indeed examination rights, and was still a part-time philosopher. His entry in the Berlin telephone directory identifies him, with factual correctness, as a "private scholar."[28] "I can't force them to love me, and they really don't like me," he would explain to his wife when he had been passed over once again for a new professorship that needed filling. He had brought out several well-regarded works, notably *The Concept of Substance and the Concept of Function* (1910),[29] and after the death of his mentor Hermann Cohen in 1918 he was considered the undisputed head of the "Marburg School" of neo-Kantianism—one of the leading experts on Kant at the time, if not the leading one. In terms of his career prospects, this description had admittedly become more obstacle than advantage, since in conservative and nationalist circles the Marburg philosophers around Cohen and Cassirer were increasingly openly suspected of dislodging Kant's teachings from their "true" (i.e., "German") roots. During the war the narrowing of national discourse had encouraged anti-Semitism in Germany, as seen with the "Jewish census" of the German army in 1916. This was further reinforced when the United States entered the war, and continued after the conflict was over. In this climate the surname Cassirer was almost paradigmatic of a class of German Jews that was viewed with increasing suspicion and hostility. The Cassirers were a well-to-do and extensive German-Jewish family whose members occupied a central place in both the commercial and the cultural life of Berlin: as manufacturers, industrialists and engineers, publishers, doctors, art collectors, and, indeed, philosophers.[30] The Cassirers were as "assimilated" as it was possible to be, and on precisely those grounds, according to the internal logic of German nationalism, they were held to be particularly suspect.[31]

ELECTRIFIED

AND THE WAR? Cassirer suffered from psoriasis, which meant that wearing an army uniform gave him such a painful rash that in the first year of the war he was declared permanently unfit for service. In 1916, however, he was given a post in the French department of the Reich press office. The writing of flyers aside, his work there consisted of reading reports in French newspapers, collecting quotes and adjusting their sense where necessary to render them useful to German military propagandists. Not an overly demanding job, but far from ideal for a firm European like Ernst Cassirer.

This occupation gave him sufficient time in the afternoons to devote himself to his own projects and studies, and to counter his duties as a producer of disinformation by writing the aforementioned *Freedom and Form*, and the essay "On European Reactions to German Culture." Come what may, Kant and Goethe should have been able to be proud of him. That was his maxim, and he had no intention of deviating from it. Not even on his grueling commute between his house in Berlin's Westend and the city center, an hour and a half each way. His wife recalled:

> I made that journey with him a few times, and was able to observe how he was capable of working even in such grotesque situations. He never tried to take a seat, because he was sure that he would soon have to give it up to women, elderly people, or injured veterans. He tried to push his way through to the back of the tram, and stood there occupying as little space as possible, with one hand reaching for a support so that he didn't fall over, and in the other holding the book that he was reading. Noise, jostling, poor light, bad air—none of it got in his way.[32]

That was what active self-formation on the streetcar looked like. We know because we have the outline for a three-volume *Philosophy of Symbolic Forms*, which Cassirer began in 1919 and completed over the next ten years, in the form of a sketch made on the streetcar. Its first version was dated June 13, 1917; written on eight small sheets of paper, it bears testimony to the brilliant ideas that the philosopher had on his journeys through Berlin—and the superhuman amount of reading that he did over the following two years, much of it on that same streetcar.[33]

In the winter of 1919, as he passed through the machine-gun fire of the Spartacist uprising, this time on his way to the university rather than the press office, he was already working on the manuscript of the first volume, concerning the phenomenon of human language as the actual basis of all symbolic forms. Cassirer was sure that he was working on something of consequence, the great idea of his life. And, as if summoned by fate, in May 1919—around the time that the corpse of Rosa Luxemburg, murdered in January, was fished out of the Landwehr Canal—he received a letter from the newly established Hamburg University. Cassirer replied as follows:

Dear colleague,

Please accept my thanks for your letter of 22 May, which was sent to me only a few days ago by the university, and to which I was unable to reply immediately since I was ill in bed with flu when it arrived. I am of course greatly obliged to you for your kind intentions, and you do not need to worry that I might be troubled by the expectation of undefined hope. Essentially—not least after recent experiences—I am quite beyond hope and hence also disappointment in this sphere. But I will not deny that in the uncertainties of the immediate future the prospect of a regular academic post would now be particularly desirable, and that I will be very grateful to you for any step in that direction.[34]

··

At last the long-awaited call to accept a chair. By the standards of the genre, the tone in which Cassirer replied to Hamburg was almost pushily unambiguous: Of course I'm coming! And yes, the money will come in handy, too! The war had made considerable inroads on his family fortune. The large cellulose factory once owned by the family, migrants from Breslau, now lay on the other side of the border, in Polish hands. But above all Cassirer was philosophically more than ready for new pastures; in a second letter he informed the developmental psychologist William Stern, director of the Hamburg appointment committee, that he had of late been increasingly devoting himself to the study of the philosophy of language. Formalities were swiftly concluded. As early as August 1919, a house was bought in the elegant district of Winterhude, and in October, Cassirer—with his wife and their three children—was on his way to a new life.

III.

LANGUAGES

1919–1920

Wittgenstein proves himself in the storm,
Heidegger learns the whole truth, Cassirer seeks his form,
and Benjamin translates God.

FIGURATIVELY SPEAKING

T
HAT'S EXACTLY WHAT ONE CAN'T SAY. You cannot prescribe to a symbol what it may be used to express. All that a symbol *can* express it *may* express," Ludwig Wittgenstein wrote in late August 1919 to Bertrand Russell.[1] At this point, in Wittgenstein's eyes, Russell was the only person alive who might be able to understand his work.

In his letter, Wittgenstein was attempting to clarify one of the basic dilemmas of linguistic philosophy, in response to a reservation Russell had expressed after reading his manuscript "twice, thoroughly." It concerns essentially the rules established within that logical symbolism, upon which, for Wittgenstein, any meaningful statement is based. Needless to say, Wittgenstein's propositions can also be read as a defiant defense of his own situation. He was ultimately determined to blaze trails on behalf of the symbol that was Wittgenstein, away from the labor, duties, and other contexts that had previously given significance to his life. Perhaps his relatives and closest friends might have been able to understand that by shedding his fortune, he had freed himself for a radical new start, but his intention to abnegate his own talent caused profound consternation, particularly among his siblings. Wittgenstein's eldest sister, Hermine, the one closest to him, recalled:

I was at first unable to understand his second decision, to opt for a completely unremarkable profession and perhaps to become a country schoolteacher. Since we, his brothers and sisters, very often communicate with each other in analogies, I told him during a long conversation that when I imagined him with his philosophically trained mind as a primary school teacher it felt to me as if someone were trying to use a precision instrument to open crates. Ludwig replied with an analogy that silenced me. He said, "You remind me of someone who is looking through a closed window and cannot explain to himself the strange movements of a passerby; he doesn't know what sort of storm is raging outside and that this person is perhaps only with great effort keeping himself on his feet."[2]

This graphic image, memorialized by the genius's sister, speaks to all the significant problems and potential solutions in Ludwig's life. First, there was the overall sensation, which he had had since early youth, of being separated somehow from the world of his fellow humans by an invisible barrier, or pane of glass—an unsettling feeling of fundamental difference, which had been further reinforced and heightened by the experiences of the war years. At its peak, this feeling slipped into a sense of intellectual exclusion (or confinement) and exposed him to the uncontrollable idea that his life was without meaning. Outwardly he could be completely unable to act, while furious storms raged within.

Recent research has suggested that Wittgenstein may have suffered from a mild form of autism, a developmental disturbance that manifests in early childhood and is often accompanied by remarkable abilities in the fields of mathematical analysis and music, and reveals itself in the form of fixed patterns of action and very restricted social skills.[3] It's entirely possible. At any rate, a metaphorical "wall" or "window" separating one's own experience from the world of others is among the most pertinent and common self-descriptions of those suffering from depression. Wittgenstein's notebooks and letters from 1919 through 1921, with their constant recourse to the idea of redemptive suicide, leave us in no doubt: during those months and years he was going through various phases of acute depression.

Setting our clinical suspicions aside, the notion that his access to the so-called world outside, and to all the others "out there," was at a fundamental level disturbed or distorted effectively sums up the founding doubt of Western philosophy: Is there something that separates us from the true nature of things? The actual experiences and sensations of others? And if so, who or what could it be?

Plato's parable of the cave already relies on the assumption that the world as we perceive it is in fact one of only shadow and appearance. About two thousand years later, in the actual founding document of modern epistemological and subjective philosophy, René Descartes's *Meditations*, written in 1641, we can see an analogy that gives concrete form to Wittgenstein's simile of the person behind the "closed window." Descartes begins one of his experiments in doubt with an initially straightforward view from his fireside seat in his own room out into the street. He questions whether all the pedestrians he sees passing in the rain outside are really people—or perhaps only "machines" wearing coats and hats.[4] What, as a thinking subject closed in behind the brain's pane of glass, do any of us know about what is really going on inside anyone else? What storms rage within them? Or perhaps there is nothing at all happening in there—is there really complete and permanent calm?

VIENNESE BRIDGES

WITH HIS RETORT TO HERMINE, then, Wittgenstein called upon one of philosophy's most distinguished images of the inescapable problem of epistemology: the extent to which we, trapped as we are entirely within the internal space of our own experiential subjectivity, can have any reliable knowledge whatsoever of the outside world, or connect with the interiority of others. As we have seen, this question was for Wittgenstein much more than an exercise in armchair skepticism. Rather, this doubt constituted a constant and burning issue even in his most mundane actions and interactions, indeed his entire relationship with the world. Here we have a man returning from the war, who has over the previous seven years devoted all of his intellectual energy to the expression of his own thoughts, *including those about this problem*, as clearly and unambiguously as possible, in the form of a logical and philosophical treatise.

In the autumn of 1919, Wittgenstein had to admit failure. Even for his most knowledgeable contacts—Gottlob Frege, Bertrand Russell, and the architect Paul Engelmann, to each of whom Wittgenstein had sent a copy of the manuscript—his work was largely incomprehensible.

As noted, however, the analogy in Hermine's memoirs reveals not only the set of fundamental existential problems with which Wittgenstein had to cope throughout his life, but also their solutions. Because with the precision of that image of the man battling the storm outside the "closed window," Wittgenstein had in fact managed to "open his window," that is, to successfully make a connection with another and thus escape from his own psychic isolation into the freedom of being understood.

Readers clearly know from Wittgenstein's image what his internal life was like a century ago; they even know it with at least the same precision and clarity with which Wittgenstein knew it himself at that moment in

1919. Thanks to the miracle of language, then, the pane of glass has ceased to exist, either for him or for us.

If we look more closely, Wittgenstein's entire philosophical oeuvre, and especially his later work, is run through with metaphors and allegories of liberation, of exits and escapes. Not just his famous answer to the question "What is your aim in philosophy?" "To shew the fly the way out of the fly-bottle!"[5]

The activity of philosophizing, and this was Wittgenstein's lifelong hope, opens the window to an active, immediate, and meaningful existence with others, the freedom that in the *Tractatus* he calls "happiness." Thus this opening is a window to "another world," because "the world of the happy is quite another than the world of the unhappy" (T 6:43).

Significantly, the route to another world uses the very medium that, without the thought-clarifying activity of philosophy, constantly threatens to undermine, obscure, distort, or even block access to an appreciation of it: language itself.

POETIC PRECISION

WHAT MADE WITTGENSTEIN'S TREATISE so incredibly difficult for its first readers (and would continue to do so for decades after) was his decision to express his thoughts through two modes of language that are so different as to seem mutually exclusive. One is the language of mathematical logic, with its entirely abstract symbols, the other a poetic language rich in imagery, concepts, allegory, and paradoxical aphorism. This stylistic obstinacy is in turn explained by the unique calibrations of the precision instrument that was Wittgenstein's philosophical intelligence. Through his studies in engineering in Berlin and Manchester, and especially his studies in Cambridge with Russell, he was deeply schooled in the construction of logical calculations and abstract symbolic connections. But, as shines through in Hermine's memoirs, his mind was also clearly whetted by the Wittgenstein family's habit of communicating "in analogies," through the poetic practices of metaphor, verbal imagery, and allegory.

This second practice was not just a peculiarity specific to the house of Wittgenstein. If there was a European cultural milieu that combined a commitment to logical analytical precision with poetic symbolization through the use of language—the two seen as distinct but mutually defining manifestations of an aesthetic aspiration to clarity—it was fin-de-siècle Vienna.[6] A profound connection between the clarity of language and the condition of the self and culture was assumed. This is the unspoken bond among works as different as the music of Mahler, the writings of Hugo von Hofmannsthal, Robert Musil, and Karl Kraus, the philosophies of Ernst Mach and Fritz Mauthner, and not least the psychoanalysis of Sigmund Freud. It was no coincidence that all this was going on at a time when the machinations of the internal political space of the imperial monarchy and the external realities of daily life in the multiethnic empire widened into a gulf of absurdity. The Palais Wittgenstein, where Ludwig spent his first fourteen years and was taught by private tutors, with its regular soirees, visits from artists, and meetings of charitable foundations, was one of the centers of that cultural milieu. The young Wittgenstein effectively absorbed it with his mother's milk.

AGAINST THE WORLD

WITTGENSTEIN'S *TRACTATUS* ASIDE, nothing better captures and defines the intellectual peculiarities of Vienna at the turn of the century than the caustic aphorisms of the writer and journalist Karl Kraus. The emperor of this milieu once complained, for example, that Freudian psychoanalysis was "in fact the very illness that it claimed to cure." Paradoxically, Kraus was skeptical about a new therapy based on achieving clarity and self-understanding through language where confusion and hopelessness had reigned hitherto (in the patient's mind). Of course Kraus was also skeptical of the value of language in and of itself for humans as cognitive beings. Is language, in the end, as the Viennese intellectuals were prone to ask, the illness that needs to be fought against? Or is it the only imaginable therapy? Does it obstruct the path to true knowledge of the world and the self? Or is it the very thing that makes it possible?

In 1918, when Wittgenstein wrote in the preface to his treatise that *the truth of the thoughts communicated here*" seemed to him "*unassailable and definitive,*" which was why he believed that "*the problems have in essentials finally been solved,*" he had in mind not only—and not even primarily—the problems involved in the construction of a contradiction-free calculus, which had been left unresolved by Russell and Frege. He meant, too, the concerns and linguistic doubts of the artistic protagonists of his own Viennese world. With the loss of the world war, however, this Viennese world had declined as definitively as the empire whose intellectual center it had previously formed. In 1919, the little that remained of it met Wittgenstein's work not only with complete incomprehension but, worse, with unadulterated indifference.

The list of publishers' rejections that the returning soldier had received by late autumn 1919 reads like a Who's Who of the former Viennese avant-garde. First he spoke to Ernst Jahoda, Karl Kraus's publisher, and then to Wilhelm Braumüller, publisher of Otto Weininger's acclaimed *Sex and Character*. Last of all he approached Ludwig von Ficker, the publisher of the avant-garde journal *Der Brenner*, which Wittgenstein had supported with financial donations before the war, and the poet Rainer Maria Rilke.

In the end Ficker passed the request on, with support from Rilke, to Insel Verlag—again without a positive result.

The only offer of publication that Wittgenstein received during those months came on the condition that he undertake to pay the costs of printing and distributing the book, which he strictly refused to do. First of all, he no longer had a penny to his name. More important, he considered it "indecent to impose such a work on the world in that way," as he wrote to Ludwig von Ficker in a letter of October 1919: "The writing was *my* affair; but the world must accept it in the normal way." But the world had no inclination to do so, at least not in Vienna. And he found no opportunities elsewhere, either. Small wonder that autumnal storms of despair raged in Wittgenstein while his days at the teacher training institute on Kundmanngasse were spent at desks side by side with students who were at least ten years younger than he was, and with whom he had nothing whatsoever in common.

The autumn of 1919 also saw a sequence of episodes that remain among the most controversial in his life. There are (or were) diary entries from this time that indicate that Wittgenstein successfully sought and found encounters in a part of the Viennese Prater park that was known for homosexual liaisons.[7] Whether these episodes really happened or happened that way remains contentious—the diary entries have been seen directly by his biographer but have not yet been made publicly accessible. What is undisputed, however, is the fact of Wittgenstein's homosexual inclinations, which were for decades kept secret by the administrators of his estate. Later diary entries also make it quite clear that throughout his life Wittgenstein had an extremely tense moral relationship with his own sexuality, and in the end considered that entire sphere of experience to be corrupt and dirty. Episodes like those in the Prater, in particular, would have been corrupt in his eyes, and indeed the supposed encounters in the park coincide with a mood that drove Wittgenstein to a new, self-destructive low that autumn.

During those months, his last hopes of being recognized as the philosopher that he was rested on Bertrand Russell. Again and again Wittgenstein urged that they meet as soon as possible so that he could explain the essential insights of his work in person. Meanwhile, the Continent lay in ruins. Wittgenstein had no money, and Russell—who had been imprisoned as a conscientious objector during the war—lacked a valid passport. At last, however, they managed to arrange a meeting for December 1919, halfway between Austria and England, in the Netherlands—where the former Kaiser Wilhelm II had fled a year earlier and remained, presumably trembling at the thought of being handed over by the Dutch government to the Entente powers.

THREE DOTS
IN THE HAGUE

THE FOUR DAYS that the two men spent together in a hotel in The Hague followed a routine: Wittgenstein would knock on the door of Russell's room in the early morning and for the rest of the day monopolize his time with discussions and expatiations about his book. The debates reached their supposed climax when Russell—in an effort to grasp the difference between *saying* and *showing*, which Wittgenstein insisted was critical for his thesis—took a sheet of paper and on it drew three dots in ink. Clutching this sheet of paper, he walked up to Wittgenstein and demanded that he admit that there were without a doubt three dots, which would make the statement "There are in the world at least three things" true and meaningful.[8] This Wittgenstein firmly rejected. By his lights, nothing meaningful could be said about the nature of the world as a whole.

According to Wittgenstein, all that could be *meaningfully* said about the sheet with the three dots was: "On this sheet of paper there are three dots." This is because the statement refers to the presence of a state of affairs in the world. It is not only meaningful but, as could be unambiguously stated in view of the sheet of paper in Russell's hand, also true.

PICTURES OF FACTS

ACCORDING TO WITTGENSTEIN'S TREATISE, meaningful—and hence, where appropriate, true—*propositions* are best grasped as *pictures of facts*, whose content, if we verbally understand these *pictures/propositions*, gives a precise idea of what kind of fact in the world must exist for them to be true.

2:221 What the picture represents is its sense.

2:222 In the agreement or disagreement of its sense with reality, its truth or falsity consists.

4:016 In order to understand the essence of the proposition, consider hieroglyphic writing, which illustrates the facts it describes.

So the truth of a proposition reveals itself when we find the picture of the facts whose existence it asserts, in the world as actually given. Or to put it another way: when that which the proposition asserts is also the case. According to the first two propositions of Wittgenstein's *Tractatus*:

1 The world is all that is the case.

1:1 The world is the totality of facts, not of things.

THE BARBER

AND WHAT IS WRONG with a proposition like "There are three dots in the world"? Russell may have asked in that hotel room, waving the sheet of paper in his hand. Well, as proposition 1:1 of the book establishes, "the world" (as a whole) is not itself a fact but only "the totality of facts."

One chief reason that Wittgenstein denied that propositions about the world could be meaningful lies in the following logic: If the world were itself a fact, it would—as only one fact among others—effectively include itself as a fact. It would be, as a world, on the one hand defined as a set *of certain elements* (here: the totality of facts) and *at the same time an element of that set* (hence: a fact). But a logical formalism that allows a set to contain itself as an element, leads—as none other than Russell himself had proved, Wittgenstein believed—to infernal logical complexities and, finally, to uncontrollable contradictions.

Russell's own favorite example of such set-theoretical paradoxes, which he conceived in 1918, is the case of a hypothetical barber, in Chiswick, say. Russell states that this barber cuts the hair of all those, and only those, people in Chiswick who do not cut their own hair. Who, if anyone, cuts the barber's hair?

The question cannot be answered without contradiction. If the barber does not cut his own hair, he is by definition part of the set of people whose hair he cuts. But if he cuts his own hair, he contradicts the set definition, "cuts the hair of all of those, and only those, people in Chiswick who do not cut their own hair." The suggestion that the barber is bald is a good joke, but it does not rid us of the set-theoretical contradictions that have arisen.

So there, in a philosophy-of-language short-back-and-sides, are Wittgenstein's reasons why the world, once defined as "the totality of facts," cannot itself be a fact. And if the world is not itself a fact, then—according to the *Tractatus*—there can also be no meaningful propositions about the state of the world as a whole, not even as simple as: "There are three things in the world." Not, for example, "The world exists." Or, "The world does not exist."

The fact that there are at least three things in the world cannot, for all of Russell's waving a sheet of paper in a hotel room, meaningfully be *said*. However—and this is Wittgenstein's key point—what this proposition states can be *shown* to be unquestionably true, through the simple fact that there are three dots on the sheet of paper. Where, then, my dear Bertrand, does the problem lie exactly? Or even your objection to it? Everything that can be said can be said clearly and without contradiction.

RUSSELL ON THE LADDER

BUT RUSSELL WAS NOT SATISFIED with these parameters of meaning. He made a very striking and pertinent counterargument, to the effect that Wittgenstein's philosophical treatise, according to the boundaries that it drew between propositions that were meaningful and those that only appeared to be meaningful, must therefore itself, for long passages, consist entirely of nonsense propositions.

"What else, my dear Ludwig, is a proposition like 'The world is all that is the case' than one that concerns the *world as a whole*?" To which Wittgenstein could have answered with complete serenity: "Of course, Bertrand, you are exactly right, and I have also expressly referred to that contradiction in the last two propositions of my book." Take up and read:

6:54 My propositions are elucidatory in this way: he who understands me finally recognizes them as senseless, when he has climbed out through them, on them, over them. (He must so to speak throw away the ladder, after he has climbed up on it.)

He must surmount these propositions; then he sees the world rightly.

7 Whereof one cannot speak, thereof one must be silent.

You see, my dear Bertrand, don't you? Correctly understood, my book *says* nothing meaningful, but it does *show* something. It is as a work nothing but a single act of showing, of "another world," that is, another vision of the world. One that is less distorted, clearer, more honest, less distorted, more modest, more astonishing and more groundless, more meaningful. But above all freer—freer because in this new world one no longer needs to debate certain questions, particularly philosophical questions—because one has in fact recognized them to be meaningless, indeed *experienced* them as such. It is a world without assertions about how the world as a whole is or is not "in reality," for example. So it is also a world shorn of ideologies and suspicions of ideologies, if you like.

My book suggests to the reader this freer vision of the world. It is as if I were to point out a cloud in the sky and ask if you, too, see it as shaped like a lion—and look, now it's more like a dragon. There's the jaw, there the tail . . . do you see, do you see it, too? There are the wings, two holes for its eyes, now closing up in the wind. . . . But eventually, of course, a point is reached where all explanations and references must end, when you simply have to see it yourself, where you grasp it yourself, when it must show itself to you. . . . It was in precisely that sense that I wrote my preface: that this work will be understood only by *"those who have already had the thoughts which are expressed in it—or similar thoughts."*

To no avail. Russell simply couldn't see it. Couldn't get it. Saw it all in a fundamentally different way from Wittgenstein. He was still clinging, not without reason, to one of the first rungs of Wittgenstein's ladder, and wanted to go no further. Wittgenstein "has become a complete mystic," Russell wrote in a letter, in summary of the discussions in The Hague.[9] He was not mistaken. Indeed, he had even touched upon something important. Likewise, Wittgenstein, back in Vienna at Christmas 1919, had the feeling that he had inched Russell closer to certain aspects of his work. The critical development was that Russell, an internationally renowned and also bestselling philosopher, had declared himself willing to write a short introduction to his former student's book. He may not have successfully clarified for his friend the difference in the philosophy of language between *saying* and *showing*, but the meeting filled Wittgenstein with fresh hope. A preface from Russell exponentially increased the chances of his book's being published and selling, as he in fact wrote to Ludwig von Ficker. But without the desired success. Ficker still considered the book to be absolutely unmarketable.

WHY THE WORLD
DOES NOT EXIST

THE PUBLISHER IN QUESTION DOUBTED whether anyone—bar a handful of logicians and set theorists—actually cared whether propositions about the world as a whole were meaningful or not. Did it really matter; wasn't it an empty dispute about vocabulary? In terms of our actual everyday life, his suspicions were not unfounded. But for the understanding that modern philosophy has of itself, and many of the problems considered central to it, a great deal hangs on this question—even, in a sense, everything. We need only think of Descartes and his skepticism, which shaped all of modern philosophy, about whether this world, as we experience it and describe it, actually exists, or whether it is instead an illusion created by an almighty demon. Does the world exist at all?

It sounds important, existential even. With Wittgenstein we can see this fundamental epistemological doubt to be a classic nonsense problem, something anyone of clear mind would do well to leave alone. Because:

> 6:5 For an answer which cannot be expressed, the question too cannot be expressed.
>
> The *riddle* does not exist.
>
> If a question can be put at all, then it *can* also be answered.

> 6:51 Scepticism is *not* irrefutable, but palpably senseless, if it would doubt where a question cannot be asked.
>
> For doubt can only exist where there is a question; a question only where there is an answer, and this only where something *can* be *said*.

The problem has been dealt with by Wittgenstein, then. Not solved or refuted. No, dealt with in the sense of having been set aside because it had already been recognized that the way in which the question was put was false. Or, to take another example considerably closer in time to Wittgenstein, we might think of Martin Heidegger startling his student audience with the most unconditional of all questions. Not the question of whether something exists (three dots on a sheet of paper, for example), but of whether there is *"anything at all."* This alternative formulation perhaps sounds more meaningful at first, but in the end it may not be. Which is not to say that Wittgenstein was deaf to the world-changing momentum that lay behind Heidegger's questioning impulse. On the contrary, he had written in his own work:

6:522 There is indeed the inexpressible. This *shows* itself; it is the mystical.

6:44 Not *how* the world is, is the mystical, but *that* it is.

Like Heidegger, Wittgenstein could not get over his original astonishment that anything exists at all. And in particular his astonishment that the "anything" in question reveals itself to us as immediately significant, even capable of truth once we open our eyes to it.

Unlike Heidegger, however, Wittgenstein did not believe that the clear and direct question about the givenness of "anything at all," let alone the world, contained a profound philosophical riddle whose true meaning needed to be expressed in language. He was instead convinced that any attempt in that direction was bound sooner or later to lead to linguistic nonsense—or worse.

UNDER PRESSURE

DURING THOSE SAME SEPTEMBER DAYS IN 1919, when the storms of meaninglessness raged in Wittgenstein and he found himself cut off from all others by a "closed window," Heidegger was in the midst of an eruption of creativity. "The visions, the problem horizons—real steps towards fruitful solutions—new ways of seeing in principle, possibilities of the most surprising formulations and character, simultaneous firing off of genuine combinations—it is all so brimming, simply overflowing, that one is, purely in terms of time, all but incapable of catching, capturing and systematically processing the flow," he wrote to his wife in Freiburg on September 9, from a farmhouse near Konstanz, where he had withdrawn for a few weeks to write.[10] The thinker of the Black Forest was, however, not free of worries closer to home. His marriage was in crisis. Only a few days previously Elfride had admitted to him in a letter that she was having a relationship with Friedel Caesar, whom she had studied alongside and who was now a physician at the university hospital in Freiburg. Heidegger's reply to her confession was at first controlled and conciliatory. He was also, however, quick to interpret the affair as a philosophical challenge, which he and he alone could solve: "Your letter arrived early this morning and I already knew its contents. It would not be fruitful to say many words about it and dissect everything. It is enough that you have told me in your simple, sure way. . . . I have known for a long time that Friedel loves you . . . and I have sometimes been surprised that you didn't tell me before. . . . It would be uncouth of me and a waste of strength if I resented him in any way. . . . I am already examining the problem of human relationships in general, a question that has preoccupied me of late when I have been meeting new people. And I notice: I am essentially indifferent to them all—they walk past outside as if on the other side of the window—you watch after them and you may think of them again. . . . The great calling to a transtemporal task must always also be a condemnation to solitude, and it is part of his nature that others know nothing about him. On the contrary, they see the lonely man as wealthy, honored, fawned over—respected and much talked about, and are then amazed when he treats them with disdain (or rather ignores them completely)."[11]

Here again are those who walk by "outside as if on the other side of the window." All those ordinary people, the all-too-numerous masses, with whom Heidegger was unable or unwilling to form any true connection. People unaware of the creative storms of thought that raged in him, people he must reject, and hence insult, in this fundamental intellectual asymmetry. The romantic image of the lone hero, condemned by fate to overcome the superhuman challenge that he alone has set himself, apart from the world and inevitably misunderstood by it: the antisocial genius. That was Heidegger's vision of himself. And would remain so throughout his life.

THE OBSCURED GAZE

IT WAS NO COINCIDENCE that Heidegger, in his reply to Elfride, should have evoked the Cartesian metaphor of the doubting philosopher behind the window, for the course of his own thought in the end called into doubt even the humanity of his fellow men. Descartes's influence on modern philosophy, as Heidegger became increasingly aware during that year, had been fatal: Descartes and his skeptical thought experiment, Descartes and his establishment of the thinking and thus ultimately calculating subject as the primary source of all certainty ("I think, therefore I am"), Descartes and his reduction of philosophy to just epistemology, Descartes and his consistent division of the world into mind and matter. . . . Descartes became the philosophical enemy par excellence, his thought marking the point at which Western philosophy went wrong.

In the euphoria of early September 1919, the "transtemporal task" that Heidegger already saw outlined ahead of him—the art of "new seeing in principle" and pushing forward into a new "problem horizon"—consists in nothing other than ridding his country, his culture, indeed his entire tradition of the bad modern-day magic of subjective philosophy and epistemology, of its purely calculating rationality and fixation on the natural sciences. Overall he saw his fellow Westerners as trapped by an understanding of themselves and an approach to the world that were fundamentally false. Their capacity to see reality had been distorted by an unquestioned adherence to false concepts. For that reason they could see themselves, the world, and one another only in a very blurred form, as if through frosted glass.

It was not enough, though, that this dim, unfocused gaze went unnoticed. No, this mode of vision had over the centuries penetrated so deeply into our culture and understanding of ourselves that by now it was itself understood as the supreme and only true form of knowledge of the world, and retrospectively celebrated as the actual breakthrough into the light of the Enlightenment. A nightmare brought to life.

A nightmare is, however, also something from which we can awaken. And that autumn Heidegger experienced himself as being fully awake: he began to philosophize independently, that is, outside the structures of the subject and knowledge as expounded by Descartes. From then on, Heidegger consistently thought "outside the box." And appropriately his first fundamental insight was that there is no box, no separate internal space of experience that separates thinking subjects from so-called reality, as a pane of glass would. Descartes's skepticism about the outside world and the related question of how reality may "in reality" be constituted, its absolute separation from the subject and object of knowledge, these were all, as Heidegger showed with an increasingly precise phenomenological approach, merely false problems and false suppositions.

When Heidegger wrote to Elfride, in that summer of breakthrough, "As you once correctly observed, I have already, and with much broader horizons and problems, exceeded him [Husserl]," he addressed his wife as a noble partner, a companion along his new path, even though they were going through a difficult time in their marriage.[12] But only a few lines later, he describes himself once again as a lonely pioneer and visionary. Heidegger's letters of September 1919 read as hopeful declarations of faith to his wife, although he is no longer certain whether he can still find loving access to her inner life. What if she had already gone over to the other side? Had she been drawn by the bourgeois affluence of Friedel Caesar to a purely conventional understanding of love, one devoted to etiquette and shallow appearances? He could no longer be sure.

At this time of uncertainty he sought and found the only certain form of refuge available: that of his work, his creation, his thought. Here nothing was separated, no crack of doubt was left open. Here all was one. All part of a great creative surge! His only regret was that he could not remain forever in that magical place of absolute Eros—and had eventually to return to the world of Friedel and his like: "This pure productivity also has its uncanny quality: *it* creates and yet one experiences oneself absolutely in the process—particularly when the state fades and a slackening follows and one tries to find one's way back into one's surroundings. Then I know that I was entirely and absolutely within myself and above all within the objective world of problems and the mind—there is no strangeness here— here nothing goes past outside. Instead one goes along oneself and makes things go—in the creative life all strangeness has disappeared—which makes it all the more disruptive and shocking when one stands on the far shore back in natural surroundings."[13]

"It" was at work in Heidegger during those days, operating with a kind of violence, carrying him away with it. What kind of "it" are we talking about here? Certainly not the "Id" that, according to Sigmund Freud's still-youthful theory of the unconscious, forms the base of the "Super-ego— Ego—Id" triad, and is hence at the root of every individual's instinctual drive. No, even at the beginnings of his philosophy, Heidegger's *"Es"* already means an effect of a different kind and category. It is the same uncanny—or we might perhaps join with Wittgenstein and say mystical— *"Es,"* which makes its first appearance in the question *"Was gibt es?"* It is an *"Es"* beyond the dualism of subject and object ("absolutely within myself and above all within the objective world"), of activity and passivity ("one goes along oneself and makes things go"), of inside and out ("here nothing goes past outside"). *"Es"* is far from easy to grasp conceptually, even for someone like Heidegger. But he had experienced it; the existence of this primordial, creative "it," the cause of all sense and being, was for him indisputable. He would spend his whole life seeking a language for it.

LONELY TOGETHER

HEIDEGGER'S LETTERS OF SEPTEMBER 1919 are powerful testimony to the serious approach with which he sought to merge philosophy and everyday life. So serious, in fact, that in the end he sought to establish a perfect parallel between the challenge of his marriage and his philosophical project. More perhaps than any philosopher before him, he equated the conjugal errors committed by Elfride with the erroneous path that modern philosophy itself was taking. Both seemed to Heidegger unreasonable demands. Demands, however, that made him stronger and more productive, since that engagement with her unreasonableness directed him toward his real purpose: to advance ruthlessly and with absolute objectivity toward the essential, to strip away all that was inauthentic, conjectural, and fanciful. As he wrote her on September 13: "I was not angry with you for your insight—how could I be, when I must experience the recklessness and hardness of knowledge every day with an attitude of absolute objectivity.... Life, in its primordial power, is deeper and fuller than knowledge, and our entire philosophy still suffers under the fact that it allows its further problems to be predetermined by things known—so that from the outset they are disfigured and afflicted by paradoxes."[14]

Piercing through superficialities, shrugging off conventions, battling falsities, advancing recklessly toward the core of the matter, enabling authenticity to break through everywhere—these and similar terms became commonplace in the years after 1919. And not only among philosophers. These concepts (superficiality, convention, appearance, distortion) increasingly became the property of an anti-Semitic strand of German culture, one with deep roots that grew stronger after the war.

At this stage, however, Heidegger's mission was not yet an explicitly political one. Its radicalism was initially restricted, as with the example of the "experience-of-the-question," to the inner space of philosophical ideas. In this case it brought forth the most universal question imaginable, one as free from all predeterminations as was possible, the question about the actual meaning of the sequence of words *es gibt*.

Seemingly no question could be asked more simply, in a manner more unhampered by convention, more universally, and above all in a way that was freer of presuppositions. And could also go unanswered. Yes, *da* (there), *gibt es* undeniably something. *Es gibt*, in fact, a whole world. And yet the abiding astonishment at its mere *Da-Sein*, its givenness, calls for anything but a natural attitude to the world. Rather, as Heidegger himself pointedly stressed, it demands a special form of immersion or meditative contemplation that has nothing to do with the everyday and largely unreflective mode with which we normally proceed through life and the world.

TWO ODDBALLS

IMAGINE, BY WAY OF EXPERIMENT, two young men strolling together through the city—and suddenly one says to the other:

"How strange that anything exists [*"dass es überhaupt etwas gibt"*]! How miraculous: There! And there! Do you see it, too?"

And the other man nods and says: "Yes, I see it. It also shows itself to me. And you know, I always think: It is not how the world is that is mystical, but *that* it is."

What curious characters! And yet it is a conversation that Martin Heidegger and Ludwig Wittgenstein could easily have had in 1919. And we may be sure that they would have understood each other perfectly. Except that Heidegger would happily have continued talking and philosophizing about the meaning of that *"Es gibt,"* while Wittgenstein certainly wouldn't. Because where one of them (Heidegger) assumed the opening question, the breakthrough to a genuinely undistorted knowledge of being, the other (Wittgenstein) saw predictable nonsense and false problems generated by language.

WORLDS AHEAD

FOR HEIDEGGER AFTER 1919, the fundamental error of philosophy, at least from Descartes on, lay in the assumption that this theoretical approach was original and authentic. Because it is precisely this that turns reality on its head, giving rise to a whole series of epistemological pseudo-problems, above all the Cartesian skepticism about whether reality in the sense of *the* reality outside exists at all. This is in itself a question that can emerge only out of a theoretical attitude, and hence in Heidegger's (and also Wittgenstein's) view is simply an interloper in philosophy:

To inquire into the reality of the environment, in the face of which all reality is already in many ways a transformed and de-interpreted deduction, is to turn all genuine problems on their head. The environment contains its own genuine self-designation. The true solution to the problem of the reality of the world lies in the understanding that it is not a problem at all, but a nonsense.[15]

For Heidegger, then, that which is primarily given is not *the* reality but *an* environment. And that "worlding" environment is already a significant totality of references that, if consistently pursued, ultimately point toward the whole world of meaning. This specific kind of givenness of the world is something to which we must, in Heidegger's view, open our eyes. We need to reclaim a philosophical point of view that we have unlearned and forgotten, with fatal consequences both for ourselves and for our culture as a whole.

Anyone who, as an existing human being (Dasein), believes that primal access to the world is solely theoretical has removed themselves from the "worlding" power of the authentic.

In 1919, Heidegger called this estrangement from the actual and the original a *"fading of significance"*: of the world, of other people, of one's own self. They are all, to return to Descartes's metaphor of the window, perceived only through the frosted glass of theory. The false life, then, in a faked world and a falsely founded togetherness.

Here the manifestly existential features of Heidegger's program for a phenomenological reconquest of the world become clear once more. Even at this early stage we can see the embryo of an ideological critique of the modern technological age and its totalizing logic of objectification and exploitation, which will continue to resonate from Heidegger into critical theory across the twentieth century and into our own. No one believed more strongly than Heidegger from 1919 onward that, to cite Theodor Adorno's perhaps most famous phrase, there is "no right life in falsehood." In his terms, the ideal existence is therefore an entirely original and undistorted, authentic "Da-Sein." (A therapeutic demand not made, however, by Adorno and his followers.) Looking back from the present day, we can even see Heidegger's influence on the postwar German ecological movement. Wholeness, environmental consciousness, the critique of technology, contact with nature—even in 1919, all these were core motifs of Heidegger's thought. In its appeal to the authentic and the genuine in all areas of life it also emphatically calls for an organic rootedness and anchoring of the self in an environment experienced as one's own, meaning: one's home, one's own landscape, with its traditions, rituals, dialects, and everything else that belongs to it. We can be completely authentic only where our roots are, in our environment. For Heidegger himself, famously, that was the Black Forest.

THE BREAKTHROUGH
OF AUTHENTICITY

EXACTLY A YEAR LATER, in September 1920, Heidegger is still (or once again) in a state of unadulterated creative euphoria—and separated from his family once again. This time he has withdrawn to the home of his brother, Fritz, in the village of Messkirch, where they grew up. From there he sends food parcels to Freiburg, where a food crisis now rages:

> What brings me joy: that I am working so well *and surely.* . . .
> I am now working . . . in one go, with the enthusiasm of "forwards"
> and "through." In the morning from 7-12 and then after a bite to
> eat from 2-7 I am absolutely free from interruption, from lectures
> and seminars and visitors—and above all in the growing cool. . . .

If I am relaxed in the evening I play—don't be startled—"66" with Father and Fritz and am entirely involved. . . . I am distracted before going to sleep—otherwise I am too preoccupied with philos.—

Many deep kisses, my dear soul—be well again soon and enjoy our boys. Give them both a loving kiss from me.

Your Möhrchen [baby carrot][16]

....

So there they sat—Martin, Fritz, and their father—playing cards. In their own way an authentic, intact Black Forest family. But that month Heidegger's philosophical euphoria was subject to a corrective. At this time not only was he in full creative flow, there was also an element of repression involved. Because in Freiburg on August 20, 1920, Elfride was still in bed, still weak from the birth of their second son, Hermann. At the time of his birth, and throughout the whole of August, Heidegger stayed in Messkirch and Elfride and little Jörg were cared for by a good friend of hers. It was only in 2005 that the secret shared by Elfride and Martin since 1920 came to light. Heidegger was not the biological father. Hermann was the issue of Elfride's relationship with Friedel Caesar. For Heidegger, for the moment, this wasn't grounds for divorce. On the contrary, he saw it as a chance to realize a truly authentic marriage—freed from the false bourgeois conventions that he so hated. Only three days after the birth he had already found language for that conviction: "I find myself thinking often how pale, untrue and sentimental all the things generally said about marriage are. And whether we do not develop a new form in our lives—without a program or intention—only because we allow authenticity to break through everywhere."[17]

Dr. Walter Benjamin from the great city of Berlin, we can be sure, would have recognized Heidegger's determination to have a free married life, though at that time he was not only out of such aspirations but also still preoccupied with other concerns.

SOMETHING IN MEDIA

A YEAR AFTER THE AWARD of his doctorate, Benjamin and his wife were trapped in the same vortex of existential uncertainty that had gripped them with the unannounced visit of his father in August 1919. In the spring of 1920, the young couple—homeless, unemployed, penniless—had no choice but to return to Benjamin's parents' house on Delbrückstrasse in Berlin. Predictably, things escalated from there.

Benjamin refused on principle to consider the move to the spacious villa permanent; his father countered by withdrawing his monthly stipend. Now cornered, the son insisted on the early payment of at least part of his inheritance. A risky strategy at best when high inflation was clearly on the horizon. But in the face of all advice, Walter insisted on his payment. In May 1920 he and his father reached a kind of agreement. In a letter of May 26, 1920, Benjamin described the situation to Gershom Scholem:

It ended in a complete argument. . . . I was dismissed from the house with an advance payment of 30,000 marks from my inheritance, a further 10,000 marks and not a single piece of furniture, that is, I left without being thrown out. . . . Of course the provisional nature of these things declares itself to heaven, and what will happen cannot be predicted. The only thing certain is that we must get a flat *somewhere*, from where we can then look around for lodgings. . . . Do you know of *anything*? . . . I would be endlessly grateful to you if you could tell me of *anything* that you hear of: apartments in the city or in the country, if possible cheap and unfurnished, country houses for two families etc.... Then, but only if I am living in a halfway human circumstance, I must start work on my *Habilitation* ... even though my prospects of finding a post as Dozent in Bern have come to nothing. My parents-in-law, now the only material support left to us, even if it is not robust, but who are willing to make the utmost sacrifices, insist that I should become a bookseller or a publisher. Now my father is also refusing me the capital. But it is very likely that I will be forced to outwardly cease the pursuit of my old profession, that I will be unable to become a Dozent and for the time being have to study in secret and at night while at the same time engaging in bourgeois employment of some kind. Again, I don't know which. (I earned 110 marks with three graphological analyses.) ... I am trying very hard to find an editorial post. Block recommended me to S. Fischer, who was looking for an editor, but he didn't choose me. Do you know of anything? I would have a very big list for a publisher.

Very best wishes, please write soon

Yours, Walter[18]

If we ignore the elegant turns of phrase, these sentences could just as easily have been written by a young Berlin postgrad in 1997, 2007, or even 2017. The housing market is an absolute disaster, my parents are totally getting on my nerves, university funding's been slashed (fuck capitalism!), there are no graduate jobs, so I'm going to have to join a creative commune in the country. . . . And my job prospects? Don't really know right now. Something in media, ideally in publishing.

It is easy to call to mind the caricature of an essentially aimless, financially cosseted, extraordinarily talented almost twenty-eight-year-old, slowly but surely figuring out that the world hasn't exactly been waiting for the genius he doubtless thinks he is. Benjamin's only independent source of income at this point in his life came from graphological analyses. Today he would be a lifestyle consultant or a feng shui adviser.

In 1920, then, this academic overachiever was heading straight for the class we call the precariat. The remnants of the 30,000 reichsmarks, which he had extorted to propel himself into a new life, would only three years later be worth less than a sandwich. If there is a constant in Benjamin's life from now on, it is his keen ability to make the wrong decision at the wrong time, but a second, life-shaping pattern also appears in exemplary form in this letter. It would go on to inform Benjamin's dealings with the people he calls friends. From 1920 onward, it would be difficult to find a single letter of his in which he doesn't attempt to persuade the friends in question to give him help of one kind or another—or offer with expansive apologies, excuses, or explanations of why he was unable to fulfill agreed arrangements or return promised favors. His friendship with Scholem, with whom he started corresponding using the familiar *Du* only in the autumn of 1920, illustrates this pathology perfectly, overshadowed as it was by incessant requests and the taint of exploitation. Benjamin was a few years older than Scholem, which gave him a certain advantage in terms of maturity and knowledge from the outset. This, too, is typical, for Benjamin preferred to maintain in his friendships a mutually acknowledged hierarchy of knowledge.

FLAPPERS

THE PAINFUL LACK of purpose and security that often follows a period of intense study—contemporary sociologists call it the "floundering phase"—can be countered either by focusing on a single grand project or with proactive openness to entirely new potential careers. Predictably, Benjamin opted for neither of these strategies. Even though the prospect of a paid position at Bern had vanished—his wife also struggled in vain to find a permanent position in Switzerland, a country that had in the aftermath of the war become very expensive—Benjamin clung to his plan for a postdoctoral dissertation. However slim his chances, a professorship at a university remained the locus of his ambitions during those three years. In keeping with the latest academic and, more important, philosophical trends, he chose an "epistemo-theoretical special subject" for his postdoctoral paper, one that "falls into the extremely problematic area of word and concept (language and logos)." Benjamin hoped to open this thematic seam, already intensely mined, in innovative fashion, by returning to a medieval scholastic philosophy of language. He believed that he had unearthed in the writings of the medieval philosopher Duns Scotus certain philosophical motifs that were not far from his own intuitions about the philosophy of language—as already set out in his "About Language in General and Human Language in Particular."[19] His plan was to legitimize his own theses with reference to a largely forgotten tradition, and to strike the sparks of systemization from the apparent disjunct among modern, logical, and analytical linguistic philosophy and medieval speculations on language that fell under the heading of theology. It was a stroke of brilliance. Except someone else had already had the idea, and executed it in 1915 as a postdoctoral dissertation. As luck would have it, the scholar in question was Benjamin's former peer and soon-to-be fierce rival at Freiburg, Martin Heidegger. Benjamin was informed about Heidegger's work by Scholem in February 1920. "I knew nothing about Heidegger's book," Benjamin admitted in his reply to Scholem in December 1920 after months of silence, then continued:

> I have read Heidegger's book about Duns Scotus. It's incredible that someone can submit as a postdoctoral thesis a work of this kind, for which *nothing* is required to write it but a great deal of hard work and a mastery of scholastic Latin, and which in spite of all its philosophical presentation is essentially only a good piece of translation. The author's abject sycophancy towards Rickert and Husserl does not make reading it any more agreeable. In this book Duns Scotus' philosophy of language goes largely unexamined, so no task is accomplished.[20]

"Abject sycophancy," "hard work," "largely unexamined." The tone is familiar, as is the unconstrained criticism of a work by some esteemed colleague in the safety of a confidential letter, but from Heidegger's pen. Benjamin's attitude here toward academia and its required dissertations is, down to the choice of words, identical to Heidegger's. The same aggressive arrogance prevails, the same exaggerated ruthlessness, the same will to annihilate others. Two members of the same generation, sworn enemies, and yet, in character and thought, extremely close, like dizygotic twins, we might say, who in terms of both personality and interest may profoundly despise each other as adults.

The thoughts that were supposed to form the skeleton of Benjamin's dissertation had also been at the center of Heidegger's postdoctoral thesis of 1916, *Duns Scotus: Theory of Categories and Meaning*.[21] Both thinkers—with Duns Scotus as guarantor—were interested in the relationship between human speech (and hence thought) and the language of God. Can the way in which God thinks, describes, and recognizes the world be compared with the human equivalent? And if so, how might that assumed relationship be more precisely defined? What if, in fact, there were not the slightest similarity between the two? How then could human beings ever truly know the world as God's creation?

Heidegger, supported by a grant from the Catholic Church, had pursued these questions in detail. Benjamin wished to examine the same questions, though with reference to the Torah and the Jewish tradition of Kabbalah—as he had done as early as 1916 in his first continuous piece of linguistic philosophy, "About Language in General and Human Language in Particular." But contrary to his initial judgment, after a deeper reading of Heidegger's book he began to doubt the promise of his own project. Only a few weeks after his assassination of Heidegger, Benjamin wrote to Scholem once again, this time with some specifics:

> Following on from my previous studies ... I have become cautious and critical about whether it is right to use the pursuit of scholastic analogies as a guideline rather than a detour, since it seems after all that Heidegger's essay sets out the essence of scholastic thought for my problem—albeit in an entirely unenlightening way—and may in some sense allow us to deduce the real problem relating to it. Perhaps for now I should concentrate on the philosophers of language.[22]

Looking around this field—the philosophy of language—in those years around 1920 prompts the question: Whom exactly was he referring to? Cassirer? Wittgenstein? Russell? Moore? Husserl? Frege? Peirce? Perhaps it was the recognition that a more thorough induction into the state of research, then exploding in all directions, would have overtaxed both his resources and his interest that soon led Benjamin to abandon the whole project. But perhaps it was also the mere existence of Heidegger's work. Since November 1920, at any rate, Benjamin had once again been living at his parents' house on Delbrückstrasse. Tormented by violent attacks of depression, during those weeks he was intellectually paralyzed and largely incapable of working. He abandoned his planned postdoctoral thesis based on the philosophy of language. After all, there were other projects in his life. The translation of Charles Baudelaire's *Tableaux parisiens*,[23] for example, which he had managed to persuade the Heidelberg-based publisher Richard Weissbach to take on—having announced, in typical Benjamin style, that he had already completed the job. There was even a little money to be had. On December 4, 1920, Benjamin wrote to his by now slightly impatient publisher: "I am hard pressed to explain my long silence concerning the Baudelaire translation. It was because of my wish to be able to give you the material in the most complete possible form and in its final versions. That took weeks because I have recently been very ill. . . . I should like to add . . . that I would be willing (if it were compatible with your possible wish to bring out a critical edition) to write a *preface*, theoretical and very general, concerning the translator's task."[24]

Why not simply use as a preface to his translation the fine preparatory work he had done for his planned postdoctoral thesis on "Speech and Logos"? It would admittedly have nothing to do with Baudelaire's poetry or indeed with his own work as a translator, but nonetheless mean that all his theoretical work would not have been in vain. The idea is typical of Benjamin, and far from his worst. Today the essay "The Task of the Translator" is seen as one of his most famous, and also one of his most thorough, cogent, and clear. In fact, it contains the nucleus of an autonomous philosophy of language.

THE TASK

ANY ATTEMPT TO ESTABLISH a systematic connection between Benjamin's translation of Baudelaire and "The Task of the Translator" will be doomed to failure. There simply isn't one, even if the readers of the first edition, who could almost be counted on the fingers of one hand, must have assumed there was, given the essay's explicit identification as a "preface." It tends toward the principle, ultimately the metaphysical, and thus could have served as a preface to any translation or, ideally, none at all. It is also a text that, regardless of its title, contains not a single concrete example or any indication of how it might be practically applied to the actual task of translation. The only reference to the translation of Baudelaire that follows is a statement by Benjamin that it is in poetry that the true essence of language appears. In poetry language is stripped of its everyday functions, its utility as a communicative device, which raises a serious paradox for the translator:

> For what does a literary work "say"? What does it communicate? It tells very little to those who understand it. Its essential quality is not communication or the imparting of information—hence, something inessential.[25]

The essence of language is most apparent in poetry, but that essence does not consist of one person's ability to communicate something to another—and hence to inform them, for example, about a state of affairs ("You left your umbrella at my place!" "The dog's sleeping in the living room"). The task of the true translator therefore cannot be to convey the content of the work as faithfully as possible from one language to the other. So what is it?

Unsurprisingly, Benjamin's interest in the translator's task is a fundamentally philosophical one, in other words, only to the extent that a phenomenon that emerges from the activity of translation is ultimately of importance to *the philosophy of language.*

> To grasp the genuine relationship between an original and a translation requires an investigation analogous to the argumentation by which a critique of cognition would have to prove the impossibility of an image theory. There it is a matter of showing that in cognition there could be no objectivity, not even a claim to it, if it dealt with images of reality; here it can be demonstrated that no translation would be possible if in its ultimate essence it strove for likeness to the original.[26]

If the modern critic, as defined in Benjamin's doctoral thesis of 1919, must become a creative co-creator of the work, the work of the translator is comparable to that of the critic. Doing justice to the work translated means neither translating its message nor producing a copy that is as faithful as possible to the original.

We can see this, though, in a slightly less nebulous form, in the motto uttered in every translation class today: "As faithful as possible, as free as necessary." Where then is the advance in knowledge, where the new philosophical impulse?

It is based on a distinction within the philosophy of language that dated back to the Middle Ages, and was granted new relevance during this period by both Husserl's phenomenological school and Gottlob Frege's mathematical and logical philosophy of language. Frege calls it the difference between "meaning" and "sense." In Husserl's phenomenological terminology, it is the distinction between the "intended object" and the "mode of meaning."

One classic example is the distinction between the "morning star" and the "evening star." Both terms refer to the same celestial object, namely the planet Venus. So in Frege's terminology they have *the same meaning* but a *different sense.* The different names for a single object stress different aspects of it: one its shining in the morning sky, the other its shining in the evening sky. The "intended object"—in the sense of the object to which the names refer—is the same in both cases, but the "mode of meaning" differs.

For Benjamin this relationship between two terms in a single language that refer in slightly different ways to a single object captures the relationship between different national languages, such as German and French, and the way they refer to each other and, above all, to the world.

> Rather, all suprahistorical kinship between languages consists in this: in every one of them as a whole, one and the same thing is meant. Yet this one thing is achievable not by any single language but only by the totality of their intentions supplementing one another: the pure language. Whereas all individual elements of foreign languages—words, sentences, associations—are mutually exclusive, these languages supplement one another in their intentions. This law is one of the fundamental principles in the philosophy of language, but to understand it precisely we must draw a distinction, in the concept of "intention," between what is meant and the way of meaning it. In the words *Brot* and *pain*, what is meant is the same, but the way of meaning it is not. This difference in the way of meaning permits the word *Brot* to mean something other to a German than what the word *pain* means to a Frenchman, so that these words are not interchangeable for them. . . . As to what is meant, however, the two words signify the very same thing.[27]

Different languages not only differ—and Benjamin derives this idea from Johann Gottfried Herder and Wilhelm von Humboldt—in terms of "sounds and signs," but are autonomous ways of seeing the world. We might also say: their own ways of discovering slightly different or even new aspects in a single object (bread, for instance). They refer to the same object, but not with the same way of meaning. And here Benjamin, as a philosopher of language, inevitably encounters a problem that had preoccupied him as early as 1916, in his essay "About Language in General and Human Language in Particular." It is all well and good to claim that two words from different languages refer in their different ways to a single object—let us say, a loaf of bread—but what they refer to in turn is really defined and given only linguistically: as bread, ultimately, by the concept "bread." In the case of the morning and evening stars, both terms refer to the planet Venus, which is also, once again, identified as such only by the name Venus. In other words: The true identity of the object referred to by both words and, for Benjamin, also by both linguistic systems assumes a single true language underlying all variants. The language of "true names." For Benjamin this ideal language is that of the Old Testament God.

As we have seen, both Heidegger and Wittgenstein, in their different ways, were grappling with this idea of a unifying, primal language that lies behind all languages and all meaning. What was Benjamin's contribution? He solved the question not by asserting, like Wittgenstein, that the world had the same logical form as language or by claiming, as Heidegger did, that the world was always (linguistically) given and infused with meaning, but by instead referring to the history of theology, claiming that what he called "pure language," or indeed "true language," was the language of God. It must therefore be the task and objective of humans as speaking, inquiring beings to come as close as possible to the immediate unity of naming and speaking with which God grasps the essence of things (God always finds the precisely appropriate expression; no possible aspect of anything escapes God). And humans do so through the creation of a language that grasps and identifies as many aspects of the world as possible in the most linguistically precise way.

For exactly this reason—and here the theoretical curtain falls, as it were—poets seek, each in their own language, to name the essence of things in their actuality and make them shine. The sacred activity of the translator does justice to this goal when the writer's chosen "mode of meaning" is accommodated as fittingly as possible within the translator's own language. The translator's task is therefore to enrich the language into which he is translating using the modes of meaning of the language under translation, and to consolidate his own target language by doing so. In other words, the task of the translator is to bring his own language, with all its density, as close as possible to the actual target language—the true language of God, because a good translation of a great poet is always a significant enrichment and gain for the power of differentiation of one's own language. It opens to it new ways of meaning—new, linguistically communicated ways of seeing the "same thing." As Benjamin puts it:

> The task of the translator consists in finding the particular intention toward the target language which produces in that language the echo of the original. . . . [Translation] calls into [the original language] . . . aiming at that single spot where the echo is able to give, in its own language, the reverberation of the work in the alien one. . . . For the great motif of integrating many tongues into one true language informs his work.[28]

True language is, so to speak, the ideal objective of all speech: speech in which every thing-in-itself reveals itself in all its clarity and differentiation and definition. It is, as Benjamin says in his 1916 essay, a state in which for everything that exists the word or name given to it by God has been found. The task of the translator is thus the task of human beings themselves.

> The human is the namer, by this we know that pure speech speaks through human beings. All nature, insofar as it communicates, communicates in language, and so, in the end, in human beings.[29]

That is Benjamin's offering to the search for the one language underlying all human speech (that search in which Wittgenstein, Heidegger, and Cassirer were simultaneously engaged). It is the language of God. All meaningful speech operates as the trace of that true language, and is thus, so to speak, on the way toward it. We cannot directly say or deduce this in our own languages but it *shows* itself in certain configurations of the use of language, especially in the translation of works of literature.

RADICAL TRANSLATION

FOR BENJAMIN the translator's true task can at this point be extended to the entirety of human speech, to each and every individual speech act. After all, each of us has our own and hence different language in a very identifiable sense. We all have our own individual and personal associations with the word "bread." Accordingly, not only is speech always translation, so is every form of understanding. In Benjamin's view, every individual is to every other individual a "French poet" whose speaking and naming are part of the great essential purpose that is the human being, and which carries us as cultured beings. This goal is to take the world to its greatest possible linguistic definition. For Benjamin, the ideal "true language," enriched by an infinite number of finely tuned translation achievements, is a kind of monad, in which every possible aspect of the world can be reflected with maximum focus and precision. Just as we imagine divine speech and thought, it is ultimately indistinguishable from the world as it is.

If Wittgenstein, as a philosopher of language, was driven from poetics into logic, in the end finding his very own unifying form for both, Benjamin slipped from poetry through logic deep into theology and Jewish Messianism. At the time Benjamin, too, was sitting, largely isolated, largely misunderstood, and profoundly depressed in his room on Delbrückstrasse. He could in his real life barely construct a significant relationship with the world that would inspire him as a philosopher to his most elegant flights of thought. "The Task of the Translator" is a masterpiece in its forging of profound connections between thoughts from aesthetics and literature and those of theology and epistemology. The essay also embodies another characteristic of this thought, one that is much less often noticed: the ability, indeed the compulsion, to take concrete, often entirely mundane problems or experiences and make them the source of a rigorous theoretical scheme.

Benjamin's translation of Baudelaire in 1920–1921 interrupted the beginnings of his postdoctoral project. But he redeployed the ideas he had developed in that project to build a theory of translation, with no aim beyond establishing the act of translation as philosophically important, the task that in fact decided everything. Whatever he did, and whatever he would do, whatever befell him, Benjamin invariably turned it into a theory, a habit that had the charming effect of ennobling whatever he happened to be doing or experiencing, revealing it to have been truly relevant and consequential, even a potentially world-saving mode of experience. There is, not only at first sight, something tremendously narcissistic about this. But there is also something enormously alert, energetic, and existential. The demand made of the creative energies of his thought is total—taken always to the absolute edge of intelligibility and thus of translatability. Meanwhile Ernst Cassirer, having safely reached Hamburg, was working on exactly the same questions. Except that his way of inquiring and meaning was quite different.

CULT AND SOUND

AS WE HAVE SEEN, the two questions "What can I know?" and "How should I live?" are for philosophers inseparable. This recognition also helps to explain the lasting impact and fascination of the protagonists of philosophy, their potential iconic status, and their capacity to influence entire eras.

The ideal of transposing one's own thought into a lifeworld—embodied in its purest form by the founding figure of Socrates—further distinguishes philosophy from other paths of knowledge, such as the natural sciences or indeed art. Being a philosopher is a way of leading one's own life consciously, giving it pull, form, and direction through constant, probing questioning. This attitude exists in perceptible tension with the objectives of a purely academic subject, with its institutionally defined goals, performance appraisals, and career paths. A healthy skepticism, indeed open rebellion against and contempt for what was first described by none other than Heidegger as "academic philosophizing," is therefore one of the few historical fundamental constants of the discipline. In fact, until the late twentieth century, a majority of philosophy's most influential minds—Spinoza, Descartes, Mill, Hume, Kierkegaard, and Nietzsche, for example—never held academic posts in the subject. But where they did, they generally cultivated the greatest possible distance from the academy, like Schopenhauer, or, in the 1920s, Heidegger, Wittgenstein, and also Benjamin. An explicit rejection of the role of the academic philosopher is an essential element of their self-description. Carefully nurtured, it creates a constellation of dramatic tensions that hover around the word "cult." And for their contemporaries, Heidegger, Wittgenstein, and Benjamin were precisely that: cult figures.

Ernst Cassirer was not, and is not. By the beginning of the 1920s his contemporaries spoke about him in a quite different register. They talked of his "Olympian" detachment or, in terms of his appearance, culture, and knowledge, his "all-encompassing" nature as the "last universal genius," or at least the "universal scholar." But also, in less benign terms, he was considered the caricature of an academic institutionalized philosopher, an intellectual bureaucrat who, in the words of his colleague Max Scheler, wrote "beautiful, sometimes also true and deep books of general culture."[30] A thoroughly decent man and thinker, then, but not a great one.

Cassirer at least never saw his rootedness in the culture of university philosophy as a problem. This is apparent in the style and form of his works, which never depart from the prevailing norms of the academic publishing of their time. Here, too, Cassirer stands in stark contrast to Wittgenstein, Heidegger, and Benjamin, each of whom sought extremely autonomous (or idiosyncratic, depending on your view) linguistic forms in which to express themselves, on the grounds that the same bond between thought and life also holds together thought and language, thought and style. The form in which thoughts are expressed is by no means an external matter, but organizes and shapes them from the beginning and from within. In this emphatically individualistic sense Cassirer's writings do not have a "sound" of their own, at least not one that is unique to him.

Cassirer's everyday life in well-to-do Hamburg-Winterhude, as before in Berlin-Grunewald, did not differ greatly from the lives of his neighbors in the district—doctors, bank managers, businessmen. His sons attended boarding school (although the family was progressive: it was the already legendary Odenwaldschule), each morning he read the newspapers (the sports pages first!) and ran through the order of the day with his wife before going to his room or the university to work. On his return, they ate dinner, played or listened to music together, read a little before bed— sometimes even a thriller. As far as we can tell, the Cassirers had a very fulfilling marriage and, with their three children—Heinz, Georg, and Anna—an essentially happy, that is, uneventful, family life.

Of our four philosophers Cassirer is the only one whose sexuality never blossomed into an existential problem, and the only one who never suffered a nervous breakdown. Nor do we know of his suffering any major creative blocks or depressive episodes. For the first years of their marriage his wife detected a "slight melancholy in the mornings," and in times of stress he was prone to feverish colds. That's it. Otherwise he thought creatively without interruption, and without making a fuss. His wife recalled: "He did not demand that any of his neighbors participate in his work. Anyone uninitiated would have been able to spend many months, perhaps years, in our circle without even guessing that Ernst was a philosopher, working from dawn to dusk on philosophical problems."[31] Cassirer's only truly radical trait was his will to equilibrium. Among the four great thinkers of this politically tumultuous decade, he was as much as anything the only explicit supporter of the Weimar Republic, founded late in 1918. Indeed, he was the only democrat.

GOETHE IN HAMBURG

WITH THE ASSUMPTION of his teaching post at Hamburg University, the newly appointed philosophy professor entered a phase of remarkable intellectual productivity. In the autumn term of 1919, Cassirer opened, naturally, with a lecture titled "Kant and German Intellectual Life." Here was a man who had, in the most positive sense, arrived: he was comfortable in himself, with his family, and also in his place of work. For Cassirer, as for the others, the form that he gave to his private life, the style of his thought, and the language of his books all perfectly embodied a single drive toward expression. In Cassirer's case, however, that drive was not engaged in an incessant struggle, but rather strove toward productivity. Cassirer embodied the philosophical life in its perpetual state; he fulfilled in his way of living the promise he had made as a philosopher.

The scale of that achievement becomes apparent when we bear in mind that Cassirer's entire philosophy consists of a productive mediation on the dualisms and apparent contrasts that lie at the heart of our culture and thought—inside and outside, body and soul, emotion and reason, mind and matter, thought and word, myth and science, empiricism and metaphysics, unity and multiplicity, human being and God, language and cosmos.

Within the possibility of this creative mediation is the flash inspiration, on which he expended all of his intellectual energy and curiosity from 1919 onward, that came to him on his long journeys through war-torn Berlin. The closing words of that project outline, produced painstakingly line by line, during those hours spent on the streetcar, include this insight:

> We know this "life" only in its "expressions": but that is itself the quintessence of all prior consideration, that the "expression" is nothing random, inessential, "external," but that it is the *necessary*, the true, and the *only* revelation of the "inside" and the essence itself. From \the/ simplest gesture, from utterance to the supreme intellectual activities and to the purest "metaphysics," this insight has now confirmed itself.[32]

What Cassirer saw in his mind's eye in 1919 was a program of research that grasped the entire space of the mind as a constantly developing continuum of human expressions. With what means and methods could it be realized? And what form of "intellectual activity" deserves closer examination? Let us follow the first years of Cassirer's project, paying particular attention to its guiding motifs.

THE FUNDAMENTAL
PHENOMENON

CASSIRER'S CENTRAL IDEA rests on the insight that what we call the "human mind" arrives "at its true and complete inwardness only by *expressing* itself. The form taken by the inner life reacts upon and determines its essence and meaning."[33]

From this perspective, the first babbling sounds and later the one-word sentences of an infant ("dadada," "ball!") are symbolic expressions of something that is experienced within, but that does not simply depict or reflect what is experienced, but rather gives it a concrete (here: acoustic) form and shape, which, in its first iterable solidity, returns to structure the child's inner life.

Our constant striving to give meaningful expression to our sensory experiences through external, materially grounded symbols thus sets in motion a dynamic that gives form both to ourselves and to the world.

Wherever we look, according to Cassirer, "we see the mark of the basic phenomenon, that our consciousness is not satisfied to simply receive impressions of the outside, but rather that it permeates each impression with a free activity of expression."[34]

Cassirer calls the sum of the continuous, mutually conditioning process of these creative formations as a whole, from the simplest gesture to the highest metaphysics, culture. And in spite of the inner diversity and multiplicity that is self-evidently involved in this process, he believes the space it opens up to be solitary and consistent: the space of signs or symbols.

THE WILL TO MULTIPLICITY

THE IDEA THAT our mind does not only depict or reflect reality but also independently lends it a format was of course the central idea of Kant's critical philosophy and his so-called Copernican revolution. According to Kant, the mind doesn't get its bearings from the laws of objects, rather the objects draw theirs from the laws of our mind. So far, then, Cassirer's project is on good Kantian, and therefore also idealistic, ground. But his "philosophy of symbolic forms" heightens an idea of Kant's. Namely the idea that there are many different ways of giving structure, form, and sense to the world we live in. Kant's fundamental world-creating categories essentially take their cues from the scientific worldview of Newtonian physics. That was the world whose "conditions of possibility" had initially to be grasped and described.

Cassirer takes his epistemological impulse for opening his project to a diversity of *essentially equal* forms of access to the world from the linguistic studies of Wilhelm von Humboldt. Humboldt examined various natural languages (German, French, Finnish, Sanskrit . . .), in the light of Kant's Copernican revolution, as different ways of giving the world a symbolically mediated structure. As Cassirer explains:

> For each form of the noticing that underlies all verbal and linguistic foundation, for Humboldt a particular kind of comprehending and understanding is found. The difference between the several languages, therefore, is not a matter of different sounds and marks, but of different world conceptions. If the moon is denoted in Greek as the Measuring One (μήν), in Latin as the Shining One, or if even in one and the same language, as in Sanskrit, the elephant is called now the Twice Drinker, now the Two-Tusked One, now the Handed One—that goes to show that language never denotes simply objects, things as such, but always

conceptions arising from the autonomous activity of the mind. The nature of concepts, therefore, depends on the way this active viewing is directed.[35]

Cassirer applies this idea of the variety of natural languages to other major cultural forms that make the world visible in a specific way and give it an action-oriented form. Alongside the sciences, for him these are in particular the worlds of natural languages, myth, religion, art, and mathematics or logic. In Cassirer's view they are all "symbolic forms," each with its own comprehensive structures and principles of construction. The epistemological turning point of his philosophy now consists in the following insight:

> None of these formations [symbolic forms] can be simply absorbed by another or derived from another, but rather each of them refers to a specific mode of mental apprehension, within and through which it constitutes its own dimension of the "real."[36]

It is no more meaningful to ask whether the Latin *luna* depicts the "moon in itself" more correctly than the Greek μήν than it is to ask whether "reality in itself" is more correctly grasped in the form of myth, art, or the natural sciences. Just as the Latin *luna* singles out one particular aspect of the moon (its shining) for emphasis, the Greek places the stress on its possible function in the measurement of time.

The processes of symbolic formation are thus not only creative, in that they go beyond the mere representation or mirroring of sensory experience; but in their particular creative formations they also adhere to specific interests and emphases that accordingly orient and guide us as acting and suffering beings in this world.

The symbolic forms of myth, religion, and art simply differ in their interests and orientation from the natural sciences: different things are important for each. So they make the world appear differently to us, giving it shape and meaning in their own ways.

> The concept of what, apart from spiritual functions, constitutes absolute reality, the question of what the "thing in itself" may be in *this* sense remains unanswered. . . . The true concept of reality cannot be squeezed into the form of abstract being; it opens out into the diversity and richness of the forms of spiritual *life*.[37]

The question of what and how something is given therefore cannot be posed independently of symbolic forms, but only *in* and *with* them. And, depending on the symbolic form in mind when it is asked, the question—measured according to the internal rules that govern the construction of this form—is *different*. The concept of "life," for example, does not appear in the world of physics, any more than "mercy" or "fate." For biology, on the other hand, the concept of "life" is absolutely central, just as mercy and fate are for most religions. The sober scientific objection that there is no mercy "in reality" because the concept cannot in the end be reduced to anything in physics reveals only one thing, according to Cassirer: that we have not understood what the symbolic form of religion—and the forms of life that bear it—is actually concerned with. These failures happen. But we should not elevate such limitations and prejudices to criteria for the "real," as happens even now with the familiar isms, physicalism, economism, materialism, biologism. In each case, according to Cassirer, the ism is based on a fundamentally erroneous account of the human capacity for knowledge and what is ultimately a narcissistic striving for power. Each presents, or rather glorifies, one cognitive perspective, one window onto reality, as the only true and fruitful one.

ONWARD

THE SUPPOSEDLY CENTRAL EPISTEMOLOGICAL QUESTION of the nature of "reality in itself" is therefore from Cassirer's point of view a nonstarter. Which is to say, it is directionless and disoriented. It is like the question of whether a particular shape of chair or a certain wallpaper pattern "fits." How should we answer? Because "fitting" is obviously a relational matter: whether something fits can be assessed only with reference to an overall arrangement into which a particular thing can be integrated. And this arrangement, if it does fit, is in turn embedded within a larger purposive system: a living room, a study, a doctor's office . . .

So in the first few years of his project Cassirer sketched out a philosophy that was not only new and autonomous but a new kind altogether. According to his approach, the philosopher must begin with the study of given symbolic forms and their specific cultural logics. Since philosophers, as researchers, cannot be active in all of these fields simultaneously—and it is not their task—they must turn with an open mind to those scholars able to show how these symbolic worlds are constructed, and the cultural laws and principles of construction they adhere to. In the case of myth, anthropologists and ethnologists; for physics, theoretical physicists . . . This is because

> if all culture is manifested in the creation of specific image-worlds, of specific symbolic forms, the aim of philosophy is not to go behind all these creations, but rather to understand and elucidate their basic formative principle.[38]

Philosophy is here the investigation of the central concepts that give our life in all its multiplicity a sense of meaning, and thus really a philosophy of culture. An activity that, if it is not to decline into what Cassirer considers to be the necessary attempt to "go behind all these creations" in order to grab "pure, undistorted life" or "pure, undistorted reality" by the scruff of the neck, must be in *active dialogue* with the sciences and other areas of knowledge. In those first years in Hamburg, Cassirer's house in Winterhude itself became a home to such dialogue, what today we would call an interdisciplinary forum. In the winter of 1921, for example, Albert Einstein delivered a lecture there on his theory of relativity (about which Cassirer, in passing and, as he put it, "for the pure purpose of clarifying it to myself," wrote a small book, of which Einstein thought very highly).

DOES *THE* LANGUAGE EXIST?

THAT IS THE PROGRAM of Cassirer's *Philosophy of Symbolic Forms*. On his journey toward it, Cassirer approached the individual findings of the aforementioned sciences from his own perspective of symbolic philosophy, and yet was obliged take their findings seriously and acknowledge when they threatened to call his overall approach into doubt.

Thus, according to Cassirer, language—and this was to be the subject of the first volume of his project—represents a particular symbolic form. But since there are many different languages, he had to assume that all their grammars and phonetic systems shared the same deep structure and the same principles—at least at a more abstract level. Cassirer labels this presumed form underlying all languages the "pure form of language." (It is an assumption that, in the form of Noam Chomsky's theory of generative grammar, would come to dominate linguistics as a science for several decades from 1960 onward.) In the autumn of 1919, however, when Cassirer was immersing himself in existing linguistic studies—according to his reading list, more than two hundred individual works—this assumption was called into doubt. It was possible, he had to admit, that the unifying fundamental structure at the root of all languages, that "pure form of language," might not exist at all, and that instead there were only several different, mutually incompatible deep structures. (An assumption that is these days receiving more and more support in post-Chomskyan linguistics.) So it may be that there is not *a single form of language*, and hence no symbolic form of language as such. But what then? In his preface to *Language*, the first volume of *The Philosophy of Symbolic Forms*, he addresses this potential crisis:

> It was necessary to seek as broad as possible a view, and not only of one
> linguistic family, but of different families widely divergent in their logic
> and structure. The linguistic literature . . . became so vast that the goal
> I originally set myself receded farther and farther into the distance.[39]

The more deeply Cassirer plunged into linguistic research, the more fragile the philosophical ground felt under his feet. And yet—or perhaps for that very reason—he kept on striding forward. He did so in the hope that the unifying structure underlying all languages would be unearthed by future linguistic studies.

A philosopher who had nothing to say about the role of language in knowledge and life in fact had actually nothing whatsoever to say. This was also true for Cassirer, and if there was a conviction that Wittgenstein, Heidegger, and Benjamin all embraced unreservedly and unconditionally at this stage (and every other stage) of their thought, it was this: The human form of life is one of speech. In this sense language is not one symbolic form among many, but the most important, and elemental, of all. It is the foundation of our understanding of the self and the world. It is the form in which philosophizing itself is undertaken and discovers itself to be, inescapably, a "discursive activity." In Cassirer's words from 1919:

It [language] stands at a central point of spiritual being, in which rays of different origin come together and go out from the principles towards the greatest variety of fields. The mythical and logical moment—the direction of aesthetic intuition and that of discursive thought: all of this is encompassed within it, although it is not absorbed into one of them.[40]

As we have seen, the fundamental question for all four philosophers was whether all the various natural languages are themselves based on a single, unifying, and unified language. If so, what is the nature of that form? And on what does its ultimate meaning rest? What does language do to us? Do we give our words sense and meaning, or is it the world-shaping power of the words and signs themselves, which call us into life, thought, and questioning? Who shapes whom? In what form? And above all: With what objectives?

IV.

CULTURE

1922–1923

Heidegger is spoiling for a fight,
Cassirer is beside himself, Benjamin dances with Goethe,
and Wittgenstein looks for a human being.

A HUT OF ONE'S OWN

I N THE AUTUMN OF 1922 real strains were making themselves felt in the Heidegger household. Even for a well-connected family in the rural setting of the Breisgau, food supplies were coming under threat. As it was for the great majority of Germans, their everyday life was starting to resemble a struggle for survival. Amid galloping inflation, time itself gained new significance. And with winter approaching, clever solutions needed to be found, especially with regard to firewood and basic food-stuffs. "Mother asks if they should send potatoes even *before* 1 Oct; I answered yes and sent the money at the same time. What should I do when the potatoes arrive," Heidegger wrote on September 27 to Elfride, who was living with their two sons in the newly built cottage in Todtnauberg, while he worked furiously on his new manuscript down in Freiburg.[1]

What was he to do with the potatoes? Store them? If so, where? Eat them himself? Share them with the Husserls? Sell them? These were is-sues of survival, for which Elfride would remain responsible throughout their life. In part to free her husband from the demands of the everyday, she had devised a plan, after a winter hike in February 1922, to buy a plot of land on the lonely slopes of the southern Black Forest and build a wooden cabin there. In the spring, to finance the enterprise, she released part of her inheritance (about 60,000 marks). Elfride designed the cabin and organized and supervised its construction. Because time was a factor here, too. For some badly needed cash, the Heideggers rented their Freiburg apartment to an American couple for a few weeks, by which time they hoped that they would be able to move into the cabin. They made it, just.

On August 9, the family of four, one son held by the hand, the other one strapped to his father's back, marched for the first time into their shelter, at an altitude of 1,200 meters. Today, *"die Hütte"* is an almost mythical site in the history of philosophy, the place where Heidegger spent nearly every spare minute from that year until the end of his life. There, on the remote heights of the Black Forest, he came into his own as a philosopher. It was all that mattered. At least if one saw and understood the world as he did.

STRANGE CALLINGS

JUST THE FIRST FEW WEEKS up there in August yielded spectacular results: "I must say that when I look at the manuscripts from the hut that I have with me, they are anything but unsuccessful," Heidegger wrote to his wife on September 11, 1922, from Heidelberg, where he was staying with Karl Jaspers to exchange ideas. Jaspers, who was actually a physician and psychiatrist by trade, had landed himself a philosophical bestseller in 1919 with his *Psychology of Worldviews*, whose resounding public and academic success ensured him a professorship of philosophy in Heidelberg.

In his book Jaspers extracts philosophical and ideological aspects from individual psychological character studies. More important, though, his depiction of human existence is one whose true essence is revealed in extreme circumstances, such as near-death experiences, which are shown to have a liberating quality. It is a therapeutic, life-based approach to philosophy, which places particular value on borderline experiences and extremity for self-discovery—a book that could have been created especially for the generation of traumatized soldiers returning from a lost war.

Heidegger, too, felt that Jaspers's great tome spoke to him directly. The two men met for the first time on a Sunday afternoon in 1920 over coffee at Husserl's house. They corresponded regularly from 1921 and, equally frustrated by the plight of academic philosophy, soon shared a firm belief in the need to make common cause in the "battle against bleakness" (as Heidegger put it).

In September 1922, Heidegger accepted with alacrity a new invitation from Jaspers to develop what he perceived to be their shared ideas in dialogue and philosophize for "a few days at the appropriate times." Heidegger spent almost a week with Jaspers, who, in view of the "present situation of both our lives" insisted on paying Heidegger's travel expenses (1,000 marks). Jaspers was a full professor with a regular income and solid financial backing; Heidegger's poorly paid position in Freiburg would expire in ten months. Heidegger urgently needed to build a reputation, lest the already precarious situation of his young family threaten to become completely untenable. Elfride was also concerned about this, and in spite of stress and exhaustion she had resumed her studies in economics earlier that year. Somebody in the house had to earn some money. And it didn't look as if her philosophically inspired husband was going to be the one to do it.

The two philosophers found the days they spent together in Heidelberg hugely enriching, and they savored the joy that comes from true friendship. Over the coming decade Jaspers would be one of the very few interlocutors whom Heidegger not only trusted as a friend but also genuinely respected as a philosopher. Nonetheless, a vocational paradox overshadowed this meeting, too. Even as they conspired to join forces in an anti-academic resistance cell, Heidegger's dearest hope was to be elevated, somewhere in the great expanses of the collapsing Republic, to a lifetime post as a state-sponsored intellectual. Husserl was one crucial advocate here, Jaspers a second.

"The eight days I spent with you remain constantly with me," Heidegger wrote to his new friend in November. "The suddenness, the apparent un-eventfulness of those days, the sureness of the 'style' with which one day grew into the next in a manner free of artifice, the unsentimental and austere step with which a friendship came toward us, the growing certainty of engaging in a common struggle, sure of itself on both 'sides'—all of that remains un-cannily in my mind, just as the world and life are uncanny for the philoso-pher."[2] That autumn, Heidegger had definitely found a language of his own to express precisely how the world must remain uncanny to a philosopher.

EXISTENTIAL
HEALTH CHECK

UNDER PRESSURE TO SUBMIT the findings of his latest research for a pro-fessorship that had arisen in Marburg, in the three weeks after his visit to Heidelberg, up in his new cabin Heidegger experienced a further philo-sophical breakthrough. Husserl's wife quickly typed up a clean copy of the manuscript. At the beginning of October, Heidegger handed in his appli-cation paper, titled "Phenomenological Interpretations of Aristotle—Indication of the Hermeneutic Situation," to Marburg (and also Göttingen). The essay has about as much to do with Aristotle as Benjamin's "Task of the Translator" has to do with Baudelaire. Instead, Heidegger was con-cerned, once again and with a curiously fresh intensity and clarity, with the question of what the actual task of philosophy might consist of. His answer springs from a few key sentences in the manuscript:

The object of philosophical research is *human Dasein* as interrogated with regard to its Being-character.[3]

Here the key term *Dasein* makes its first appearance in Heidegger's writing. It is understood as a specific way in which humans have always felt meaningfully addressed and challenged by this world.

The world always meets with a particular way of being-addressed (*Angesprochensein*), of appeal (*Anspruch*).[4]

In this sense philosophizing is a questioning process of continuous self-enlightenment. The conceptual innovation of "Da-Sein," however, expressly includes the idea that this task cannot be delegated: all must be themselves, in their own place, in their own time. There is no alibi in existence. At any rate not in philosophical existence. In Heidegger's words:

Factual Dasein, whatever it is, is only ever the fully own, not the just-being of general humanity.[5]

Of course this process, thoroughly uncomfortable and not certain in its results, can also be dismissed or diverted by the Dasein in question. Human Dasein would not be human, it would not be free, if that choice were not open to it. To describe the more or less conscious overlooking of this possibility, Heidegger chooses—as Wittgenstein does in the *Tractatus*—the theologically tinged concept of the Fall (*Verfallen*). A regrettable drama, albeit an all-too-current one for Heidegger:

It is because of an inclination toward falling (*Verfallensgeneigtheit*) that the factical life, which is always in fact that of the individual, is not usually lived in that way.[6]

The majority's susceptibility to "falling" is not, for Heidegger, due to a lack of intellectual ability. Rather it is the result of an inclination toward existential comfort. To put it plainly: Most people would rather spend their lives avoiding themselves than seriously seeking themselves. This deliberate self-avoidance is not necessarily either particularly painful or unpleasant. Indeed, it is without a doubt the safer path and, in a very dull sense, the one that guarantees happiness. It means never really becoming who we are or who we could be. It leads to a life of self-imposed and permanent impoverishment, one whose chief concern cannot therefore be with things that are important or on which a life might rest, in Heidegger's sense. In the realm of the material these are consumer goods; in the social sphere, career goals; in relationships, friendships without actual conversation, marriages with a great deal of routine and little love; in religion, a learned faith without a true experience of God; in language it is apparent in the continuous, thoughtless repetition of clichés and received wisdom; finally, in research, it is a deliberation of questions the answers to which we already believe we know for certain.

Not so Heidegger. He heard another appeal from his surroundings. It called for nothing less than a fundamental critique of all those concepts, categories, and structures that guided reflection on human Dasein over the previous twenty-five hundred years, from Aristotle onward, give or take. He finally wanted to take the gloves off in the "interrogation of Dasein with regard to its Being-character." And thus in his "Phenomenological Interpretations of Aristotle" he reaches the insight that the purpose of this opening interrogation must in the end be the complete *destruction* and wholesale replacement of those very conceptualities and categories.

In this, his first unquestionably independent piece of writing, Heidegger already styles himself as a kind of conceptual wrecking ball, blasting through the hopelessly distorted and obfuscatory interrogations of Dasein in pursuit of a perspective free of precisely that.

STORMY WEATHER

AT THE MOMENT when the centrifugal forces set in motion after the war by the Treaty of Versailles threatened to tear his country apart once and for all, Heidegger also opted for the existential tactic of a return to supposed fundamentals. He countered the seemingly inevitable fragmentation that was the spirit of his age with a concentration on the roots and origins of all Dasein. In terms of philosophy, this focus took the form of a startlingly clear-sighted revelation of its fundamental question. Conceptually, it is determined to renew the distorting and all-too-unquestioningly accepted vocabulary of tradition in contemporary terms, and bases it in the actual experience of Dasein. It is existential in the emphatic personalization of its project of self-illumination via the appeal to questioning contemplation, which every Dasein senses and hears within itself. Finally, in terms of its concrete application to real life, it is his solemn retreat to the cabin, buffeted by autumnal storms, up on the peaks of his native Black Forest.

Over the years that followed, Heidegger would time and again equate life in the cabin, especially with the storms that raged there, with the experience of thinking. In the supposed security of the wooden cabin, the uncanny and the primal powers of nature were more exposed, and could be felt all the more keenly. The essential uncanniness of philosophizing, of which Heidegger speaks solemnly in his November letter to Jaspers, reveals itself to Dasein, precisely there, in its full power and intensity, where its roots run deepest.

Philosophizing, as Heidegger saw it, did not seek to calm Dasein permanently, or to instill any tranquillity of the soul. On the contrary: it expressed itself in the steadfast will to resist the storm of radical questioning; to perceive, with courageous investigation, a bottomless abyss where, it had once been imagined, and hoped, a secure foundation lay. The path of this thought cannot be an easy one. It welcomes nothing more than moments of great tension and danger.

In the political sphere, this posture runs naturally into an emphatic affirmation of crisis and danger, situations that demand genuine contemplation and resolution, offering no alternatives.

As burdensome as the disaster years of 1922 and 1923 might have been in the real world, Heidegger welcomed them unconditionally as what we might call a configuration of the social climate. And as a moment of openness held out the prospect of a radical rethink. He already felt it in the winter of 1922–1923, just as he would do precisely ten years later, another time of extreme controversy and radicalism, which would see Heidegger in a quite different position.

WARS OF ATTRITION

BUT IN THE HERE AND NOW of the autumn of 1922, the immediate thing was to find himself a permanent academic post. Heidegger was well aware of the philosophically explosive power contained in his "Phenomenological Interpretations of Aristotle." "The work has struck home in Marburg," he reported, with military-style understatement, to Jaspers in November, closing his letter: "I have been hard at work collecting wood and storing it for the winter."[7]

Heidegger waited, lamenting, understandably enough, the "appalling state" in which this "endless rambling" of "half-constructed views, gushing praise and so on" put one. Finally, in March 1923, he had indirect word from Marburg. They didn't want him. Not yet, at least, or probably not. Elfride, stretched to the limits of her abilities, had abandoned her studies once and for all in January 1923. Now the situation was serious. "We're not about to starve," Heidegger wrote encouragingly to her that March, but only a month later he set the bar at the barest minimum: "It's enough if we and our children make it; otherwise I have more important things to do than strive for a great career or the like."[8] For that something else needed to happen, if necessary without an academic post. As he had written so rightly in September: "The factical life with a troubled livelihood is *circuitous*."

Meanwhile inflation soared ever higher. Heidegger found a new source of income working as tutor to a Japanese aristocrat, Count Kuki. But his financial troubles were still great. Then, on June 18, the news arrived of his successful application for an "associate professorship with the status and rights of a full professor." "At last the spell is broken," Jaspers congratulated him from Heidelberg, advising him paternally that even though the pay was poor, he'd reached the limit of what he could ask for. In fact—and entirely in accordance with his nature—Heidegger had no intention "of being a seemingly elegant and cautious professor who takes his income 'as it comes.'" Instead, in his letter of July 14, he openly informed a colleague at Marburg, a neo-Kantian and friend of Cassirer's, Paul Natorp (who had resolutely supported Heidegger's appointment), that he would henceforth "with the manner of my presence give (them) hell; a combat troop of sixteen is coming with me, among the inevitable fellow travellers some of them quite serious and hard-working."

So Heidegger's plan was to take Marburg by storm. Indeed, the whole thinking world.

BAD NEIGHBORS

AS WE KNOW, it was not easy to make Cassirer lose his composure. His labors were completely unaffected by the challenges of the financial crisis of 1922–1923. He finished the first volume of his *Philosophy of Symbolic Forms* and immediately set about preparing for the second part, which would be devoted to mythical thought. Myths and their associated rituals and taboos have from ancient times provided a form of orientation through the world and a guide for action; indeed, they constitute the origin of symbolic formation as such. "You really don't need to worry about me: not only am I bearing my solitude well, as ever, I am seeking it out, since it is the best and absolutely tried and tested salve for my nerves, which have recently been subject to a certain amount of stress," he wrote on July 5, 1922, from the study of his Hamburg villa, where he was buried under tomes about religious history and ethnology, to his wife, who was staying, along with the children, with relatives in Vienna.[9] Yet the events of the previous month had left their impression on him. By then his children, particularly Anna, age fourteen, had already been subjected once or twice to "shouts from neighbors' houses" on the way to school, but the recent occurrence had crossed another line. It was too much for even the imperturbable Ernst Cassirer:

....

Hamburg, 10 June 1922

Dear Sir,

Yesterday afternoon you used my absence from home to approach my wife and father-in-law, engage in a conversation with them and in the end shout some insults across the canal. Such behaviors toward a lady to whom you have not even been introduced and toward a 76-year-old man speak for themselves: it would be otiose to add anything about the nature of such actions. I have, as your neighbor, drawn clear and distinct boundaries between us—and I must most urgently ask you to make no further attempts to traverse those boundaries. Hitherto I have always successfully sought to avoid any dealings with people of your kind, and I must also urge other fathers from our neighborhood, in the interest of the upbringing of my children, to avoid any contact with your son.[10]

....

What had happened? The day before, a neighbor named Hachmann, from the other side of the tributary of the Alster, whose garden abutted the Cassirers' property, had responded furiously to a request from Frau Professor Cassirer, doubtless with the greatest politeness, as to whether the Hachmanns' seven-year-old son might not wish to play a little more quietly, or indeed somewhere other than in his own garden, since the shrill and irritating noises he was producing disturbed the summer reading of Frau Cassirer and her father, who was staying with the family in Hamburg. The retort, shouted as they sat in their sunlit garden, was vicious: "Do you think you don't disturb us? The mere sight of you—you all belong in Palestine."[11]

Looking back from her American exile, Toni Cassirer recalled that dispute between neighbors as a crucial turning point: "From that day I began to free myself from Germany." The unabashed directness of Hachmann's hatred was probably not the factor here, as much as Toni Cassirer's keen sense that in those early critical years of the Weimar Republic an explosive mixture of anti-capitalism, anti-communism, and anti-Semitism was brewing, all the while finding more and more followers even in the circles of the cultured elite.

Ernst Cassirer believed, as his letter makes clear, that he could escape the acts of impertinence associated with this shift in public mood, even as it increasingly made itself felt in everyday life, with clearly delineated boundaries between public and private, buttressed by impeccable bour-geois etiquette, and by what he saw as a scholarly retreat into his own social circles and his own four walls. During that summer, nothing could have been further from his mind than the idea of bidding farewell to his Ger-man homeland, and particularly to Hamburg. After all, possibly for the first time he now felt acknowledged, fully and entirely accepted by his peers. This was not least because Cassirer had recently discovered his true thinking space. In his case it was not a lonely cabin on a hillside in the Black Forest, but the library of a private scholar of cultural science who had collected several tens of thousands of rare studies in intellectual and scientific history on his shelves, and organized them in a very idiosyncratic way. This was the library of Abraham ("Aby") Moritz Warburg, the scion of one of the world's most influential banking families, which Cassirer first entered in the winter of 1920 and which for the next ten years would be the site of inspiration for his work.

GOOD NEIGHBORS

HE WAS IN SHOCK: "I can never return to this place, or I will lose myself forever in this labyrinth," Cassirer murmured after Dr. Fritz Saxl, head li-brarian of the Warburg collection, led him past the shelves and stacks, ele-gantly if very eccentrically arranged.[12] The richness of this literature as well as the precious rarity of the volumes acquired from all over the world was one thing. But for Cassirer what was miraculous was the idea of this library itself, and the intellectual objective behind its compilation and organization.

In fact, the volumes were not ordered alphabetically—Warburg orga-nized them instead according to a taxonomy of his own devising, based on what he called "good neighborliness." This measure was in turn based on a special research program into the true nature of human culture, its distinguishing features, and the dynamics that had determined its development over millennia.

The whole collection was accordingly divided into four sections, each of which corresponded to a fundamental philosophical concept.[13] These were, and remain:

ORIENTATION   IMAGE   WORD   ACTION

Warburg, as director of the library, had initially used the rubric "Orientation" to reflect the fact that the world is for us far from self-explanatory. We come into the world largely helpless, without instincts, and also, crucially, without bearings. Our basic need to orient ourselves in thought and action, in our entire relationship with the world, gives rise to what we call culture. This was already the point of departure for Kantian philosophy. Not only was this view expressly shared by Cassirer, but it represents the true foundation of his major work, still in its early stages. Under the rubric of Orientation, Warburg's library variously included works of superstition, magic, religion, and science—considered central cultural products of our fundamental human need for orientation.

However, the sections labeled "Image," "Word," and "Action" according to Warburg's system implicitly answer the question of the structural forms through which this orientation is achieved: through what Cassirer, in his system, calls "symbols" and "symbolic systems."

Under "Image," Warburg included works about "ornaments, prints, or painting." Under "Word," spells, prayers, epics, and imaginative literature. Under "Action," finally, books that investigated the human body itself as a medium of symbolic formation—treatises on festival and dance culture, on theater and erotica.

For that reason, on his first visit Cassirer had to overcome the uncanny and fantastical feeling that this library had been designed and organized precisely according to the strictures and emphases that had governed his own work since those fateful streetcar journeys of 1917: the arrangement of the Warburg Library corresponded exactly, in terms of both form and content, to his own philosophy of symbolic forms.

As if that weren't enough, in one sense the library went a step further than the systematic architectural plan that was Cassirer's work. Rather than proceed in a chronological fashion, according to the development of culture from its cultic beginnings in totem, rite, and myth through to the modern natural sciences in one continuous arc culminating in true knowledge of the world, what prevailed on the shelves of Warburg's library was the internal organizational principle of "good neighborliness." It saw works from a tremendous variety of disciplines and eras placed side by side in such a way as to suggest scarcely imaginable connections between them, potential similarities of approach, and lines of influence that seem inconceivable. Consequently, foundational works of chemistry rubbed shoulders with books on alchemy; studies in ancient haruspicy with books about astrology and modern algebra.

UTOPIA ON THE BOOKSHELF

WARBURG'S COLLECTION IS FOUNDED on the idea of a continuous cultural non-simultaneity of the simultaneous, in which a great variety of approaches from a great variety of sources influence and also contradict one another. At the same time, his taxonomic system is based on the conviction that there is something like an unconscious cultural memory that lurks behind the various epochs and the objects of their scholars' attention, with significant though subtle effect. Symbols and people—and this was Warburg's central idea—constantly educate one another, and the symbols with which we think, speak, curse, and pray, with which we make predictions, inquire, and research—in short, find our orientation in this world—are generally much older and in a sense wiser than we, the creatures who use these symbols only in our own time and appropriate them in line with our own interests. So much could be revealed, if only the innumerable tacit connections and alignments among these symbols could be given a voice. It was only logical, then, that Warburg should have placed his library under the tutelage of the Greek goddess of memory, Mnemosyne.

From his first day in that library, Cassirer's way of thinking grew closer to the ordering of its vision of culture. In small steps at first, but then continuously and with ever greater intensity. On Warburg's shelves there were no clearly demarcated individual disciplines, areas of study, or even clearly defined realms of culture. It was a space completely free from taboo, and its arrangement encouraged the visitor to embark on a glorious search for ideas as yet unexplored—whether from the future, the present, or the past.

Imagine it. A world in which Frau Cassirer and Herr Hachmann, having transcended borders, inherited categorizations and prejudices, could live side by side like the books in Warburg's library. The library embodies a utopia of communality and connections among all things, and sometimes it takes only a small step or a leap across the waters of oblivion to perceive and acknowledge as much.

Cassirer was caught completely off guard in 1920 by the discovery of the Warburg Library of Cultural Studies. When he accepted his place in Hamburg and moved there from Berlin, he had no idea the library existed. The same could not be said, however, of the library. Dr. Saxl knew exactly whom he was dealing with when Cassirer first stepped into Warburg's domain. Cassirer was expected—and subsequently he was deliberately lured. Saxl says of Cassirer's first visit to Warburg:

> I started in the second room, with the cabinet marked "Symbol," since I assumed that Cassirer would find it easier to approach the problem there. He immediately gave a start and explained to me that this was the problem that had long preoccupied him, and one on which he was currently working. But he was only familiar with a small part of the literature that we own on the concept of the symbol, and he knew nothing of its visual configuration (the visualization of symbols in gesture and art). Cassirer immediately understood and asked me to spend over an hour showing him how one shelf was lined up next to another, one thought next to another. It was lovely to guide a man of such substance for once.[14]

After only a few months, the initial, humble reaction to this labyrinth, to which he had said he would never be able to return without losing himself, was replaced by an express desire to spend years there.[15] And indeed he would go on to do just that. Cassirer had discovered the intellectual space of his dreams, and the library had found precisely the researcher for which it had originally been conceived. A perfect symbiotic relationship came into being, one that also included the management of the library. Cassirer's requests for books expanded the holdings of the collection, while Dr. Saxl and his subordinates, whenever a new research question arose, approached Cassirer and encouraged him to write a response to it in the spirit of the library. The first result of this enormously fruitful collaboration, Cassirer's essay "The Conceptual Form of Mythical Thought," was published in July 1922.

THE OUTCOME OF MYTH

IN THIS ESSAY, a milestone in his thought, Cassirer assessed the properties of concepts and the world as constructed in myth as opposed to the modern natural sciences. Meanwhile, in his investigations into Aristotle, Heidegger pursued the question of how much certain fundamental differences shape or distort the whole of our thought, as an archaeologist or indeed a demolitionist might; similarly, with his investigation, Cassirer also returned to a notional beginning of our cultural history, revealing the extent to which that unconventional primal layer of thought continued to influence our understanding of the world in the present.

Rather than seeing mythical thought as purely random and irrational, Cassirer recognized that it was characterized by great rigor, expediency, and consistency. In the end its conceptualities establish a fixed and rigid place for everything and everyone in the universe. At the heart of this process are fundamental and absolute core divisions that follow a logic of the totem. It begins with dividing a social community—generally one's own tribe—into two, and fixing that division with the attribution of rigid qualities, properties, and, above all, taboos. From this fundamental distinction, it becomes possible to form subgroups, so that for example "the men of one class who have a particular totemistic emblem . . . can marry only the wives of a very specific clan marked by a particular totem." In this way a first order is created. That is, however, never enough:

> In fact the difference between the individual clans according to their totems extends further and further out from the closer social circle in which it first applies, passing in the end to all circles of existence, the natural and the spiritual. Not only the members of the tribe but the

whole universe with all that it contains is encompassed in groups by the totemistic way of thinking.[16]

This monumental task of translation—assigning a fixed place and value to everything in existence—is also accomplished in mythical thought through relationships of similarity. Thus it is the defining characteristic of mythical thinking that this similarity "is never grasped as a 'mere' relationship with its origin in our subjective thinking, for example, but points back to a real identity: things cannot *appear* similar without in their essence somehow being one and the same."[17]

If we acknowledge that totemistic distinctions of value are highly value-laden, and thus encourage logics of absolute exclusion and inclusion (this is their first act of ordering), the political and moral controversy of this form of thought, as the foundation of our cultural evolution, also becomes apparent. We can see it in our everyday language even today. Take the word *sinister*, Latin for "left," reflecting the low value given to the left hand relative to the right, a fundamental distinction that runs through the whole of Western culture. So the evaluative power of the mythical conceptual form is linguistically all around us. Indeed, whether we like it or not, it speaks to us from every word—and above all: from us.

THE NEW ENLIGHTENMENT

FOR CASSIRER, shedding light on such origins through analysis meant enlightenment in the best Kantian sense of the word. That is, "leading human beings out of their self-imposed immaturity," an immaturity that expresses itself primarily in our desire to avoid examining the true roots of the concepts that orient us in our thought and, hence, in our entire access to the world.

Heidegger, too, struggled against this same complacency or, as he termed it, unconcernedness, in his 1922 essay "Phenomenological Interpretations of Aristotle." Here, however, Heidegger spoke expressly of a necessary "destruction" of extant concepts, particularly in philosophy. By contrast, Cassirer's analyses are not aimed at their wholesale destruction—where could that lead but to a new yet also inevitably mythical set of formulations? Rather, they were fostered by a growing awareness, in itself radically enlightening, of the possibilities and impossibilities inevitably imposed by every conceptual form, whether it be mythical, religious, or scientific.

Cassirer perceived two central dangers that every culture is exposed to at every point in its development. First, every culture is manifestly susceptible to relapse. Every developmental step it takes can be reversed. Second, it is at times of greatest crisis, tension, and confusion—as during the years 1922 and 1923—that the danger of an unburdening relapse into a rigid and judgmental pattern of interpretation is at its greatest.

ACROSS THE RIVER

IN THIS LIGHT, the dispute between Frau Cassirer and Herr Hachmann is a textbook example of a momentary relapse into mythical thinking. Hachmann was fully in thrall to mythic stages of thought when, from an ultimately totemistic distinction between "the Germans" and "the Jews," he perceived Frau Cassirer's very proximity to be an insult, a disturbance, even a contamination, while at the same time taking it for granted that all human beings have a fixed and given place in the world on the basis of their group or tribe—a There where they absolutely belong, and only there. For the Jews: Palestine.

And that was the spirit in which Frau Cassirer took it: "When Herr

Hachmann shouted to me across the canal that we all belonged in Palestine, from his lips this was exactly the same as saying we belonged on the dung-heap. At the time, in the minds of those people Palestine was just a curse. For us it was the place to which Jews closely connected with tradition, or Russian and Polish refugees, turned to find a new fatherland."[18]

The Cassirers emphatically did not feel any close connection with Jewish tradition or indeed with Orthodox Judaism—and they did not want to have that way of thinking imposed upon them by people more primitive than themselves. At the same time, and perhaps this was the actual point of Cassirer's philosophy of culture, the criterion for philosophical primitivism lies not in the conceptual form to which one feels absolutely allied, but rather in the pursuit of a fixed idea that there should be something like a single unified, all-encompassing, exhaustive form.

But no single conceptual form is rich enough to exhaust the space of the real. On the other hand, each conceptual form—by its very nature—has a certain invasive quality. Each strives for total order and appropriation and thus a hostile takeover of all the others. It is in this impulse that Cassirer sees the potential calamity that could blight our cultural life:

> A certain clear, emotional and intellectual difference does not stop at the point where it first came into being, but has a tendency to go on working from it, drawing greater and greater circles and in the end encompassing the whole of being and in some way "organizing" it.[19]

That applies to myth just as much as it does to modern science and its totalizing isms (biologism, physicalism, economism). It applies to religion and its psychotic fundamentalisms. It applies to works of art that strive toward aesthetic totality in the one-sided sense of Wagner's *Gesamtkunstwerk*. For Cassirer, this insatiable urge to invade precisely those fundamental differences that are the most telling must be addressed by the difficult but invariably enlightening business of revealing the hidden connections and obvious designatory limitations in the description of each symbolic form. An endless, labyrinthine business—as endless and labyrinthine as the creation of culture itself.

In 1922 and 1923 Cassirer set about this project with gusto. He now had not only the support of his family, his Free Hanseatic City, and its university faculty, but also the library of his dreams. Financially, too, the light at the end of the tunnel was beginning to emerge. In April 1923 he reassured his wife, who was concerned about the future of the household, and indeed about feeding her children:

> Today Bruno [Cassirer's publisher] sent me the accounts for the first quarter of 1923. During those three months he sold 1,240 copies of my books, which has brought me in a royalty of over 1 million marks. So not only is my advance paid back, but I've also got over ½ million out of it.[20]

Home found. Mortgage paid. Book supply assured. And half a million marks! The same, alas, could not really be said of Benjamin.

IN THE MAELSTROM

THE YEAR 1922 SHOULD—once again—have been that of his breakthrough. At the instigation of the Heidelberg publisher Richard Weissbach, who also promised to publish Benjamin's translation of Baudelaire, in the autumn of 1921 Benjamin planned, with high hopes and not a little ambition, to bring out a journal called *Angelus Novus*. Its writers were to be drawn from his closest circle of acquaintances, and its goals were set out in a note from the editor in chief, Dr. Walter Benjamin, to Gershom Scholem, one of his potential writers:

> The plan, which is entirely my own, is to found a journal which does not have the slightest concern for the *paying* public, so that it can serve the intellectual public all the more resolutely.[21]

The first issue of the journal, named after a drawing by Paul Klee (bought by Benjamin in Munich in 1921), was in principle ready for the printers early in 1922. In spite of Benjamin's tireless urging, however, Weissbach held it back. The economic risk to the publisher was too great. The publication of the Baudelaire translation (along with the preface "The Task of the Translator") dragged painfully on throughout the whole year, and Weissbach still had no firm publication date planned. To make matters worse, mounting inflation was driving up the price of paper and forcing caution on the entire publishing industry. To an esoteric outsider, as Benjamin was—and was determined to remain—that development effectively ruled out the possibility of bringing out the journal. In 1922, when asked to list his book publications, he could give only one honest answer. Apart from his dissertation, which had enjoyed no attention whatsoever: none.

The gap between his self-image and reality was therefore as wide as it could possibly be. Much the same applied to his academic ambitions. The year 1922 saw him become a restless traveling salesman of postdoctoral dissertations. There was hardly a major German university at whose door he had not knocked in one way or another. He thought he had a chance in

Heidelberg, though he couldn't say precisely which subject and with whom. Philosophy, German studies, sociology . . . Jaspers, Emil Lederer, Alfred Weber? Benjamin sought closer contact with all of them.

In the late autumn his predicament grew more acute. The bond with his parents' household now seemed to be definitively severed. Benjamin's father insisted that his son should become a bank clerk, while Walter had declared himself open in principle to all forms of gainful employment as long as they didn't get in the way of his postdoctoral dissertation. Without any clear postdoctoral prospects, however, that possibility hovered in the void. And without sufficient time and freedom to make that ambition plausible, the threat of life as a bank clerk or an inevitable—though equally impossible—approach to his parents for funding loomed. Benjamin was unable to show any income of his own for the whole of 1922.

The depths to which someone in such circumstances could sink were revealed in crushing detail in October by his friend Erich Gutkind (the same Gutkind with whom the Benjamins had envisaged a bucolic communal existence on a farm in southern Germany):

> Our situation is bad. At the Gutkinds' it seems to be becoming disastrous. As his mother is still in the same condition, a few days ago Erich decided to become . . . a traveling margarine salesman. . . . But if that's to work out, God's going to have to do some selling too.[22]

Only a short time later Benjamin noted:

> Gutkind's . . . business is heading for catastrophe—earnings of 150 Marks in four days—that means, taking travel expenses into

account, that he almost ended up making a loss. I have set off on a similar but easier course and had a go at buying and selling books, buying them in the north of the city and selling them in the west, for which some knowledge of old books is coming in useful. . . . It can be so enthralling looking for treasures in flea markets or little antique shops . . . and the work is in danger of faltering so that I have to keep at it.[23]

Throughout his life Benjamin saw "work" as meaning nothing other than the development of his own thoughts in writing. However precarious, or even hopeless, things might have seemed, he saw no room for compromise, no alternative. A postdoctoral thesis—ideally with a paid lectureship attached, which appeared for the first time to be a possibility—still seemed the only realistic way for him to rescue this way of life, and his willingness to make sacrifices and humiliate himself was accordingly great.

The obstacles in his case were considerable. There was, among German professors, something like an unspoken rule never to employ more than one Jew at a time as a postdoctoral candidate. It was also quite clear to those professors from Benjamin's CV that he had conned his way out of military service, which certainly didn't help. For many professors, it ruled him out from the start. You just don't support someone like that.

THE THIRD MAN

DECEMBER 1922 saw Benjamin knocking on doors in Heidelberg once again, this time in a particularly regrettable situation. It was becoming increasingly difficult to find accommodation appropriate to his budget. For the whole of the Christmas season he rented a room in a primitive but warm flat

---

> that has the great disadvantage of being beside the kitchen of a proletarian family that has a two-month-old child. . . . But I address the task with a stoicism unfamiliar to me—even though the child 1) also sleeps beside me at night; 2) was born at seven months and therefore raises a bitter war cry against life. Today, Sunday, when everyone was at home, it was entirely as if all hell had broken loose.[24]

Like the Cassirers, Benjamin struggled with the neighbors' children. He could, however, neither keep his distance nor make a calm appeal to bourgeois etiquette. Which was not to say that Benjamin and his family, even in these most difficult times, were really about to fall into the financial abyss and lose their home. Significantly, Dora's family was still giving them help and support. While Benjamin spent 1922 on the road as an editor in chief, serious critic, antiquarian book dealer, and would-be postdoctoral candidate, complaining all the while without a hint of irony about the "unfamiliar whirl of multifarious occupations," Dora retired for whole months with Stefan to her aunt's sanatorium at the foot of the Semmering in Austria—not far from the vacation home of Toni Cassirer's parents.

No, there was further to fall. In September 1922, the month when Jaspers provided Heidegger with 1,000 marks to finance his trip to Heidelberg because such an expense threatened to sink the family budget, Benjamin, on his expeditions through the antique shops of Berlin, Göttingen, Frankfurt, and Heidelberg, wouldn't have hesitated to spend the same amount on some rare book for his private collection.

Jaspers was in fact a significant reason why Benjamin was staying in Heidelberg again that December. "I don't yet know how things stand at the university," Benjamin told Scholem on December 6. "I will do everything I can to be introduced to Jaspers." It is highly unlikely, if not quite inconceivable, that Benjamin knew anything about the "community of struggle" newly forged between Jaspers and Heidegger. And if he had, would it have discouraged him, or even bothered him?

Benjamin had made contact with Jaspers in 1921 (he had liked him "quite well"[25]), and after the setbacks of the previous few months, he saw the recently appointed philosophy professor as one of his last real hopes. Jaspers, whose wife was Jewish, represented a more unconventional and freer vision of philosophy, far from the scholastic strictures and the traditional straitjackets of what all young thinkers would have agreed was the common enemy: neo-Kantianism. And like Heidegger, desperately seeking a post in 1922, Benjamin had a new and extremely ambitious application in his suitcase that winter. An essay so powerful, so theoretically rich and methodically refined that, as he clearly sensed and also openly declared, it "marked the method of his future works." It was his hundred-page critical analysis of Goethe's novel *Elective Affinities*.

GOETHE IN WEIMAR

AS ALWAYS WHEN BENJAMIN TURNED his hand to philosophy, this essay was about simply everything, not least a piercing interpretation of his own living arrangements. Because the centrifugal forces of those years had taken his marriage to Dora to a breaking point. Certainly, at the time, Heidelberg University was one of the Continent's intellectual beacons. It was where the brothers Max and Alfred Weber had laid the foundations of

modern sociology. Where the lawyer and philosopher of law Gustav Radbruch achieved renown. Where the young György Lukács had written his
theory of the novel. Friedrich Gundolf dominated German studies from
Heidelberg. In the summer of 1921, Stefan George was still wandering
lost in thought through the castle ruins that had once inspired Hölderlin
and Hegel to reach their greatest heights. And among the philosophers,
too, a newborn star was flickering to life in the form of Karl Jaspers.

But the actual reason, from 1921 onward, that Benjamin regularly spent
weeks at a time creeping down the alleyways of Heidelberg's old town was
the sculptor Jula Cohn. When they first met among friends in Berlin, Benjamin had fallen heavily in love with her—unhappily, of course, and for a
long time without a hint of reciprocation. But that wasn't all. Jula Cohn
had at the same time fallen for Benjamin's school friend Erich Schön, with
whom—and it's almost too banal to be true or even just interesting—
Benjamin's wife, Dora, had been quite openly in a relationship since 1921.
A tricky quadrangle whose classical model any child in Germany could
actually have identified: Goethe's deeply complex novel about relationships, *Elective Affinities*.

In the closing days of 1921, when Benjamin sat down at his desk in
Berlin to have another run at his postdoctoral project, his own complex
network of relationships became the crucial impulse to bundle his lifelong
preoccupation with Goethe's work and worldview—based on his conviction about the actual tasks and methods of literary criticism—into a treatise of just a hundred pages.

This extraordinarily dense text, celebrated today as one of Benjamin's
major works, titled "Goethe's *Elective Affinities*," is dressed up as a classic,
and therefore purely interpretative, essay.[26] But in fact Benjamin's engagement with Goethe's novel, not unlike the novel itself, is the most comprehensive imaginable critique of—we might even call it a meditation on—the

institution of bourgeois marriage and hence the supposed core of bourgeois society as a whole. In other words, it is an exercise in myth-busting,
which reveals all the hidden forces and dynamics that actually hold a modern bourgeois society together, with all its constituent promises of freedom
and self-involvement. For the Benjamin of "Goethe's *Elective Affinities,*"
these are in the end *mythical forces,* patterns of thought and dynamics—and
hence inevitably inauspicious, disabling, and constraining. Building on this,
he answers the question of how the supposedly free and self-determining
subject is to liberate himself from the subtly pernicious effects of these
forces and ideas and thus lead a life in which a true and fulfilling marriage
might be possible.

Benjamin's essay amalgamates—of course without any knowledge of its
contemporaries—the two central ideas and impulses of Cassirer's book
about mythical conceptual form and Heidegger's "Phenomenological Interpretations of Aristotle" into an autonomous theory of his own. The theory concerns the conditions necessary for a true marriage—or, more
broadly understood, a true, free, and authentic form of life. Like Cassirer,
Benjamin saw the need to reveal the cryptic and invariably present effects
of mythical patterns of thought on our civilization through the liberating
process of consciousness raising. And like Jaspers's friend Heidegger, writing in the same year, Benjamin directed his attention at certain openings
that become apparent in extremely heightened situations, and make possible the courageous leap into another and more essential form of existence.
All three authors showed themselves (like Kant) to be firmly convinced: a
person, a subject, an existence that is not clear about the true conditions of
its orientation in the world cannot make a truly free decision. It is not truly
mature. And only the mature, Benjamin would add, should marry each
other—indeed only they *can* be married to each other in the true sense.

MORE LIGHT

ALL THREE AUTHORS here recognize the obligation to philosophically submit the modern rational subject to a conceptual *process of unlearning* in order to render the linguistic forces at work in and through it visible and thus, if necessary, also treatable: to bring them into the light.

Benjamin begins his essay with the four protagonists, highly cultured and intrinsically bourgeois, of Goethe's novel:

> At the height of their cultivation ... they are subject to the forces that cultivation claims to have mastered, even if it may forever prove impotent to curb them.[27]

Benjamin is thus expressing the suspicion, shared by Cassirer, Heidegger, and Wittgenstein, that the modern subject's emphasis on consciousness, precisely where it imagines itself to be entirely free and sovereign, masks only processes of repression and obscurity that, if they are not worked through, can only lead to misery, if not to social destruction. But the prime example of a free choice made by the modern bourgeois subject on its own terms is precisely that of marriage. Here, as the title of Goethe's novel suggests, the mature subject can escape the bonds of nature and confidently opt to find affinities with complete strangers.

FREEDOM OR FATE

THE TWO CENTRAL CONCEPTS that bracket each modern life, according to Benjamin, are "freedom" and "fate." If true freedom is to exist, the forces of fate must ultimately pale in the face of human desire. If fate gains the upper hand, all freedom and choice are merely illusory, and the morally charged concept of "guilt" in particular becomes empty in its application. Fate knows no guilt, only atonement. Freedom knows no atonement, only responsibility.

For Benjamin, Goethe's *Elective Affinities* portrays the necessary failure of the modern bourgeois way of life. In the end, bourgeois life has been unable to free itself entirely from the notion of destiny, which it presents as natural. Bourgeois individuals are accordingly incapable, despite their own supposed self-determination in the choices they make, of assuming full responsibility for the consequences of their actions.

This ambivalence, which shapes the whole of bourgeois existence and hence the whole of modern life, even and especially in the Weimar Republic, is particularly apparent in the concept of romantic love and its inevitable consequence, marriage. Because this love must, it is commonly held, always have something fateful about it, something vaguely predetermined and inexplicable (often the myth of how improbable the lovers' first meeting was, in retrospect). On the other hand, that fateful event must be transferred, by the conscious choice of marriage, and hence the signing of the relationship into law, entirely into the realm of reason and self-determination. *I do!* But having both at the same time, once we grasp the situation in this way, is contradictory and existentially unattainable.

The necessary consequence of this dilemma is, in Benjamin's words, a way of being that is distinguished by a "lingering, at once guilty and guiltless, in the precincts of fate." And it inevitably leads, as Goethe shows us in exemplary fashion in *Elective Affinities*, to catastrophe. In this state of lingering, both inconclusive and tragically unresolved, the "powers that emerge from the disintegration of the marriage must necessarily win out. For they are precisely those of fate."[28] In Benjamin's reading of Goethe, these are mythical powers in the sense of nature and natural forces (the environment, water, premonitions, astrology, curses . . .) that exceed the human will and in this sense disempower human existence.

Benjamin sees the tendency to attribute the failure of one's own marriage—while that failure is unfolding—ultimately to "higher powers" as a prime example of the very same existential laziness and lack of concern that Heidegger saw, in his "Phenomenological Interpretations of Aristotle," as the origin of the modern loss of self. In Cassirer's terms it is the voluntary withdrawal into a form of thought—the mythical—in which truly self-determined action and hence responsibility become impossible.

Wrapped up once again in mythical thought, in which every event in nature augurs or reveals a plan predetermined by fate, or indeed fate itself, we lose ourselves as free beings. And in Benjamin's view we lose ourselves all too willingly, because by doing so we escape one of the greatest of all impositions: truly having to accept responsibility for our own actions. It is an aversion that even Goethe, as he was only too aware, felt powerfully. Benjamin describes that state as follows:

> The human being petrifies in the chaos of symbols and loses the freedom unknown to the ancients. In taking action he lands among signs and oracles. They were not lacking in Goethe's life. . . . Indeed, in *Poetry and Truth*, he recounted how, while on a walk, torn between his calling to poetry and his calling to painting, he set up an oracle. Fear of responsibility is the most spiritual of all those kinds of fear to which Goethe's nature subjected him. It is a foundation of the conservative position that he brought to the political, the social, and in his old age, probably the literary, too. It is the root of the missed opportunities in his erotic life.[29]

This is, then, one kind of disempowerment that Benjamin reveals through Goethe, using the example of the marital crisis: a relapse into descriptions of and perspectives upon the world that yield to the lazy urge to self-disempowerment. It exemplifies the fall into the mythical form of thought, which for Benjamin (and indeed for Cassirer) includes all forms of deterministic and interpretative superstition, particularly that of astrology.

But the shortcoming addressed—and here Benjamin, unhappy in both love and marriage, is also addressing himself—refers to the state of a cravenly neglected and essentially irrevocable chance at a fresh experience of love and the chance of a new life.

CHOICE OR DECISION

ISN'T IT ALL A LITTLE BIT TOO PAT, and above all too gloomy? Isn't the absolute *I do* uttered voluntarily by spouses the textbook example of a mature promise, a durable self-tethering, a willingness to assume lifelong responsibility not only for their own life but also for the life of their chosen partner?

One Benjaminian answer to that is: If marriage is really a choice, then that choice is not the one on which the institution is supposedly based, namely true love. Because, according to Benjamin, we cannot choose love, insofar as "choice" here means something like a selection deliberately made from established alternatives (like the choice between two pairs of shoes, for example). The complete erasure of fate from the course of love seems inevitably to mean the extinction of love. Such relationships even have a contemporary name: rational marriage. This may exist, indeed it may even today be the most widespread form of the institution. But by definition it does not fulfill the ideal of a true marriage. Even from this point of view, then, an ultimately liberating escape from mythical thought is obstructed by the same bourgeois-romantic ideal of marriage. In these matters we cannot be entirely rational and self-determined. Anyone who really wants to be struck by Cupid's arrow cannot have fired it himself.

But above all, in Benjamin's view, when we say *I do* and enter a bourgeois marriage as someone who is capable of love, we inevitably find ourselves plagued by thoughts of guilt and sacrifice. For what is the meaning of *I do*, if not the promise to deny ourselves, in the future and for the rest of our lives, that singular event that opened up our lives, the true foundation of the promise we have just given? And are we then supposed to act as if that is where the actual, rational happiness of life is to be found? As if it were really possible for us to reconcile ourselves with this self-chosen state of permanent self-denial? This is precisely what Goethe did not believe. His flesh-and-blood experience as an erotic natural being was fundamentally different. As Benjamin maintained:

> In the tremendous ultimate experience of the mythic powers—in the knowledge that reconciliation with them cannot be obtained except through the constancy of sacrifice—Goethe revolted against them.[30]

Goethe's novel is thus, for Benjamin, the most artfully composed testimony imaginable for rebellion against two equal forces: the myth of Eros (in which we are passionate natural beings) and the allure of mastering these forces by means of reason, law, and voluntary moral education (in which we are linguistic rational beings capable of cultivation). In Goethe's day this was the classic opposition between "Sturm und Drang" and "Enlightenment." What the example of marriage clearly shows is that reconciliation between these forces is ultimately impossible, and that there *cannot* be something like a truly successful, truly self-determined life under the premises of the bourgeois plan of life. The bourgeois promise of freedom is inevitably deceptive, distorting, and hampered by fate. Its freedom is also purely notional:

For what the author shrouds in silence a hundred times can be seen quite simply enough from the course of things as a whole: that, according to ethical laws, passion loses all its rights and happiness when it seeks a pact with the bourgeois, affluent, secure life.[31]

There is no true marriage on bourgeois terms, no right life in the false. Bourgeois marriage, by virtue of its stability, leads to a state of irresolution, a "lingering, at once guilty and guiltless, in the precincts of fate." Furthermore, for both Goethe and Benjamin that stability can only be illusory, as any form of stagnation can only be a concealed form of falling, and in the end it unleashes the mythical forces with all their destructive power and leads the bond, chosen by lovers, to its destruction.

THE DIVORCED REPUBLIC

IN 1922 ALL THIS WAS, for anyone capable of reading it, now far more than merely a dazzling analysis and decoding of the philosophical content of Goethe's novel. The open-minded reader could see that Benjamin was using the institution of marriage—as the supposed foundation, indeed the kernel of all bourgeois society—as a cipher for the state of bourgeois democracy, meaning the Weimar Republic; his prophetic and philosophical verdict on the predictable fate of precisely this republic had been committed to paper. This republic, if it continued doggedly in its present form, constantly stalling and refusing reparation payments, a typically Weimar form of "lingering, at once guilty and guiltless, in the precincts of fate," would inevitably fall back under the spell of mythical forms of thought—and in the end be destroyed by them.

LEAP OF SALVATION

WAS THIS PROCESS really inevitable? Was there really no way to escape the forces ranged against one another, no chance of a universally liberating extirpation of guilt, a leap into freedom, into a happy "marriage"? According to Benjamin, such a possibility certainly did exist. It is at least hinted at in Goethe's novel, or more precisely in the novella "The Curious Tale of the Childhood Sweethearts," which lies at the novel's center and is completely uncoupled from the actual plot. The marriage of those "children" is, in Benjamin's reading, the only truly successful one in the novel, because it is based not on a *choice* in the conventional sense, but instead on a *decision* in the existential sense. A decision made in the midst of a perilous, life-threatening situation.

The female sweetheart, in extreme hardship due to the oppressive power of bourgeois convention, resolves to make a *leap* from a moving boat into a supposedly lethal river, only to be rescued by her future bridegroom, who is likewise resolved to end his life. Benjamin offers—on occasion quite directly and deliberately addressing Jaspers, as the intended reader of what was, after all, an application essay—the whole repertoire of existentially urgent rhetoric as necessary for true self-discovery:

> In the novella a brilliant light holds sway. From the outset everything, sharply contoured, is at a peak. It is the day of decision shining into the dusk-filled Hades of the novel. . . . Because these human beings [the sweethearts] do not risk everything for the sake of a falsely conceived freedom, no sacrifice falls among them; rather, the decision befalls within them. . . . It is the chimerical striving for freedom that draws down fate upon the characters in the novel. The lovers in the novella

are beyond both freedom and fate, and their courageous decision suffices to tear to bits a fate that would gather to a head over them and to see through a freedom that would pull them down to the nothingness of choice.[32]

REDEEMING
TRANSCENDENCE

HOWEVER, IN THE CONSCIOUSNESS of Benjamin's approach to the existential leap into true freedom lies an essential difference between him and Heidegger. Heidegger's leap resolutely renounces any form of a Beyond or transcendence, and hence renounces all religion. Dasein can acquire liberation only from the structures of false (i.e., bourgeois) existence, from the false (Aristotelian-Cartesian) foundations of the modern subject, from within itself. As Heidegger established quite clearly in 1922: "Philosophy is fundamentally atheistic." The self-enlightenment of one's own facticity must be accomplished in full knowledge of one's own finitude (Heidegger speaks of the "having-imminently" [*Bevorstehendhaben*] of death). Benjamin, on the other hand, explicitly interprets the leap of the young sweethearts—perfectly harmonizing with that of the existentialist philosopher-king, Søren Kierkegaard—as a leap into belief in God, belief in the possibility of salvation from the ultimately false alternatives that condition and devastate all non-transcendent existence.

> Goethe said this expressly in the novella, since the moment of shared readiness for death through God's will gives new life to the lovers, following which old rights lose their claim. Here he shows the life of the two lovers saved in precisely the sense in which marriage preserves

it for the pious ones. In this pair he depicted the power of true love, which he prohibited himself from using in religious form.[33]

Yes, for Benjamin, every decision worthy of the name refers to the transcendent sphere of the Beyond, because "choice is natural and can even belong to the elements; decision is transcendent."[34] There is in decisions always more at stake than we want and are capable of. And in 1922, this transferred quite neatly to Benjamin's *political theology*. He sees the Weimar Republic as trapped inside the same unholy maelstrom as that in which Goethe describes his couples. Choices are incapable of salvaging this mess. Rather than return to the polls, always with less hope than last time, we need to summon the courage for a quasi-religious leap into a different system, to make a decision in favor of a radically new form of coexistence, one predicated on the experience of a Messianic salvation.

At a personal level, things with Jula Cohn hadn't worked out. She just hadn't made that leap. And that year Benjamin lacked both the strength and the funds necessary to make a brave escape from the bourgeois structures of the academic career. Neither could he have described the form of government that the Weimar Republic should have adopted to save itself. Nor, for that matter, could Heidegger. In this context Cassirer's desire to cling to his perfectly conventional, if perhaps also slightly passionless, marriage to Toni Cassirer also acquired a distinctly political edge as a rejection of confused adventures, revolutions, or civil wars, particularly in a time of crisis. They would only make everything much, much worse.

And Wittgenstein? Well, as we have seen, following in the footsteps of Kierkegaard and Tolstoy, he had taken the leap into a new life of his own. Now he had to live with the consequences of that decision.

RUTHLESSNESS

"LET US PRAY." The teacher reverently sets his watch down on the lectern, his stick on the other side. He folds his hands, closes his eyes, and in a deep voice recites the usual morning verses to the forty pupils in his classroom:

> Holy Spirit, come and shine
>
> Your light of mercy on us,
>
> So that we may make our progress,
>
> our duty always to learn.
>
> To retain what we have learned
>
> And always strive to do good.[35]

It was a sacred ritual for him. This week, as every week, Wittgenstein would tell stories "in which the battle for religious convictions placed the faithful in situations of extreme danger."[36] His eyes, normally hidden behind his hands as they dug furrows in his brow, begin to shine with enthusiasm. Each of his pupils understood that this teacher was different from all the others in the school. The day before, he had struck one pupil on the head with his exercise book until it fell apart and the pages fluttered loosely to the floor of the classroom. The boy's misdeed had been to answer Wittgenstein's question "Where was Jesus born?" by saying, "In Jerusalem."[37]

Every day Wittgenstein battled to hold on to what he had recognized philosophically and then chosen religiously, while still striving to do good, but without losing his self-control or the possibility of a meaningful life.

As he had written in January 1921, from his first teaching post in the little mountain village of Trattenbach, to his friend Paul Engelmann:

> I ought to have turned my life to the good and become a star in the sky. But I have remained stuck on earth and now I am gradually fading away. My life has actually become meaningless, so it only consists of superficial episodes. The people around me don't notice and wouldn't understand either; but I know I lack something fundamental.[38]

By now, in November 1922, he had already switched posts twice, and he hoped—or pretended to hope—that he would find conditions at least tolerable in the school in the village of Puchberg.

His doubts about the meaning and above all the value of his life were increasingly taking their toll on his colleagues and even his friends. "To my great shame I must admit that the number of people I can talk to is becoming smaller and smaller," he had admitted to Engelmann that August. During this phase, the criterion of connection was determined by his devotion to the Catholic faith: Wittgenstein feared that he would no longer be able to make himself intelligible to those who lacked it—above all Bertrand Russell, the author of the future international bestseller *Why I Am Not a Christian*.[39] As a result, their friendship entered a serious crisis. That terrible encroaching suspicion about everything human, which Wittgenstein described to his friend and patron at the start of his time in Trattenbach, applied increasingly to his closest circle of friends: "It's true that people on average aren't worth much anywhere; but here they are far more useless and irresponsible than elsewhere. . . . Trattenbach is a particularly inferior place in Austria and the *Austrians* have—since the war—fallen abysmally low."[40] In his first two years of teaching, Wittgenstein was trapped in a downward spiral of misanthropy in which self-hatred and hatred of others increasingly came to reinforce each other.

THREE-QUARTERS
UNDERSTOOD

IN THE AUTUMN OF 1922, when he was transferred to the neighboring village of Hassbach, Wittgenstein stuck it out there for just a few weeks, since the locals seemed to him to be "not human beings at all, just repellent maggots." It was not until he was moved to Puchberg in Lower Austria in November 1922 that things took a slight turn for the better. Not that the people there struck him as more agreeable than anywhere else. In Puchberg, too, he saw himself surrounded by creatures that were at best "three-quarters human, but one-quarter animal." But that month Wittgenstein, then still a trainee teacher, took his final qualifying exam. From now on he had greater freedom in designing his courses. His status among his colleagues was also more secure than before. Yet this period of relative relaxation may have had something to do with developments in the life that he had abandoned. While their friendship might have become increasingly fraught, Russell, after his return from China in August 1921, had, as promised, stepped up his efforts to find a publisher for Wittgenstein's book, and had in the end succeeded. On or around November 15, 1922, the first copy of Wittgenstein's treatise, printed in German and English, arrived in Puchberg, under the now definitive title *Tractatus logico-philosophicus*.

Wittgenstein was delighted. The fact that he received not a single shilling, or indeed penny, for the book from his publisher Kegan Paul mattered not in the slightest. Neither did the fact that he was still waiting for someone to understand it. It had been published in England, was as free of errors as possible, and the translation wasn't bad. The work now existed in this world, it was universally accessible, a publicly available fact: it was the case. And it was not inconceivable that someone would comprehend the actual therapeutic aim of his treatise, motivated as it was entirely by ethical concerns.

IN THERAPY

THE OBJECTIVE OF THE WORK was simply "to see the world correctly" and, with this clarified way of seeing, which relied on drawing a sharp boundary between what can be said meaningfully and what cannot, to lead a more clarified life. It was also this objective approach that had led Wittgenstein to accept G. E. Moore's suggested title of *Tractatus logico-philosophicus*. It was a reference to Baruch Spinoza's *Tractatus theologico-politicus*, and hence a book written in the seventeenth century with the explicit aim of liberating its readers from false assumptions based on errors of thought and concept about the nature of the human spirit—above all, errors involving the use of divine revelation as a supposed foundation for ethical and political action. For Spinoza, philosophizing meant first and foremost exposing existing confusions as such, and exposing false assumptions through a clarifying logical analysis that enabled readers at last to "see correctly" the world of which they are a part. Spinoza's program, too, was initially a destructive or decivilizing one—in the sense of liberating us by linguistic means from false assumptions that are themselves linguistically determined, which permanently distort our vision of the world.

As far as Wittgenstein was concerned, however, by 1922 these false assumptions were not solely, and not even primarily, religious convictions.

Rather, they were the fundamental assumptions of the supposedly enlightened scientific vision of the world. This vision revealed itself (although its acolytes were not aware of it, and had no wish to be) to be trapped in extremely primitive and, according to Wittgenstein, demonstrably groundless convictions, which in the end fell short of even clarified religious faith. The scientifically enlightened modern age, with its foundational belief in the unconstrained power of natural laws, from which it imagined everything that was, is, and could be causally explained and even predicted, was based on a conceptual self-deception. It lay in an inability to distinguish between the concepts of "logical necessity" and "the necessity of natural laws."

Confronted with the same problems that preoccupied Heidegger, Cassirer, and Benjamin, Wittgenstein might be said to have been concerned more than anything with clarifying the relationship between "guilt" and "fate," "freedom" and "necessity," "faith" and "knowledge," "being there" and "being like this" as the central concepts of any truly mature life. And these ideas were set out as clearly as possible in the very book that Wittgenstein was now able to hold in his hands:

> 6:36311 That the sun will rise to-morrow, is an hypothesis; and that means that we do not know whether it will rise.

> 6:37 A necessity for one thing to happen because another has happened does not exist. There is only *logical* necessity.

> 6:371 At the basis of the whole modern view of the world lies the illusion that the so-called laws of nature are the explanations of natural phenomena.

> 6:372 So people stop short at natural laws as at something unassailable, as did the ancients at God and Fate.

And they both are right and wrong. But the ancients were clearer, in so far as they recognized one clear conclusion, whereas in the modern system it should appear as though *everything* were explained.

The truth was, however, that nothing was explained, least of all the question of why the world exists, with its laws that we believe we are able to explain. And no explanation of it would ever be possible, because any explanation would have to fall back on something *outside* this world and thus inevitably make us say things that were nonsense. A truly religious individual of the kind Wittgenstein imagined, and considered himself to be, was someone able to take that crucial clarifying step, advancing ahead of all those who put their faith in science.

That was not to say that no locus of meaning might be found beyond the boundaries of the sayable, only that what can be sensed beyond those boundaries was unsuited to justifications or explanations concerning *this* world—if those justifications were of a factual or an ethical nature.

6:41 The sense of the world must lie outside the world. In the world everything is as it is and happens as it does happen. *In* it there is no value—and if there were, it would be of no value. If there is a value which is of value, it must lie outside all happening and being-so.

TOP DOWN

THEN AGAIN, these were all propositions that, according to Wittgenstein's own criteria, were completely meaningless. But that was precisely the brilliant trick that formed his program of conceptual decivilization. How can a confusion created by language be clarified except through the means of language itself?

In the end, therefore, all that remained was to push away the clarifying ladder of propositions that had just been laboriously climbed.

But what next, at such a height, in the absence of a ladder? What chance do we have of returning to solid ground? There is in fact only one option: the decision to make the leap! The leap into faith! The leap into a truly ethical existence, the leap into freedom! Granted, this leap is distinguished by the fact that it is performed in the full awareness of its fundamental instability and groundlessness. A leap into nothingness, then, if its opposite "something" means a solid ground or a fact within the world. Only a genuinely groundless leap grants a true footing in faith, because only such a leap is from the outset free of any justifiable expectation of a potential reward, of justice, spiritual salvation, immortality, or anything else usually promised by religion. This is also set out, word for word, in the *Tractatus*:

> 6:422 The first thought in setting up an ethical law of the form "thou shalt . . ." is: And what if I do not do it. But it is clear that ethics has nothing to do with punishment and reward in the ordinary sense. This question as to the consequences of an action must therefore be irrelevant. At least these consequences will not be events. For there must be something right in that formulation of the question. There must be some sort of ethical reward and ethical punishment, but this must lie in the action itself.

The value of the decision to lead a free life, if there is one, is justified by the experience of living that life itself (and can therefore not be grasped externally as its consequence). And it must be understood as a leap into this concrete life and no other, not even a later or indeed an eternal one:

6:4312 The temporal immortality of the soul of man, that is to say, its eternal survival also after death, is not only in no way guaranteed, but this assumption in the first place will not do for us what we always tried to make it do. Is a riddle solved by the fact that I survive for ever? Is this eternal life not as enigmatic as our present one? The solution of the riddle of life in space and time lies outside space and time.

The very decision to make the leap into faith or, more broadly, into a truly ethical existence, presented by Heidegger, Benjamin, and Wittgenstein to their readers in 1922 with the full force of their rhetorical and conceptual acuity, seeks no other guarantee and no other basis than the living of life itself. Those who now seriously ask why we should opt for such a life—is it, for example, easier, more pleasant, more comfortable, more carefree?—reveal only their misunderstanding of the *purpose* of that leap. Indeed, it shows that they have in the end understood nothing at all. Not about themselves, nor about the world. That, at least, was how Wittgenstein saw it—and he wasn't alone.

Wittgenstein's clarification of motive and expectation sheds light on the difference between "choice" and "decision" that was also crucial to Benjamin's, Heidegger's, and even Cassirer's writings from this time. A choice seeks justification in predictable consequences, while a decision does not. In this sense a choice is always conditional, a decision unconditional—and hence in fact free. A choice remains entangled in myth, while a decision— ideally—breaks away from the supposedly existence-guiding, rational logic of cause and effect, fate and necessity, guilt and reconciliation. This liberation in itself bestows sacredness of a kind. That was the philosophical and educational liberation theory (or liberation theology?) set out by Wittgenstein in the 1920s.

But there was one thing that Wittgenstein could not deny, fully aware as he was of having undertaken the leap into a new life as a primary school teacher: the possible meaning of that existence did not appear to him in his daily living of that life. At any rate it did not fulfill him, but left him for days and weeks at a time with that numb feeling of emptiness from which he had in fact hoped to escape, redeeming himself by making his decision. He found himself not only seriously troubled in Puchberg; he had had enough of this "it." His letters from this period testify with monotonous regularity to his awareness of the impossibility of escaping the dark forces of his own character and nature. Time and again he was drawn inexorably inward, back to the deeper, unilluminated strata of himself.

He did make sincere attempts to connect with others; indeed, he was at this time spending his lunches with his colleagues at the pub, and in Rudolf Koder he even found a person who shared his tastes in music and with whom he was soon playing duets for piano and clarinet by Brahms and Mozart every afternoon. But in the end he and everyone around him clearly sensed that that invisible and, for precisely that reason, impenetrable pane of glass—which he had once described to his sister Hermine— still stood between him and the rest of the world. Throughout the winter and spring of 1923, Wittgenstein was above all: painfully lonely.

The publication of his book did nothing to relieve his plight. On the contrary: it must only have reinforced and intensified his sense of constant, fateful isolation. As he sat in his sparsely furnished room, what else could the sight of that volume, day in and day out, convey to him but the simple truth that there were limits, clearly and firmly drawn, on his ability to liberate himself from his own troubles by philosophizing. What is the point of seeing this world "correctly" if there is no one anywhere to share it with?

V.

YOU

1923–1925

Wittgenstein curses, Cassirer heals,
Heidegger becomes demonic, and Benjamin porous.

THE IDIOT

WITTGENSTEIN NEVER FOUND the inner peace he hoped for in Puchberg, let alone anything approaching happiness. Within the narrow community of school and village he remained an outsider, and the subject of the strangest legends. Then as now, the line between village saint and village idiot was extremely fine. For some he was the "baron" or the "wealthy lord"; others said he had "voluntarily renounced all his riches." A third group confidently reported that Wittgenstein had suffered a brain injury during the war, that "the bullet was still in his head and causing him great pain."[1] None of this was entirely correct—or entirely false. But one cannot feel fully accepted under such conditions. Like the monk he really wanted to be, Wittgenstein shared a spartan, bare-walled room with nothing but a bed, chair, and table. His lodgings, which were very important to him, were to be free of any kind of comfort, free from the so-called achievements of modern civilization. His clothes, which during this phase consisted of a leather frock coat, lederhosen with wrap puttees, and heavy mountain boots, accorded perfectly with this quest. His colleagues were struck, and not necessarily pleased, by the fact that he never adapted his outfit to the weather conditions of the day or season, or even changed them. He smelled. There were mutterings.

When, on his increasingly sleepless nights, as he stared out of his bedroom window at the starry sky above Puchberg, Wittgenstein's thoughts turned to the few happy episodes he had known; he was always taken back to his prewar years as a student in England. There he had found not only true kindred spirits but, in David Pinsent, also the love of his life. Wittgenstein even dedicated his *Tractatus* to the memory of his friend, who had perished as a test pilot during the war. He and Pinsent had once ridden through Iceland on ponies, and in Norway they had traveled together to a lonely cabin. With Pinsent he had sensed a possible meaning in life.

In early 1920, Wittgenstein had written of his enduring grief: "I'm no longer in any condition to acquire new friends and I'm losing my old ones. It's terribly sad." Every day, he said later, he remembered his lost love: "I think of Pinsent. . . . He took half my life away with him. The devil will take the other half."[2] Three years later, even his friendship with Russell was fading, as the failed meeting of the previous summer forced them to admit. Wittgenstein objected on moral grounds to Russell's divorce, and to his long, "wild" affair with Dora Black, which was legalized only shortly before the birth of their son, while Russell's understanding of the pious mysticism of his brilliant student waned.

IT'S COMPLICATED

WITTGENSTEIN COULD CLEARLY SEE that he was in danger of losing the final few connections that tethered him to anyone else. And for all the determination with which he had embarked on a radical new path, that prospect did not attract him. This fear of loss in turn made him still more prickly and sensitive, as a letter to John Maynard Keynes from the spring of 1923 reveals:

Dear Keynes!

Thanks so much for sending me the "Reconstruction in Europe." I should have preferred though to have got a line from you personally, saying how you are getting on, etc. Or, are you too busy to write letters? I don't suppose you are. Do you ever see Johnson? If so, please give him my love. I should so much like to hear from him too (not about my book but about himself).

So do write to me sometime, if you will condescend to do such a thing.

Yours sincerely
Ludwig Wittgenstein[3]

Precisely the tone that renders a reply most unlikely. Particularly since at the time Keynes was tremendously busy. This Cassandra of the impending catastrophe became, during these postwar years, the most influential economist in the world. Just as he had warned, both as a member of the British delegation at Versailles and as author of the book *The Economic Consequences of the Peace*, hyperinflation was bringing Germany and Austria to the brink of political collapse. The fate of the Continent was once again at stake. War between France and Germany threatened. Ailing Lenin's revolutionary Soviet Union was sinking into a civil war the outcome of which no one could predict. Keynes advised the British government, publicized his own opinions to a global audience, and also taught economics at King's College, Cambridge. As Wittgenstein taught elementary mathematics to his pupils in Puchberg, Keynes sat in gilded conference rooms, explaining to the great and the good the criminally neglected fundamentals of economic dynamics. Wittgenstein struggled daily to stay sane;

Keynes struggled to set Europe on a new economic foundation. Wittgenstein played Mozart with Rudolf Koder in a back room in Puchberg. On weekends, over strawberries and Pimm's, Keynes ruminated about the possible forms of these and many other experiential worlds with his old Cambridge friends from the Bloomsbury Group—among them Virginia and Leonard Woolf, E. M. Forster, and Lytton Strachey.

In the spring of 1923, Wittgenstein's existential cul-de-sac was becoming more and more restricting. What of that young, unusually alert mathematician who had translated his *Tractatus* "so excellently" from German into English, and of whom Charles Kay Ogden, the editor of the series in which Wittgenstein's book was published, had nothing but good things to say? What was his name again?

....

Dear Mr Ramsey,

I've got a letter from Mr Ogden the other day saying that you may possibly come to Vienna in one of these next months. Now as you have so excellently translated the Tractatus into English I have no doubt you will be able to translate a letter too and therefore I am going to write the rest of this one in German.[4]

....

The rest of this letter from the spring of 1923, originally written in German, has not been preserved, but clearly it contained an invitation for Ramsey to visit Wittgenstein at some point in Puchberg. For Frank Ramsey, just twenty years old and the son of a Cambridge academic, it was the opportunity of a lifetime—a chance to be on first-name terms with Wittgenstein and review with him the *Tractatus*, the work that had so gripped and disturbed the young intellectual elite of his university within only a few weeks of its publication. By September 1923 the time had come. Ramsey traveled to Puchberg and—for two long weeks—went through the *Tractatus* sentence by sentence for four or five uninterrupted hours after school each day. Ramsey's expectations are understandable enough, but Wittgenstein's motivation must have seemed considerably less so. Ramsey told his mother how the visit unfolded:

It's terrible when he says "Is that clear" and I say "no" and he says "Damn it's *horrid* to go through that again." Sometimes he says, I can't see that now [and] we must leave it. He often forgot the meaning of what he wrote within 5 minutes, and then remembered it later. Some of his sentences are intentionally ambiguous having an ordinary meaning and a more difficult meaning which he also believes.[5]

A few days later, Ramsey wrote a postcard to Ogden, the publisher of the *Tractatus*, in a markedly different tone:

L.W. explains his book to me from 2 [to] 7 every day. It is most illuminating; he seems to enjoy this and as we get on about a page an hour I shall probably stay here a fortnight or more. He is very interested in it, though he says that his mind is no longer flexible and he can never write another book. He teaches in the village school from 8 to 12 or 1. He is very poor and seems to lead a very dreary life having only one friend here, and being regarded by most of his colleagues as a little mad.[6]

This rather overweight, pallid young man with his moon face and metal-rimmed glasses, his carefree attitude, curiosity, and, not least, obvious intellectual brilliance, was in Wittgenstein's eyes the first reader of the *Tractatus* who truly understood it. A unique opportunity and experience for Wittgenstein, too, then, the full potential of which may have become apparent to him only during those two weeks in September. After all, while his work had been enthusiastically received by the inner circles of philosophy, which were extremely formal and logic-focused, as far as Wittgenstein could tell, they had received it in entirely the wrong way.

Indeed, none other than Wittgenstein's publisher, the man of letters, linguist, and philosopher C. K. Ogden, in March 1923 had released a book titled *The Meaning of Meaning*, which sought to capture core insights of Wittgenstein's thought by explaining the foundations of meaning through language. Ogden proudly sent a copy to Puchberg—only to receive the following reply from Wittgenstein:

> I have now read your book and wish to admit quite openly that in my view you have not correctly grasped the actual problems on which—for example—I have been working (regardless of whether my solution of them is correct or not).[7]

Ogden's suggestion (which is still popular among philosophers of language) that the riddle of linguistic meaning be solved via the category of causality and a conscious reference by the speaker to the denoted object is, in Wittgenstein's view, too wrongheaded to seriously consider a potential answer. Hadn't he clearly shown that the actual sense-founding relationship between logical sentence structure and the logical construction of the world itself had nothing meaningful to say or even to explore, but that they were simply as given and hence at best to be marveled at?

> 4:12 Propositions can represent the whole reality, but they cannot represent what they must have in common with reality in order to be able to represent it—the logical form.
> To be able to represent the logical form, we should have to be able to put ourselves with the propositions outside logic, that is, outside the world.

> 4:121 Propositions cannot represent the logical form: this mirrors itself in the propositions.
> That which mirrors itself in language, language cannot represent.
> That which expresses *itself* in language, *we* cannot express by language.

But expression through language was exactly what Ogden had aimed to achieve with his causal theory of meaning. He wanted to express *through* language what was expressed *with* language. In any case, according to Wittgenstein it was impossible to assume something like causality or indeed the laws of causality as final categories capable of providing final clarifications.

> 6:36 If there were a law of causality, it might run: "There are natural laws."
> But that can clearly not be said: it shows itself.

With similar suspicion Wittgenstein may have heard, by the time of his stay in Vienna on holiday in August 1923, that his *Tractatus* was now also beginning to inspire seminars and discussion groups (later known as the "Vienna Circle") at the city's university. The Vienna group wanted to save and heal society by adhering to a strictly scientific view of the world. This certainly did not correspond to Wittgenstein's approach, since he saw the purely scientific worldview as yet another wrong track that his era had placed itself upon, and one that was, in its supposedly value-free and enlightened clarity, based on particularly stubborn misunderstandings.

However painful it might have been to go through that damned book again, proposition by proposition, there were some things that needed clarifying. In 1923, though, the most painful problem tormenting Wittgenstein on an existential level certainly lay not in the possibility that he would be misunderstood as a philosopher, and would in all probability remain so, but in the severity of his isolation and loneliness. He recognized Ramsey's appearance in Puchberg as an opportunity to sound out the chance of some kind of return to England—even, if necessary, to rejoin academic life there. After his visit, the wunderkind Frank Ramsey, sponsored and nurtured by all the leading figures in Cambridge—Moore, Russell, and Keynes—became Wittgenstein's English emissary. His first task consisted in determining whether Wittgenstein, as a former student and now the author of the *Tractatus*, might graduate from Cambridge University. "I haven't yet met Keynes to ask about your graduation," Ramsey reported in telegraphic style to Puchberg in October 1923. Only a month later he clearly had more concrete information.

....

Dear Wittgenstein,

Thanks for your letter.

I have good news for you. If you will pay a visit to England, there is £50 (= K16,000,000) available to pay your expenses. So do, please, come. I imagine you would prefer to come in your summer holiday, which I think you said was July and August. The disadvantage of that time is that it is vacation in Cambridge, and the time when people in England take their holidays, so that the people you would like to see might be scattered all over the place. It occurred to me that if, as you said was possible, you were leaving your present school at the end of the academic year, you might perhaps leave two months earlier, and come to England for May and June, or longer, or part of those months. The Cambridge summer term is April 22nd to June 13th.

I asked Keynes about your degree, and the position seems to be this. The regulations have changed so that it is no longer possible to obtain a B.A. by keeping six terms and submitting a thesis. Instead you can obtain a Ph.D. by 3 years and a thesis. If you could come here for another year, you could probably get permission to count your two previous years and so obtain a Ph.D.[8]

The fifty British pounds put at Wittgenstein's disposal, calculated to be 16 million Austrian krone at the time, came from Keynes, who didn't want to be mentioned by name as the donor, in the fear that it would be immediately refused. As he emphasized to Ramsey, under no circumstances would Wittgenstein be willing to accept alms or handouts. Neither was he concerned with an official degree or any kind of documentary testimony to his philosophical competence. Keynes now found this out, too, when he sat down at his desk after more than twelve months of silence, to invite Wittgenstein to join him in England. The exchange between the two deserves to be quoted almost in its entirety:

46, Gordon Square
Bloomsbury

29 March 1924

My dear Wittgenstein,

A whole year has passed by and I have not replied to your letter. I am ashamed that this should have been so. But it was not for want of thinking about you and of feeling very much that I wanted to renew signs of friendship. The reason was that I wanted to try to understand your book thoroughly before writing to you; yet my mind is now so far from fundamental questions that it is impossible for me to get clear about such matters. I still do not know what to say about your book, except that I feel certain that it is a work of extraordinary importance and genius. Right or wrong, it dominates all fundamental discussions at Cambridge since it was written.

I have sent you in a separate package copies of the various books which I have written since the war. Probability is the completion of what I was doing before the war,—I fear you will not like it. Two books on the Peace Treaty, half economic and half political, a book on Monetary Reform (which is what I most think about just now). I should like immensely to see and talk with you again. Is there a chance that you will pay a visit to England?

Yours truly and affectionately
J. M. Keynes

I would do anything in my power which could make it easier for you to do further work.[9]

But this time Keynes failed, precisely because he desired to speak politely and with great care, to strike the requisite tone and address Wittgenstein's main concern. Wittgenstein replied to Keynes:

....

Puchberg am Schneeberg

4:7.24.

My dear Keynes,

Thanks awfully for sending me your books and for your letter dated 29./3. I have postponed writing to you so long because I could not make up my mind as to whether to write to you in English or in German. Writing in German makes things easy for me and difficult for you. On the other hand if I write in English I am afraid the whole business may become hopeless at MY end already. Whereas you might find somebody to translate a German letter to you. If I have said all I've got to say I'll end up in English.

Also: Zuerst möchte ich Ihnen noch einmal für die Bücher und Ihren lieben Brief danken. Da ich sehr beschäftigt bin und mein Gehirn für alles Wissenschaftliche ganz unaufnahmsfähig ist, so habe ich nur in *einem* der Bücher gelesen ("The economic consequences [of the peace]"). Es hat mich sehr interessiert, obwohl ich von dem Gegenstand natürlich so gut wie nichts verstehe. Sie schreiben, ob Sie etwas tun könnten, um mir wieder wissenschaftliches Arbeiten zu ermöglichen: Nein, in dieser Sache läßt sich nichts machen; denn ich habe selbst keinen starken inneren Trieb mehr zu solcher Beschäftigung. Alles was ich wirklich sagen mußte, habe ich gesagt und damit ist die Quelle vertrocknet. Das klingt sonderbar, aber es ist so.—Gerne, *sehr* gerne möchte ich Sie wiedersehen; und ich weiß, daß Sie so gut waren, mir Geld für einen Aufenthalt in England zuzusichern.

Wenn ich aber denke, daß ich von Ihrer Güte nun wirklich Gebrauch machen soll, so kommen mir allerlei Bedenken: Was soll ich in England tun? Soll ich nur kommen um Sie zu sehen und mich auf alle mögliche Weise zu zerstreuen? I mean to say shall I just come to be nice? Now I don't think at all that it isn't worth while being nice—if only I could be REALLY nice—or having a nice time—if it were a VERY nice time indeed.

But staying in rooms and having tea with you every other day or so would not be *nice enough*. But then I should pay for this little niceness with the great disadvantage of seeing my short holidays vanish like a phantom without having the least profit—I don't mean money—or getting any satisfaction from them. Of course staying in Cambridge with you is much nicer than staying in Vienna alone. But in Vienna I can collect my thoughts a little and although they are not worth collecting they are better than mere distraction.

Now it wouldn't seem impossible that I could get more out of you than a cup of tea every other day that's to say that I could really profit from hearing you and talking to you and in this case it would be worth while coming over. But here again there are great difficulties: We haven't met since 11 years. I don't know if you have changed during that time, but I certainly have tremendously. I am sorry to say I am no better than I was, but I am *different*. And therefore if we shall meet you may find that the man who has come to see you isn't really the one you meant to invite. There is no doubt that, even if we *can* make ourselves understood to one another, a chat or two will *not* be sufficient for the purpose, and that the result of our meeting will be disappointment and disgust on your side and disgust and despair on mine.— Had I any definite work to do in England and were it to sweep the streets or to clean anybody's boots I would come over with great pleasure and then nicety could come by itself in course.

There would be a lot more to say about the subject but it's too difficult to express it either in English or in German. So I'd better make an end. I thought when I began to write that I should write this letter altogether in German but, extraordinarily enough, it has proved more natural for me to write to you in broken English than in correct German.

Herzliche Grüße! Yours ever
Ludwig Wittgenstein

P.S. Please give my love to Johnson if you see him.[10]

....

For now, at least, Wittgenstein was not coming back to Cambridge. But the exchange reveals a fundamental contradiction that would have a lasting effect on the mutual expectations of both parties in the years before his actual return, and in fact far beyond: Wittgenstein wanted his friends back, and the Cambridge group wanted their philosophical genius back, too. The group was ready to do everything within its power to achieve this. And Wittgenstein showed surprising flexibility. He would even consider returning to philosophy. Anything was better than sitting alone in his cell in Puchberg and waiting for his wits to finally abandon him.

HOSPITALITY

IT WAS A MATTER OF HONOR for Cassirer to guide his guest—who had traveled from Marburg, where he had recently been appointed professor—through the rooms of the Warburg Library. The previous evening, December 17, 1923, at the invitation of the Kant Society of Hamburg, of which

Cassirer was president, Heidegger had delivered a lecture on "Tasks and Paths of Phenomenological Research." In sight of the rare treasures that occupied the cabinets and shelves around them, the two men could expand upon the conversation they had begun the previous evening. Of course, Cassirer said, assenting to the core of his guest's thesis, the foundations of man's relationship with the world cannot be the sole preserve of the empirical sciences, of only psychology, anthropology, and biology. In the end, for example, the conceptual form of myth as an early way of approaching the world is shaped by categories and assumptions fundamentally different from those of the scientific worldview.

Of course, Heidegger nods, precisely such "primitive phenomena" can help reveal existing distortions of Dasein's self-interpretation. On the other hand, concentrating only on the mythical form of thought always risks mistaking the primitive for the primordial. Seen correctly, is the use of signs in myth not based on a form of world disclosure that it does not, for example, generate itself but rather interprets in a particular way? And if that is so, will it not, in the descriptive acquisition of a truly primal concept of the world, inevitably be a matter of describing that concept in terms of everydayness? As a fundamental orientation that must be given and disclosed to Dasein even prior to any symbolic formation? Does primitive Dasein not also have an everydayness, just as modern scientific Dasein does?

"Certainly," Cassirer replies, as the tour ends, and they both halt by the cabinet devoted to the subject of the "Symbol," "except not before or independent of all symbolization. How else could we imagine and explain the orientation apparent in the everyday?" "That is precisely," Heidegger says with a pursed smile, "what I wonder myself."

Portrait of Ludwig Wittgenstein on the occasion of the awarding of his research grant, 1929.

Martin Heidegger, 1922.

Ernst Cassirer after his election as rector of Hamburg University, 1929.

Walter Benjamin, 1925.

(Left to right) Hermine, Paul, Helene, Ludwig, and Margarete Wittgenstein.

The Wittgenstein family, gathered to celebrate Ludwig's parents' silver wedding anniversary on May 23, 1899, at the family seat in Neuwaldegg. Ludwig, in a sailor suit, is at the front toward the left.

Wittgenstein as a primary school teacher with his pupils
in Puchberg, 1922.

The Great Court of Trinity College, University of Cambridge.

The house built by Wittgenstein on Kundmanngasse
in Vienna, 1928.

Margarete Stonborough
(née Wittgenstein) in a 1905
wedding portrait by Gustav Klimt.

Martin Heidegger with his wife, Elfride, and their sons, Jörg and
Hermann, 1924.

Hannah Arendt, 1927.

Martin Heidegger, ca. 1922.

View of Marburg with the university, 1930.

Ernst and Toni Cassirer, 1929.

The reading room at the Warburg Institute Library in Hamburg, 1926.

Ernst Cassirer at home at 26 Blumenstrasse, Hamburg, late 1920s.

Walter Benjamin, 1924.

Dora and Stefan Benjamin, 1921.

Asja Lacis, 1924.

Zum Kater Hiddigeigei (the Tomcat Hiddigeigei café) on Capri, 1886.

Davos in winter 1929.

Audience at the Davos University Conferences, 1929.

Martin Heidegger at the Parsenn ski
resort, 1929.

Ernst Cassirer and Martin Heidegger in Davos, 1929.

Group around Heidegger and Cassirer in Davos, 1929.

Early days of the economic crisis in Berlin, 1929.

FROM HAMBURG TO BELLEVUE

THAT, OR SOMETHING LIKE IT, is how the first lengthy personal discussion between Heidegger and Cassirer must have gone in Hamburg, in the rooms of the Warburg Library. At any rate, this is the context in which Heidegger would later recall that meeting in the winter of 1923, in his masterpiece *Being and Time*.[11]

It seems inconceivable that during his guided tour Heidegger didn't wonder about its actual founder, the mind behind the library. Was he still alive? If so, where was he and what was he doing?

Even to someone as worldly as Cassirer, it wasn't an easy situation to explain. In fact, Aby Warburg was several years into psychiatric treatment for a severe nervous condition that had led to a complete breakdown in 1918. Since the spring of 1921 he had been in a Swiss institution in Kreuzlingen on the shore of Lake Constance. The Bellevue Sanatorium, one of the most renowned and progressive on the Continent, was run by the Binswanger family—since 1910 by Ludwig Binswanger, the eldest son of Robert Binswanger and grandson of Ludwig Binswanger the Elder, who had founded the sanatorium in 1857 on the grounds of an abandoned monastery. Bellevue was less a closed institution and more a wooded estate of houses and apartments in which patients were intended to enjoy the greatest possible degree of freedom and dignity, and were in most cases assigned generous living areas as well as personal nurses. Aby Warburg resided in an apartment with his own bedroom, study, and bathroom—not least because of the severity of his schizophrenia. Its core symptoms were paranoia and obsessive-compulsive disorders, leading in its more intense phases to severe eruptions of rage and violence. One defining feature was Warburg's constant fear of being poisoned, along with the suspicion that he was being fed the innards of his wife or children, or else that he would soon be killed with his family. Warburg's episodes of anxiety were accompanied by powerful compulsions to wash himself and to engage in repetitive activities, mostly to do with arranging and tidying certain areas of his apartment. Compulsions that had, before he referred himself for treatment in 1918, already begun to dominate the course of his day.

Over the years of his stay in Kreuzlingen, Warburg alternated between phases in which he spiraled out of control and phases of zest and mental clarity, during which—mainly through his continued correspondence with Dr. Saxl—he kept himself up-to-date about developments in his research library. Cassirer's arrival in Hamburg aroused particular interest.

SNAKE EXPERIMENTS

WARBURG PRESENTED a rare but clinically fascinating phenomenon—a mental patient haunted by the same delusions, obsessive ideas, and episodic anxieties that had formed the center of his cultural-historical research. According to Warburg's theory of culture, which was based primarily on the medium of the image and pictorial representation, the human urge to give symbolic expression to our deepest and most existential anxieties—to give them a solid form and by doing so to make them amenable to innovation or treatment—is actually the source of all culture and learning. Even in its most sublime and abstract achievements, in art and science, the human mind can never entirely overcome culture's origins, the feeling of existential anxiety and of being subject to the overwhelming forces of nature that, we suppose, surround us and overpower us.

This dynamic of overcoming fear is especially evident in the spiritual symbols or rituals of "primitive"—or, as we would say today, indigenous—

peoples and cultures. And hence also the extent to which these guiding symbols are similar and overlap with one another, transcending all continental and temporal boundaries. The case is made in exemplary fashion in Warburg's "A Lecture on Serpent Ritual," his study of the Pueblo Indians, prepared at Kreuzlingen at his doctor's suggestion and delivered to the patients and staff of the institution on April 21, 1923.

In his lecture Warburg describes the mythically charged snake (always with an eye on the biblical fall in the book of Genesis) as "an international symbolic answer to the question: Whence came destruction, death, and suffering into the world?"[12]

The fears, demons, and obsessions that, for Warburg, underlie the whole of our civilized existence and, in the early stages of their development, constitute an instructive regime of magic and ritual had in the form of an illness also taken over his mind, as Warburg was in his more lucid moments only too aware. They defined his thoughts, his feelings, the whole of his everyday life.

The crucial question, of course, was whether his treatment would enable him to free himself from these compulsions by means of scientific reflection and analysis. Whether, deputizing for humanity as a whole, so to speak, he would once again be capable of liberating himself from the constrictions of a primal symbolic consciousness, with its magical and totemistic charge. Or would his relapse be a permanent one?

TUNNEL AND LIGHT

THE LECTURE ABOUT THE SERPENT RITUAL thus marks a crucial turning point in Warburg's private mythology, since in it, for the first time in many years, the liberating spirits of enlightenment and analysis triumph over the magical-mythical forces of fear and obsession. Cassirer was one of very few people whom Warburg allowed to see the written notes for his lecture. It was an act of trust encouraged by Dr. Saxl, on the understanding that a personal meeting between the two researchers might prove an important step in Warburg's recovery and thus bring about his return to Hamburg.

It was an invitation to deliver a lecture in Switzerland in the spring of 1924 that gave Cassirer the opportunity to visit his colleague and patron Warburg in person in Bellevue.[13] The meeting required careful preparation. Both Saxl and Warburg's wife, Mary, traveled to Kreuzlingen days before Cassirer's arrival to support the highly expectant and hence also overexcited patient. This was Warburg's first lengthy research meeting with a stranger, and one whom he greatly respected and (rightly) assumed capable of fully grasping his own approach toward the history of images.

Warburg spent several days in intense preparation for the meeting, noting down and arranging questions and problems on pieces of paper and, minutes before Cassirer's arrival in Kreuzlingen, declaring that all the notes carefully arranged on his desk were taboo. In the face of patient encouragement from his caregivers, he insisted that the whole room be cleared of these and other unlucky objects. It *had* to be done. Meanwhile Cassirer waited to be allowed to cross the threshold of the study.

Despite these initial complications, the two were quick to speak freely. Cassirer understood man's development through symbols as a continuous process of liberation that found its starting point in conceptual forms from which mythical thought derived. Warburg was fully in accord with this vision, and was particularly concerned to demonstrate the inextinguishable energies and impulses of mythical image-worlds within that advancing process. It was a rare meeting of minds, which Warburg shortly afterward described as follows: "I felt as if I could hear someone knocking on the other side of the tunnel."[14]

Their discussion almost inevitably concentrated on the Renaissance and its status as a transitional phase in European thought. The era was marked by an exciting simultaneity of mythical and magical ways of thinking; developments in astrology were matched by rather more logical and mathematical ones in astronomy. As they strolled in the park, their conversation was centered on Kepler's (re)discovery of ellipses in the orbits of heavenly bodies, with regular interruptions by Warburg about which of the many buildings of the institution his wife—who was walking arm in arm with him at the time—was being held in.[15] The essential bipolarity of all existence, which Warburg saw as reaching its clearest expression in the figure of the ellipse—a geometrical body with two focal points—did not leave his mind even on that remarkable afternoon of April 10. He experienced himself in three dimensions, as a mixture of complete rationality and irrationality, of brilliant scientific intuition and delusional restriction of thought. Nonetheless he was filled with fresh hope: of a new community of researchers, a continuation of his life project, with an interlocutor in the form of Cassirer, who would follow his intellectual impulses and interpret them in his own way.

Back in Hamburg, Cassirer immediately dispatched to Kreuzlingen bibliographical references and sources on the problem of ellipses. On the very evening of Cassirer's departure, meanwhile, Warburg sat down to write a letter to the "directors of Bellevue Sanatorium," inquiring "where my good doctors stand with regard to the symptom of returning scientific work as a subjective healing factor. . . . It is probably not overstating the case—perhaps Cassirer has spoken to you about this—to say that I could still outline a truly workable method of cultural-psychological historiography."[16]

Warburg now wanted only to get back to his library, and for the first time in years he felt strong enough to do so. By August, his doctors concurred.

Binswanger noted on his discharge date, August 12: "*Set off this morning for Frankfurt with the consultant, welcomed there by Dr. Embden, before traveling on to Hamburg. . . . Preparations for the journey made calmly and matter-of-factly, departure too free of agitation. On the journey to Frankfurt strikingly orderly, obliging and calm.*"[17]

Warburg had once again found support and security in the struggle against his demons. He might not have been free from a profound fear of death, but he was no longer its slave—the ideal for anyone honest in analyzing his own being-in-the-world. Reassurance of any other kind would be false and fatal. At least that was how Martin Heidegger saw things that autumn, shortly before his existence, too, was seized by a new and previously unknown demon.

WEIMAR TOPPLES

HEIDEGGER SPENT HIS FIRST AUTUMN as a professor apart from his family. Finding a place to live was extraordinarily difficult. A wave of refugees from the Ruhr, currently occupied by French troops, meant that even in Marburg any accommodation was assigned to homeless families by emergency decree. At the same time the economic crisis was worsening. The purchasing power of wages could halve in a few hours, if indeed the university accounting department possessed sufficient banknotes to pay its staff. Nonetheless, late in October 1923, Heidegger managed to send home "three times 20 billion." He immediately inquired of Elfride whether the money had actually arrived in Freiburg.

It seemed to many as if the war had only now been truly lost. People were starving in the streets. Riots and looting were rife. That autumn the Weimar Republic was on the brink of collapse. Bavaria independently

declared an emergency in September and effectively installed a dictator-
ship led by the conservative Gustav von Kahr. Other parts of the Republic,
such as the young *Bundesländer* of Thuringia and Saxony, threatened to
follow. In the larger cities, communist brigades and nationalist Freikorps
engaged in daylong street battles. It was in essence a civil war. The state
was barely capable of action and had forfeited its monopoly of power.

Chancellor Gustav Stresemann of the liberal nationalist German People's Party (DVP) declared a military emergency at the end of September
1923. Catastrophe seemed to be programmed in. The only question seemed
to be what form it would take.

In Bavaria in particular, a revolution was brewing. On November 8,
1923, things came to a head in Munich's Bürgerbräukeller when Adolf
Hitler, protected by a large shock troop of his AS militia, interrupted a
speech of von Kahr's by firing a shot into the ceiling, forcing him to flee
the hall, and—following the glorious example of Mussolini and his Fascist
movement in Italy—called on the crowd to "march on the capital" the next
day. Thousands followed Hitler's appeal. But the revolution ended only a
few kilometers away, in the center of Munich. Mobilized by von Kahr, the
regional police were under orders to fire at the marchers. Twenty lives were
lost, with Hitler managing to escape in an ambulance.

In Berlin, Stresemann still refused to admit defeat. To combat runaway
inflation, his government introduced the new "Rentenmark" only a week
later. This was a maneuver that, to much surprise, proved successful and
contributed to a distinct stabilization of the situation. The following year,
the French announced their withdrawal from the Ruhr. The Weimar Republic had gotten away with it again. There were political forces that saw
precisely that as the real catastrophe.

MIGHTY FORTRESSES

THE HEIDEGGERS' SITUATION had also stabilized at the start of 1924. Finally, an apartment was found near the home of Heidegger's professor colleague Nicolai Hartmann. The location was not ideal and their new home unfortunately lacked a yard, but by January the family was happily reunited in Marburg, whose name even reminded them of Freiburg. The mountains weren't as high, their slopes not quite as steep, the churches not as venerable, and the alleyways not as quaint, but it was familiar in its provincialism. It wasn't exactly love at first sight, but it was familiar and provincial enough for the Heideggers.

At the university itself—which in the preceding decades had been turned by Hermann Cohen, Paul Natorp, and Ernst Cassirer into the stronghold of neo-Kantianism known as the "Marburg School"—Heidegger, along with his "shock troop," were well received in their first year. The list of students that Heidegger won over with his thinking in Marburg contains some of the most famous names in German postwar philosophy and philosophical writing: Hans-Georg Gadamer, Gerhard Krüger, Karl Löwith, Walter Bröcker, Hans Jonas, and Leo Strauss.

During those first chaotic months Heidegger found support in Gadamer, who was a native Marburger, with highly regarded parents who were suitably placed to help with local difficulties, big and small. Philosophically, Heidegger found a precious kindred spirit in the Protestant theologian Rudolf Bultmann. Influenced by Kierkegaard and Jaspers, Bultmann was concerned with regaining the true existential momentum of Christianity—shorn of all myths and fake erudition, and of all institutional constraints—and also with demystifying Christianity. He wanted to strip human existence down to its naked absurdity, thereby making it receptive to the power of the Christian message of liberation.[18] That was precisely what the former church philosopher Heidegger wanted to do, too, but without the accompanying Christian promise of salvation.

BEING AN EVENT

INSIGHT INTO OUR FUNDAMENTAL GROUNDLESSNESS, as Heidegger became increasingly aware during his first months in Marburg, is made possible by the knowledge of mortality, which is always a concomitant part of existence. But we cannot find our own salvation from without, from elsewhere, as something promised or even revealed to us; we can acquire it only with an open and hence also fearful gaze into the abyss of our own finitude. For human Dasein, in the end, there is only one fact that is truly unavoidable and at the same time always certain: the approach of death, which accompanies us as a possibility at all times. The Christian faith promises to free all human beings from that imposition forever. That was what made it so thoroughly suspicious from Heidegger's point of view.

In their teaching in Marburg, both Bultmann and Heidegger were therefore concerned with forging a path for the individual toward a decision in the profound sense—as a first step to a free and authentic way of life. The similarities in their thinking were apparent to both, as were their differences. This philosophical and theological configuration had an electrifying effect on the young listeners in both faculties. Something intellectual was stirring in Marburg in 1924. It was soon the talk of the student body, not only in the intellectual circles of Marburg, but as far as Berlin and even beyond.

The intensity that Heidegger sought in his thinking, which he was also able to evoke as a teacher, was intolerant of intercessions or false promises. Here any kind of compromise would appear lazy. Intellectually lazy. Heidegger's mobilization of "anxiety" [*Angst*] and "Dasein's running ahead of itself into its own death," as he put it to his students in the summer of 1924, might also have had a compensatory element. He was thirty-five years old, married, he had two children, he was in the middle of his life and work. And yet deep down he knew very well that unlike the overwhelming majority of his generation, he had never personally experienced having his life in danger, or running ahead toward death. Still, something sparked and flashed when he entered the lecture theater wearing a specially designed pair of tight breeches and a long frock coat—half traditional costume, half suit—and quietly, almost in a whisper, gazing out of the window, without notes or any discernible preparation, began philosophizing with ever greater density and penetration. The man was the event that he wanted to be.

YOU, DEMON[19]

IT WAS NOT until the winter term of 1924–1925 that Heidegger had, for the first time, personal experience of something of which he had hitherto only inspiringly spoken and written about. Nothing like that has ever happened to me before, he admitted to himself—and not just himself—on February 27, 1925. It was as if he had been struck by the demonic. But what Heidegger was heralding here was not dread or the proximity of death as invoked in his lectures, and also not *purely* emergency. On the contrary. It was the experience of another person, it was the experience of love: "The fact of the Other's presence breaking into our life is more than our disposition can cope with. . . . Human fate gives itself to human fate, and the duty of pure love is to keep that self-giving as awake as it was on the first day."[20] He wrote to his lover:

Everything between us must be simple and clear and pure. Then alone are we worthy of being allowed to meet. That you became my pupil and I your teacher is only the cause of what befell us.

I will never be able to possess you, but you will belong in my life henceforth, and may it grow with you.[21]

The person whom Heidegger was addressing so unguardedly was the nineteen-year-old Hannah Arendt, a student of Ancient Greek, philosophy, and Protestant theology from Königsberg. Arendt, shortly after her arrival in Marburg in the autumn of 1924, was recognized also by her fellow students as a special case, an event of a kind. And not only because of her extraordinary beauty and her extravagant, colorful fashion sense. Just like Heidegger, who had brought what he called a whole shock troop of undergraduate and graduate students from Freiburg to Marburg when taking up his post in 1923, the singularly brilliant student had—as their leader and intellectual ruler—persuaded a whole circle of friends and compatriots to follow her from Berlin to Marburg. She had come to see with her own eyes what was being whispered among philosophy students all across the Republic: that someone new and brilliant had appeared in Marburg, someone who could teach you to "learn thinking anew." The prophet of Dasein, Martin Heidegger.

IN THE MIDST OF BEING

THE ESSENTIAL CHARACTERISTIC of Heideggerian "Dasein" is the fact that it is not and cannot ever be plural. "Dasein" is always only something individual, discrete, or, as he puts it, "in each case mine" (*Jemeiniges*). If it truly wishes to liberate and claim itself, it must do so entirely of its own volition. Suddenly, however, there is another Dasein, a You who—from their very first encounter, at a consultation in November 1924—had reached deep inside him with a single glance. As he in turn had reached inside that You. No wonder he was left incapacitated, unable to deal with this event. As Heidegger records in his letters to his new love, we can never know what kinds of things, what kind of damage, a loving You that has broken into the depths of our own I can do. Would it split that I from within? And thus estrange us from ourselves? Would it effect a hostile takeover? Or, more fatally, philosophically speaking, grant us unquestioning security?

Suddenly all of this seemed possible in a real sense. Because Martin loved Hannah as he had never loved anything before. The next spring he confessed as much to her in almost daily letters: Something new has appeared to me, a big You in the middle of my Self, my Being.

In practical terms, classical solutions were quickly found for this development: Heidegger planned their meetings with very great care. Primarily for Hannah's protection, of course. They communicated via a flashing light at a window or a chalk symbol on their favorite park bench. Arendt followed Heidegger to lectures he delivered at other universities, waited where necessary two streetcar stops farther on, or outside country taverns a few kilometers out of town.[22] The things one does in such situations.

It was clear to both of them from the outset that they would "never fully own each other"—at least not in the sense of a bourgeois marriage. At no point did Heidegger consider or mention the possibility of separating from Elfride. But ending his relationship with Hannah was also out of the question. The attraction was too strong, the erotic rapture too thrilling. The pull of this love brought the young student in particular to the brink of self-loss. In a long, allegorical confessional letter, which she titled "Shadow," Arendt showed Heidegger the exhilarating conflict within her. She felt on the one hand liberated from dark isolation and inauthenticity; her Dasein brought out at last, as if from a cave into the light of day. On the other hand, she expresses serious doubts about whether she can ever find her way to herself under the intoxicating influence of this very demon.

TO THINK
THE HARDEST THING

DURING THOSE SPRING DAYS Heidegger's philosophical sensibility constantly oscillated between liberation and oppression: "There are ways, help, boundaries and understanding for everything else—here alone everything means: to be in love—to be pressed into Existence," he writes to Arendt on May 13, 1925.[23] Remarkable words, especially compared with Heidegger's letters of previous years to his wife. In those he consistently portrayed philosophizing as the most difficult and deepest challenge in his life. Now it was love itself. Through his relationship with Arendt, Heidegger felt forced into a new, dialogical form of authenticity. If his philosophy was to be sustained, that had to stop.

After only a few weeks, he invented in his letters an interpretative arrangement that he also imposed on Arendt: the conflict that was experienced was now to be taken as proof of true self-discovery. The incursion of the Other was the most authentic form of liberation. The feeling of helplessness, of having-to-let-it-happen, typical of love was the demonstration of the supreme resolution. In other words: Rather than acknowledging the full, Dasein-splitting power of the incursion he had experienced, Heidegger sought by dialectical means to find a place for it in his philosophy of radical individualization. In the name of his ideal existence of heroic authenticity, he refused to acknowledge the experience of the You. That seemed to satisfy him. But not so the young philosopher Hannah Arendt, who loved him. Without warning, she left Marburg in the summer of 1926 for Heidelberg to start work on a doctorate there with Karl Jaspers. Her subject was "Love and Saint Augustine." Arendt was particularly interested in the question of what part the experience of love played for beings whose Dasein was always and ineradicably related to the existence of others. An actual reversal of Heidegger's starting point.[24]

AMOR MUNDI

ARENDT'S DISSERTATION, which she concluded in 1928 (when she was still meeting Heidegger in secret), marks the start of an intellectual journey whose autonomy and significance are not diminished by its deep connection with Heidegger's work. From now on, Arendt's philosophizing is distinguished by the ability to trace, illuminate, and elaborate all existential dimensions of the event of "You"—to which Heidegger, in the dwelling of his thought, had to remain blind if he was not to risk complete exile and homelessness. But that was exactly the role in which Arendt would see herself throughout her life: she would write to Heidegger years after the end of the war as "a girl from abroad" whose thought forced its way into the houses and dwellings of others and unlocked them from within. As his biographer Rüdiger Safranski accurately puts it: "To [Heidegger's] 'running ahead into death' she will reply with a philosophy of being born; to his solipsism of *Jemeinigkeit* (each-one-ness) she will reply with a philosophy of plurality; to his critique of *Verfallenheit* (helpless addiction) to the world of *Man* (one/they) she will reply with her *amor mundi*. To Heidegger's *Lichtung* (clearing) she will respond by philosophically ennobling the 'public.'"[25]

Unlike Heidegger, Hannah would prove to be a philosophical match for the event of their shared love. Heidegger, on the other hand, never found an essential place in his thought for the demonic incursion of the You that he invoked as an existential liberation in his letters to Hannah. This dialogical deficit—like the existentialism that goes with it—limits and heavily burdens his philosophy.

As a lover, Heidegger never got beyond Arendt. But for Arendt—incidentally, just as he had hoped in his early letters—he became a point of departure for her own journey from 1925 onward.

HUNGER CURES

IN THE AUTUMN OF 1923, the postdoctoral student Walter Benjamin also declared himself prepared for the most extreme outcome: "At any rate I am resolved to prepare a manuscript, that is, I would rather be dismissed with insults and shame than withdraw into myself," he wrote at the end of September in a letter to the theologian, politician, and writer Florens Christian Rang.[26] Now, after more than two years of nomadism, Benjamin had both a solid subject and a faculty that could at least imagine accepting a work from his own hands. Stoically sponsored by a great-uncle, the mathematics professor Arthur Moritz Schoenflies, and the family friend and sociologist Gottfried Salomon, he had spent the whole spring of 1923 in

Frankfurt, with a view to joining the university there. Admittedly, his hope of submitting his essay on Goethe's *Elective Affinities* as a postdoctoral thesis had proved to be a vain one, but his efforts had won over the historian of German literature Franz Schultz as an advocate and supervisor. Schultz suggested a treatise on the "form of the Baroque tragic drama," focusing on the so-called Silesian School in particular. It was for Benjamin anything but a desirable subject, since he had little knowledge of the period—the late seventeenth century—or of the plays and playwrights in question. So rather than plowing on with any conventional approach, he turned the topic into a completely new subject area with extensive initial readings.

But what alternative did he have? As far as aesthetics at Frankfurt was concerned, the possibility of collaborating with Professor Hans Cornelius was out of the question. Even the advocacy of an extremely gifted doctoral student with whom Benjamin had become friends during his months in Frankfurt, a young man by the name of Theodor Wiesengrund Adorno, failed to change this. Consequently, Professor Schultz, with whom Benjamin was not well acquainted, and whom he did not hold in especially high esteem, was his only hope. "I am now in the middle of the work that you have particularly encouraged about the form of the tragic drama," Benjamin reported to his new patron from Berlin—a city wracked, in October 1923, by battles over barricades, by blackouts and riots over food shortages. In the late autumn his finances were worse than ever. Dora, who had found a job that brought in hard currency, working as a secretary in the foreign department of the American Hearst media group, lost her post only a few weeks after finding it. The loathed house on Delbrückstrasse, where Benjamin's father was close to death after the amputation of his right leg, once again became the family's final refuge. From there Benjamin wrote to his friend Rang: "Anyone who does serious intellectual work in Germany is threatened with grievous hunger. . . . Certainly there are many different ways of going hungry. But none of them is worse than doing it in the midst of a starving people. Everything here consumes, nothing now feeds. My task, even if it were here, could not be fulfilled here. This is the perspective from which I view the problem of emigration. I pray to God that it may be resolvable."[27]

The Benjamins no longer saw a future for themselves in Germany. But the United States, the destination of Dora's dreams, was out of the question for Benjamin. He barely spoke a word of English. Palestine, to which Gershom Scholem immigrated with his wife in the autumn of 1923 to take up a post as a librarian, was not an option, either, since Benjamin once again lacked the language. Learning Hebrew would take several months, if not years, of intense study. He didn't have the time or energy to bring his thesis to its successful conclusion. Because here, too, he was under enormous pressure. Gottfried Salomon was unequivocal in recommending its swift delivery, ideally within the next twelve months, the window of opportunity for Schultz, as dean at Frankfurt, to make appointments. Rumors were circulating, particularly that autumn, that the whole university—still a young institution, founded after the war—would be forced either to close down or to merge with Marburg on economic grounds.

In spite of all the insecurities and rejections, Benjamin continued to see the writing of a postdoctoral thesis as the sole productive route for him, if only because of the hope that it would enable him at least "to take out a private loan." Like a snared fox, which was how he saw himself at the end of 1923, Benjamin opted to chew off one of his own legs and hobble as far away as possible. Meaning: In less than four months he finished his source work on the Baroque tragic drama, took out a good six hundred quotable passages, and arranged them in the form of a catalog. With this foundation, which was "remarkably—yes, incredibly—narrow" and "included only the knowledge of a very few dramas, by no means all the ones in question," he drew up a plan.[28] He would write at great speed in monastic solitude somewhere in a "free setting," ideally in a southern and hence affordable foreign country, far from the family feuds he detested, far from Germany, which he found vexatious, far from all the everyday distractions and seductions of the city. Nothing so clearly conveys the level of Benjamin's determination as his willingness to sell parts of his library in order to put the plan into effect.

GOODBYE DEUTSCHLAND

WITH ENCOURAGEMENT from the Gutkinds and the Rangs, similarly enthusiastic travelers, he chose the Italian island of Capri. Wandering as a flâneur through Berlin on April 1—and this may only have been a joke, albeit one that was diabolically close to reality—Benjamin read a headline at a newspaper kiosk, about a threatened ban on emigration, proposed to prevent the flight of capital abroad. He decided to travel right away. On April 9, 1924, Benjamin and his six hundred quotations arrived in Capri.

Intoxicated as he was by the beauty of the Mediterranean spring and the glories of the island's landscape, concentrated work was naturally at first unthinkable. Particularly since the Gutkinds and the Rangs, married couples both, had arrived in Capri as well. They all lived together on the same floor of a summer villa that had one of the highest balconies on the island. These were for Benjamin "some of the most beautiful and strangest days" of his life. After only three weeks, though, when the Rangs were due to go home and the Gutkinds planned to travel northward, Benjamin, still without having committed a single line to paper, was dragged back to face reality. There was no money. All that could help now was a letter to his publisher in Heidelberg, Weissbach:

Dear Herr Weissbach,

... Unforeseen circumstances have cost me part of my travel budget, so I am sitting here in an urgent predicament. Please do not think ill of my question as to whether you might be so kind as to send me the equivalent of 60 Marks—in hard currency, whether as an advance or as a loan (repayable on 1 July 1924)—to my poste restante here.[29]

It is hard to guess what these "unforeseen circumstances" might have been (if they even existed). But it is easy to imagine that on his first excursion to Naples across the bay, his "money and papers vanished in the wink of an eye."[30] Be that as it may. A miracle occurred. Weissbach actually transferred the money, and Benjamin immersed himself more and more deeply in the enchantments of the island. His days were marked by hikes and outings, more and more frequently to Naples, which exerted a special, morbid fascination on him. In May the university there celebrated its seven hundredth anniversary. To coincide with this, a large international philosophical conference was held, and this, too, attracted Benjamin. But the course of the conference led him to conclude "that philosophers are the worst paid because they are the most superfluous lackeys of the international bourgeoisie, but the fact that they should demonstrate their own subaltern status with such dignified shabbiness is something that I have never seen before."[31]

Benjamin could barely endure a day with his own people.

GRAPES AND ALMONDS

CONVERSATION ON HIS FANTASY ISLAND was, however, distinctly more exciting. Rather than for the international bourgeoisie, as they had now come to describe themselves, Capri had by the turn of the century become an aspirational site and a health resort for the left-wing intelligentsia. The Russian writer Maxim Gorky, a literary icon of the Revolution, had even founded his own (albeit short-lived) academy there. The low cost of living and the newly stabilized Rentenmark meant that for the summer of 1924, Capri was a major meeting point for German thinkers and artists. Benjamin was by no means the only financially precarious thinker hoping to find a better quality of life and space for intellectual contemplation in the eternal spring of Capri. The locus of this scene was Zum Kater Hiddigeigei, the Tomcat Hiddigeigei café, run by a German couple. After his friends left, Benjamin went there increasingly often for his first coffee of the day. He would then collect his thoughts as he watched the busy activity of the piazza, or, while reading the newspaper, congratulate himself on witnessing the imminent decline of the West from a distance, in the delectable warmth of this glittering paradise that May.

But even here not everything was rosy. He was under intellectual and psychological pressure, mostly because he still hadn't begun writing his thesis. Under stress as he was, as ever, Benjamin's illness resurfaced, a particular problem in a small Italian island village. That month he searched frantically for affordable lodging, and to avoid the oppressive heat of the day put off working until the evenings. But unfortunately "the birdlife also stirs at night." And then there was that young lady whom he watched for several weeks from his seat in the café, as she shopped with her little daughter or sunned herself while her daughter danced around the fountain in the piazza, ice cream in hand. She wasn't German, that much was certain. Her high cheekbones and rounded though narrow face suggested another origin. Her wide eyes, moreover, became tiny slits whenever she laughed, giving her face an almost Asian appearance. Benjamin was enchanted, and probably toward the end of May, when he saw the beautiful stranger trying to buy a bag of almonds from a street vendor but unable to make herself understood in Italian, he seized his moment:

"Excuse me, madam, can I help you?"

"Please do."

The man before her had thick, dark hair and wore glasses that "flashed like little headlights,"[32] a thin nose, and hands that had never done a stroke of real work. She knew the type: "a classic bourgeois intellectual, presumably one of the affluent kind." His financial status aside, it was a highly accurate appraisal, and one that was swiftly vindicated. Benjamin clumsily dropped the bags that he had helpfully offered to carry, leaving her groceries rolling around the piazza. "Let me introduce myself: Dr. Walter Benjamin."

Benjamin walked mother and daughter home and invited himself over for spaghetti and red wine the following evening. At the start of June, he wrote to Scholem in faraway Palestine, his evening labors had been postponed a little further into the night: "Over time, particularly since Gutkind's departure, in Scheffel's Café Hiddigeigei (about which there is nothing unpleasant apart from the name), I have been meeting one person after another. . . . The most remarkable is a Latvian Bolshevik woman from Riga, an actress and director, a Christian. . . . Today is the third day that I've been writing this letter. I talked with the Bolshevik until half past twelve and then worked until half past four. Now I am sitting in the morning beneath an overcast sky with the sea wind on my balcony, one of the highest in the whole of Capri."[33]

On occasional evenings things may have run still later. Talking isn't everything, after all. And Benjamin fell in love—more deeply in love than ever before—in love with Asja Lacis, whom he now praised in his letters to Scholem as a "Russian revolutionary from Riga" or an "outstanding communist who has been working for the party since the Duma Revolution," but mostly as "one of the most brilliant women I have ever met."

Lacis, then thirty-two and a year older than Benjamin, had, like him, traveled to Capri from Berlin. She had come with her then partner, the German theater director Bernhard Reich, principally to cure her three-year-old daughter, Daga, of a respiratory infection. Reich returned to Germany in May, and Asja and Daga remained on the island to complete the cure. Before going to Berlin, Lacis had been part of the Russian avant-garde scene, as both an actress and a director, and in the early 1920s had founded her own youth theater in the city of Orel in central Russia.

For Benjamin, a German abroad, this relationship opened new horizons of experience, both intellectual and erotic. He described to his friend Scholem, during those magical summer days, the island's vineyards, nocturnal miracles: "You must have encountered that, when fruits and leaves are submerged in the blackness of night, and one reaches carefully—so as not to be heard and chased away—for the big clusters of grapes." And he added, so that his actual message might be understood: "But there is much more besides, which might be explained by commentaries on the Song of Solomon."[34]

Lacis would later jokingly recall those days to Benjamin as a time in which he was able to "lie on top of me twenty-four hours a day."[35]

NEW BEGINNINGS

THE EFFECTS OF THIS AFFAIR on Benjamin's entire relationship with the world should not be underestimated. He spoke often of having been effectively transformed by it. Since early adulthood he had been a regular visitor to brothels—inaugurated during a trip to Paris. His marriage to Dora had been platonic for years. His crush on Jula Cohn remained unrequited and unfulfilled. So it is no exaggeration to say that his relationship with Lacis—a woman whom he found extremely attractive physically, and impressive intellectually—was for Benjamin an erotic awakening, practically an initiation into sexual experience, a love completely fulfilled. His conversations with this avowed communist and activist were like an initiation into new intellectual realms and perspectives: Lacis's relationship with theory and practice, art and politics, commitment and critique was almost precisely the opposite of Benjamin's. The Russian activist was for her part entirely unable to understand how, in a Europe brimming with revolutionary activity, anyone could focus his attentions on seventeenth-century German Baroque theater, of all things. For her it was a textbook example of that very bourgeois escapism of which Benjamin had accused his own fraternity at the Naples conference. With Lacis, communism entered Benjamin's thought as a theoretical alternative with practical relevance. He would spend the rest of his life battling to achieve intellectual domination over that incursion. In vain, incidentally.

Soon the two were regularly seen strolling together, child in tow, along the paths and trails of the island, chatting and joking. Signs of mutual affection wouldn't have been difficult to spot. They also made increasingly frequent outings to that city on the other side of the bay that exerted an almost hypnotic effect on both of them: Naples. But where Lacis recognized revolutionary potential in the emotional excess of everyday life there, Benjamin saw primal and unspoiled symbolic forces at work. Where Lacis glimpsed a multistage avant-garde event in the witty role-play in the piazza, Benjamin found the allegorical mystery play of the Baroque being freely acted out. Where Lacis analyzed materiality and improvisational art,

Benjamin was drawn to eternal configurations of ideas embodied in the moment. They were each all too keen, as new lovers so often are, to see the world with the other's eyes, to absorb the perspective of the other into the center of their own selves.

Our best account of this summer is a portrait of the city, *Naples*, which was jointly written by the pair.[36] It is a unique document of what happens when a view of the world shaped by communism and avant-garde theories blends and merges with the timeless configurations of esoteric idealism. So much that it seems consistent only for *porosity*[37]—seen as a kind of productive fragility that overcomes rigid dualisms—to be the key concept by which the nature of the city is revealed and interpreted in all its profundity. Porosity is the principle of the true life of Naples:

> At the base of the cliff itself, where it touches the shore, caves have been hewn. As in the paintings of hermits from the Trecento, a door appears here and there in the cliffs. If it is open, one looks into large cellars that are at once sleeping places and storerooms. Steps also lead to the sea, to fishermen's taverns that have been installed in natural grottoes. Faint light and thin music rise up from there in the evening.
>
> As porous as those stones is the architecture. Buildings and action merge in courtyards, arcades, and staircases. The space is preserved to act as a stage for new and unforeseen configurations. What is avoided is the definitive, the fully formed. No situation appears as it is, intended forever, no form asserts its "thus and not otherwise." . . . Because nothing is finished and concluded. Porosity results not only from the indolence of the southern craftsman but above all from the passion for improvisation. For that space and opportunity must be preserved at all costs. Buildings are used as a popular stage. They are divided into innumerable theaters, animated simultaneously. All share innumerable stages, brought to life simultaneously. Balcony, forecourt, window, gateway,

staircase, roof are at once stage and theater box. Even the most miserable wretch is sovereign in his dim, twofold awareness of contributing, however deprived he may be, to one of the images of the Neapolitan street that will never return and, in his poverty, the leisure of enjoying the grand panorama. What is played out on the stairs is the highest school in theatrical direction. The stairs, never entirely revealed, but closed off in the dull northern house-box, protrude in places from the houses, make an angular turn, and disappear before reemerging.[38]

There can be no doubt, the language is Benjamin's. But the vision guiding it comes from Lacis.[39] Pure pleasure in existence, eternal excess, and a delight in transformation had hitherto been entirely absent from Benjamin's writing. In the dialectic of this new vision, indissoluble opposites continuously interpolate each other: good and evil, outside and in, work and play, death and life, theory and practice. Rather than advancing toward the authentic by stripping away layer after layer, here the layers are laid atop one another, and wholly new aspects and qualities are drawn from the materials employed. In this new figuration, the tendency to liquefaction and evaporation, which, according to Marx, characterizes capitalism and must in the end lead to the destruction and leveling of all traditional relations, undergoes a clearly utopian reinterpretation: Naples becomes the symbol of another modernity, one that is worth living and always revolutionary. And as if in a secret dialogue whose true meaning is known only to the two lovebirds, every paragraph in this cityscape was soon interpolated with the favorite concepts of the other. That is how two strangers, now happily together, write abroad.

In the summer of 1924, after this breakthrough, Benjamin found a new way of writing, a new vision, that would carry him henceforth. In contrast to the love of Heidegger and Arendt, Benjamin was in his love porous and plastic enough to experience the shocking incursion of the beloved into his own self as a fundamental renewal, not least philosophically.

This opening of a new way of thinking came at a time when Benjamin's primary concern must have been to apply his usual approaches, as clearly and methodically as possible, to a collection of themes only partially accessible to him. The result, of course, was further stress and greater time-pressure. By late September, when Lacis traveled with her daughter from Capri back to Berlin and to her companion Bernhard Reich, barely a third of Benjamin's work was completed, and he was also seriously behind on the translation of a novel by Proust that he had been commissioned to do. If we believe his letters to his publisher, whom he continued to ask, although now without success, for financial support, this delay was primarily the result of an unfortunate case of blood poisoning (contracted through either insect bites or bad food—Benjamin was vague in his explanations). Still, in August and September he was cheerful enough to visit the ancient Greek temples at Paestum, and to give the Marxist philosopher Ernst Bloch, who had recently arrived in Capri, guided tours of the island. Late in the evening he would return to the desk in his new home, chosen to conserve money: a former storage room with whitewashed walls, the size of a monk's cell, but still with a "view of the most beautiful garden in Capri."

A cool autumn breeze now blew in through the windows. It was time to go back, time to leave the dream. On October 10, Benjamin departed Capri. After some time in Rome and Florence he returned to Berlin in mid-November. Back to Dora—and now to Asja, too. But above all to the German tragic drama, as yet unmastered, which stood between him and any prospect of a better future.

VI.

FREEDOM

1925–1927

Benjamin mourns, Heidegger begets,
Cassirer becomes a star, and Wittgenstein a child.

RED STARS

WHAT THE NEAPOLITANS STROLLING across the piazza must have made of the four Germans sitting at one of those street cafés that Benjamin had been so enthusiastic about the year before is hard to say. Even if these seemingly respectable members of the bourgeoisie, clothed in their summer suits, had been yelling at one another in Italian rather than German, the locals would hardly have understood a word. However authentically Neapolitan the style of debate may have appeared, the topics of discussion were specifically German. Concepts such as "alienation" and "objectification" played a central role, along with "inwardness" and "cognition of essences." "Origin," "revelation," and "delusion" were tossed around. And inevitably, "class consciousness."[1]

Theodor Wiesengrund Adorno, one of the debaters, in a letter to his teacher the composer Alban Berg, recalled "a philosophical battle, in which we were able to conquer the field, but at the same time found it necessary to regroup our forces."[2] By "we" he meant himself—a twenty-two-year-old postgraduate student in the Frankfurt University Philosophy Department—and his friend and companion Siegfried Kracauer, fourteen years his elder and editor of the *Frankfurter Zeitung* arts and opinion supplement. While their relationship, always difficult, might by now have become porous, given the power of the enemy at the café table, it was still important to show solidarity. The enemy in question was none other than Walter Benjamin, Neapolitan in spirit, and his acquaintance of many years, Alfred Sohn-Rethel, who had left Germany several years earlier for the village of Sorrento on the Amalfi Coast, to devote himself to the study of Marx's *Das Kapital.* So the Red faction clearly had the home advantage and also— a view of the piazza was enough—a practical vision on their side.

Since Kracauer had a stammer and was thus not entirely fit for combat, the burden of the defense of an avant-garde attitude intended to align, albeit not straightforwardly, with a Kierkegaardian ideal of "inwardness" and "individuality"[3] fell entirely to the star student, who had successfully completed a doctorate in Frankfurt under Professor Hans Cornelius, titled *The Transcendence of the Objective and the Noematic in Husserl's Phenomenology.* Young Wiesengrund—as Adorno was teasingly known—might have had many shortcomings, but he wasn't slow with a smart retort. And during his years of study in Frankfurt he hadn't exactly been distinguished by an excess of theoretical modesty.

The members of the group knew one another from the previous spring in Frankfurt, where similar coffeehouse discussions had formed the germ— indeed, to be more precise, the core—of these extremely bourgeois intellectual lives. Now here they were: gifted thinkers on a school trip.

Benjamin's debating tactics in Naples would be remembered as particularly unyielding, lacking even a trace of desire for consensus. Small wonder, since his postdoctoral thesis *The Origin of German Tragic Drama,* which he had submitted only two and a half months before, had in July 1925 been rejected, largely on the basis of an appraisal by Cornelius, Adorno's supervisor. To spare Benjamin the shame of a documented failure, the faculty had advised him in a letter of early August to withdraw his candidacy, which after several days' struggle he did. Classic Benjamin, then. Once again.

CRITICAL PROLOGUES

HOW HAD IT COME TO THIS? After all, he had written to Scholem in Jerusalem, a month before submitting the first parts of the work: "Things are not unfavorable: Schultz is dean; and in other respects as well, some things are in good shape, practically." That was in fact the case, at least until his thesis was submitted. Benjamin was still tinkering with it in February and March, so it had been trickling in to Professor Schultz through the spring. It was not until May 1925 that the whole thing had been delivered. By this point the literary historian Schultz had already made his judgment after a first, presumably slightly cursory glance at the "Epistemo-Critical Prologue."[4] As the adviser who had chosen the subject of the thesis, he declared its content inadequate, and passed the case on to his colleague Hans Cornelius, professor of philosophy and aesthetics. Now, rather than being submitted as a work of literary history, it would be a postdoctoral thesis in aesthetics. But Cornelius, too, despaired of the text. Benjamin's "Prologue" so stubbornly resisted Cornelius's attempts to understand it that he was unable to reach a reasonable assessment of the work's contents. The same applied to the assistants Dr. Max Horkheimer and Dr. Adhémar Gelb, who were brought in as special advisers. In the words of Cornelius's appraisal, passed to the faculty for their information: "For all my benevolence toward the author, whom I otherwise know as being both profound and wise, I cannot conceal my impression that, in his unintelligible manner of expressing himself, which must be interpreted as a sign of a lack of clarity, he cannot be a leader to students in this field."[5]

Where the "Prologue" was concerned, this was an absolutely understandable judgment. Quite apart from anyone else, Benjamin had reached it himself when he described it to Scholem as the "brittlest part of the whole." In fact, the degree of clumsiness and the lack of strategic think-ing with which Benjamin had constructed his work aroused the suspicion that he was being deliberately obstructive. At any rate, given its extreme complexity and the esoteric nature, which far exceeds that of the preface to his translation of Baudelaire, it is difficult to avoid the feeling that its au-thor, for fear of experiencing rejection, preferred instead to take his fate into his own hands by providing himself with impeccable grounds for its dismissal. At the same time it is worth considering seriously whether it would have been still more devastating for the author's academic prospects if the prologue's meaning had been even partially revealed to its appraisers. Benjamin described this part of the work to Scholem as "unmitigated chutzpah—that is to say, neither more nor less than the prolegomena to epistemology, a kind of second stage of my early work on language (I do not know whether it is any better), with which you are familiar, dressed up as a theory of ideas."[6]

A CASE FOR ADAM

WHEN HE SAYS "early work on language," Benjamin is referring to his essay written in 1916 and published only posthumously, "About Language in General and Human Language in Particular."[7] It is an analysis, run through with motifs from Jewish theology, of the age of modern philosophy and particularly the philosophy of language, an age of decay, which holds it to be removed from the truth. As a consequence, a shroud of mourning has settled over the whole of nature and also over humanity. These are also ideas, then, that absolutely inform the "Epistemo-Critical Prologue" to Benjamin's thesis on tragic drama.

The term "epistemo-critique" [*Erkenntniskritik*] that gives the prologue its title refers to an understanding—still prevalent in 1925—of modern philosophy as epistemology. It was a view entirely in the spirit of Kant's first and supposedly central fundamental question: "What can I know?" Instead of trying to answer this question directly, Kant—and this was the epoch-making brilliance of his approach—first examined the conditions and boundaries of the human capacity for knowledge in the context of his *Critique of Pure Reason* (1781).

Benjamin's "Epistemo-Critical Prologue," however, isn't yet another critique of epistemology *within* this discipline, but rather a frontal poetic and analytical attack on the widely held belief that the task of philosophy in the future must lie first and foremost in a Kantian form of epistemology. In other words, what Benjamin is criticizing is the narrowing of modern philosophy to epistemology itself. For him this constriction was completely misguided and had a devastating effect on culture as a whole.

Benjamin's thesis is concerned primarily not with an analysis of the "form of baroque tragic drama" and its supposed origin, but with a fundamental critique, wrapped up in the form of academic literary analysis, of the tragedy that modern life had in his eyes become. It was therefore only consistent that its prologue should be concerned not with revealing the true *conditions of the possibility of knowledge*, but on the contrary with distilling the *conditions of the impossibility of true knowledge* that originated in the modern age.

In Baroque tragic drama, these negatory conditions are now—and herein lies the key to Benjamin's analysis—given artistic representation in a curiously concentrated form. They *show* themselves with exemplary clarity in Baroque tragic dramas and are paradigmatically embodied in them. In 1919, Benjamin had already recognized the true function of criticism as the revelation of truths that had for centuries remained hidden in works of art.

Once the intention of the work has been fully disclosed, only three questions remain, mirroring the structure of Benjamin's thesis. They are: Why is the reduction of modern philosophy to epistemology so devastating; what are its core mistakes? ("Epistemo-Critical Prologue.") What form of grief is produced by the understanding of the world contained within it? (Part I: "Trauerspiel and Tragedy.") And to what extent does allegory, as a linguistic medium and artistic form, assume a particular epistemological function within the analysis of this dejection? (Part II: "Allegory and Trauerspiel.")

Like an artist's sketches, the prologue provides the textual foundation for analyses that far exceed it. It ranks as one of the darkest, but also richest, works of the German language. If we treat it analytically and, in accordance with the author's instructions, concentrate on the role of language as a condition of knowledge per se, we can see it arrange itself into a concentration of all the core philosophical convictions that shaped and guided Benjamin's intellectual journey from 1916 onward. The prologue is in this light a profound, sphinxian riddle for readers to solve individually, if they wish to move freely within the space of their thought. So it may be worth the trouble.

GRIEF WORK

FOR BENJAMIN, the original sin of the philosophy of language in the modern era lies first of all in the acceptance of the fundamentally arbitrary nature of linguistic signs. For example, that the word "table" stands not in an essential but rather in a completely gratuitous relationship to the object it denotes. Against this fundamental tenet of modern thought, rarely questioned, Benjamin musters an Adamic or even paradisiacal conception of language. In the original language, the one that creates meaning, what

Benjamin calls "pure language," the signs/names of things had a relation-ship with the signified that was anything but gratuitous, and instead nec-essary and essence-defining:

> Adam's action of naming things is so far removed from play or caprice
> that it actually confirms the state of paradise as a state in which there
> is as yet no need to struggle with the communicative significance of
> words.[8]

Consequently, the second fundamental false assumption of the philos-ophy of language lies in seeing the purpose of language—its essence, in fact—as communication. For Benjamin, language is expressly not a *means* for conveying valuable information to others but a *medium* in which we become aware of ourselves and all the things that surround us—recognizing both by naming them. We don't express ourselves through language, but language expresses itself through us:

> It is fundamental that this spiritual essence communicates itself *in* and
> not *through* language. Hence languages have no speaker, if this is taken
> to mean someone who communicates *through* language. Spiritual es-
> sence communicates itself in, not through, a language.[9]

What Benjamin still described, in 1916, as "spiritual essence," he called in the prologue to his thesis "idea," in keeping with his desire to "dress everything up as a theory of ideas." His argument was that language facil-itates not mundane communication but the revelation of being. This sense of a revelation, not communication, happening in language harmonizes perfectly with Wittgenstein's *Tractatus* and the thought of Heidegger, slowly developed in the years around 1925, concerning the essence of language.

But revelation is not something that individuals with a thirst for knowledge can somehow instigate themselves. Instead, awareness of it calls for a certain—in a sense passive—attitude of listening toward being. An attitude that runs precisely counter to the activity of modern scientific investigation into nature (for example, scientific experiment), and the assembling of knowledge by the modern thinking subject.

Benjamin rejected the idea of a sudden redemptive or illuminating event that was plainly not of this world and could not be actively brought about in the world. In its place, in the age of modernity, he posited a philosophy of history grounded in gradual progress, including social progress toward truth, freedom, and justice.

Against this image of continuous human progress, which inspired the whole Enlightenment, not least the philosophy of Kant, Benjamin places the logic of disruptive intervention, later called "Chok" (shock). The quintessential Chok events, which both bring down extant entire images of the world and create new ones, are "origins" (*Ur-Sprünge*, literally "primal leaps"), as described in *The Origin of German Tragic Drama*:

> The term origin [*Ursprung*] is not intended to describe the process by which the existent came into being, but rather to describe that which emerges from the process of becoming and disappearance. Origin is an eddy in the stream of becoming, and in its current it swallows the material involved in the process of genesis [*Enstehung*].[10]

For Benjamin, origins are not events *in* historical time but beginnings of new calculations of historical time and also relationships with the world.[11] The origin of modern philosophy—and all the previous configurations of knowledge that it drags down into its maelstrom in order to be able to assert itself—is the actual object of Benjamin's whole developing thought.

REMEMBERED PERCEPTION

WE CAN ALREADY DISCERN here how far removed Benjamin's text is in approach and character from the requisite tasks—or presumptions—of academic writing. No wonder that its appraisers were shocked and infuriated. They had, quite rightly, commissioned and, quite rightly, expected a work of scholarly balance and qualification. What they got instead was a philosophical confession. A confession not about the author's own intellectual poverty but about that of the whole of the philosophy of his era. Benjamin's "Epistemo-Critical Prologue" itself sought to be an event—an exhilarating leap into new thought that opened up and overcame modern philosophy. Unmitigated chutzpah, indeed.

Particularly so in light of the seemingly reactionary alternative origin to the age of modern philosophy Benjamin proposes. Ultimately, for him, only God—an event as divine as the phenomenon of speech itself—can supply true salvation. Just as language—as the foundation of all meaningful access to the world—cannot in Benjamin's view be of human origin, the healing shock of the perception of truth (in "pure language") cannot be, either. Like Wittgenstein, Benjamin insists time and again that the miracle of language cannot be explained *in* language. At most, its essence can be *shown* through particular linguistic modes of representation.

The endeavor to give language to what he calls "original perception" via the observation of his own concrete period of time is what Benjamin calls philosophy. And in the form of remembering:

> It is the task of the philosopher to restore, by representation, the primacy of the symbolic character of the word, in which the idea is given self-consciousness, and that is the opposite of all outwardly directed communication. Since philosophy may not presume to speak in the

tones of revelation, this can only be achieved by recalling in memory the primordial form of perception.[12]

This remembering, which consists of immersion in thought-pictures created especially for this purpose, is in perceptive terms rather passive—unlike cognition. In this context, which—as he himself stresses—grants insight only into an impossibility, Benjamin speaks of a "fruitful skepticism." This gives rise to a heightening, based on contemplative repetition, of one's own perception that opens it to all phenomena in their empirical richness. It is a process entirely comparable to contemplating a Buddhist mandala, into whose allegorically charged pattern one must plunge, erasing all illusory images. In Benjamin's words:

> This can be likened to a pause for breath, after which thought can be totally and unhurriedly concentrated even on the very minutest object without the slightest inhibition. For the very minutest things will be discussed wherever the work of art and its form are considered with a view to judging their content. To snatch hastily, as if stealing the property of others, is the style of the *routineer*, and is no better than the heartiness of the philistine. In the act of true contemplation, on the other hand, the abandoning of deductive methods is combined with an ever wider-ranging, an ever more intense reappraisal of phenomena, which are, however, never in danger of remaining the objects of vague wonder, as long as the representation of them is also a representation of ideas, for it is here that their individuality is preserved.[13]

To understand Benjamin's diagnosis of decline we have to understand the kind of judgment to which such a prelapsarian "return to phenomena," to "the things themselves," will never lead: a value judgment in the moral sense.

The arrogance of modern "subjects capable of judgment" in appointing themselves arbiters of good and evil in the face of creation (thus propagating the idea that ethics are founded on phenomena—or indeed the phenomenon of language itself[14]), signifies for Benjamin modernity's actually fatal and universally distorting fall from grace. In keeping with the theme of his thesis, he equates this fall with another finding in the German Baroque tragic drama as an exemplary stage in the decline of a genre:

> The enormous, anti-artistic subjectivity of the Baroque converges here with the theological essence of the subjective. The Bible introduces Evil in the concept of knowledge. The serpent's promise to the first men was to make them "knowing both good and evil." But it is said of God after the creation: "And God saw everything that he had made, and, behold it was very good." Knowledge of evil therefore has no object. There is no evil in the world. . . . Knowledge of good and evil is, then, the opposite of all factual knowledge. Related as it is to the depths of the subjective, it is basically only knowledge of evil. It is "nonsense" [*Geschwätz*, also often translated as "prattle"—translator's note] in the profound sense in which Kierkegaard conceived the word. This knowledge, the triumph of subjectivity and the onset of an arbitrary rule over things, is the origin of all allegorical contemplation. . . . For good and evil are unnameable, they are nameless entities, outside the language of names, in which human beings, in paradise, named things, and which they forsake in the abyss of that problem.[15]

The triumph of subjectivity and, born out of the spirit of immanence, an arbitrary dominion over things—not least over nature, which from this perspective becomes a thing itself—is what in the end also leads to the reification of humanity. This is precisely the basis of the real tragedy of modernity, whose gloomy origin Benjamin's work explores. The knowledge of good and evil has "no object," it is "not *in* the world." To speak with Benjamin's curious ontology of names: it is "outside the language of names."

But whereof we cannot speak, thereof we must remain silent. And that is precisely what modern subjects, in their will to empower themselves, do not do. Instead they "prattle on," in the process becoming ever more desensitized to perception with the effect, albeit only dimly, of grief.

These diagnoses of the state of culture and of philosophy as a discipline were, as we have seen, shared by Wittgenstein and Heidegger. Just as they also shared the conviction that ethics do not exist in philosophy, and any attempt to explain such a thing from the spirit of immanence is nothing but the clearest symptom of the degree to which human beings, as naming agents, have already entangled themselves in prattle. None of these thinkers ever wrote about ethics in the conventional sense, or even tried to do so. Not even Cassirer. They had their reasons.

TRISTES TROPIQUES

FOR BENJAMIN, the specific grief that, with the origin of modernity, increasingly overshadows and mutes the whole of being-in-the-world affects not only those human beings who see themselves as judging subjects. It affects also the supposedly mute objects of so-called nature, which humans believe they can dispose of as freely and capriciously as they do the arbitrary signs with which they name the objects. But for Benjamin nature is not fundamentally mute. Rather, in the age "after the fall" it has been increasingly silenced. But it has been silenced only for us.

In the "true language" nature speaks to us as we speak to it. Neither side gives meaning to the other; instead meaning produces itself.

The distorted conditions of knowledge in the modern age produce between the two poles of this reciprocal listening (nature and human) a mutually accentuated loss of resonance. The total loss of meaning and language that results ("Nothing speaks to me anymore") is something Benjamin calls, appropriately, grief:

> Yet the sadness of nature makes her mute. In all mourning there is the deepest inclination to speechlessness, which is infinitely more than the inability or disinclination to communicate. . . . In the language of men, however, [the things of nature] are overnamed. . . . [Overnaming is] the deepest linguistic reason for all melancholy and (from the point of view of the thing) for all deliberate muteness.[16]

The age of the Baroque sought compensation for this muteness, born of the modern spirit of "overnaming," through art.[17] And it did so in the most helpless and formally overwrought way imaginable in the German *Trauerspiel* (literally "mourning play"), by making *everything* on stage speak; by making everything, however remote and insignificant, the object of a dramatic communication to the audience. It is like a blind fury provoked by the original loss of meaning and the vertiginous fall that results from it. This tragedy repeats itself from the beginning of the 1910s in the linguistic excesses of Expressionism, which Benjamin expressly compares with those of the Baroque.

Against this background we can begin to see the significance of allegory as the characteristic means of artistic representation of the Baroque. First of all, an allegory (a woman holding a set of scales as a depiction of justice, or more recently, *One Hundred Years of Solitude*, as an allegory of the fate of colonial Colombia, for instance), rather than saying something directly, symbolizes it indirectly. As the preferred means of representation of the Baroque tragic drama, however, allegory achieves one thing above all in Benjamin's eyes: it is the clear and naked representation of extreme despair, and hence ideally suited to displaying the consistency of the world *after* the fall. In a world that obeys the laws of complete (semiotic) randomness, allegory as a "diabolical means of knowledge" is the artistic means of knowledge par excellence. In Benjamin's words:

> The intention which underlies allegory is so opposed to that which is concerned with the discovery of truth that it reveals more clearly than anything else the identity of the pure curiosity which is aimed at mere knowledge with the proud isolation of man.[18]

Insofar as the task of philosophy consists of a "remembering that is first and foremost a return to primordial perception," after the modern "fall" it can consist of nothing but the revelation of the impossibility of true knowledge. And what means of knowledge could display this better than one that depicts with elaborate grandeur the complete randomness and disparity that defines its age.

It is an epistemological method so completely at odds with the pursuit of truth underlying all investigation that it quite clearly reveals the abyss of the loss, *showing* it in the manner of a photographic negative.

After the fall into the modern age there is no longer a direct way of expressing the truth. Language is far too entangled and empty to do so. But within that entanglement there are ways of making the primordial level of perception visible and memorable.

Allegory, through the "thought-picture," would define the writing and knowledge of Benjamin's work in the years 1924 and 1925, guiding it toward a new formal peak.

CRITICAL ALBUM

TO UNDERSTAND the entire philosophical project, in its completely systematic conception and execution, it is crucial to stress that Benjamin's concern with the allegorical method of depiction is about a medium of anti-knowledge. Other means, given the overall linguistic state of things, are not available (and perhaps never will be again). Just as Wittgenstein must climb his ladder of propositions, which are, as he acknowledges, meaningless and as far from the truth as can be imagined, in order to "see the world correctly," Benjamin uses allegory and allegorical reading as a tool in a truth-oriented critique of the state of his age, the age of modernity. Even Benjamin cannot express the truth in language in the cultural context to which he is irrevocably confined, but he can indicate it.

As with the allegorical thought-picture, logically stringent argumentation makes way for the practical logic of the album. This is concerned with traveling through a broadly divergent area of ideas, zigzagging over hill and down dale and along specific passages, and constantly examining the same points, or almost the same, in different directions, composing new configurations that offer the viewer a clear image of the situation, his own included. Benjamin's own "Epistemo-Critical Prologue," with its grandiosely complex scatterplot of arguments, itself has the character of an album or a sketch. Those who cannot assemble this riddle for themselves cannot understand the signs of their own time. The "Epistemo-Critical Prologue" can therefore also be seen as a kind of test. Those who fail it would be better off saying nothing. But under no circumstances should they judge, or deliver judgment.

From this point of view, it wasn't Benjamin's work that was failed by Frankfurt, it was Frankfurt that was failed by his work. As, incidentally, are many of the members of the Benjamin cult today, who seem to prefer to place him on a pedestal as an esoteric figure rather than respond to his highly consistent, deeply systematic impulses and to his forward-looking, independent way of thinking. In that sense the age of grief is not yet over.

PALESTINE OR
COMMUNISM

BENJAMIN'S IDÉE FIXE, reinforced by economic need, of having an academic career—an idea that in moments of clarity "merely terrified him"—lay at the origin of his own tragic drama. After the entirely understandable rejection of his thesis—a fundamental rejection by those academic disciplines and institutions for which he had formally sought to qualify—Benjamin felt released from the pull of what had been the gravitational center of his adult life. In spite of all the dark emotions that inevitably accompanied his rebuttal, he saw Frankfurt's judgment as a liberation. As he wrote to his "manager" and sole advocate in Frankfurt, Gottfried Salomon-Delatour, in August 1925, "If my self-esteem depended even slightly on those positions, the careless and impulsive manner with which the crucial authority in question treated my case would have given me a shock from which my productivity would not quickly have recovered. The fact that none of this—in fact the opposite—is the case remains a private matter for me."[19]

So by the middle of 1925, Benjamin was for the first time a truly free man—his newfound liberty being the freedom to starve. The future direction of his work and the associated direction of his life going forward called for a decision. In his study of tragic drama, all of the central insights of his works—"About Language in General and Human Language in Particular," "Fate and Character," the preface to his translation of Baudelaire, and the essay on *Elective Affinities*—were closely interrelated and interwoven with singular density. In 1925, Benjamin had a philosophical vision that was very much his own, and also a voice that was beginning to articulate itself more and more freely and intuitively in his earliest thought-pictures, such as the piece on Naples. His systematic analyses of tragic drama revealed to him two paths, both equally important to the course of his life and his investigations, but also mutually incompatible. The two can be neatly reduced to the decision between Palestine and Moscow.

Palestine of course signified immersion in Jewish theology, in the sense of a relentless search for the lost language of Adam and the preservation of Messianism in Judaism and the prospect of a truly transcendent salvation that it held out. This path was represented by his closest and most loyal friend, Gershom Scholem, who had immigrated to the Promised Land in 1923 and attempted to entice Benjamin to join him. But the necessary condition for this was Hebrew, which Benjamin so far neither spoke nor read.

On the other hand, as Benjamin had realized in his pillow-talk introduction to communism during his dreamlike stay in Capri in the summer of 1924, many of his insights pointed toward a diagnosis of the age, not unlike that practiced in the early works of György Lukács—above all in his book *History and Class Consciousness*, published in 1923 and one of the subjects of Benjamin's intense discussion, as it was for Adorno, Kracauer, and Sohn-Rethel.

The dark mythical powers, which, in Benjamin's essay on *Elective Affinities*, conspired to govern the bourgeois sense of self, could without much difficulty be decoded or rewritten as those of the class struggle. The core accusation that Benjamin levels at the tragedy of the whole of the modern age and its philosophy is "objectification"—of nature and, in particular, of humanity.

Lukács saw capitalism's central sin as lying in the alienation it causes with "the increasing exclusion of the qualitative, human-individual properties of the worker."[20] This critique, of the system's objectification and subsequent alienation of the proletariat, fits splendidly with Benjamin's notion of the de-differentiation and interchangeability of all things in the wake of a philosophy of language that declares every sign arbitrary and refuses to acknowledge any significant connection with sacred naming of the original. The allegorical art of the Baroque had been distinguished, in Benjamin's view, by its attempt to interpret a confusion created by the forgetting of individuality:

> Every person, every thing, every relationship can signify anything else. This possibility delivers a devastating but just judgment on the profane world: it is designated as a world in which details are no longer of great importance.[21]

And therefore neither is the individual as an individual. Which way to go? Benjamin saw this parting of the ways clearly, and in May 1925, when the failure of his postdoctoral application was already apparent, wrote: "For me everything depends on how publishing connections are made. If I am unsuccessful, I will probably become more concerned with Marxist politics and—with the prospect of traveling at least temporarily to Moscow within the foreseeable future—join the Party. At any rate I will take that step in the longer or shorter term. The horizon of my work has changed and I cannot artificially limit it. Of course this and my study of Hebrew must first enter into a monstrous conflict of forces (my own) and I cannot make a fundamental decision, but must make the experiment of starting here or there. I can only acquire the totality of the horizon that I can discern, dimly or more clearly, in these two experiences."[22]

The theorist of the state of emergency remained in "real" life a hesitant character. Like the paradoxical flea that with each jump covers only half the distance to its destination, he managed only a half leap. That was how things stood in the autumn of 1925.

Benjamin's "publishing connections" had improved enormously, to the extent that he signed a contract with Rowohlt Verlag. The following year

Rowohlt wanted to publish the essay on *Elective Affinities*, the work on German tragic drama, and another book (published as *One-Way Street*), and granted Benjamin a monthly income, although not one that he could live on. He was also commissioned to translate further volumes of Proust's *In Search of Lost Time* for Rowohlt.

Facing the actual, and in his eyes inevitable, choice between Moscow and Palestine, in November he traveled for several weeks to Riga in Latvia. The reason was Asja Lacis, who was working on a number of plays there. Eros triumphed over his friendship with Scholem. Evidently struggling with his conscience, Benjamin told Lacis that he was now busily learning Hebrew (over the following years he would repeatedly claim to be doing so), and in fact he had already seen some "Eastern Jews" in the dark, wintry city on the Baltic Sea.[23] Without question a sign. But of what?

NEIGHBORS

AS WALTER BENJAMIN awaited judgment of his *Origin of German Tragic Drama* in Frankfurt, in the early summer of 1925 Martin Heidegger was in a state of constant of erotic anticipation. Not even the dreary, foggy dump of Marburg and his increasingly tiresome teaching responsibilities could dampen it: "Someone has ambushed me with a completed dissertation. . . . I hope I'll have finished by the time you come. . . . I always like to be close to you through my work. . . . Please come on *Friday* evening, like last time," Heidegger wrote to his Hannah on July 1.[24] It was a good time, as Heidegger's wife, whose birthday was two days later, was on a trip to her parents' in Wiesbaden with their son Jörg. Elfride, too, received a letter from Heidegger; it offers a glimpse of the now rather functional character of their marriage: "I send you my warmest wishes for your birthday. On this day I should like to thank you for your care for me and your assistance. But this consists—alongside phenomenological criticism—precisely in the hardest thing: in renunciation and waiting and believing. And when I consider such a semester from your point of view, it calls for a considerable deployment of strength. Here it is still a difference between what duty requires and what you can give in terms of your goodness and strength. And while I might not talk about it, you still know that I'm thinking about it. However disagreeable it is in itself that you are away on that day, it will give me the opportunity to express my thanks even more comprehensively. And conversely I will be glad if I can bring you and your dear parents pleasure with my renunciation."[25]

Decades later Arendt would say that Heidegger did not have a bad character, in fact he had none at all. If we read these two letters, very probably written on the same day, it's easy to see what she meant. At any rate, in the finest bourgeois tradition, Eros and marriage remained firmly distinct spheres. No less clear from these two letters is the fact that Heidegger doesn't address his correspondents as autonomous individuals but only praises them in terms of their functional subordination—as a means to a sacred end. This grand purpose is the task of his thought, and his thought forms in his eyes his primary connection with his fellow human beings, if he even acknowledges them at all. That summer the philosophical task urgently required him to give his ideas concrete form in an autonomous work. Because so far, the "secret king" of German-language philosophy had published only fragments and test samples. Nothing mature, nothing finished. Nothing that carried any weight of its own.

TO WORK

IN JULY 1925, Nicolai Hartmann, Ordinarius (professor with a chair) in Marburg, was offered a position at Cologne University. As much from the appreciable pressure of Heidegger's presence as anything, he immediately accepted. While Heidegger soon agreed, in a letter to Jaspers, that Cassirer would be "the best without question" to fill the vacancy in Marburg, the faculty, under Hartmann's aegis, identified Heidegger as the ideal successor to Paul Natorp, the Ordinarius who had died the previous year. But this demanded that he finally publish a work of his own. Otherwise any advocacy to the ministry responsible for appointments in Berlin would be fruitless. Thus Heidegger, too, was caught in the institutional trap. If he wanted to do justice to his self-image and his status, he would have to deliver.

Only eleven months later, on June 18, 1926, the Marburg faculty sent the first printed pages of *Being and Time* to Berlin. Heidegger would endlessly complain of the terrible time pressure under which he had to commit his masterpiece (in fact the only autonomous book-length work that he would ever publish) to paper. The writing of this work must be seen as one of the great bursts of creativity in the history of philosophy. Setting aside term-time obligations in Marburg, when Heidegger wouldn't have been able to write uninterrupted, the 450 or so pages of his book were written in less than five months—at a rate of 30 printable pages a week.

Heidegger was able to fall back on detailed preliminary studies, particularly talks and lectures he had given over the previous six years. *Being and Time* thus constitutes the hiatus of a conclusion, a pit stop on one continuous movement of thought and disclosure extending from the first lectures of the emergency semester in 1919 through "Phenomenological Interpretations of Aristotle" to the Marburg lectures on Plato's *Sophist* and those on the "History of the Concept of Time." He wrote the latter in the summer term of 1925 (working twice a week, between seven and eight in the morning).

EXPOSING THE QUESTION

IN TERMS OF CONTENT, at the center of Heidegger's intellectual journey lay the exposure of the meaning of a single question: the question of being, or more precisely, the *sense of being*. But before this primordial question can be (re)examined, well before any attempt may be made to answer it, Heidegger argues, we must expose the specific mode of being of the only creatures known to us that can meaningfully ask that question: human beings.

We alone can make sense of being the object of questioning. We alone are capable of being surprised that "there is something rather than nothing." We alone, as life-forms capable of speech, can ask wherein the sense of our specific Dasein might lie. To separate what he calls his "fundamental-ontological" method of investigation from all biological, anthropological, psychological, and even transcendental investigation in Kant's sense, Heidegger therefore speaks of the human being as Dasein:

> Dasein is an entity which does not just occur among other entities. Rather it is ontically distinguished by the fact that, in its very Being, that Being is an *issue* for it. But in that case, this is a constitutive state of Dasein's Being and this implies that Dasein, in its Being, has a relationship which itself is one of being. And this means further that there is some way in which Dasein understands itself in its Being, and that to some degree it does so explicitly.[26]

If, as Heidegger maintains, each Dasein understands itself more or less expressly in its Being, this also means that this very understanding of

Being cannot be taken for granted but has to be examined and possibly made explicit. False analyses and ill-thought-out concepts can obscure and distort Dasein's relationship with itself. And this, according to Heidegger (referring to the entire cultural configuration in which he finds himself), has occurred.

For Heidegger, a permanent "falling" was under way by the time of Aristotle, and a new and crucial phase of darkness was impelled by Descartes at the beginning of modern philosophy. Consequently, not only was the meaning of the question of the "sense of Being" either consigned entirely to oblivion or rendered taboo, but Dasein itself became blind to the actual sources and foundations of its relationship with Being, and hence did not in the end become a meaning of life.

In this context Heidegger diagnoses a comprehensive *oblivion of Being* in modern culture and particularly in modern philosophy, when understood as epistemology.

In essence, then, his analysis pursues precisely the same objective as Benjamin in his *Origin of German Tragic Drama*. Both works start with the present state of our own culture and declare that it would be premature and a mistake to attempt to give answers. All that can be done and that can matter is the attribution of loss, of the fall into oblivion. Heidegger is concerned with its exposure in *Being and Time*, initially only to prepare for the question: for that reason he calls his enterprise a "preparatory fundamental analysis of Dasein."

"Analysis" should be understood here not just in a descriptive sense but also in a therapeutic one. Self-understanding Dasein should be led back by a generally insightful redescription, as close to phenomena and as free of prejudice as possible, of the obscurity that it had entered, into the liberating light of its authentic fundamental relationship.

As in Freudian psychoanalysis, or indeed Wittgenstein's philosophy as set out in the *Tractatus*, the objective of describing the subject's situation (in the broadest sense) in the most precise and structurally revelatory manner goes hand in hand with the subject's transformation of the conduct of his life.

This project required that Heidegger either entirely avoid the ubiquitous but fundamentally false concepts used to describe the modern state of the world (subject, object, reality, individuality, value, life, matter, thing) in his own philosophy or replace them with new creations (Dasein, environment, being-in-the-world, each-one-ness [*Jemeinigkeit*], concern [*Sorge*], equipment [*Zeug*]). There can be no right speaking in the false, so Heidegger brought a new kind of speaking into the world.

THE TIME OF DASEIN

AMONG THE MOST SIGNIFICANT ASPECTS of Heidegger's philosophy to be affected by his bid for proximity to experience and eschewing of prejudice, picked up from his phenomenological training in the wake of Husserl, is his understanding of time and temporality. Rather than accepting a neutral "vulgar concept of time," mathematically clear and hence fragmented into unambiguously measurable units, seconds and minutes, Heidegger sought an understanding of time that was entirely illuminated by the specific way in which Dasein experienced its temporality. The kind of time Heidegger wishes to discuss in his analysis of Dasein is strictly limited to the space of the immanence of experience. In other words: The time that can contribute to the enlightenment of Dasein in the distorted possibilities of its being is understood as finite. Its meaningful horizon is death. Any reference to transcendence, whether in the form of an afterlife or an openness to Messianism in Benjamin's sense, is part of a process of distortion, not one of revelation. And as for Wittgenstein, for Heidegger death is not an event in life. But unlike Wittgenstein, who was willing to undertake a "leap" into faith, Heidegger saw the intuition of death as a guarantee that the sense of the "riddle of life"[27] could be investigated and, if necessary, grasped only *within* the perspective of temporal finitude.

The immediate proximity to experience that is supposed to distinguish Heidegger's philosophy is apparent in this work not least in the fact that to illustrate its analyses it repeatedly refers to contexts, states, and liminal situations that directly affect him—and enable him to demonstrate the living of his own daily existence. This applies particularly to the three key concepts that organize his philosophical illumination of Dasein: *Zeug* (equipment), *Angst* (anxiety), and *Tod* (death).

PHILOSOPHIZING WITH A HAMMER: THE STUDY OF EQUIPMENT

THE ONSLAUGHT OF WRITING can be dated to around August 8, 1925. In order to work, Heidegger withdrew to the cabin in Todtnauberg, where his family would also spend the whole of the summer. "On 1 August I am driving to the cabin and very much look forward to the strong mountain air—that soft, light equipment down here ruins one in the long term. Eight days of wood-work, then writing again," he informed Jaspers from Marburg. Only at a high altitude could he breathe and think clearly. The proximity in this passage of woodwork and writing is no coincidence. Here Heidegger is consistent in presenting himself as someone who in spite of his professorial position stays true to his peasant (not proletarian!) upbringing and the robustness that goes with it. He transferred the image of himself directly to philosophical analysis when it came to exposing the original world-relation of Dasein. Because how can a quite normal peasant boy who works energetically on the farm every day come as a thinking subject from a supposedly meaningless world of objects? Certainly not from his own experience, since as someone active and constantly working he is already "in the world," as Heidegger says. And not in the sense of a spatial relationship (like a canned fish in its tin), but in the sense of a relatedness steeped in meaning with the concrete environment he experiences. At the very beginning of his analysis of Dasein, Heidegger imagines a Cartesian (disembodied) subject that, through pure reflection from its armchair, wishes to assure itself of the reality of its world, and he compares it to a cheerful peasant from the Black Forest who leaves his cabin to chop wood, fully absorbed, as the sweat pours down his face. In Heidegger's words:

> The Being [Dasein] of these entities which we encounter as closest to us can be exhibited phenomenologically if we take as our clue our everyday Being-in-the-world, which we also call our *"dealings"* in the world and *with* entities within-the-world. . . . But the kind of dealing which is closest to us . . . is . . . not a bare perceptual cognition, but rather that kind of concern which manipulates things and puts them to us; and this has its own kind of "knowledge." . . . For the kind of Being which belongs to such concernful dealings is not one into which we need to put ourselves first. This is the way in which everyday Dasein always *is*: when I open the door, for instance, I use the latch.[28]

For all those "things" that we use in circumstantial acts in our daily lives, rarely in a conscious and reflective way, Heidegger introduces a new concept taken from the everyday peasant idiom of the Black Forest. He calls them *Zeug* (tools, equipment).

> We shall call those entities which we encounter in concern *"equipment."*
> In our dealings we come across equipment for writing, sewing, transportation, measurement. The kind of Being which equipment possesses must be exhibited. . . . Taken strictly, there "is" no such thing as *an*

equipment. To the being of any equipment there always belongs a total-ity of equipment, in which it can be this equipment that it is. . . . Equipment—in accordance with its equipmentality—always is *in terms of* its belonging to other equipment: ink-stand, pen, ink, paper, blotting pad, table. . . . These "Things" never show themselves proximally as they are for themselves, so as to add up to a sum of *realia* and fill up a room.[29]

Just as Heidegger, with earthy pragmatism, rights the epistemological presumption of the pure observer, he also inverts the explanatory trend of classical Cartesian-influenced epistemology by revealing tools to have al-ways been part of a totality of tools. This epistemology proceeds from the assumption of individualized, atomized things, to ask how a whole could be assembled from the parts. For the phenomenological pragmatist Heideg-ger, however, this atomization always presupposes the disappearance of a world in which objects are experienced primally, prior to all theoretical reflection, as integrated into a meaningful whole. The integration of equip-ment into a whole is something that, by practical use, we can grasp with our hands. Because in the pursuit of the question of "Being" that guides his investigation, Heidegger makes it unmistakably clear where the Being of equipment—and hence of all the things we interact with in our everyday life, and use to organize and orient ourselves—actually shows itself. For this hut-dweller and woodcutter chooses, appropriately enough, the exam-ple of a hammer:

> The less we just stare at the hammer-Thing, and the more we seize hold of it and use it, the more primordial does our relationship to it become, and the more unveiledly it is encountered as that which it is—as equipment. The hammering itself uncovers the specific "manip-ulability" [*Handlichkeit*] of the hammer. The kind of Being which equipment possesses—in which it manifests itself in its own right—we call *"readiness-to-hand"* [*Zuhandenheit*].[30]

Because the essence of this equipment lies in its use, it is not only *present-at-hand* (*vorhanden*) for Dasein (as a "thing" whose use was still to be disclosed would be), but *ready-to-hand* (*zuhanden*). The methodological foundation of Husserl's phenomenology lay in concentrated, epistemologically motivated staring at (and describing) something that was purely present. Heidegger's work is thus, among other things, a frontal attack on the philosophy of his teacher and patron. This fact did not escape him when he first read the printed pages, and as Heidegger would report, not without a certain pride, to Jaspers: "The work [*Being and Time*] will not bring in any more than what I possess already: that I have come into the open for myself and can with some certainty and direction ask *questions*. . . . If this treatise is written 'against' someone, then it is against Husserl, who saw that right away, but from the outset clung to the positive."[31]

STURM UND ANGST

AS BOUNTIFUL AS THE EVERYDAY ABSORPTION of peasant Dasein in its dealings with its equipment may seem, for Heidegger, on a philosophical quest for meaning, it is still fatally flawed. Such a Dasein remains essentially unquestioning, precisely in the assumption of its own rootedness in its environment and, in fact, in the smooth execution of the tasks ahead. Its relationship with the world is so original, so direct, and so filled with meaning that it never becomes questionable to itself. Those who are absorbed entirely in their own world ask neither the question about the sense of Being nor the question about the Being of their own lives. It is only the concrete experience of a loss of meaning and therefore, in whatever form, a disturbed relationship with the world that raises the question for the concerned Dasein of the sense of Being and the sense of its own existence: What is it all for? Why am I here?

No human life, however protected and homebound, passes without such disturbances of existence and hence questions of meaning. But these questions become inevitable for Heidegger in the experience of a particular feeling or, as he would put it, a particular "mood of Dasein" ("*Gestimmtheit des Daseins*"). It concerns the experience of anxiety, which Heidegger clearly differentiates from fear, the dread of something definite and concrete:

> That which anxiety is anxious about is Being-in-the-world itself. In anxiety what is environmentally ready-to-hand sinks away, and so, in general, do entities within-the-world. The "world" can offer nothing more, and neither can the Dasein-with of Others. Anxiety thus takes away from Dasein the possibility of understanding itself, as it falls, in terms of the "world" and the way things have been publicly interpreted. Anxiety throws Dasein back upon that which it is anxious about—its authentic potentiality-for-Being-in-the-world. Anxiety individualizes Dasein for its ownmost Being-in-the-world, which, as something that understands, projects itself essentially upon possibilities. Therefore, with that which it is anxious about, anxiety discloses Dasein as *Being-possible*, and indeed as the only kind of thing which it can be of its own accord as something individualized in individualization.[32]

For Heidegger, anxiety is the model for the experience of a comprehensive loss of meaning, which in the resulting emptiness and disconnectedness lays bare the true foundations of each Dasein. And lays it bare in such a way that this foundation itself is not present, does not exist, is not given, and is secured and guaranteed by nothing. In the mode of anxiety, Dasein experiences the factical bottomlessness and possible nothingness of its own existence, indeed of all that is. But the question of meaning thus bears no delegation to second or third parties, no relegation to transcendence and no self-reassurance through use, tradition, or home. Instead Heidegger is concerned to keep this question about the existential tension permanently open in all its radicality:

> When in falling we flee *into* the "at-home" of publicness, we flee *in the face of* the "not-at-home," that is, we flee in the face of the uncanniness which lies in Dasein—in Dasein as thrown Being-in-the-world, which has been delivered over to itself in its being.[33]

The anxiety-inducing experience of being-not-at-home, and of the secret sense of the uncanny, becomes increasingly acute and intense in contexts that convey the greatest security and familiarity to Dasein—particularly within the four walls of the home. For Heidegger the exemplary form of this is the wooden hut in Todtnauberg. It is here that anxiety unfolds its actual Dasein-opening and hence philosophically stimulating effect. Thus, in April 1926, when large parts of *Being and Time* had been completed, Heidegger wrote to Jaspers: "As you see, we are still up here. I began work on printing my treatise *Being and Time* on 1 April. It consists of about 34 sheets. I am making good progress and am only annoyed about the coming term and the petty-bourgeois air that will surround me again. The faculty wants to recommend me once more, bringing the printed sheets. . . . The boys both survived scarlet fever in the hut. It is already deep night—the storm sweeps over the summits, the beams creak in the hut, life is pure, simple, and as big as the soul."[34]

Heidegger experienced the uncanny inhospitality of a hut in the mountains beneath a raging storm as being entirely appropriate to that great and imperturbable intensity that was, for him, the very experience of philosophizing. The ideal image of a Dasein tensed for thought.

THAT CERTAIN SOMETHING: RUNNING AHEAD INTO DEATH

BUT NO BLACK FOREST STORM lasts forever. Eventually even the greatest thinker must return to the bourgeois air of everyday concerns. In order to forestall the slackening of Dasein that went hand in hand with that equally unquestionable fact, Heidegger referred to another fundamental of human life that was all too present, indeed ultimately unavoidable. It is the finitude—and this characterizes what it means to be human, in contrast to all other living creatures—of which Dasein is aware. Aware with a certainty that accompanies us throughout the course of our own lives. Indeed, if we look at it correctly, of all the possibilities that can define a Dasein freely projected upon the world, there is only one whose realization is truly certain: the possibility of no-longer-being-there.

As a possibility that is entirely uncertain in terms of both time and content, and yet one that will inevitably occur, Heidegger speaks equivocally about death as the "certain possibility." Unlike anxiety, death is also a constant certainty for Dasein—and thus not a mood that might descend or depart. As a certainty that can be concretely experienced, death is the constant condition of the possibility of all the possibilities that can be concretely grasped by Dasein in the course of a life. In other words: Death is the portal to freedom.

Death can fulfill that function only insofar as it remains completely indefinite: for Heidegger, any assumptions and speculations—or even just hopes—of a life after death should therefore, in the context of his efforts to lay bare the question of meaning, be rejected. They distort Dasein's perception of its own possibilities of being. Precisely as something openly tensed to this world, and hence something authentic, Dasein is thus a continuous running ahead into death:

With death, Dasein stands before itself in its ownmost potentiality-for-Being. This is a possibility in which the issue is nothing less than Dasein's Being-in-the-world. Its death is the possibility of no-longer-being-able-to-be-there. If *Dasein* stands before itself as this possibility, it has been *fully* assigned to its own most potentiality-for-Being. When it stands before itself in this way, all its relations to any other Dasein have been undone. This ownmost non-relational possibility is at the same time the uttermost one. As potentiality-for-Being, Dasein cannot outstrip the possibility of death. Death is the possibility of the absolute impossibility of Dasein. Thus death reveals itself as that *possibility which is one's ownmost, which is non-relational, and which is not to be outstripped.*[35]

Rather than looking back from the certainty of death and complaining of the nothingness of all Being and in particular our own existence—like the age of the Baroque analyzed by Benjamin, for example—the uncertainty of one's own inevitable nothingness goes hand in hand with an appeal to a self-defined grasping of all of our own possibilities of Dasein. Rather than lingering constantly in the contemplation of one's own finitude, as in some Christian—and indeed classical—doctrines, for Heidegger we should resolutely go toward it. Rather than consoling ourselves with the idea that the world would keep on turning after our death, as they say, for Heidegger running ahead into death became an uncatchable impulse to catch up with one's ownmost uncatchable possibility of Dasein.

Each of us dies in our own way. Our own death cannot be delegated any more than our life can. But the most profound misunderstanding of Heidegger's conception of Dasein as running ahead into death would be to see it as an appeal to suicide. Because those who die by their own hand are once and for all stripping from themselves the possibility that might actually be grasped in this running-ahead. This continuous process of resolute grasping—which for Heidegger must always have about it something of the openness of an as yet inadequately understood question (precisely the question of the sense of Being)—Heidegger now calls existing. Anyone who exists in this sense lives as a Dasein should live: authentically. Only a few people do that. Far too many don't.

Small wonder, then, that Heidegger finds more true authenticity embodied in the company of the "simple folk" of the Black Forest than in the deformed academic milieu: "I don't long for the company of professors. The farmers are much more pleasant and even more interesting," he confided to Jaspers. And: "I often wish that you could be up here at such times. Sometimes I can no longer understand how one can play such curious roles down there."[36]

In the rapturous creative phase of *Being and Time*, Jaspers the philosopher of existence also remains the only academic contact with whom Heidegger spoke as an equal. This applies not least to the practical question of dealing with the matter of dying itself, because even in the midst of his investigation into the question of death and the anxiety of the dying, new areas of experience opened between 1924 and 1927 that affected him deeply. In May 1924, several weeks after suffering a stroke, his father died. Heidegger's most powerful impression as this devout Catholic battled death was of his fear of hell and the Day of Judgment, which persisted right up to his death. Almost exactly three years later his mother succumbed to intestinal cancer, also after months of suffering. She had found it particularly difficult to deal with Martin's fall from faith, and told him as much on her deathbed. On February 5, 1927, Heidegger told his wife about his final conversations with his mother, who was already dying: "I am of course a great source of concern to the poor woman and she always says she is responsible for me. I reassured her—but she still found it hard to bear. The forces that are coming to light especially in these hours are so energetic. My mother was very serious, even harsh, and it was as if her true being had been hidden. She said to me: 'I can no longer pray for you, because I have to think about myself.' I must bear this, and my philosophy shouldn't just be on paper."[37]

Heidegger would put the first printed copy of *Being and Time* on his mother's deathbed on May 3, 1927. The conscious isolation of the dying mother, whose view of her life after death made her willing to foreclose the spiritual salvation of her son—"I have to think about myself"—may have made such a particular impression on him that the mood of anxiety and the certain possibility of death in Dasein chiefly led to the effect of radical isolation in his philosophy as well. But with a view to life *before* death.

The authenticity that, according to Heidegger, Dasein had to attain could be truly effective only through this experience and through the awareness of radical solitude. The presence and concern of other people were no help in that respect. Heidegger's appeal to authenticity and hence to self-discovery is thus based on a pervasive asociality of Dasein. It is only as something fully uncoupled, unique, and thus isolated that we attain insight into our true possibilities.

In the summer of 1926, Hannah Arendt had moved on to Jaspers's much more social philosophy of life, and Heidegger felt forlorn and abandoned in his foggy Marburg hideaway. Still a new, brighter apartment with a yard had at last been found for the family. And even the stubborn ministry in Berlin would now, since *Being and Time* was beginning its meteoric rise in German philosophy, no longer be in a position to resist the faculty's express wishes. Professorship called—a consolation, but not a reason. Heidegger's time in Marburg, as was becoming obvious with deathly clarity, had run out for good. With equal certainty, in his home in Hamburg, Cassirer imagined himself to be at the start of a new intellectual era.

THE HAMBURG SCHOOL

TO CALL IT AN OFFICIAL CEREMONY would be an overstatement. It was more of a circle of close friends and co-researchers who met at 116 Heilwigstrasse in Hamburg on May 1, 1926, to open the new building of the Warburg Library. Shortly after his return to Hamburg in the autumn of 1924, Aby Warburg had started planning it. There was no longer room for his collection of over 30,000 volumes to be arranged in an orderly manner in the old location. Funds were not in short supply, and neither were vision and enthusiasm. In less than two years, on the plot of land right next to Warburg's house, a research center unequaled anywhere in the world had been built. With "26 telephone connections, pneumatic post, conveyor belts and a special lift for books as well as another for people,"[38] the Kulturwissenschaftliche Bibliothek Warburg (KBW) broke new ground, not least in terms of its technical equipment. Moreover, it wasn't just that: the building itself, which filled the whole plot, was an architectural masterpiece. The pinnacle was the large ellipse of its reading room, where Cassirer now stepped onto the podium to deliver a lecture about "freedom and necessity in the philosophy of the Renaissance."

In the face of the reservations of his engineers, Warburg, in whose intellectual world every geometric shape had a specific symbolic, indeed philosophical, significance, had insisted that the largest, most important room in the building be elliptical. Cassirer was not entirely innocent. In particular their discussion in Kreuzlingen about the significance of the ellipse in Johannes Kepler's astronomical calculations had restored Warburg's intellectual resilience as a researcher.

For Warburg, Kepler's discovery that the orbit of Mars was elliptical—and not circular—represented the actual breakthrough from mythical, medieval thinking into the freedom of modern, scientific thought. The ellipse, as a circular form with two focal points, did not appear among the ideal geometric bodies set out by Plato in his dialogue *Timaeus*, which were fixtures in the geometric study of nature well into Kepler's time. Kepler's extension, motivated by astronomy and mathematics, of this formal canon— born purely out of the spirit of ancient myth—represented for Warburg nothing less than the emancipation of the human mind. It was both exemplar and embodiment of the move from the formal concept of myth to that of science, and therefore constituted a stride toward freedom and the making of a new epoch: the breakthrough to the modern worldview.

Marking this origin and disclosing its place in culture and history, with all the possibilities it generated, was now clearly set out as a core part of Warburg's program. The framing of the question alone indicates that this was in line not only with the major works of Heidegger and Benjamin— which were also autonomous anamneses of modernity—but also of course with the interests that guided the investigation of the philosopher and historian of philosophy Ernst Cassirer, as "number two" in the Hamburg School, in the newly constructed KBW building, with its elliptical reading room.

THE HIDDEN ORIGIN

WHAT HAD BECOME of the modern vision of the world? In the spring of 1926, Ernst Cassirer investigated that question in a work titled *The Individual and the Cosmos in Renaissance Philosophy*, dedicated to Aby Warburg for his sixtieth birthday.[39] At the inauguration of the library building, Cassirer read aloud the third of its four chapters to the assembled guests. His study of the Renaissance was by no means "only" a history of philosophy. Rather, by unearthing the intellectual roots of the Renaissance, he also sought to find restorative impulses and sources of inspiration for the philosophy of his own time.

Even this quiet work, then, warns of a loss and analyzes a crisis, but not with a view to showing that the modern age has taken a wrong turn, toward cultural forms that mourn the world or forge existence. Instead, Cassirer wanted to make a clear profession of faith, a philosophical celebration of the origin of the Renaissance as a milestone in self-liberation and the reshaping of the world. The essential impulses of this immense event were overshadowed, from the seventeenth century onward, by the abstraction-fixated, anti-corporeal, consciousness-obsessed modern age of René Descartes and his methodical successors—with profound consequences well into the philosophy of the 1920s.[40] While it might have been dressed up in elegant Hanseatic garb, Cassirer's *Individual and the Cosmos* is an appeal for a fundamental renewal of modern philosophizing by the return to its original sources: those of the Renaissance. This is an interpretation in the spirit of the same philosophizing that Cassirer had practiced and developed in his *Philosophy of Symbolic Forms*. Expressed theoretically, and hence more directly than Cassirer's style allows: The renewal of philosophy in the spirit of the Renaissance as the real and still pioneering origin of our modern age must assume the shape of a philosophy of symbolic forms!

PLURALITY OF OUTCOME

FOR CASSIRER—paradoxically—the most important feature of the Renaissance is the fact that philosophy did not play a significant part in it. Having ossified into the doctrines—kept in place by church institutions—of scholasticism, philosophy proved incapable of conceptually keeping up with the furious pace of innovation in both the arts and the sciences in the fourteenth and fifteenth centuries or even adequately reflecting them. Like large areas of analytic philosophy today, scholasticism, too, preferred to busy itself with the fetishization of fine distinctions on an apparently secure investigative foundation, rather than engaging in the adventure of providing a relevant contribution to the understanding of its own age, with its shifting foundational structures. In Cassirer's words: "Thus it appears that precisely in philosophy, the spiritual force of the age—that of clear delineation and formation, separation and individualization—either exercises no influence or falters at its first steps."[41]

On the very first pages of his book, Cassirer thus expressly turns against a characteristic assumption of Heidegger's analysis of the fall in particular. It might be called the assumption of "an overestimation of the civilizing power of philosophy."[42] Anyone who seeks the supposed origins of an age, and particularly the modern age, in philosophy alone, will get to neither the peculiarities of the age nor its philosophy. In his analysis of the Renaissance, Cassirer sees philosophy more as one innovative voice among many, and one with the function of connecting different disciplines. It is precisely this understanding that guides his philosophy of symbolic forms throughout the rapid artistic, scientific, and technical innovations of the 1920s. That decade rightly saw itself as a time of unprecedented, world-changing innovations, above all of a technical kind. The automobile, now mass-produced, began to determine the shape of cities; radio became a global medium of communication in the public sphere, the telephone in the private; cinema became an art form; the first commercial airlines were launched; now not only steamships but soon also zeppelins and even airplanes crossed the oceans, with Charles Lindbergh paving the way. The twenties witnessed the birth of an age of global communication facilitated by and in turn facilitating leaps in technical innovation. It persists into our own time. No individual and no individual discipline could keep interpretative pace. Not even philosophy. Precisely in the German-speaking world it saw itself as being propelled forward by progress; it wanted at best to act as its critical brake, not its driving engine.

So it may be more than a polite beneficence when Cassirer, in dedicating his book to Aby Warburg, indicates that it should be understood as the product of collaboration by that interdisciplinary group of researchers, working through close exchange with one another, who embraced the library as the intellectual center of their labors. In 1926, the close circle included Gertrud Bing, Ernst Cassirer, Edgar Wind, Erwin Panofsky, Joachim Ritter, and Fritz Saxl—to name only the most influential. Let the construction and the spiritual structure of the library—Cassirer continued in his dedication—embody the idea of a methodical unity of all areas of research and trends in intellectual history.

According to Cassirer, one of philosophy's essential tasks lay in identifying, beyond different disciplines, a common core that runs from one era to the next. If only to give all the forces and trends involved in this event a vision of their own limitations, and also of the connection among the different disciplines in the concert of the great whole. Without clues to define unity, especially in its more dynamic eras, the polyphony of disciplines threatened to descend into cacophony. And all participants suffer from that in the end.

SELF-FASHIONING THROUGH OPENNESS

FOR CASSIRER, the unifying central motifs of the Renaissance cluster around a new definition of the place of humanity in the cosmos, then freshly revealed to him. Hence the title: *The Individual and the Cosmos*. The

Renaissance individual sees himself or herself first and foremost as someone discrete, someone whose individuality consists and persists in a capacity for, or openness to, active and undogmatic self-fashioning, and the cosmos is to this individual like an open, infinite space whose laws prove to be almost unbelievably accessible through this practice of active, questing self-fashioning.

In Cassirer's speech the concept of freedom represents the human capacity for self-examination and self-making. The concept of necessity stands for the process of knowing the world and thus disclosing the laws of nature.

Seen in this way—and for Cassirer, this is one particular charm of the Renaissance (and indeed of his own philosophy of symbolic forms)—the twin concepts of freedom and necessity are no longer mutually exclusive. From this point of view, the seemingly terrifying question "If everything is governed by natural laws, how can free will exist?" loses its existential charge. Freedom and necessity are instead complementary concepts that condition each other at the source: only works of self-fashioning—which encompass the experiments of the sciences and the arts, and also include engineering and medicine—reveal the laws that allow us to speak of something like causal necessity. For Cassirer, modern freedom and causal necessity thus share an origin—and not as the origin of a tragedy in which everything is mute and deaf, but in the sense of a celebration of knowledge of the whole wealth of creation, in which all things are made to speak and sound together, just as Leonardo da Vinci was able to act and experience as an artist, a scientist, a poet, a philosopher, an engineer, a physician, and an individual with many interests of the mind and the flesh, all in the same single person.

For the Renaissance—as for Cassirer's own philosophy—the foundation of all this opening of the self and the world is the ability to give symbolic expression to our own experience. It is this that enables our entirely individual vision of the world to take shape in the form of a work, even if it is only a matter of playing the flute, making a gesture, a drawing, or a calculation. Having become a sign, and having been placed in the public sphere, a "work" can then be a starting point for others, for successors to open up themselves and the world: this is culture as a continuous process of symbolically guided orientation, or indeed an opening up, even in the humble form of a whistle, a movement, a sketch, or a calculation. It is here, for Cassirer, that the actual "logic of research" of the Renaissance lies. It is no coincidence that the construction of this uniquely creative world corresponds precisely with that of the content in the Warburg Library.

THE FAULT IN OUR STARS

FOR CASSIRER, one particular characteristic of the Renaissance as an age of transition and breakthrough into a new understanding of the world is the cultural simultaneity of "mythical approaches" and "modern scientific" approaches. This is especially visible at the boundary, still blurred at the time, between astrology and astronomy. Astrology sees us as subject to secret forces and constellations that we can at best interpret, but not steer and change at will. Astrology is a discipline governed by especially strict rules: the laws of nature are considered valid and apply, but the nature in question is disclosed and grasped primarily through myth and not mathematical calculation. This relationship is reversed with astronomy, and it is the particular merit of transitional figures such as Kepler and Copernicus that in the course of the Renaissance they effected the breakthrough from astrology, which still strongly influenced them, to the new way of thinking of astronomy. Cassirer describes the effects on humanity's self-image associated with this change, and our new position in the cosmos:

> A man is born under a certain star and has to conduct his life under its
> dominion; but it is nevertheless up to him to decide which of the powers and possibilities contained by this star he will develop and bring to
> full maturity in himself. Indeed, according to the intellectual tendencies and aspirations that he allows to flourish and nourishes within
> him, he can place himself now under the influence of one star, now
> under the influence of another.[43]

This leads to a reversal in direction of thought: the perspective no longer moves from cosmic natural forces down to the individual, but from the microcosm of the individual up into the macrocosm, of which it sees itself as being part. This is not to deny that the individual's natural integration into the cosmos imposes certain boundaries and conditions. The individual's capacity for self-determination in the Renaissance view of the world is therefore not unconditional, not fully autonomous. No one on earth can alone create the laws that determine their own development. Total autonomy is an illusion. The Renaissance sees an awareness of what we might call conditional freedom, and hence the possibility of self-fashioning within certain parameters. But the deeper the individual's insight into the conditions that determine development, the greater the space that opens up within that acknowledged system of conditions.

One technical example: No human being is born with the ability to fly. Not even Leonardo da Vinci. But once the laws of gravity, inertia, and air resistance have been revealed, with certain calculations and techniques, spaces open up for us to modify and circumvent our supposedly inalterably flightless fate. As creative shapers of our own access to the world, we play our own constellation (a law) off against another constellation (another law). And end up flying.

If the Renaissance, thus understood, does not emerge from the unconditional freedom of the individual, neither does it emerge from an unconditional necessity of "natural laws." In this sense human beings are very much given the chance to take their fate into their own hands, and to do so through the investigation and the use of dynamics that govern the course of their own development. Once again, the relationship between "freedom and necessity in the Renaissance" as set out by Cassirer is none other than that of his own "philosophy of symbolic forms."

Cassirer's search for the origin of the modern age in *The Individual and the Cosmos*, as with Benjamin's and Heidegger's works, indicates a loss. Cassirer sought to show, equally clearly but in a different way, the location of that loss later in the modern age. Intoxicated by the explanatory and predictive power of the natural sciences in the seventeenth and eighteenth centuries, the physical laws of nature assume an absolute determinative role as the forces behind all cosmic events—including humanity, as a purely material species. The problem of our freedom (of will) could then be solved only by extricating our essence from the world in the form of Cartesian philosophy of consciousness: the human being as a purely thinking entity separated from the body.

In a natural event determined entirely by blind chains of causality, we can see ourselves as free only if we are removed from the world and stylized into a kind of little god, with the mysterious capacity to conjure our own chains of causality out of nothing, with only the power of the mind.

In Cassirer's terminology the diagnosis of this *later* modern age and thus the Enlightenment in particular is as clear as it is seemingly paradoxical: once again, a culture relapses into mythical categories of thought—albeit at a distinctly higher level. A rigidly mythical necessity is replaced by the causal laws, and the whims of sovereign celestial bodies or merciful God by the "autonomous" human transformed into pure being of consciousness.

This is the true dialectic of the Enlightenment that Cassirer names and laments—not because the fundamental impulse of the Renaissance inevitably had fatal consequences, but because it was itself concealed and distorted in the course of its development. Cassirer's philosophy of symbolic forms attempts to reverse the process of concealment, at a time when the relationship between freedom and necessity, determinacy and uncertainty, as understood by classical physics, was radically called into question. Werner Heisenberg published his thesis on the "uncertainty principle" in 1927, the same year Cassirer published *The Individual and the Cosmos*.

Grasp your freedom, and do so on the basis of a scientific vision of the world, with a clear awareness of its limits, misunderstandings, and dogmatic interpretations. That was likewise the mission of the *Tractatus logico-philosophicus* and its author, the primary school teacher and intellectual guide into a "better" time: Ludwig Wittgenstein.

OUT OF THE MOUTHS OF BABES

Even here in idyllic Otterthal my birthday, which I would have much preferred to have kept quiet, was celebrated by the locals with a massive parade. From every district in the Waldmark thousands and thousands come streaming in; to greet their beloved teacher on the day of his celebration and express the wish that he might work for many more years for the good of the fatherland's youth, and thus also give the younger generation—such as yourself—an example and inspiration of dutiful self-sacrifice. Today I myself will speak about the eight-hour working day, peace among nations, and the unemployment benefit.[44]

Shortly before the end, only sarcasm helped. And the end, teacher Ludwig Wittgenstein felt more clearly than ever on his thirty-sixth birthday, was near. Sending such nonsense to his closest friends, as here to Rudolf Koder, was hardly unusual. Anyone who wanted to map the limit of sense, as he did, had also to be familiar with the many different varieties of nonsense. Asked seriously, in the spring of 1925, whether he saw his own culture as headed toward a new nadir, Wittgenstein would certainly have mentioned that mixture, as explosive as it was typical of the time, of the political Führer cult, mass stupidity fostered by the mass media. It was the year Hitler's *Mein Kampf* was published; the year Stalin definitively assumed power; the year a young Spanish army officer by the name of Francisco Franco—to the battle cry of "Long live death!"—invaded Morocco; the year the Conservative Paul von Hindenburg replaced the Social Democrat Friedrich Ebert as president of the Reich; the year Kafka's *Trial* was published. Wittgenstein was on his fourth and, it would turn out a year later, final teaching job in Otterthal. But the universally "beloved teacher" wasn't yet ready to admit defeat. While Heidegger, Benjamin, and Cassirer were drawing up their own analyses of the fall of the modern age, Wittgenstein was working on the resistance.

ENGINEERS OF SPEECH

HE HAD NO ILLUSIONS about the therapeutic suggestions of his *Tractatus*. They would always be reserved for a minority. Seeing the world "correctly" as he meant it was not something that could be taught as such. This was due primarily to the fact that the ladder of the *Tractatus*, particularly in its decisive beginning, was connected with specific experiences and intuitions. Experiences and intuitions whose substance went far beyond what could be said and hence discursively communicated. Thus the book's preface expressly stated that it was "not a textbook." The philosophical origin of the *Tractatus* lies in an unsharable experience, given as a gift, rather than an argument that could somehow be reconstructed with transparent clarity.

On the other hand, Wittgenstein, as a pedagogue, like other icons of Viennese modernity—Ernst Mach, Karl Kraus, Sigmund Freud—saw an entirely therapeutic potential for intervention in the sphere of everyday language. For him, too, the crisis in culture was also primarily a crisis of the public use of language. To grab this evil by the roots, one did not only need, like Heidegger, Benjamin, and Cassirer, to return to fallacious formations in the historical past. In fact, every new day delivers new beings untainted by any culture and the susceptibilities and confusions it entails: isn't every bright child living proof of the ability to learn a better, clearer way of speaking, and therefore one that fosters autonomy? To the extent that enlightenment is "emergence from self-imposed immaturity," this "self-imposed" dynamic can also be interpreted pedagogically. This "self-imposition" pilloried by Kant then becomes visible as a generational relationship, and also as a catastrophe: we bring up our children in a common immaturity by giving them and teaching them our own use of language and concepts, in an insufficiently clarified form, as the basis for their orientation in the world. That is not a destiny. That can be changed. If not in the parental home, then at least in school.

The conviction that language, out of its internal logic, bears within itself at every stage and every state of culture the forces needed to heal those very misunderstandings and misinterpretations that language itself constantly provokes and creates was already the foundation of Wittgenstein's therapeutic program in the *Tractatus*. And it would also become the guiding assumption of the whole of his late philosophy from 1929 onward, particularly in his second major work, *Philosophical Investigations*. This book, which takes dialogical form, is dominated by the voice of a stubbornly inquisitive child. Large parts consist of an endless game of question-and-answer between a philosopher and an imaginary, inner child. Almost every page depicts exemplary scenes of education into our way of life, in which a paternal philosophical voice attempts to explain to a child what language is, what it is based upon (and what not), and the role and significance certain key words truly assume in our lives.

The very first entry of this work, loosely arranged in a sequence of paragraphs, quotes just such a scene. And it does so with the express aim of rebutting the image of the nature of human language set out by no less than Saint Augustine, one of the Fathers of the Church, in his *Confessions* (I.8):

> §1. . . . When they (my elders) named some object, and accordingly moved towards something, I saw this and I grasped that the thing was called by the sound they uttered when they meant to point it out. Their intention was shewn by their bodily movements, as it were the natural language of all peoples: the expression of the face, the play of the eyes, the movement of other parts of the body, and the tone of voice which expresses our state of mind in seeking, having, rejecting, or avoiding something. Thus, as I heard words repeatedly used in their proper places in various sentences, I gradually learnt to understand what objects they signified; and after I had trained my mouth to form these signs, I used them to express my own desires.[45]

Wittgenstein's commentary on this primal scene is as follows:

> These words, it seems to me, give us a particular picture of the essence of human language. It is this: the individual words in language name objects—sentences are combinations of such names.—In this picture of language we find the roots of the following idea: Every word has a meaning. This meaning is correlated with the word. It is the object for which the word stands.

Augustine does not speak of there being any difference between kinds of word. If you describe the learning of language in this way you are, I believe, thinking primarily of nouns like "table," "chair," "bread," and of people's names, and only secondarily of the names of certain actions and properties; and of the remaining kinds of word as something that will take care of itself.[46]

Wittgenstein's therapeutic efforts now turn to countering the false images that linger in memory with other, alternative memories and thought-pictures, so as to see the world and our place in it "correctly." The reference to childhood as the stage when we absorb the largest amount of information about our relationship with the world is absolutely central here, as becomes apparent as early as paragraph 5:

§5. If we look at the example in §1, we may perhaps get an inkling how much this general notion of the meaning of a word surrounds the working of language with a haze which makes clear vision impossible. It disperses the fog to study the phenomena of language in primitive kinds of application in which one can command a clear view of the aim and functioning of the words.

A child uses such primitive forms of language when it learns to talk.[47]

Translated into pedagogical-philosophical action, this is expressed in paragraph 11.

§11. Think of the tools in a tool-box: there is a hammer, pliers, a saw, a screw-driver, a rule, a glue-pot, glue, nails and screws.—The functions of words are as diverse as the functions of these objects. (And in both cases there are similarities.)[48]

Any fourth-grader knows this. So Wittgenstein's therapeutic solution is clearly to go "back to the roots"—to the actual beginnings of speaking, to the concrete contexts in which speech is learned. And not in a historical or metaphysical sense—as is particularly the case with Benjamin and Heidegger—but in terms of real life, as when we teach children.

Wittgenstein was very familiar with this idea from 1920 onward. In the figure of the speaking child, a signature of his later work, we can see biographical experiences and philosophical insights drawn directly from his time as a primary school teacher. References focus in particular on his time in Otterthal from 1924 onward. Because it was there that Wittgenstein—at the same time as Heidegger, Benjamin, and Cassirer—wrote a new work that explicitly posed the question of the linguistic roots of our relationship with the world. The guiding question of that book (the *Tractatus* aside, the only one that he would publish under his name) is quite simply: What are the three thousand words that signify the world to an Otterthal schoolchild in 1925? Hence the extremely direct title: *Dictionary for Primary Schools*—by Ludwig Wittgenstein.

A LITTLE LIST

THE PROBLEM THAT NEEDED to be solved, and to which this basic work owed its existence, was anything but philosophical. Austria at this time lacked a dictionary accessible to pupils in the poorer regions of the country. Wittgenstein thought this could easily be remedied. In autumn 1924, he made contact with a Viennese textbook publisher, which immediately registered an interest in putting the project into action. What was required was an alphabetically arranged, orthographically correct list of the most common and important words in the vocabulary of a rural child of primary school age. The book was intended to enable pupils, if they were unsure how to write a word, simply to look it up, and thereby improve their spelling by themselves. Not earth-shattering in itself, it might seem. *Abend-mahl* (evening meal) was in there, as was *Abendbrot* (supper). But what about *Abendstern* (evening star) or even *Abendland* (the West)? *Pfau* (peacock) and *Pfeil* (arrow) needed to be in there, but what about *Promenade?*[49] Or would the introduction of that concept to a young rural mind already represent the beginning of a cultural decline?

Surely, if the borders of language are the borders of the world, it must be the duty of the pedagogue to draw those borders as carefully as possible, and also to guard them? Questions, and questions about questions, all of them with values attached. The Wittgenstein test still applies even today. Tell me which three thousand words are most important in your life, and I will tell you who you are. The dictionary project, in terms of both content and execution, was a prime example of Wittgenstein's whole pedagogical approach.

In the fastness of his bedroom, he selected words without asking or consulting his pupils. He included vernacular words, since they were part of the natural linguistic usage of his pupils. In Otterthal he also turned the dictionary into a project that the children put into practice step by step in the course of the school year: from laboriously writing out the lists of words by hand, often for hours at a time, to copying them out in beautiful hand-writing, then binding the pages into a book. (Wittgenstein had the material sent from Vienna at his own expense.) For many of his students their handwritten volume would have been the first and only one they owned.

Wittgenstein was a project-based teacher. He always tried to make his subject matter visible in objects. He was particularly keen on animal skeletons, which he prepared and assembled with his pupils. The carcasses, which included cats and other roadkill, he collected from the village streets, skinned and disemboweled them himself, before boiling the bones for several days. Even in Trattenbach the resulting foul stench led to fierce complaints from the neighborhood. But this didn't keep Wittgenstein from persisting with all the further stages of these projects. In the end he wasn't doing it for himself, he was doing it for education. Moreover, he couldn't have cared less about the opinions of his fellow villagers, unlike those of the children under his tutelage. Whenever complainants showed up at his house, he slammed the door in their outraged faces and told them that if the smell bothered them so much, they should simply leave, ideally forever!

THE RESPONSIBILITY PRINCIPLE

HE MIGHT HAVE BEEN SEEN as an eccentric, but as a rural pedagogue Wittgenstein had clear educational ideas and ideals: to recognize what we are, explore what we want, and experience what we can. To avoid plain nonsense errors of logic where possible. Anything that can be said can be said clearly. Practice trumps theory. And if there is anything here on earth that needs to be saved and healed, then it is our own soul, but not the whole world.

Boiled down to his daily dealings with fourth-graders, this focus was neither particularly complicated nor lofty—nor was it wayward. And yet pedagogically, Wittgenstein felt largely isolated in Otterthal. For all his declared desire to address the "simple people," to follow in the footsteps of Tolstoy, and indeed to be absorbed by their bounteous modesty, his own educational style was characterized by a robust, meritocratic obstinacy. As a "leader of youth" he was concerned primarily with the production and promotion of capable individuals who were familiar with their own per-sonalities and sound in their morals. For this reason his pedagogical goodwill was always devoted to the few, not the many. As Heidegger was praising the primordial wisdom and natural integrity of his Black Forest farmers, the provincial teacher saw his fellow adults only as cattle, maggots, or, at best, three-quarters human. Wittgenstein loved the idea of the "simple people," but not the reality, just as he loved the idea of life as a teacher, but not the rapidly changing job of teaching in Austria under the educational reforms instituted by the Social Democrats. His revulsion at the teaching methods that were being introduced was clear in the preface to his *Dictionary for Primary Schools*:

> But it is absolutely necessary for the pupil to be able to mark his essay by himself. He should feel like the sole author of his work, and also assume full responsibility for it. Only self-correction enables the teacher to form a correct image of the knowledge and intelligence of the pupil. Swapping exercise books and marking each other's work gives what we might call a blurred picture of the abilities of the class. From the work of pupil A I don't want to learn at the same time what pupil B can do, I want to know that from the work of B. And marking each other's work does not even, as is sometimes claimed, give a correct picture of the general level of the class (for that each pupil would have to correct the work of all his fellow-pupils, which is of course impossible).[50]

To have an idea of Wittgenstein's popularity in Otterthal, we need only imagine him informing his colleagues, over their regular lunches in the Golden Stag, about the fundamental incoherence, from a purely logical point of view, of aspects of the educational reforms. From a purely argumentative point of view he might have been right. But as we know, that isn't everything. And often not even the most important thing. Particularly for a philosopher who had gone pedagogically astray. Firm reservations were expressed about his dictionary, not least by the educational authorities. The assessor specially appointed to evaluate the work, one Herr Bux-baum, reached the following conclusion:

> From the methodological point of view it must be considered vexatious that the author mentions in the preface that he dictated the dictionary to his pupils. That should not be understood to mean that words that were already known, learned through the key word method, and frequently written were written down after dictation to be checked for their spelling. . . . In the present version the book can, in the view of the undersigned, hardly be recommended to a school authority.[51]

Incomprehension again. No textbook again. Even in the world of reference books and dictionaries Wittgenstein remained a problematic author for the publishing industry. In the end, however, the book was issued without major changes—but not until the autumn of 1926, more than eighteen months after it was delivered. Too late for Wittgenstein as a teacher, or as a human being. Like the *Tractatus* before it, this book would testify to an existence from which its author had moved on by the time it was published. Or rather: one from which he should have moved on.

A FAINTING FIT

HIS PUPILS AT THE TIME would not have called him a disciplinarian. His moods were too erratic for that, his eruptions too rare, and his punishments—usually knuckle taps to the head delivered swiftly to pupils at their desks, or blows with a stick—too irregular. And whatever Josef Haidbauer, eleven years old, had or hadn't done on the morning of April 10, 1926, to attract the fury of his teacher, in retrospect none of his classmates could say for certain. The boy, who had never known his father, and whose mother worked as a maid for a farmer, Herr Piribauer, certainly wasn't one of the class troublemakers. In fact, he was generally remembered as having a quiet temperament, as tall, not particularly bright, and above all rather green around the gills. Three years after the event that still bears his name—the "Haidbauer incident"—he would die of leukemia. The disease might already have weakened his constitution years before. There is no way of telling. At any rate, during class Wittgenstein dealt Josef Haidbauer two powerful disciplinary blows, not with unusual violence, but still brutally enough that the boy fainted as a direct consequence, and lay motionless on the classroom floor for several minutes. Wittgenstein immediately left the classroom, called a doctor, and carried the still-unconscious boy to a quiet room on the second floor of the building—and waited. When the doctor finally arrived from Kirchberg, four kilometers away, Josef had come to. His mother and Herr Piribauer, one of the wealthiest property owners in the region and also a member of the board of school governors, were already present. From the corridor, Haidbauer's foster father loudly accused Wittgenstein of being "inhuman" and an "animal trainer," and threatened to "report" him so that he would never teach again. And Wittgenstein? He put Josef in the care of his mother and the doctor, left the building by another exit, packed a suitcase (he had no furniture or books of his own), and took the first available bus out of idyllic Otterthal. In other words, he fled.[52]

By the time Piribauer went to the police the following day, Wittgenstein was already far away in Vienna. No criminal complaint was ever filed. Neither did the internal procedures of the school authorities establish serious misconduct on the part of one of its teachers. And yet: April 10, 1926, remained Wittgenstein's final active day as a primary school teacher. As he had predicted in numerous letters to friends over the years, "the worst" had in the end happened.

"I lost the connection with my class," he explained to District Inspector Wilhelm Kundt in a personal conversation. In spite of persistent requests by the inspector for the matter to be reconsidered, Wittgenstein asked to be released from teaching immediately. The request was officially granted on April 28, 1926. Two days after his thirty-seventh birthday.

In leaving for the provinces, Wittgenstein had never really been concerned with the youth of his fatherland, eight-hour days, or improvements in the material living conditions of the poor. Rather, what he wanted was a new and more healing contact with his pupils and himself, but in vain. Precisely seven years after his return from the First World War he was forced to acknowledge that his plan had ended in failure on every level. From now on it was shame alone that kept him alive.

VII.

ARCADES

1926 – 1928

Wittgenstein builds on, Benjamin breaks through,
Cassirer is tempted, and Heidegger goes home.

TECHNICAL TALENT

I KNOW THAT SUICIDE is always a dirty business, because one *cannot* want one's own destruction, and everyone who has imagined the process knows that suicide is always an *ambush* of oneself. But nothing is worse than having to ambush oneself. It all comes down to the fact that I have no faith."[1] Wittgenstein wrote these lines, eighteen months after the end of the war, in a state of great despair, to his friend Paul Engelmann. They had met in training for the front in Olmütz and remained in contact after the war. While Wittgenstein was working as a primary school teacher, Engelmann, who as a younger man had been a private secretary to Karl Kraus and later a student of the architect Adolf Loos, was setting up his own architectural practice in Vienna. Engelmann must have been aware that his friend Ludwig, after his flight from Otterthal, would once again be unraveling mentally.

Wittgenstein received the news of his mother's death on June 3, 1926, in the monastery of the Merciful Brethren in Hüttersdorf, where he had withdrawn with a view to entering the order. It is difficult to imagine the consequences for philosophy over the course of the twentieth century if the prior there had agreed to Wittgenstein's wishes. It became all too clear to him during their conversation just how lost and confused the lapsed philosopher was, however. Still, Wittgenstein was granted lodgings, in the gardener's cottage of the monastery, where he spent the summer distracting himself in the only way that he found truly effective: through hard physical labor as an assistant gardener.

Luki's state of inner turmoil was also a serious concern, as it had been seven years before, to his family. Above all to his sisters, Hermine ("Mining") and Margarethe ("Gretl"), who now, after their mother's death, were the de facto heads of the house of Wittgenstein—and of its still considerable fortune. Hermine was now the oldest in the family. Margarethe, eight years her junior, and married since 1905 to the American businessman and banker Jerome Stonborough, had spent the war in Switzerland and the United States, and went back to Vienna only sometime afterward. By now living separately from her husband, she returned to her life as patron of the arts and society lady, roles she had held to great effect before 1914, as can be seen in Gustav Klimt's famous 1905 portrait of the young Margarethe Stonborough-Wittgenstein.

What Gretl lacked in Vienna, when it came to playing this part in her own way, was a home of her own in the style of the old Palais Wittgenstein. Engelmann was chosen as the architect. Through his lasting friendship with Ludwig he had also become a friend and confidant of the family, and had planned and executed various conversion works for Hermine. Now he was to design a new townhouse for Margarethe. Money was irrelevant, as were prevailing conventions and fashion. In the winter holidays of 1925–1926 he corresponded with Ludwig about the project, and now drew up a plan about which Margarethe was immediately enthusiastic, given the desolate state of his friend. In June 1926 she wrote to her son Thomas Stonborough in the United States:

Engelmann has just had the brilliant idea of offering Luki a partnership. Can you imagine the enormous advantages that would offer all involved. Luki's great gift as a moral authority, as an instituter of logical principles exploited at last. His technical talent, replacing a consultant engineer for Engelmann. And again giving Engelmann the opportunity to build without having to renounce moral activity.[2]

His friend was kept busy, his client happy, and his costs reduced. Ludwig's involvement in the project looked like a win-win. A plot of land had been found and bought. This was, following Margarethe's express wishes, not in the city's classic villa quarters like the first or third district, but in the then petit-bourgeois or proletarian area of Vienna-Landstrasse. The chosen locality was a statement. And even more so, in line with the client's wishes, was the building to be erected there.

The final plan for a three-story residential villa at 19 Kundmanngasse was at last submitted on November 13, 1926. The responsible parties under construction law were "Paul Engelmann and Ludwig Wittgenstein, Architects, 18 Parkgasse, Vienna III." From ousted primary school teacher to star architect in six months—such things were still possible in Austria in 1926. At least if you had the right name and the right friends.

The problem brother now had an official profession and even a salaried occupation. And it would be understating the case to claim that he was a passenger in the project. In fact, Ludwig hurled himself into the task. After only a month everyone involved was under the yoke of this uncompromising and compulsive character. Engelmann, whose plan had been largely finished beforehand and was executed unchanged, remembered the twenty-four months leading up to the completion of the building as "very hard for me." In the end, he admitted, "collaboration with a man of such will" had even "put me in a deep inner crisis." Their friendship would never recover. At any rate, the orders quickly came solely from Ludwig, who would assume the role of architect, construction engineer, and, not least, interior designer: "Ludwig drew every window, every door, every window bolt, every radiator as exactly as if they were precision instruments, and in the most elegant proportions, and then, with an uncompromising energy, he ensured that the things were also executed with the same precision. I still think I can hear the locksmith saying to him, talking about a keyhole: 'Tell me, does this millimeter really matter to you?' and, even before he had finished speaking, there was a loud and energetic 'Yes' that almost made the man jump out of his skin."[3]

Even as a master-builder Wittgenstein was impelled by an ideal of precision that extended down to the millimeter. Imagining a new building from the ground up and erecting it—wasn't that what philosophers did, anyway? Could it be a coincidence that Kant spoke explicitly of an *architectonics* of reason? That Goethe's Faust turns into a master-builder in the second (and actually philosophical) part of the play? That Viennese thought in the Wittgenstein era was dominated by new "foundations" and "basic propositions"? All Wittgenstein's talents and also his longings seemed to find an active synthesis in this new role: exact, mathematical planning with an aesthetic aspiration, faithfulness to detail as an enabling principle, creative transposition of pure thought with materials from the environment. . . . And all with the goal of granting a secure shelter to humans, beings placed in the world without reason. In this case Wittgenstein was even free of the usual material and above all financial constraints that inevitably went hand in hand with the architect's profession, as Engelmann, after years of independent work, knew only too well.

Gretl gave her brilliant brother completely free rein in the process. No matter was too small—apart from time and money. After all, what she wanted was something more and something other than just a residence. It was to be the expression of a specific moral and aesthetic sense of the world.

Hermine might have been his favorite sister and the person he most trusted, but when it came to extravagance and self-dramatization, Ludwig had more in common with his sister Gretl than he could admit. Wittgenstein's desire for monkish austerity is, from this perspective, no more than an inversion of the inclinations of Gretl, for whom, from early youth, "everything that surrounded her had to be new and big."

FOR GODS ALONE

AT FIRST SIGHT of the building, which has barely changed in the intervening years, outwardly at least, comparisons with the idiosyncratic form of the *Tractatus* are hard to avoid. Completely lacking in ornament, the villa on Kundmanngasse looks, in Hermine's words, like "logic made house." An arrangement of ashlars create a cold impression and, with the building's narrow windows, convey a sense of arcane exclusion rather than one of inviting openness.

The doors of the huge hall, and copies of those in the old Palais Wittgenstein, are alarmingly high, like the metal screens that, in place of roller shutters, descend mechanically from the ceiling to block off any views of the interior. Even though from within the house is striking in its complete transparency and the exposure of mechanisms, such as the elevator cable, from the outside it looks like a riddle whose answer you can guess without being able to formulate the question. Then as today, the house was detached from its surroundings, like one of those anonymous offices in which Kafka's hero K might have striven for definitive resolution of his fantastical case. If "to dwell" means really to feel at home in a building, the villa on Kundmanngasse could effectively be described as an anti-house. In Hermine's always telling words, it was "more a dwelling for the gods than for . . . tiny mortals like myself."

A dwelling for the gods—in the Wittgenstein case the family resemblances between written and built work are in fact very striking. Except that a house entirely consistent with the architecture of the *Tractatus* would have no foundation to secure it in the earth or bear its weight, but would float magically, without visible support yet with inviolable stability, fifteen meters above the ground. The laws of physics do not correspond to those of metaphysics. The latter don't, in fact, exist. So there are clear earthly limits to the analogy. And even Wittgenstein could perform magic only as a thinker, not as an architect.

Even today the appropriate stylistic classification of the house on Kundmanngasse remains a subject for discussion—classic Loos school? Bauhaus style? Cubism, or, as Russell wrote, a building after Le Corbusier?—in much the same way as the classification of the *Tractatus* within the philosophical tradition: empiricism? logicism? idealism? existentialism? An argument that can never be meaningfully concluded, since Wittgenstein's personality, like his essentially aesthetic vision of the world, is a brilliant amalgam of radical modernity and rock-hard conservatism, perfect geometry and unsettling disproportionality, proof-based severity and aphoristic ambiguity, not least total transparency and mystical concealment. The man was not suited to any school. Either as a teacher or as a founder.

A CIRCLE
WITHOUT A MASTER

PROFESSOR MORITZ SCHLICK, of the Philosophy Faculty at Vienna University, experienced firsthand the difficulty of understanding the Wittgenstein phenomenon. Over long years he had gone through the *Tractatus* sentence by sentence, until, in mid-April 1926, after a series of failed attempts to make contact, he bestirred himself and, with a number of students, set off on a hike to Otterthal to seek out the genius hidden away there. Having reached their destination, the rucksacked pilgrims discovered that they had arrived a few days too late. Wittgenstein no longer taught at the school and had left, destination unknown.

As in Cambridge, Wittgenstein in Vienna had in his absence become an omnipresent figure, his work analyzed and questioned by the most innovative thinkers of the day. Every Thursday the philosophical avant-garde of Vienna met at Schlick's villa to work together on the deep reform of philosophy, indeed of European culture as a whole. They wanted to put an end once and for all to fake metaphysical arguments, laments of philosophical decline, and religiously impregnated appeals to authenticity. The new path of reason passed not through opinions but through arguments, not through dogmas but through facts, not through windy prophecies but through repeatable experiments.

"Logical empiricism" soon became the nom de guerre of this Vienna Circle, whose key figures, apart from Schlick, included Rudolf Carnap, Friedrich Waismann, Herbert Feigl, and Otto Neurath. The only missing piece of the puzzle was the group's master, the figure who had inspired it: Ludwig Wittgenstein.

It was another whole year before Schlick's request for an audience with him finally found a hearing. Their first meeting, carefully engineered by Gretl, happened in the spring of 1927. They had lunch together. Wittgenstein, intellectually entirely devoted to the building of the house on Kundmanngasse, wasn't sure if he was even a worthy partner in a philosophical discussion. Immediately after the lunch he passed on his impression of the conversation: "Each of us thought the other must be mad."[4] But from the first there was something like an underlying sympathy. The usual reasons may explain it. Like Wittgenstein, Schlick came from a wealthy family, even a blue-blooded one. The old Protestant Schlick family had been among the most important aristocratic families of the fallen empire.[5]

MUCH TO LEARN
YOU STILL HAVE

THAT WAS ETIQUETTE TAKEN CARE OF. And with Wittgenstein that was half the battle. Nowhere was he more uncompromising and irritable than in matters of conversational style. Schlick grasped that immediately. When, in the summer of 1927, he had finally persuaded Wittgenstein to meet the other core members of the circle, he pleaded with them "not to start discussions of the kind to which we are accustomed in our circle."[6] Instead, they were to listen raptly to the disquisitions of the master, and afterward, if necessary, carefully request further explanations. But there was one thing that this circle of logicians, mathematicians, and philosophers, who had influential futures ahead of them, had not grasped: Wittgenstein did not at first have the slightest desire to hold court, or indeed to talk to them at all about his work or philosophical questions narrowly defined.

At one of the first of those Monday meetings, which would become the stuff of legend, he set the tone. Without explanation or introduction, Wittgenstein stood with his back to his audience in the middle of the room and recited poems by the Indian poet Rabindranath Tagore, a cult figure of the 1920s popular in certain circles because of his broadly spiritual writing, but now largely forgotten. To interpret this entrance solely as the irritating tic of a self-involved genius would be to underestimate Wittgenstein's sense of the dramatic presentation of his persona as a thinker. In fact, this kind of gesture stands in a long tradition of initiations by masters in Asian contexts. Rather than reciting poems, the wise man from the mountains could have asked his curious pupils to clap with one hand or meditate on the extent to which the nature of the Buddha resembled a dirty stick. The message conveyed, at any rate, was clear: I am not your master. I have no method. *The* question does not exist. And neither does the answer. So if you think you've understood, it shows only that you really haven't understood anything at all.

The result was total perplexity. But predictably in such a situation, the offensive refusal of the role of the master is taken as an irrefutable indicator of true mastery. The same was true of the Vienna Circle around Schlick. Particularly since Wittgenstein, once the prevailing tone had been set, proved over the following meetings entirely willing to pursue philosophical questions, albeit in his own way. Rudolf Carnap, only ten years later a crucial figure in the creation of so-called analytic philosophy in the United States, recalled:

> He was hypersensitive and easily irritated. Whatever he said was always interesting and stimulating and the way in which he expressed it was often fascinating. His point of view and his attitude toward people and problems, even theoretical problems, were much more similar to those of a creative artist than to those of a scientist; one might almost say, similar to those of a religious prophet or a seer. When he started to formulate his view on some specific problem, we often felt the internal struggle that occurred in him at that very moment, a struggle by which he tried to penetrate from darkness to light under an intense and painful strain, which was even visible on his most expressive face. When finally, sometimes after a prolonged arduous effort, his answers came forth, his statement stood before us like a newly created piece of art or a divine revelation. Not that he asserted his views dogmatically. . . . But the impression he made on us was as if insight came to him as through divine inspiration, so that we could not help feeling that any sober rational comment or analysis of it would be a profanation.[7]

The Vienna Circle had hoped for something that coincided with their ideal of objective research but were instead left to grapple with an extremely idiosyncratic style of thinking that, in both execution and results, seemed directly contrary to it. The impression gradually grew until at last it was undeniable: if they were being addressed by a master, he was clearly not a master of logical empiricism. Because far from providing the foundation for rigorous claims to knowledge, Wittgenstein saw the technique of logical formalization solely as an aid to avoiding erroneous assumptions new and old. Chief among them was, for him, the view that only problems that could be understood through empirical experiment were worth exploring. As in Kant, Wittgenstein's limits on meaningful speech are established primarily to remove the central questions of metaphysics from the requirements of supposedly objective methods. Indeed, for him the immaturity of modern culture, which he was convinced he could subject to therapeutic treatment, lay in the assumption that with regard to truly philosophical questions there existed something like verifiable methods, academic professionalization, and above all measurable progress in knowledge. In Wittgenstein's view, philosophy was not akin to legal writing, and neither was it intellectual engineering; in fact, it wasn't a teachable or thematically definable science. But those were the precise convictions that lay at the heart of the Vienna Circle.

The only area of agreement still discernible between master and pupils is the fact that metaphysical and religious assertions must necessarily burst the bounds of verifiable meaning. For the Vienna Circle this meant that they were philosophically obsolete, for Wittgenstein that they were in fact crucial. For the Vienna Circle, logic was a firm foundation necessarily underlying all thought. For Wittgenstein, on the contrary, that same meaning-inducing foundation floated inexplicably forever in the air, as a lasting miracle of creation that should be devoutly revered rather than analytically grasped. For the Vienna Circle, metaphysics was nothing but a permanent ideological ambush of culture—with entirely fatal consequences. For Wittgenstein, on the other hand, the notion of banishing its questions consistently and declaring them void amounted to a desire for cultural suicide. So each party thought that the other was in need of further enlightenment. Except that the goals of that shared effort were diametrically opposed.

The Monday meetings were in a sense a tug-of-war, in which the Schlick faction—supposedly in the name of his mentors, Gottlob Frege and Bertrand Russell—sought to drag their master over the demarcation line of the "verification criterion" (Schlick: "The meaning of an assertion lies in the method of its verification"), while a famously indefatigable Wittgenstein held his ground at the other end of the rope with Schopenhauer, Tolstoy, and Kierkegaard, waiting for the whole positivist troop to collapse. As if he wanted to give the Vienna Circle one last fatal blow, Wittgenstein announced on the occasion of another session:

> I can imagine what Heidegger means by being and anxiety. Man feels the urge to run up against the limits of language. Think for example of the amazement that something exists. Astonishment cannot be expressed in the form of a question, and there is no answer. All that we can say can *a priori* only be nonsense. Still we run up against the limits of language.[8]

Defending Heidegger? That was going too far!

The grotesque miscommunication typical of the Monday meetings in Vienna offered everyone present the opportunity to recognize the relationship between Wittgenstein the master and his would-be disciples for what it doubtless was: one of the strangest misunderstandings, not without its comical side, in the history of philosophy. But rather than finding common ground in the comedy of the situation, this scene has been repeated almost daily in the most dispiriting way ever since, with the result that two tribes have formed—that of "analytic philosophy" and that of "continental philosophy"—which, identified by their war paint, are dedicated to leveling mutual accusations at each other without having understood even half of what philosophizing really means.

After nearly a hundred years of playing out this scene, it seems like nothing more than a farce. It now has barely anything to do with the living philosophizing of which Wittgenstein was most convinced from the beginning. But even today, his work and teaching form the essential focus or axis in the context of this tribalism. For decades, in "Wittgenstein research," every inch of interpretation has been fought over as if it were a matter of transposing the architectural plan of a brilliant master without the slightest deviation, rather than continuing to think in terms of the clearest possible vision of our relationship with the world. Precisely as if philosophers were engineers of the soul rather than creative seekers in an open space without a final foundation or a protective cover.

From his brief spell as an architect from 1927 to 1928, we can say of Wittgenstein: The ideal of total precision that he sought in thought was not one that could be expressed purely through mathematics or language. It demanded an extremely subjective feeling for space and one's own unrelinquishable positioning in which one wanted to find and understand oneself creatively within it. Only in this conviction he was, both as philosopher and as engineer, equally unforgiving. And while he was forcing the adepts of the Vienna Circle to rethink their methodical construction of logical empiricism from the ground up, despite the fact that its leading voices considered themselves absolutely conclusive and unalterable, he was at the same time working as site manager on Kundmanngasse. In November 1928, when cleaning had begun on the building that had been declared finished, Ludwig ordered the "ceiling of a hall-like room" to be raised by three centimeters, because he thought that only then would it feel right. No objective explanation for this assessment has been passed down. And what might it have been?

There was plainly something else that he sensed during that winter in Vienna, with mounting subjective certainty: his philosophical mission was far from over. Perhaps it was only beginning.

INSTABILITY

"I HAVE HAD (as they so nicely put it) a nervous breakdown; or rather one after another; the intervening periods during which I felt better only made it worse in the end," Benjamin wrote from Marseille on September 14, 1926.[9] He had retreated there from Paris with the intention of "barely picking up my pen." His autumn was also tense: intellectually, socially, and financially. No hint of any consolidation of his position. Throughout the spring he had commuted between Berlin and Paris in an "elliptical way of life." In mid-June, practically at the same time Benjamin completed his so-called Book of Aphorisms, his father died. The work on which Benjamin had been laboring more or less continuously over the previous two years was originally supposed to have been called *Road Blocked!* Now it was titled *One-Way Street*.[10] In terms of his personal life that autumn, an equally appropriate title might have been *Cul-de-sac*.

Still, the new work—a collection of sixty sketches of memories, most of them biographical, arranged as in a magazine—showed, according to his estimation, the way into a new form of writing and hence of thinking. He traced the crucial impulses behind it back to the summer of 1924 in Capri, and accordingly gave the book the following dedication:

This street is called

Asja Lacis Street

after her who

as an engineer

cut it through the author.

The breakthrough attributed to Lacis is the attention paid toward objects from everyday life and their use as launchpads for philosophical reflection. The essence of the author's own epoch was to be conveyed no longer via theories or classical artworks but directly through contemporary objects and behavior. The key objective was the revelation of those "mechanisms . . . with which things (and relationships) and the masses work together."

The very first entry in *One-Way Street* explicitly announces the consequences of this new direction. It is called "Filling Station": under given social conditions, it says,

> significant literary effectiveness can come into being only in a strict alternation between action and writing; it must nurture the inconspicuous forms that fit its influence in active communities better than does the pretentious universal gesture of the book—in leaflets, brochures, articles and placards. Only this prompt language shows itself actively equal to the moment.[11]

And in the form of recorded situations that, once they have been committed to paper, appear like leaflets, brochure texts, or poster slogans, according to their genre. The very title, *One-Way Street*, contains an ambivalence that reveals each of these thought-pictures, indeed every sentence they contain, to be a literary gem that invites the reader to produce very different, ideally even mutually exclusive, interpretations. *One-Way Street* offers travel in a straight line with a clear direction and no oncoming traffic, but also the fear, typical of the age, of being fatally on the wrong track with no adequate exits or opportunities to turn. The sense of a "lost generation," like the one identified around this time by Gertrude Stein in conversation with Ernest Hemingway in Paris: lost, chronically indecisive—and precisely for that reason inclined to extremes.

Benjamin's thought-pictures are also quite deliberately conceived as literary complements to those reversible images that were particularly popular in Gestalt theory and psychology at the time, and show different objects, depending on how you look at them: the line drawing of the head of a duck, for example, that, from one moment to the next, appears as the head of a rabbit, and goes on switching indistinguishably between the two, neither being in the end definitive. Only someone able to perceive both figures at once sees "correctly." Benjamin also saw this dynamic, of an "identity that is demonstrated only in a paradoxical switch from one to the other," as a key effect of his new, object-centered writing.[12] Indeed, if the times did not deceive him, this flickering "free change" between two mutually exclusive states even corresponded to the paradoxical law of those subatomic particles from which everything that existed was constructed: what the physicist Max Planck called quantum particles.

These quantum particles, at least as claimed since 1923 by the group of researchers around Werner Heisenberg, Niels Bohr, and Max Born, lacked any fixed observable identity. Instead their nature, difficult to grasp, consisted precisely in the fact that, according to the perspective of the observer, they appeared now as a wave and now as a particle. The law of observation-dependent "switching from one to the other" was hence the fundamental motion of the developing universe itself. This was a process, furthermore—as Heisenberg and his colleagues claimed to have demonstrated—that did not follow any strongly deterministic laws, but at best followed statistical laws. It wasn't just social life that was based on an ineradicable ambivalence and uncertainty; the physical world was, too.

Benjamin's thought-pictures attempt to provide for this ontological vagueness of all things by describing as precisely as possible the world of commodities around him, penetrating its deepest structures. In turning toward concrete everyday objects as the starting point of his reflection, he was also turning philosophically toward materialism, but not dialectical materialism in the sense meant by Marx or Lenin. After all, Benjamin's concern was quite explicitly not exposing the contradictions that were predictably contained in the object. On the contrary. What was at play here was the insight into the impossibility of doing exactly that.

The actual "thing" that Benjamin wanted to turn around and examine under the microscope with the tiny plaquettes of his *One-Way Street* in 1926 was nothing other than the historical world in all its developing wholeness. The particular charm, indeed enchantment, of his materialism, which we should call "magical," is the use of concentrated description to "penetrate ever deeper into the interior of objects" until these "finally represented a universe only within him"—and hence precisely in that focus to create the possibility of an accurate, effectively monadic depiction of the whole historical process, permanently tipping between momentary salvation and eternal damnation.

His investigative immersion in the total immanence of the here and now was to open a window into the transcendence of salvation. With Benjamin, the categorical imperative associated with this epistemological (anti)program was as follows:

> The task is to decide not once and for all, but at every moment. But to *decide*... Always proceeding in a radical and never a consistent fashion

with regard to the most important things would also be my way of thinking were I one day to join the Communist Party (which I would in turn make dependent on a last-chance impulse).[13]

Something else that was consistently absent, of course, was the experience of such a decision. Particularly in his life. Since April 1926 he had been victim of severe depressions. Now, with the completion of the *One-Way Street* project and the loss of his father, in his hotel room overlooking the Mediterranean he seriously considered suicide. Ernst Bloch, who had originally traveled with him from Paris to Marseille, remembered how openly Benjamin had contemplated it. Suicide, the ultimate decision! A person cannot actually in the end "choose" it, since in Benjamin's view suicide is preceded by a form of unconditional self-definition whose radicality lies precisely in excluding any further rational consistency.

It didn't happen, ultimately. Rather than bring his life to a premature end, Benjamin locked himself away in a hotel room for three weeks and read Laurence Sterne's novel *Tristram Shandy*. The constantly ironic, sometimes simply silly tone of the work may have saved Benjamin's life in the late days of September 1926. Literature can do that.

His mood remained gloomy. Early in October we find him back in Berlin. If an old and caring friend had offered him a "partnership" as an architect, Benjamin—creator of *One-Way Street*—would presumably have leapt at the chance. But he didn't have such a friend. And he didn't have the right name. At least not in Berlin. And certainly not in Paris, where he had spent the previous few months striving in vain to gain access to the inner circles of the French literary scene.

Not one of his major works had appeared in book form. Even though the galleys were ready and everything had been agreed upon contractually for more than a year, Rowohlt held both the essay on *Elective Affinities* and the book on German tragic drama. *One-Way Street* was also supposed to be published on this list. But when, how, and whether this would ever happen was now more doubtful than ever. The only continuity in Benjamin's life consisted in his translation work on Proust's cycle of novels, which—since he thought Proust's artistic intentions very close to his own—was increasingly causing "something like inner toxic phenomena."[14]

MOSCOW OR BUST

IN NOVEMBER 1926 news reached Benjamin that Asja Lacis, still the love of his life, had also suffered a severe nervous breakdown. Critically weakened, she was being treated in a Moscow sanatorium.

Moscow. Winter. Mental hospital. Precisely the kind of configuration in which Benjamin imagined he could see a possible way out of his crisis. What more effectively inspires someone prone to attacks of meaninglessness than looking after a beloved Other who is clearly in a worse state? He also faced an existential decision, and hoped he could get considerably closer to its definitive solution by staying put. In Moscow, the still-swirling laboratory of the communist revolution, he would be able to see with his own eyes what the future state, and his own state, might look like.

Of course he had no close contacts or liaisons in the Soviet capital, and no functioning knowledge of Russian. Asja aside, the only person he knew there was the theater critic Dr. Bernhard Reich—Asja's partner. Reich had risen to a position of some seniority in the Moscow theater and, as a member of the Russian Association of Proletarian Writers, was an official part of the state apparatus in the way that Benjamin imagined as a possible alternative existence for himself.

United in solidarity, for the first few days the two men sat by Asja's bedside every afternoon, and brought the temperamental patient cakes or tea, scarves or soaps, magazines or books. They passed their time together, on Reich's initiative, playing dominoes. Even though Benjamin hardly had a minute alone with Asja, at first he put a brave face on things, particularly since in the remaining hours Reich generously introduced him to the most important places, theaters, and cultural institutions of Moscow.

As a visually oriented person, Benjamin had to adjust his technique of looking in the megapolis of Moscow, not only because the windows of the "unheated electric tram" at temperatures less than minus 20 Celsius were permanently covered with ice. In particular, walking "on completely icy streets," and on narrow pavements to boot, required so much concentration that he could barely raise his head, flâneur that he was. But from the first day his impressions were so overwhelming that he believed he could capture them only in the form of a continuous diary:[15] sleds rather than cars; instead of multistory high-rises, ramshackle summer villas as colorful and irregular as the swarming army of street traders and beggars; Mongols in ragged furs; Chinese vendors of paper flowers; tobacco-chewing Tatars on every street corner, above them gigantic billboards with revolutionary slogans or the visage of Lenin. On the left bank of the Moskva, Red Army soldiers marched back and forth between a church and a building site; children played soccer among them, with nothing but tattered felt shoes on their feet . . .

The concentration of what he recorded into thought-pictures—that would have to wait for some later time. Because here "everything is being built or rebuilt and every moment poses critical questions. The tensions of public life—which for the most part are actually of a theological sort—are so great that they block off all private life to an unimaginable degree. . . . It is totally impossible to predict what's going to come of all this in Russia.

Perhaps a truly socialist community, perhaps something entirely different. The battle that is going to decide this is still in progress."[16]

That winter, three years after Lenin's death, Stalin had definitively triumphed over Trotsky and assumed control. The socialist experiment thus took its totalitarian turn. Within only a decade, millions of Soviet citizens would fall victim to him: through resettlement, ethnic cleansing, arbitrary exile, torture, forced labor in gulags and ore. A harrowing episode that even now has yet to be grasped theologically.

As a tourist, Benjamin did not anticipate all this. Neither did Reich, a resident of Moscow, though he had told his guest on their first evening together how worried he was about the "reactionary turn that the party was taking particularly in cultural matters." In Moscow in 1926, the feeling that one could in an instant switch from one extreme to the other dominated and menaced all spheres of life and all social milieus, reaching even into the highest levels and circles of the party. Rather than emancipatory resolution and radicalism, this configuration inclined toward radical remoteness, and Benjamin noticed not least within himself a tendency toward God-fearing fatalism: "Nothing ever happens as planned or expected—this banal formulation of life's complications is borne out so implacably and so intensely in every single instance here that you quickly come to grasp the fatalism of the Russians."[17]

But for now, looking on the bright side, everything was still open, everything was new, everything was in revolutionary motion. On the first day, a hopelessly exhausted Benjamin—Asja had argued with Reich over living conditions—had withdrawn to his hotel: "I'm reading Proust in my room, and wolfing down marzipan."[18]

In Moscow, by Benjamin's estimation already the "most expensive city in the world," housing was the pressing problem, as he would soon find out for himself. The state-registered co-resident of Dr. Reich's apartment was plainly mentally ill, which was why Reich spent much of the coming weeks sharing Benjamin's hotel room. Reich spent the night in the bed, snoring loudly, while Benjamin slept in an armchair installed by Asja specially for that purpose. It was only a tactical maneuver, perhaps. But for Benjamin, in this context very much the fifth wheel, truly private moments with Asja were now out of the question. In triangular relationships the private becomes a means of power politics.

THE HELL OF OTHER PEOPLE

BENJAMIN'S NOTES from his eight-week stay bear witness to a constellation of relationships that, absurd and excruciating in equal measure as they might be in their fundamental arrangement and development, are mortifying to read even today. *Moscow Diary* stands as an object lesson in the mutual humiliations to which essentially well-meaning people can subject themselves when negotiating a supposedly shared love. Asja fought with Reich, Benjamin with Asja, Reich with Benjamin, Benjamin with Reich, and Asja with Benjamin. Causes ranged from the cut of evening blouses, to dripping faucets, cash-flow problems, and supposed careerism, to the threat of sending Asja's daughter Daga to a state-run children's home on the edge of the city. But their most intense disagreements concerned the role of the writer in communism, the latest theatrical production by Meyerhold, Bulgakov's drama, the closing scene of *Metropolis*, and indeed the question of how often the term "class conflict" needed to appear in a Soviet encyclopedia entry on Goethe. They would go for days at a time without talking to one another, they would variously suffer heart attacks, before finally reuniting as a trio to sit side by side in the front row of the theater. Benjamin didn't understand a word at the theater, so a translation was whispered in his ear to keep him abreast. On particularly good evenings he might get a little kiss as well, although only if Asja was in the mood and her chaperone Reich was otherwise occupied. So hardly ever. "One only knows a spot once one has experienced it in as many dimensions as possible. You have to have approached a place from all four cardinal points if you want to take it in, and what's more, you also have to have left it from all these points," Benjamin noted on December 15, 1926, while Reich was right beside him in the hotel room.[19] An observation that applies also to human relationships. As early as December 20, Benjamin made the analogy between cities and people explicit: "For me, Moscow is now a fortress; the harsh climate which is wearing me down, no matter how healthy it might be for me, my ignorance of the language, Reich's presence, Asja's utterly circumscribed mode of existence, all constitute so many bastions, and it is only the total impossibility of advancing any further, only the fact that Asja's illness, or at least her weakness, pushes our personal affairs into the background, that keeps me from becoming completely depressed by all this. Whether I will achieve the secondary purpose of my journey—to escape the deadly melancholy of the Christmas season—remains to be seen."[20]

On December 31, this question also seemed to have been answered. Benjamin was standing in front of a theater poster with Asja when he admitted: "If I had to be sitting alone somewhere tonight, I would hang myself with misery."[21]

A MAN WITHOUT A FRAMEWORK

AT THE START of the new year it wasn't just the temperature in Moscow that reached a new low: Asja, whose fevers had returned again, was assigned a new roommate—one who was as noisy as she was passionately vulgar. To make matters worse, she spoke German, and eagerly butted into every conversation. Reich was still living with Benjamin at the hotel, which he was now also using as an office and a study, rendering even arguments impractical. The situation was too messy, the protagonists too weary. On January 8, Reich suffered a severe heart attack; Asja's health had deteriorated. In the increasingly defensive isolation of his hotel room, Benjamin experienced a painful moment of self-understanding.

It is becoming clearer and clearer to me that my work needs some sort of solid framework for the immediate future. Translation can obviously not provide this. In fact, this construction depends first and foremost on my taking a position. Only purely external considerations hold me back from joining the German Communist Party. This would seem to be the right moment now, one which it would be perhaps dangerous for me to let pass. For precisely because membership in the party may very well only be an episode for me, it is not advisable to put it off any longer. But there are and there remain external considerations which force me to ask myself if I couldn't, through intensive work, concretely and economically consolidate a position as a left-wing outsider which would continue to grant me the possibility of producing extensively in what has so far been my sphere of work. Whether this production can move ahead into another phase without a break, that is the question. And even in this case, the "framework" would have to be propped up by external circumstances, an editorial position, for example. At any rate, the period that lies ahead seems to me to distinguish itself from the previous one in that the erotic is becoming far less of a determining factor. My observation of Reich's and Asja's relation has, to a certain extent, made me more conscious of this. I note that Reich manages to weather all of Asja's ups and downs and is, or seems to be, rarely ruffled by patterns of behavior that would make me sick. And even if this is only an appearance, that's already a great deal. It's because of the "framework" he has found for his work here.[22]

Benjamin's life in the late 1920s in a nutshell, then. What the monastery was for Wittgenstein, the Communist Party was for Benjamin. With unsparing candor, introspection into abortive stabs at maturity intermingle freely with the nakedly opportunistic considerations of a socially and economically déclassé individualist. If there was no ultimate reason for deciding one way or another, utility would in the end settle it. The choice now was radical pragmatism, and the bourgeois daydreams of an "editorial position" flickered through his consciousness. Anything but continuing as he was! Benjamin, now in his mid-thirties, had to acknowledge that he lacked any support in life, indeed lacked a life as such. Even Asja and Reich were better off in that regard. At least they had each other, and Asja her communist mission, apparatchik Reich his days full of meetings:

> Further considerations: join the Party? Clear advantages: a solid position, a mandate if only by implication. Organized, guaranteed contact with other people. On the other hand, to be a Communist in a state where the proletariat rules means completely giving up your private independence. You leave the responsibility for organizing your own life up to the Party, as it were. . . . As long as I continue to travel, joining the Party is obviously something fairly inconceivable.[23]

Continuing to travel. Always Benjamin's favored option. Neither in the winter of 1927 nor subsequently would he join any political party. The will to independence always triumphed in the end, as a necessary precondition of the possibility of the life of a freethinker. He left Moscow on January 30. His final minutes with Asja took the form of an ambiguous emotional scene à la *Doctor Zhivago*: "Displeasure with her and love for her leapt

continue until noon the following day. All without Benjamin. By the mid-1920s some 40,000 Americans, attracted by the cheap franc, had taken up residence in Paris.[24] Most of them young, ready to party, and with artistic interests of some kind. Far from home and backed by a ludicrously favorable exchange rate, they painted the town scarlet.

Benjamin, too, dipped his toes every now and again into a *palais de danse et de baiser*. A moderate white-wine drinker throughout his life, he would occasionally take to the dance floor, where his ungainliness earned the mockery of his literary colleagues Franz Hessel and Thankmar von Münchhausen, who were likewise connoisseurs of the city's brothels. But that was as far as it went. The French franc was not so weak that Benjamin could indulge as he might have wished. Despite his liking for prostitutes and gambling, he was no party animal or lounge lizard. The time he spent in Paris in 1926 and 1927 wasn't some hedonistic blur of champagne, literary salons, and sexual adventure. On his good days, immediately after getting up—without washing, eating, or drinking—he would work for several hours on his translation of Proust or a review for the *Frankfurter Zeitung* or the *Literarische Welt*. Having fulfilled his quota, he could stroll through the city's arcades and alleys, spending as little as possible, with an eye on the side streets for a cheap Chinese restaurant with a halfway decent budget menu.

Though his French was fluent and largely error-free, his standards for his own linguistic expression exceeded it. When he requested meetings with French writers, they always agreed unconditionally—but of course he never quite managed to escape his role as a journalist. As a writer he forged barely any lasting or useful connections. At no point does he seem to have taken the slightest interest in the vibrant British and American scene. He couldn't read English and didn't speak it, either. It is a curious gap in his interests, and one that seems almost willful or defensive. Perhaps this is due to the fact that his wife still earned much of her livelihood for herself and her son as a literary translator from English. Dora visited him with Stefan in June 1927—a happy interruption. Otherwise Benjamin felt that he and his talent had been shamefully spurned by the two golden cosmopolitan cities of the decade, Paris and Berlin.

"Right now I am more or less utterly on my own, and in a fortnight I will be sitting here in total isolation," he wrote to Scholem in July. Coming from Jerusalem, where he was now teaching at the Hebrew University, which opened in 1925, Scholem was on a research trip to London and Paris. After four years apart, the friends wanted to spend a few weeks together in August. Benjamin, ashamed of the precariousness of his situation and intimidated by Scholem's "ostentatious self-confidence," dreaded the encounter at first, but overall their reunion was positive. They usually met in the evenings in the cafés around Boulevard Montparnasse, "in the Dôme and La Coupole," Benjamin's favorites. Scholem had now found his framework; Benjamin was still mulling over his. In the meantime he had started a new project, about the Paris shopping arcades, intended to complement the thought-pictures of *One-Way Street*. At the time, Scholem later remembered, "he talked about completing that work over the next few months." The manuscript, barely fifty pages long, from which Benjamin read to his friend in the cafés forms the embryo of the Arcades Project, a fragment of the work over which he would labor for the next decade. It would remain a (gigantic) fragment.

Benjamin told Scholem about Moscow; Scholem, fully aware of Benjamin's precarious situation, told him about Jerusalem, about the building of a new state for the Jewish people and the role of the Hebrew University in the consolidation of a Jewish identity. By chance, Judah Leon Magnes, the university's chancellor and a fluent German speaker, was in Paris as well. Scholem arranged a meeting. "So," he recalled, "there was a two-hour conversation between the three of us, in which Benjamin, who had obviously prepared well for this meeting, set out his intellectual activities in grand phrases, his wish to approach, through the medium of Hebrew, the great texts of Jewish literature not as a philologist but as a metaphysician, and declared his willingness to come to Jerusalem if necessary, whether temporarily or permanently. . . . He wanted to devote his productive work to the Judaic world."[25]

This was yet another moment of transition from one extreme to the other. Endlessly radical, ceaselessly inconsistent! Scholem concludes the passage: "I myself was surprised by the definite and positive form in which Benjamin set out these thoughts, which of course had been uttered often enough before in one form or another, and in which I was to a certain extent involved."

That same evening Benjamin secured Chancellor Magnes's financial support for a yearlong visit to Jerusalem to study Hebrew full-time. In what was perhaps the most fantastical turn of the whole evening, Magnes believed Benjamin's every word and promised to see things through on his side. As his sole condition he requested written appraisals of Benjamin's works—ideally from the pen of high-ranking authorities. All of a sudden Benjamin saw a genuine future opening up before him. If not in Moscow, Jerusalem. Had he not written to Scholem that he wanted to make a final decision dependent upon chance?

In Berlin, too, things had suddenly taken a positive turn. His books were to be published by Rowohlt at last! Benjamin traveled there in November to assist with the publication in person, only to spend three long weeks in bed with jaundice. Enough leisure time to think about who might appraise his works. For his travels to Jerusalem. For a new life, with a framework.

Hugo von Hofmannsthal, for years his only loyal admirer, was his first choice. The second appraisal was to come, if it could be arranged, from

Ernst Cassirer. No small hurdle. By March 1928, Benjamin had not advanced a step further, and in his usual manner he had even begun to perceive a grand conspiracy ranged against him—as he told Scholem: "The importance of Cassirer's vote would be obvious to me, but you are aware of the hostility of my cousin William Stern in Hamburg. And Warburg is surrounded by fog, no one can clearly see what could come out of there. As soon as I learn what Cassirer thinks about me, I will tell you."[26]

What Cassirer thought about Benjamin? Good question.

HIGH SEAS

ON OCTOBER 30, 1927, Ernst Cassirer made a passing observation about himself, which could apply to the description of his whole philosophy: "I can express everything I need without difficulty," he wrote to his wife from London. One could plow through all the diaries and letters of Wittgenstein, Heidegger, and Benjamin without coming upon such a sentence. Where the limits of languages, the limits of the world are concerned, Cassirer was always the thinker of the possible, not the impossible.

Basically his contented surprise was a response to his safe arrival at the capital of the Empire. He had prepared for the expedition at the invitation of King's College by taking some private classes in the weeks before his departure, having barely spoken a word of English in his life. Only a few days later, on November 3, he proudly told his wife that he was able to "understand the language of scholars quite effortlessly." The philosopher as genius in the use of symbols.

Of course, during that autumn of 1927 there could hardly have been a single person in the world who spoke and understood more languages fluently than Ernst Cassirer. Because Cassirer saw the actual task of his philosophy as lying in the mutual illumination of as many "languages" as possible. Not just English, French, Sanskrit, and Chinese; as far as he was concerned, myth, religion, art, mathematics, even technology and law, were also languages, each with its distinct internal form and world-shaping force. Accordingly, he saw the goal of his "philosophy of symbolic forms" as the "directing of one's gaze in all directions in order to understand the world," and, for each of the various forms of the world,

> to assign to each of them its own specific and peculiar index of refraction. The philosophy of symbolic forms aspires to know the special nature of the various refracting media, to understand each one according to its nature and the laws of its structure.[27]

In the autumn of 1927, Cassirer brought this project to a temporary conclusion by finishing the first draft of the third volume of *The Philosophy of Symbolic Forms*. Any "normal" person would have had a nervous breakdown after the conclusion of such a life's work, or at least suffered from some sort of illness, but Cassirer just carried on. The only thing he allowed himself by way of celebration, so to speak, was a two-week trip to England and the Netherlands. All by himself, without his children and also without his wife. Toni had been hit by a car in September, and needed months of intense rehabilitation, chiefly physical therapy.

On board the passenger ship *New York*, which was to take him from Hamburg to Southampton, Cassirer sent several reports on the progress of his journey.[28] Only a few minutes after moving into his "fabulously luxurious and comfortable cabin" he felt a great temptation to travel on from Southampton "all the way to New York." It is inconceivable that Cassirer would have missed the near-perfect allegorical coincidence between the form of his philosophical project and his journey on an oceangoing steamer.

Only a few days before, in the closing passage of his introduction to the third volume of his major work, he had described himself as a curious explorer on the sea of symbolic forms: "But this 'journey round the world' must really embrace the whole of the *globus intellectualis*."

Nietzsche, in his command "To the ships, Philosophers!" had not been the first to use nautical metaphors. The sea, as a provisional space constantly in motion and spanning the whole of the globe, is well suited to use as a symbol of contemporary knowledge-production that can scarcely be grasped, let alone tamed. In the 1920s in particular, the sensation of lacking solid ground under one's feet permeated the fields of economics, art, politics, and science. Even physics and logic had been afflicted by crises that threatened to make a mockery of all attempts to give the edifice of human knowledge a solid and rational foundation. Otto Neurath, one of the most important members of the Vienna Circle, would soon describe the philosophical predicament as follows, possibly in part because of his disillusion with Wittgenstein's séances: "We are like mariners who must rebuild their ship on the open sea without ever being able to dismantle it in a dock and rebuild it from the best component parts."[29]

IN THE EYE OF THE STORM

"THE TRANSITORY, THE FLEETING, THE CONTINGENT," which Baudelaire had identified as the central properties of the modern age, also fully characterized philosophy. Not all protagonists found it equally easy to welcome this new feeling of existence. If such a mariner's life was to be enjoyed at all, and steered calmly through each storm, then surely it would be aboard a modern ocean liner like the one on which Cassirer now sailed, and whose internal construction and workings he immediately began to explore with almost childlike curiosity, as if the steamer were nothing but another symbolic form and hence a way of being in the world.

After only six hours on board he had "viewed everything from top to bottom—I have even been to third class, where I had everything shown and explained to me down to the smallest details by a quickly acquired 'friend.' Here, too, for all the striking contrast with the incredible luxury in first class, everything is comfortable and in excellent order." It would not have occurred to Cassirer that in third class he might not have seen all the sleeping accommodations available on the ship, any more than he inquired into the presence of stowaways or rats in the galley. Where other observers, like Bertolt Brecht at around the same time, saw the transatlantic steamer as the perfect backdrop to illustrate the dramatic social differences of the age, starting with the gap between "top deck and lower deck,"[30] Cassirer allowed himself to be shown around by a "friend," and judged the vessel to his own general satisfaction: in principle, everything was in perfect working order.

He was accommodated "almost in the highest part of the ship," to which he was "conveyed by elevator." He described traveling inside it as "entirely unreal," particularly since the ship glided along "with a tranquillity that sometimes makes one lose the feeling of being in motion at all."

Even when a storm raged over the North Sea at night, so violently and so powerfully that all of Toni Cassirer's close friends "called me with tearful voices," her husband offered a further textbook example of existential resilience:

....

> I was woken at about three o'clock in the morning by the wailing of the wind. . . . You can imagine what a storm at night sounds like up there. As I couldn't get back to sleep again

immediately, I read for a while, then grew tired and slept through until eight—still quite a decent achievement. I don't feel the slightest bit seasick. . . . In spite of the strong waves the sea voyage is wonderfully calm.[31]

....

AN EMERGENCY
IN FRANKFURT

IT WASN'T UNTIL JUNE 1928, when Cassirer's international reputation was approaching its zenith, that we can discover anything approaching an existential wobble. Frankfurt University (later renamed after Goethe), a recently founded institution like Hamburg University and still under construction, invited him to take up a post with a remit to "reshape the whole of the philosophy department."[32] A unique opportunity and a well-funded one, too. Cassirer immediately informed the Hamburg authorities of the offer he had received. He wanted to make his decision in July and be sure that the negotiations had been concluded by both parties.

There was much at stake, particularly at the Hanseatic end. Above all for Aby Warburg and the "crew" of his library. Perhaps out of concern for the survival of his own research in the future, Warburg wrote an open letter in the *Hamburger Fremdenblatt*, titled "Why Hamburg Must Not Lose the Philosopher Ernst Cassirer." With the publication of this appeal, which Warburg also distributed to "seventy influential persons all over Germany,"[33] the struggle to retain the most renowned philosopher in Germany became a public, even a political, matter. It wasn't long before both mayors joined in the debate with invitations of their own ("Come to Frankfurt and help us give Frankfurt University the position and the significance appropriate to the unique geographical situation of the city, its cultural tradition, the intellectual agility and inner freedom of the population"[34]).

Warburg, too, remained active on all fronts, asking the Kurator (chief academic administrator) of Frankfurt University, Kurt Riezler, who had issued the invitation, to bear in mind "what a violent attack it would be on the roots grown with such effort in the difficult soil of the North Sea coast" for Cassirer to depart.[35] Hamburg was financially willing and able to match Frankfurt's offer. (Warburg had been busy in this area as well.) But would that be enough to keep Cassirer in a city that was then, as now, famous for a great number of things, though few would count academic excellence among them?

Cassirer increasingly realized that he had become something more than an academic philosopher. He was a radiant symbol of a liberal, republican attitude—something that could not be taken for granted among the great German minds of his day. As the most significant living neo-Kantian, as a student of Hermann Cohen, as an internationally regarded authority on the work of both Kant and Goethe, he was one of the figureheads of German-Jewish patriotism. In the context of such accolades it is almost ironic that Walter Benjamin, who had failed noisily with his attempt to have his postdoctoral thesis accepted in Frankfurt, should have run aground in attempting to land in Hamburg. Through Hugo von Hofmannsthal he had personally sent his *Origins of German Tragic Drama* to Erwin Panofsky in Hamburg. The reply, which returned via Hofmannsthal, was so brusque that Benjamin even felt the need to apologize to his middleman for having compromised him to such a pointless end.

What form would Benjamin's career have taken if his application to be admitted into the Warburg circle had been accepted? Like other members, he probably would have been exiled to London or the United States early in the 1930s. And hence he would never have been dependent on the economic support, or the patronage, of the Institute of Social Research, later run by Adorno and Horkheimer, which would have such an influence on his work.

Much more interesting, however, for the trajectory of future German-language philosophy, is the question of what might have happened if Cassirer had actually accepted the invitation to Frankfurt to rethink the philosophy department according to his very own ideals. With Cassirer at its intellectual helm, could the tendency known as "critical theory" or the "Frankfurt School" ever have come into being there? That Frankfurt School whose founding father would, in the early 1960s, be sanctified and revered as none other than Walter Benjamin?

Cassirer, the seafaring pilot of linguistic diversity, remained on board, however. He remained loyal to Hamburg and to Warburg, and, not least, to the love of stability that was his nature. In late July 1928 he informed all concerned about his decision. The cost—or was it the gift?—consisted in greater relevance for the cultural and political life of Hamburg.

At the same time negotiations for his retention began, and possibly as part of a deliberate flanking maneuver, he was invited by the Hamburg Senate to deliver an address marking the ten-year anniversary of the Weimar Constitution. This was generally held to be an outstanding idea. Only Toni refused to join in with the choir, partly because it threatened to delay their summer holiday in the Engadin valley in Switzerland by two whole weeks. But also because—as someone with a chronic fragility, and thus unlike her husband with a particularly keen sense of the vicissitudes of existence—she saw this overt declaration of allegiance as unwise, indeed almost dangerous, in the political climate. Especially as a German Jew. A storm of unprecedented magnitude, she sensed, was on the way. Her husband didn't share these concerns. And if he did, he considered himself strong enough, and well protected, to weather the coming storm.

INDIVIDUAL AND REPUBLIC

THE MATTER WAS CLEVERLY RESOLVED, as it had to be. After all, the aim of the speaker—with his snow-white professorial mane, wearing an academic gown, and singing along to the third verse of the German national anthem with the others—was nothing less than to turn the prevailing narrative about the origin and birth of a constitutional republic on its head in forty-five minutes.

If a scandal was to be avoided, it had to be done with many voices and through many different channels. But above all with the noblest of guarantors. For Cassirer, on this day, these were the same as they had been throughout the whole of his intellectual life: Leibniz, Kant, Goethe. No culture, at least not German culture, could need anything else to return to rude health. But where this intellectual legacy was slandered or despised, an abyss of barbarism would open up.

The skepticism with which too many Germans regarded the Weimar Republic wasn't primarily the result of its questionable efficacy. By August 1928, less than ten years after it had come into existence, it had gone through no fewer than ten chancellors, yes. But over the past two to three years it had undoubtedly made economic advances. The resentment of the great nations defeated in the First World War lay not in the realm of finance but in cultural memory: the republic itself, with its democratic form of government, was held in the dominant narrative to be foreign, imported from the histories of the victorious nations of the United States (Declaration of Independence, Bill of Rights), France (French Revolution), and, with a great deal of historical benevolence, England (Magna Carta). Even Switzerland had its Pledge of Allegiance to the Confederation, but in terms of democratic creation myths, on the other hand, Germany pretty much drew a blank. From this point of view the Weimar Constitution was not a gift but an accident of the country's own history, a kind of permanent collateral damage from the outcome of the war, along with the reparations imposed at Versailles, and not much easier to bear. For this reason a truly self-defined Germany would—on the basis of its own history—be many things, but not actually a republic. This view was shared by the incumbent president and former field marshal Paul von Hindenburg. The problem with Weimar was thus that of its historically formed self-image—a sore point that Cassirer addressed right at the start of his speech to the Hamburg Senate. As one might have expected of a philosopher if he didn't share the conviction that

> the great historical and political problems that dominate and agitate
> the present day cannot in the end be separated from the great funda-
> mental questions that systematic philosophy asks itself, and which it
> has tirelessly struggled to solve throughout its history.[36]

This reveals a first, important part of the trick. Here history becomes the history of philosophy, a history that, as with its political counterpart, always must revolve around the same systematic questions: What is the correct relationship between individual and community? And between true self-determination and a free, public use of reason? And what of the supposed rights attributable to any rational being, which may not be in-fringed upon? For Cassirer, as a self-declared Weimarian, these were all genuinely German questions, at least where the philosophy of the modern age was concerned. Once the matter had been framed in these terms, with some precise knowledge of the relevant sources, it became clear that no less a figure than Gottfried Wilhelm Leibniz—a systematic philosopher, not particularly associated in those days (or indeed today) with democratic ideas—was in fact "the first of the great European thinkers to represent, with great energy and resolution, in the foundations of his ethics and his philosophy of the constitutional state, the principle of the inalienable rights of the individual."[37]

Leibniz, of all people! The philosopher to princes! It would have seemed no less unlikely if one pulled a giant rabbit from Foreign Minister Gustav Stresemann's top hat.

Cassirer, a magician of sources, mentioned a telling passage from a treatise on the rights situation of slaves and serfs, which had gone almost unnoticed by students of Leibniz in the past. Far from questioning the practice of slavery itself, this passage instead granted these subjects certain unconditional minimal rights.

There were still a number of giant steps to be taken from these minimal rights to the fully mature subject of the modern constitutional state. According to Cassirer, this was exactly what happened. Leibniz's impulse from this point—via Enlightenment philosopher Christian Wolff—influenced the whole political philosophy of the Continent, and—via William Blackstone, the British legal philosopher and reader of Wolff—led directly to the 1776 American Declaration of Independence, which in turn served as a model for the French National Assembly.

Admittedly, Cassirer does not prove this in philological and historical terms, but it remains a concise German counternarrative, which on that fifteenth day of August 1928 reached its truly inspiring climax, of course, in Immanuel Kant:

> In Kant's text "Idea for a Universal History with a Cosmopolitan Purpose," which was written in 1784, five years before the outbreak of the [French] Revolution, the goal of the political history of mankind is identified as the achievement of an internally—and to this end also externally—perfect state constitution. "Although this state body," Kant adds, "stands before us for now only in the form of a very tough project, nevertheless already a feeling begins to stir in all members, each of

which has an interest in the preservation of the whole; and this gives hope that after many transforming revolutions, in the end that which nature has as its aim will finally come about—a universal *cosmopolitan condition*, as the womb in which all original predispositions of the human species will be developed." Thus it is only the repetition of this original demand of his, not the influence of external events in the world, when Kant, over ten years later, in his essay "Perpetual Peace," determines the first definitive article of eternal peace to be that the civil constitution in every state should be republican. Because in his view only such a constitution corresponds to the idea of the "original covenant" on which all rightful legislation of a people must in the end be based.[38]

The American Constitution, the French Revolution, the Weimar Republic, all given foundations in a new and essentially German way! And not only those: there was also the League of Nations, highly controversial in the country, to which the German Reich had been granted access only two years previously. So a little magic trick of historical philosophy, admittedly of highly dubious construction, but delivered so pleasantly and so elegantly by Cassirer at this ceremony that no one was struck by it. Instead the content set out here was applauded as the most naturally self-evident, particularly when Cassirer reached the historical moral of his lecture:

> What my reflections were intended to convey to you was the fact that the idea of the republican constitution as such is by no means a stranger within the whole of German intellectual history, let alone an invader from without, that instead it has grown on its own soil and fed on its very own powers, the powers of idealist philosophy. . . . "The best that we have from history," Goethe says, "is the enthusiasm that it stimulates." So immersion in the history of the idea of the republican constitution should not only be turned backward but should strengthen in us

the faith and confidence that the powers from which it originally grew will also point its way into the future, and that it will help it do its part in bringing about that future.[39]

He finished speaking and left the podium to thunderous applause. Aby Warburg, easily excitable by nature, who was of course among the audience, even claimed to have recognized the lecture as a "preface to the Magna Carta of the German Republic," and hence precisely "what this poor Germany of the present day, which is still unable to assuage its hunger for freedom" now needed. Once again he requested permission to produce a special edition.[40]

Only Toni Cassirer reserved the right to skepticism. "After the ceremony in Hamburg City Hall, I did not meet many who had been 'affected,'" she remembered, "and those who were convinced remained as always the ones who wanted to be convinced. Shaking up Germany in those days required other means than those which Ernst was used to applying and willing to apply."[41]

An assessment with which both Walter Benjamin and Martin Heidegger would definitely have agreed. That same evening the Cassirers boarded their night train for the Swiss mountains. This time for a well-deserved vacation.

BUILDING WORK

IN OCTOBER 1927, Heidegger was still awaiting a clear signal from the ministry in Berlin. *Being and Time* had attracted a huge amount of attention in the few months since publication, and was being celebrated as an event itself, but still he had not been called to accept the chair in Marburg vacated by Natorp. The redeeming letter finally arrived on October 19. Heidegger was then staying with his brother in Messkirch—sorting out the last of their mother's affairs after her death—while Elfride remained with the boys in the hut. For three years now the family had alternated between the flat in Marburg and the hut in Todtnauberg. The arrangement could not last, especially since their sons were by now of school age.

With his appointment as professor, completely new horizons opened up. "I could tell by your voice on the telephone the day before yesterday how happy you were. The minister's decision is a welcome sign of objectivity. The [education] ministry itself must feel liberated.... [Husserl], now that I am the successor to Natorp's chair, has quite another trump card in his hand.... The very great good fortune of the Heideggers seems still to be alive.... Now we will be able to breathe a little and allow ourselves some cheerfulness—but above all 'the house' is taking definite shape not only in the plans but in the possibility of its realization."[42] Möhrchen (baby carrot) Martin wrote this to his Seelchen (little soul) Elfride on October 21. If everything went according to plan, Marburg would be only a brief stop on their journey back to Freiburg, where Husserl wanted to retire the following year. Despite seeing the heretical independence of his master student all too clearly, Husserl wanted Heidegger and no other to be his successor.

AGE OF THE DEMON

HE HAD CHILDREN, he had written a book. . . . To complete the traditional trinity of a fulfilled existence (a requirement even for Heidegger), he needed only to build a house. Especially as he was just now, in his thirty-ninth year, really beginning to feel like an adult. Such a house, if it was really to be considered his own, could stand only in his home, and hence had to be built there. Dwelling comes before building, in the end, the homey relationship with the world before the accepted vision of the world, but thought precedes everything else! Here, too, after the intoxicating process of writing *Being and Time*, he felt new stirrings in the winter of 1927–1928: "The tensions of 'publication' had been followed by a rest—now I notice that it is over, and the demon is beginning to rummage and push me again," Heidegger wrote to his wife from Marburg on January 21, 1928.[43] Elfride and their sons were now lodging with a family of farmers near the hut. Going to school in Marburg, they had decided, was no longer worth it.

The stirring of this demon of thought within Heidegger, whenever it occurred, also drove him into new erotic adventures—or vice versa. A Greek in spirit, he saw Eros and thought as essentially one in terms of the history of philosophy, but also as sharing a common origin in an existential sense. So, unable to re-create the event that was Hannah Arendt, he once again made Elisabeth Blochmann the object of his ardor. By now she was living and working as a teacher in Berlin, but she repeatedly visited the Heideggers at the hut (and received return visits from Martin). Their correspondence became more intense.

While Heidegger the house-builder might have seen the warmth of the family as the firm foundation of his existence, a dramatic escape from the structure of the bourgeois marriage also remained for him a necessity. As he saw it, not just as a philosopher, a truly free existence would shape and be shaped by a dynamic of foundation and escape, and of finding and searching. The basis for this had been established with the Dasein analytic in *Being and Time*. Admittedly, the book as it had been published remained a fragment. Not even the first of its two parts had been completed. One rather glaring omission resulting was a clear answer to the question of what the titular connection between *Being* and *Time* might be. In essence, the published part of the work had not gone beyond a descriptive exposition of the being-in-the-world of the very being that could ask the question of Being: the human. But this "analysis of Dasein" was chiefly preparatory in nature. *Being and Time* was really *Hamlet* without the prince. The stage had been set, but the leading question itself had not appeared. The question that needed clarification was not "To be or not to be," but what was meant by the word "be."

To employ Heidegger's terminology, the "analysis of Dasein"—a descriptive "disclosure of the internal possibilities of the understanding of Being"—needed to be followed by a "metaphysics of Dasein."

At the center of this metaphysics would be two questions: (1) How does the human in general understand what we call Being? and (2) What is the relationship between that understanding and time?

In 1927 and 1928, as he yielded to fresh assaults from the demon, Heidegger's task was "with a view to solving the problem of Being and, guided by it, to demonstrate temporality as the fundamental constitution of Dasein."

Here again, the path of ontology (what is the meaning of "Being"?) must, as in all of Heidegger's explorations during this period, take what appears to be a detour through the concrete understanding of Being by questioning Dasein. Dasein could not ultimately be deduced from the nature of Being, but rather: Being could be deduced from the nature of questioning Dasein. And Dasein, on closer inspection, was profoundly conditioned by temporality.

AFTER BEING

DASEIN'S UNDERSTANDING OF BEING, however it may be defined in concrete terms, is undoubtedly this: It is in fact always *present*. It is already there, it is given and shows itself in its entirety as something already disclosed, independent of the various kinds of *Sein* that may enter a Dasein's defining field of vision (houses, fir trees, chairs, mushrooms, hammers, nails, bacteria, quantum particles . . .). So Being, unlike concrete entity (*Seiendes*), has at least one property: a *pretemporality* that must be explored in greater depth. In Kantian terms it has the character of an a priori: "Being is already understood in advance in all grasping of entity; the previous understanding of Being sheds light, so to speak, on all grasping of entity."[44]

This experience of pretemporality was already an important highway in ontological thought, at least for anyone concerned with gaining a clearer understanding of *Being* and *Time*. Because one distinction must be established by every human being, even by every child: there is a clear difference between entity (*Seiendes*) and Being (*Sein*); entity is everything that appears before us, everything found in the world as something concretely definable (houses, dogs, chairs, hammers, nails, quantum particles . . .)—so in the end, everything. In the background, however, there is also the apparently meaningful question: What distinguishes the Being of all entity? The ontological question that is the eternal mother of philosophy: What is this "Being" in itself? "Is" it, even? And if so, is it in the same way as entity or in an entirely different way? Heidegger calls this the question of "ontological difference." And the only obvious thing in relation to this difference is that Being always precedes entity, so it is in a *temporally* founded relationship of this fundamental difference. On this point Heidegger, in his role as a Dasein-centered ontologist, can now continue to ask: In which experiences does this difference appear in the most impressive form for Dasein?

Or to put it another way: In the end, inquiring into ontological difference itself—that is, the metaphysical question about the meaning of Being—makes Dasein what it essentially is: philosophizing. In a letter to

Elisabeth Blochmann, Heidegger wrote: "It is part of the essence of human Dasein that, insofar as it exists, it philosophizes. Being human *already means* philosophizing, and because that is the case, that is why the liberation of *authentic* and *explicit* philosophy is so difficult."[45]

Precisely because this world is always experienced as fundamentally disclosed, and because of the prior nature of Being, the question of the reasons for this disclosure does not arise for most people, or does not do so any longer. They live in an unquestioning disclosedness, and hence a disclosedness that is not disclosed to them. This could take the form of an accepted worldview or an assumed worldview, such as a religious, mythical, scientific, or dialectical materialist one. But above all they are trapped in the everyday worldview of so-called healthy common sense, in which as a rule there are subjects and objects, natural and cultural things, edible and inedible, useful and irrelevant, sacred and profane . . .

This background, which generally goes unquestioned, and in which the various images of the world (also known as "philosophies") are rooted, has to be separated from its implicit assumptions and explicitly questioned (as Ernst Cassirer did, for example). More than that, though, we need, like Heidegger, to be even more radical and investigate fully the ultimate background lying behind these various internal ones, to ask the fundamental ontological question: Why is there something like a prior disclosure of the world, on the basis of which sciences, images of the world, languages, and symbolic forms were able to take shape?

In concrete terms: Are all the reasons we give one another and ourselves for our everyday actions and knowledge, questions and answers, ultimately founded on another reason? That is the actual question of metaphysics, whose core is ontology, or the theory of Being.

The concept of the *ground* thus dominates all of Heidegger's lectures and works in the phase directly following *Being and Time*: these include the lecture "Metaphysical Foundations of Logic," delivered in Marburg in the summer term of 1928, and lectures such as "On the Essence of the Ground" of 1929, the talk "The Fundamental Concepts of Metaphysics" from the winter term 1929–1930, and indeed the interpretation that also appeared in 1929, *Kant and the Problem of Metaphysics*, whose four chapters all revolve around the problem of "laying the ground for metaphysics."

FOUNDATION AND ABYSS

THERE HAVE BEEN OF COURSE many potential candidates within philosophy for an ultimate metaphysical foundation; God, for instance, or Platonic ideas, eternal substances, fundamental laws of pure logic such as the law of identity (A=A), and certain other fundamental categories of thought abstracted from the structure of declarative propositions, as in the work of Aristotle and Kant. These candidates had to be eternal or even extratemporal: they had to be grasped as prior to and possibly even independent from humanity. And all of them, not only according to Heidegger, demonstrated at least one of two problems: either it was simply impossible to prove by means of finite human understanding and the limits of its experience that they existed (God, substance), or else the relationship between these supposed primordial grounds and the world in which a living Dasein was always present and capable of action would necessarily remain unclear. Finally, Immanuel Kant's supposed impulse that classical metaphysics and its ontology in particular were best left alone and that it would instead be better to investigate the categories of human understanding that were what made the world a world for us (objects conform to the categories of the understanding, rather than the other way around) assumes a separation as absolutely given. It assumes the separation between conscious subjects and the objects of knowledge. But according to Heidegger, the apparent absoluteness and givenness of that separation itself needed to be unmasked. Didn't the distinction between subject and object assume that very experience of primordial disclosure that it set out to explain with clearly established boundaries in the course of the Kantian project?

BACK TO THE ORIGIN

AS IN THE 1922 ESSAY on Aristotle that paved the way for his analysis of Dasein, Heidegger's 1928 ontological investigation—in the narrower sense—into logic and metaphysics was aimed at the *destruction* of the entirety of Western metaphysics. Because ontological questioning traditionally emerged from fundamentally false assumptions. Either it left open the issue of how finite beings subject to temporality could reach a definition of or even just know things or foundations that are infinite hence unbound to temporality, or else it proceeded on the basis of assumptions that had to be called into question at the very outset (the separation of subject and object, for example, or epistemology). So once again it was necessary to return to the origin of the ontological problem itself, to the question already posed by Parmenides about the meaning of being. But for Heidegger every worthwhile question of Dasein was ultimately based in the experience of a troubling being-called-into-question for Dasein.

To return to the origin of philosophizing, then, it wasn't a case of transporting oneself some twenty-five hundred years back in history, physically or culturally (which for beings as deeply embedded in history as ourselves is impossible). Rather, the specific experience of disturbance that forms the foundation of that question must be created. A metaphysics of the concept (or substance or logic or categories) makes way in Heidegger for a *meta-physics of experience*, the experience of Dasein, finite and aware of the fact.

The particular experience of disturbance that for wakeful Dasein lies at the root of the ontological question has everything, really everything, to do with the specific form of a constantly unfolding temporality in which human beings stand: precisely with the experience of *their* temporality, which is always also an experience of their finitude.

This experience was situationally bound to particular, exposed moments of existence in which the question of Being appeared, posed, and imposed itself in a particular way: we are not the ones, in Heidegger's view, who ask the questions. The questions ask themselves to us.

But what kinds of experiences are those? According to Heidegger, they are, once again, radical and existential experiences of groundlessness or even of the abyss. Near-death experiences in particular, or experiences of anxiety, or the tug of conscience.

What underlies our metaphysical questioning and hence metaphysics itself is not a foundation but an abyss. It is not solid ground, it is nothingness. Our essentially metaphysical existence is grounded on fundamental groundlessness! For precisely this reason it is truly possible and amenable to experience. It is ontologically abysmal, like the existence of each individual Dasein.

In this sense the ideological and philosophical structures that human beings construct for themselves to cling to as a guide in Dasein—to equip themselves for this world, and make it as bearable as possible—distract from the *essence* of existence. They are part of seeming, not of being. Only the gaze into the abyss produces authenticity.

Real experience of nothingness is the true condition of the possibility of all meaning of Dasein. This "nothingness" "is" not in the actual sense any more than "Being" is. Both "are" not for Heidegger, rather "it gives" them (*es gibt sie*). Gives them as *experiences* for finite, temporal existences.

Anyone who philosophizes, of course, inevitably—and Heidegger would have been the first to admit this—"runs up against the limits of language." However, it is in precisely this way that Dasein produces what is commonly called meaning: as the experience of a full, freely self-grounding, deciding life.

Would Wittgenstein have contradicted him in this respect? In the Vienna Circle, at any rate, he expressly did not. And was not Benjamin, at the same time, singing a metropolitan hymn to chance, chance as a producer of meaning, which waits upon the ground of all groundlessness for the way to open up into a different, redemptive way of being?

HOMECOMING

SO HEIDEGGER WAS MAKING PROGRESS. He was striding forward, at any rate, not least in his professional life. In the spring of 1928 the last institutional bastions of resistance to his Freiburg professorship had been overcome. Only a few days after his successful appointment on April 16, 1928, a plot of land at 23 Rötebuck in Freiburg-Zähringen was purchased for the construction of his family's house. The building was due to be completed in the winter term of 1928–1929, to coincide with Heidegger's succeeding Husserl. Elfride was responsible for the design, site management, and interior decoration, as she had been with the construction of the hut in 1921. Heidegger brimmed with anticipation and gratitude, even though the plain contradiction between his program of total metaphysical "de-housing" and the complete embourgeoisement of his own existence plainly gave him pause: "In recent days I have been thinking a great deal about 'our house'—that in our hearts we are also renewing and enriching the old building of our love. And I thank you warmly for giving me the whole strength of your trust. I know that I am only slowly really learning how to live, and living according to what my inner voice always unambiguously says to me. Admittedly we must never rely on external help and yet I believe that our house, because it is by no means external—particularly since it arose out of your maternal desire—will reinfuse our community and our community with the children. Our journey is only beginning," as Heidegger wrote from the hut on September 27, 1928, to Elfride the master-builder.[46] At least by the family's own standards, the result could be described as a success: part hut, part family home. Half Black Forest, half suburbs, wood paneling within, shingles without. The largest room was, of course, Martin's study.

DIZZY HEIGHTS

HEIDEGGER FELT THAT BEING ROOTED in Freiburg would, as both starting point and foundation, propel to new heights and down to new depths. He said as much to Elisabeth Blochmann during the summer he spent in the hut while the house was under construction: "Now I am gradually adapting to Freiburg, but during these days of relaxation I perceive above all a deepening of tasks or a slow advance into something which was still inaccessible to me during my first time in Freiburg. . . . The last course in Marburg this summer was a new path, or rather a description of the paths which for a long time I was only allowed to glimpse. . . . The house was roofed before a single drop of rain had fallen."[47]

Where "the liberation of philosophy" from the structures of pure scholarship was concerned, not only were new paths necessary to access the areas now being explored, but a different kind of walking was required. In fact, a thinker such as Heidegger could no longer proceed by setting an example. Instead he had to be an authentic existential guide for his audience, someone who could ensure that the absolutely essential and authentically human experiences that he proclaimed were personally available to others. In other words, Heidegger's declaration that the abyss and nothingness were the only conditions under which true philosophizing was possible also imposed a new understanding of the philosopher's role as a teacher: one definitively relocated from instruction to performance, from tutoring to proselytizing. The academic teacher had to become a master, the seminar leader an existential guide—and one capable of dragging others with him into the void. Onward, forward, beyond all false discursive solutions and distorting attempts at communication, into the radical depths of authenticity. The critical thing was not to ossify into pure pedagogy, into pure discursiveness.

For Heidegger, charismatic as he was and always had been, this was perhaps the easiest part of the exercise, though the riskiest. Unlike the patriotic defender of the constitution, Ernst Cassirer, this prophet of the liberating plunge, had in that summer of 1928 everything he needed to "shake up Germany." The battlefield had been prepared, the position adopted, the house inhabited—and the opportunity itself was irresistible. "In March," he wrote to Elisabeth Blochmann two days before Christmas 1928, when he was already in the new house, "I have been invited to the Davos University Conferences and have already agreed, not least because of the prospect of high-altitude outings."

VIII.

TIME

1929

Heidegger and Cassirer at the summit, Benjamin looks into the abyss, and Wittgenstein discovers new paths.

SLALOMING

HAVING CLIMBED TO THE SUMMIT, Heidegger was then "a little afraid of what was to come." Twenty-seven hundred meters above sea level was higher than he had ever been before. The air was thin up there. Did he have the skill, and would the equipment he had brought from Freiburg be able to withstand the challenge? Here, now, he would have to prove himself. It was too late at any rate for self-doubt and hesitation. *Hic Davos! Hic salta!*

Things went surprisingly well. Even after the first few turns it was clear to Heidegger that he was in fact "far superior" to all the others—even those with more experience on these slopes. The Parsenn descent, some 800 meters into the valley below, as he wrote to Elfride, on March 21, 1929—from the middle of the Davos conference—was the highlight of his stay in the Swiss Alps so far. Cassirer couldn't come on the hiking tour. His colleague, Heidegger reported, "fell ill after the first lecture, he came down with a cold." The Kurator of Frankfurt University, Kurt Riezler, however, joined the climb. The same Riezler whom Ernst Cassirer had tried to headhunt from Hamburg less than twelve months previously with carte blanche to redesign the philosophy department in Frankfurt. The chair in question had been occupied after Cassirer's resignation by Max Scheler, whose *Position of Man in the Cosmos* was published in 1928, less than a year after

Cassirer's *Individual and the Cosmos in Renaissance Philosophy* and before the third volume of his *Philosophy of Symbolic Forms*. Scheler had died unexpectedly in May 1928.

AMONG PEOPLE

SO WHILE CASSIRER SAT with his wife, Toni, swaddled in warm camelhair blankets, on the balcony of his hotel room, hoping like Hans Castorp in *The Magic Mountain* that he would soon be cured, Heidegger spent every free minute with his new Alpinist friend Riezler. It was a chance to make academic advances, and not just in passing: "I am with Riezler a lot, he told me he very much hoped that I would be receiving a call to Frankfurt—it was just a matter of time." Everything else had for Heidegger been more or less disappointing—not least Davos itself: "It is dreadful: boundlessly kitsch architectures, absolutely random confusion of pensions and hotels. And then the invalids."[1]

Reading *The Magic Mountain* in Marburg with Hannah Arendt, he had formed a rather more attractive image of the town. In terms of content, too, the course of the conference and its participants had hitherto left him cold. Admittedly, he considered his two lectures on Kant's *Critique of Pure Reason*—each of which he had delivered in a free slaloming style, "for over 1½ hours without notes"—to have been "a great success," particularly since he had had the impression that "the young people feel that the roots of my work lie in a place that today's city people no longer have—indeed no longer even understand."

But he was also horrified to note "how torn, how insecure and deprived of instinct, the young people are. And they cannot find their way back to the simplicity of Dasein."[2] Cassirer, he added in a letter of March 23, "will try to get up today, so that the 'working group' will not take place until Monday or Tuesday."

The disoriented "young people" who attended Heidegger's and Cassirer's lectures in Davos included a considerable number of the future greats of global postwar philosophy, such as Emmanuel Levinas, Norbert Elias, Joachim Ritter, and the no longer quite so young Rudolf Carnap. Like almost all of the rising generation of German and French philosophers, Carnap was particularly impressed by Heidegger: "University Conferences. Cassirer speaks well but somewhat pastorally. . . . Heidegger serious and sober, very attractive in a human way," he recorded in his diary on March 18. Then, on March 30: "Went for a walk with H. His position: against idealism, particularly in national education. The new 'question of existence.' Need of redemption."[3]

With Cassirer now on the way to recovery, Carnap did his rounds of the conference hotel. The discussion focused mostly on which academic posts would be vacated in the near future. Cassirer had been engaged in a long and intense exchange of research with Carnap's Viennese mentor, Moritz Schlick: networking, bowing and scraping, forming and nurturing new contacts, collecting and recording impressions. Then as now, this business was at least as important for the career of an academic philosopher as thinking itself. Lucky are those who can maintain their balance on that waxed and polished parquet. That was how Heidegger saw it, too: "I am very pleased, even though there is not in essence very much for me to learn, to be a part of something of this kind—agility, dealing with people and having a certain outward confidence."[4]

It may be that those days in the feudal Belvédère were the first that Heidegger had ever spent in a grand hotel. But for this milieu, extremely sensitive to etiquette, only those who had fully grasped and mastered its rules could afford to break with convention. This Heidegger also learned quickly: "Tired and satisfied, full of the sun and freedom of the mountains, still with the rhythms of those sweeping descents in our bodies, we always turned up in the evening in our skiing outfits among the elegance of the evening wear."[5]

Toni Cassirer was appropriately irritated, all the more so because she enjoyed what was for her the distinctly dubious privilege of being right next to Heidegger in the seating arrangement imposed in the grand dining room. "The problem I encountered," she remembered, "was how I would spend the next fourteen days as neighbor of this curious enemy if I acknowledged him as such." Since her husband was ill in bed for practically the whole of the first week, that meant that twice a day she "sat with that strange character who had undertaken to drag Cohen's legacy through the mud and, if possible, to destroy Ernst."[6]

Toni Cassirer's memories of Davos (written in 1948, when she was in exile in New York, and thus likely embellished) are the only ones we have that really speak of any kind of noticeable "enmity" or visible "destructiveness." Other available testimonies, especially those of participants, are on the contrary united in their depiction of a cooperative, benign, and open atmosphere. And yet from the beginning, as all the participants knew, a shadow lay over the conference, and particularly over the upcoming debate between Cassirer and Heidegger.

ON THE EVE

ONLY A MONTH BEFORE, on February 23, 1929, as part of an event for the Combat League for German Youth, the Viennese sociologist Othmar Spann had delivered a lecture on "The Cultural Crisis of the Present Day" at Munich University. In it he expressed regret at the fact that "the German people had to be reminded of their own Kantian philosophy by foreigners." Among these "foreigners" he included philosophers of the rank of Hermann Cohen and Ernst Cassirer. In Spann's words, "The explanation of Kantian philosophy by Cohen, Cassirer, and others is . . . very lacking," since "the true Kant, who was in fact a metaphysician, was thus not presented to the German people."[7]

"Professor Spann's lecture," the correspondent of the *Frankfurter Zeitung* reported on February 25, "was essentially a polemic . . . against democracy. . . . He spoke in fleeting but clear reference to the Prussian culture minister about the stifling of the intellectual freedom of German students, scholars and artists, and slogans about individualistic democracy and class struggle."[8]

Spann's appearance in Munich became a scandal for a number of reasons. First, the Combat League for German Youth was an organization founded by Alfred Rosenberg, the future Nazi ideologue, with the aim of representing and disseminating the political goals of the National Socialist Party. In Munich, as elsewhere, university guidelines prohibited the use of the institution's space for political events. Before Spann stepped up to the podium, Adolf Hitler had entered the auditorium to a "noisy ovation" from his many "swastika-wearing followers," and at the end of the lecture the two exchanged "a handshake and deep bows."[9]

The occasion of Spann's lecture represented a spectacular infringement of university regulations. But the substance of it fell explicitly within a line of thought, promulgated by nationalist-leaning Kant scholars such as Bruno Bauch, that held there were two traditions of Kant interpretation, one genuinely German and one Jewish, the latter characterized by Cohen and the neo-Kantian school at Marburg. In the wake of this talk, philosophical circles had been in uproar. Cassirer threatened privately to renounce his membership in the Kant Society if Bauch did not immediately resign his presidency, which he subsequently did. This was the backdrop for the toleration by Munich University of a völkisch-nationalistic, rabble-rousing attitude, applauded by Adolf Hitler, itself only four weeks before an international conference—guided by the Kantian question "What is a human being?"—at which Heidegger would present his own distinctly metaphysical reading of Kant's major work. Whether it suited the protagonists or not, the Davos conference now held a distinctly political charge.

RELAX!

DURING HER HOURS WITH HEIDEGGER, Toni did everything she could to soften the brittle atmosphere:

> Then it occurred to me to outwit the sly fox—because that was his reputation. I began a naive conversation with him, as if I didn't know the slightest thing about his philosophical or his personal antipathies. I asked him about all kinds of mutual acquaintances, above all his knowledge of Cohen as a person, anticipating even with the tone of my question what was going to be an obvious answer. Without his asking, I told him what Ernst's relationship with Cohen was like; I talked to him about the shameful treatment that this eminent scholar had experienced as a Jew; I told him that no member of the faculty had attended his funeral in Berlin. I told him, certain this time of his acquiescence, all kinds of important details about Ernst's life, and had the satisfaction of seeing that hard crust dissolving like a soft roll in warm milk. When Ernst rose from his sickbed, it was difficult for Heidegger, who now knew so many personal things about him, to maintain his planned attitude of hostility. Admittedly, Ernst, with the kindness and respect that he showed him, did not make it easy for him to launch a frontal attack.[10]

Even in advance, Heidegger, too, was plagued by fears that the whole thing might become "a sensation," in which "I was the center of attention more than I would personally have wished." Particularly since Cassirer proved determined—probably to avoid a direct argument about Kant—to direct his lectures primarily at Heidegger's *Being and Time.* While Heidegger, precisely out of fear of being too much the center of attention, decided to devote himself, given his fundamental ontological interests, entirely to Kant's *Critique of Pure Reason.* The tactical dance had thus begun long before the actual debate. And Heidegger seemed to have taken the lead: with Kant as his subject he would meet Cassirer on his own turf, where he had more, or indeed everything, to gain. Although it was by no means openly hostile, the meeting of the two at ten in the morning on March 26, 1929, was decidedly tense, as eyewitness Raymond Klibansky recalled. In front of the next generation of philosophers of both Germany and Switzerland, they were about to begin a debate that "in a sense concerned the future of German philosophy."[11]

VERBAL STORMS:
THE DAVOS DEBATE

CASSIRER BEGAN, determined to sweep the subject of Neo-Kantianism—an explosive issue, once again—out of the way. *"What does Heidegger in fact understand by Neo-Kantianism? . . . Neo-Kantianism is the whipping-boy of newer philosophy. I feel a lack of existing neo-Kantians."*[12]

Cassirer had scored a point. Particularly since Neo-Kantianism had in any case never been a *"dogmatic doctrinal system, but rather a direction taken in posing questions."* And, he continued, *"I must admit that I am surprised to have found a Neo-Kantian here in Heidegger, which I would not have expected.*" A dexterous start. First: I'm not a Neo-Kantian! Second: If I am, Heidegger is too!

Now Heidegger, who begins by naming some names: *"Cohen, Windelband, Rickert . . ."* He was not out for reconciliation, that much was already clear. That said, Cohen was Cassirer's thesis supervisor, and Rickert was Heidegger's. So in fact the two were cut from the same cloth. But what cloth might that have been? Heidegger went on. Neo-Kantianism was at root more of an embarrassment than an autonomous direction of research. And around 1850 that embarrassment was the following: *"What remains of philosophy if the totality of beings has been divided among the sciences? All that remains is knowledge of science, not of entity."* That hit home. And introduced the counterattack: philosophy as the pure maid of the sciences? Wasn't that exactly what Cassirer was striving for with his "philosophy of symbolic forms": knowing the systems of knowledge according to its internal structure? Epistemological theory rather than ontology? On it went, attack met with attack, now with Kant enlisted as token witness: *"Kant sought not to provide a theory of the natural sciences, but to demonstrate the problems of metaphysics, and indeed of ontology."* In other words: Kant was not a Neo-Kantian, but a fundamental ontologist. Like me: Heidegger.

Cassirer was now clearly on the defensive. Distance himself from Cohen? Out of the question in the present circumstances. Better to attack Heidegger with Kant! His open flank was ethics. They were at least central for Kant, but a void for Heidegger. Cassirer: *"If we consider Kant's work overall, major problems arise. One problem is that of freedom. That has always been the actual main problem for me: How is freedom possible? Kant says the question cannot be grasped, we grasp only the ungraspability of freedom."*

The moral: Kant was a metaphysician, not at the service of ontology, however, but at the service of ethics! He was concerned with finite, active humans, not with Being. But precisely in Kantian ethics—and now Cassirer prepared to deliver a powerful blow—a breakthrough, an incursion, into metaphysics occurred: *"The categorical imperative must be constituted in such a way that the law thus established applies not only to human beings but to all rational beings. Here there is suddenly this curious transition. . . . Morality as such leads beyond the world of phenomena. That is the decisive metaphysical aspect, that the breakthrough occurs at this point."*

A breakthrough from the sphere of the finite into the infinite, from immanence into transcendence. Here was something about which Heidegger had nothing whatsoever to say. And it implicated the problem with his whole design of *Being and Time*, his whole analysis of Dasein, his fundamental ontology. Or, as in a sequence of questions: *"Heidegger has stressed that our cognitive power is finite. It is relative and it is bound. But then the question arises: How does such a finite being come by knowledge, reason, truth? . . . How does this finite being reach a definition of objects which are not as such bound to finitude?"*

That was the fundamental question of metaphysics. That was Kant's real question. And Cassirer's, too. But was it also Heidegger's? Cassirer now went all in: *"Does Heidegger want to give up all of this objectivity? Does he want to withdraw entirely to the finite being, or if not, where does he see the breakthrough into that sphere as taking place?"*

Good questions. Body blows. Heidegger was now cornered. He needed to call upon Kant. Or at least upon himself. Ethics were not exactly his specialty, but needs must: *"Cassirer, then, wants to show that finitude becomes transcendent in the ethical writings. There is something in the categorical imperative that goes beyond finite being. But precisely the concept of the imperative as such shows the inner reference to a finite being."*

True! A child could have understood it: God needs no imperatives, only finite rational beings do. And God doesn't need ontology, so this is also essentially, Heidegger added, an *"Index of finitude."* This, then, was not a breakthrough, quite the contrary. Now Heidegger came back powered by Kant: *"This going out to a higher being is also only a going up to a finite being, one that is created (angel)."*

Davos, 1929, and the two most important philosophers of the modern age are debating categorical imperatives for angels on a public stage? Yes indeed. But Heidegger's actual point is: *"This transcendence, too, still remains within creation and finitude."*

Therefore Kant's transcendence is only an immanent one, which retreats to finitude, is limited by it, and is indeed only made possible by it! Heidegger is now heading upstream: if we wish to understand Kant, metaphysics, philosophizing, at all, the direction of the questioning must be radically reversed: the actual question is not how, from the transcendence of entity, and thus from its temporary disclosure to us as human beings, one reaches the finitude of Dasein as the actual origin of the whole. That leads, of course, directly to the question of the Being of Dasein. The real question is: *"What is the inner structure of Dasein itself; is it finite or infinite?"* Everyone in the auditorium knows Heidegger's reply to that: The inner structure of Dasein is radically finite, and its possibilities are determined from within by temporality. That is the core of *Being and Time.*

No reply from Cassirer. So Heidegger continues: *"Now to Cassirer's question about universally valid eternal truths. If I say: Truth is relative to Dasein, that proposition . . . is a metaphysical one: truth can only be as truth and as truth has only one meaning, if Dasein exists. If Dasein does not exist, there is no truth, there is nothing at all. But it is only with the existence of something like Dasein that truth enters Dasein itself."* What is important for Heidegger: it is not, for example, that the truth of individual statements is relative to what a particular person may think; rather, the concept, the idea of truth itself, is essentially related to the finitude of *Being*, indeed it finds its true origin in its finitude. For God there is no question of truth, any more than there is for elephants or dogs. The question of truth arises only for Dasein. Metaphysics, developed from Dasein.

This was a tough one to counter. What about the supposed eternity of the known? Heidegger went on digging: *"I ask the counter-question. . . . How do we know of this eternity? . . . Is this eternity not only what is possible on the grounds of an inner transcendence of time itself?"* Inner transcendence of time itself? What did Heidegger mean by that? Simply put: Time, as something fluid, constantly refers beyond itself, and that is precisely what its essence is: *"An inner transcendence lies within the essence of time; that time is not only what makes transcendence possible, but that time itself has a horizonal character; that in future, recollected behavior I always have at the same time a horizon of present, futurity, and been-ness in general; that a . . . definition of time is found here, within which something like the permanence of the substance is constituted for the very first time."*

Not all that complicated, in essence: for Heidegger, time is not something external or a containing vessel but a process that underlies all experience. Yet just because this process essentially denies with its essence the dynamic by which it is actually constituted—its constant state of flux— Dasein is led to think that there is something like permanent stability, indeed eternality. Eternal substances are therefore a metaphysical illusion, a deception from the spirit of Dasein. In truth, only the process itself is real. And that process is not a thing, it is not eternal, but "given." And it "gives" in turn. Ultimately it "gives" everything that in its course becomes and passes. Being *and* time.

Bergson and Proust saw things similarly, incidentally. And Benjamin. And Husserl. And William James. And his brother, Henry. And Alfred North Whitehead. And Virginia Woolf. And James Joyce. And Salvador Dalí. And Charlie Chaplin . . . The idea defines the spirit of the 1920s. It is itself a child of the time. (What else could it be?) And for that very reason the important thing is to draw the correct metaphysical conclusions from it in a fully radical fashion. Heidegger is now in his element. Not another word about Kant. Heidegger is concerned with one thing only: *"To stress the temporality of Dasein with regard to the possibility of the understanding of Being. And all problems are oriented with respect to this. In one direction, the analysis of death has the function of stressing the radical futurity of Dasein. . . . The analysis of anxiety . . . has the sole function of preparing for the question: On the grounds of which metaphysical sense of Dasein itself is it possible that the human being in general can be placed before something like Nothingness? . . . It is only possible for me to understand Being if I understand Nothingness or anxiety. . . . And only in the unity of the understanding of Being and Nothingness does the question of the origin arise of Why. Why can humanity ask about Why, and why must they ask?"*

That is what metaphysics is concerned with. The experience of Being is bound up with the experience of the Nothing. It gives the groundless ground of all questioning. It shapes human beings into human beings, and brings them into actual existence for the first time! Human beings are the only creatures open to the experience of the Nothing at the ground of being. An eternally questioning origin, then. Infinite only in its ultimately unceasing questioning, but never in its cognitions.

Still no response from Cassirer. So on Heidegger went. And on. He now launched into a stormy counterattack: *"Cassirer says: We do not grasp freedom, but only the ungraspability of freedom. . . . It does not follow from this, however, that to a certain extent the problem of the irrational pauses here. Rather, because freedom is not an object of theoretical apprehending but is instead an object of philosophizing, this can mean nothing other than the fact that freedom only is and only can be in the liberation. The only appropriate relation to freedom in humanity is the self-liberation of freedom in humanity."*

Freedom is a factual truth. And hence, by its essence, bound not to any given timeless law but to the groundless decision made in the moment, to make it work for ourselves. Is that still Kant? Kant reborn? Essentially German and metaphysical, the true Kantian Kant.

A student whose name has not been passed down to us took pity and brought Cassirer back into the ring. His questions were very simple. And aimed directly at the center.

Questions for Cassirer

1. *What path do human beings have to infinitude? And can they participate in infinitude?*

2. *To what extent is the task of philosophy to be able to become free from anxiety? Or is its task not to surrender human beings, even radically, to anxiety?*

Everyone in the auditorium, even Cassirer, sensed it was now time to break cover. He didn't hesitate to give all he had. What path did human beings have to infinitude? *"Solely through the medium of form. This is the function of form, that while humans change the form of their Dasein, that is, while they must now transpose everything in them that is lived experience into some objective shape in which they are objectified in such a way, to be sure, that they do not thereby become radically free from the finitude of the point of departure (for this is still linked to their particular finitude). Rather, while it arises from finitude, it leads finitude out into something new. And that is immanent infinitude."*

This is the metaphysical core of his philosophy of symbolic forms: the embodiments of our own experiences in symbolic forms create an autonomous realm of their own, which transcends the boundaries of their own finitude and possibly even finitude itself. Like the realm of logic, for example, or mathematics . . . systems of symbolic form, created by humans as cultured beings, but in their laws and their validity presumably not limited to it. Ergo: *"They [human beings] possess their infinitude solely in this form. 'From the chalice of this spiritual realm, infinitude flows to them.' The spiritual realm is not a metaphysical spiritual realm; the true spiritual realm is just the spiritual world created by human beings themselves. That they could create it is the seal of their infinitude."*

Once again, as ever in a time of emergency, the same combination: Kant—Goethe, Schiller, Goethe—Kant. Is that enough? It didn't look particularly radical, at any rate. And in 1929 it looked even a bit stale. But it was certainly one thing: idealism embodied, "typically" German in character (insofar as that term means anything at all). It might also be true. Cassirer believed it was. He faced the music. Here he stood. He could not do otherwise.

Now to anxiety—and to philosophy: what was his position? Cassirer summoned his strength and stood a little straighter: *"That is a very radical question, which can be answered only with a kind of confession. Philosophy must allow humans to become sufficiently free, to the extent that they can just become free. While it does that, I believe, it frees human beings—in a certain radical sense, to be sure—from anxiety as a mere disposition. I believe, even according to Heidegger's disquisitions earlier today, that freedom can properly be found only along the path of progressive liberation, which indeed is also an infinite process for him. . . . I would like the sense, the goal, in fact the freeing, to be taken in this sense: 'Anxiety throws the earthly from you.' That is the position of idealism, to which I have always pledged myself."*

Pause for breath. Powerful emotion. Tense expectation. How would

Heidegger react? Where did he see philosophy's actual task as lying? Where was the actual liberation, the breakthrough? Nothing, that much was clear to everybody, could be considered certain and lasting in his view. Not even questioning itself. Rather, according to Heidegger, humans were, *"in an ultimate sense, accidental . . . so accidental that the highest form of the existence of Dasein can only be traced back to very few and rare glimpses of Dasein's duration between life and death, that humans exist only in very few glimpses of the summit of their own possibility, but otherwise move in the midst of their entity."*

Such moments are the ones that count, not least and in fact particularly in philosophizing. For that reason, Heidegger continues, *"the question of the essence of human beings . . . makes sense and can be justified only insofar as it derives its motivations from philosophy's central set of problems, which leads human beings back beyond themselves and into the totality of beings in order to make manifest to them there, with all their freedom, the Nothingness of their Dasein. This Nothingness is not cause for pessimism and melancholy. Instead, it is the occasion for understanding that authentic activity happens only where there is opposition and that philosophy has the task of throwing human beings back, so to speak, into the harshness of their fate from the shallow aspect of human beings who use only the work of the spirit."*

Theses like fists. Silence. How could all that be summarized? Which of the two directions should judgment take?

What the philosopher Cassirer wanted: Cast off your anxiety as creative cultural beings, liberate yourself from your original constraints and limitations.

What the philosopher Heidegger wanted: Cast off culture as a rotten aspect of your essence, and sink as the groundlessly thrown beings that you are, each in your own way, back into the truly liberating origin of your existence: the Nothing and anxiety!

Davos, the debate of the century, the monad of a decade. Stretched to bursting from within, on March 26, 1929, it gave birth to two radically different answers to the same eternal question: Where can we find the essence of philosophizing? Or indeed: What is a human being?

Even Cassirer, chronically well disposed, now saw no chance of agreement: *"We have reached a position where little is to be accomplished through mere logical arguments."* What Heidegger had known from the outset. At root it is not about arguments but about the courage to leap. But nothing hinders the necessary courage more than tepid deliberation and yearning for consensus: *"Mere mediation will never contribute anything productive."* Now he turned away from Cassirer, and delivered his conclusion to the students in the room: *"The important thing is that you take one thing with you from our debate: Do not orient yourselves to the variety of positions of philosophizing human beings, and do not occupy yourself with Cassirer and Heidegger. Rather, you have reached the point where you have felt that we are once more on the way toward getting down to business with the central question of metaphysics."*

If they probably hadn't fully understood everything, hopefully they had sensed it. It. The abyss. The first necessary step on the way into total authenticity! Was that the case?

Yes, they sensed it. They took the first precipitous step. Deep within. Most of them, at least. Heidegger left the hall certain of his victory.

LICKING WOUNDS

IT WAS ELFRIDE who would find out first: "I have just had a two-hour debate with Cassirer, which went very well and apart from its content made a big impression on the students."[13] In time Heidegger's judgment grew a little more sophisticated, as his report to Elisabeth Blochmann reveals: "Cassirer was extremely elegant and almost too obliging in the discussion. So I encountered too little resistance, which kept the problems from being given the necessary focus in their formulation. Essentially the questions were far too difficult for a public discussion. The only essential thing is that the form and guidance of the discussion could work through mere example."[14] Once again it becomes apparent: guidance was Heidegger's new form of argument. That was a core insight of the days in Davos. At least for him.

It had not in fact come to a real battle, or even to real combat. The gloves had been kept on, the head guard, too. The correspondent of the *Neue Zürcher Zeitung*, sounding a bit bored, reported with a hint of disappointment: "Rather than seeing two worlds collide, at best we enjoyed the spectacle of a very nice person and a very violent person, who was still trying terribly hard to be nice, delivering monologues. In spite of this all members of the audience seemed to be very gripped, and congratulated one another for having been there."[15]

Still, the young guard of students seemed to find the dispute exciting enough to rerun it as a satirical sketch during the closing evening on the peak at Davos. Emmanuel Levinas, with white ashes on his head, took the role of Cassirer. To lend theatrical expression to the complete outdatedness of Cassirer's idealistic sense of culture, he let ash trickle from his trouser pockets throughout the reenactment, while stammering: "Humboldt, culture, culture, Humboldt . . ." (If there are actions that deserve lifelong shame, in Levinas's case this was surely one of them.) Only two months later, in June 1929, Heidegger published *Kant and the Problem of Metaphysics*[16]—an elaboration of the theses, delivered in book form. In 1932, Cassirer would return in written form to Heidegger's Kant interpretation, but otherwise he handed down no further statement concerning the debate. Perhaps he simply didn't consider the event important enough. Or else, years later, he had a painful sense that it was too important. At any rate, he remained silent about it for the rest of his life. After the debate he left Davos with a group of students for a day trip to the Nietzsche House in Sils-Maria. Heidegger didn't join them. He preferred to continue hurtling down the snow-covered slopes.

SPRING AWAKENINGS

IN LATE MARCH 1929, when Martin Heidegger delivered a second Kant lecture in the Grand Hôtel Belvédère, and Ernst Cassirer, still weak from what appears to have been a bad case of flu, rose once more from his sickbed, Benjamin was hunting for a capable Hebrew teacher. "I will write to Dr. Magnes daily, as soon as the lessons—daily ones—have begun," he promised in a letter of March 23 to Gerhard Scholem, who had now been waiting impatiently in Jerusalem for news on the subject for some time. That spring wasn't trouble-free, but problems were distinctly thinner on the ground than usual. Because in the grand scheme of Benjamin's fiasco-strewn career, the previous twelve months were the most successful of his adult life: the book on tragedy and *One-Way Street* actually materialized late in 1928, winning an intense and even largely positive critical reception. He was praised to the skies in *Literarische Welt* and the *Frankfurter Zeitung*, his home ground. But he also found admirers in the *Vossische Zeitung* and as far away as Austria and Switzerland. No less a figure than Hermann Hesse contacted Rowohlt unprompted to express spontaneous enthusiasm for *One-Way Street*. A Berlin bookshop near Potsdamer Brücke decorated its entire window with Benjamin's collected writings—along with a bust of his head made by Jula Cohn. Even though sales of each book barely exceeded a thousand copies, within a year of publication Benjamin had gained widespread recognition as an author of considerable originality.

THE THREE-HUNDRED-PENNY OPERA

HE WAS ALSO ENJOYING considerable stability in his role as critic. Both the *Literarische Welt*, run by Willy Haas, and the arts section of the *Frankfurter Zeitung* kept him firmly on their roster. Indeed, if we look a little closer, Benjamin was now a fixture, if not a major influencer, of an arts-page clique that happily took the liberty of reviewing one another's books in the relevant media. Kracauer reviewed Benjamin, Benjamin reviewed Bloch, Bloch reviewed Benjamin . . . Adorno, too, still going by the moniker of "Wiesengrund," was a rather established member of the circle.

For the first time in his life, Benjamin, now also a contributor to the radio schedule of Hessischer Rundfunk, had a professional network and a measure of financial stability. He no longer seemed desperate, but could confidently turn down work every now and then; he didn't have to beg for review copies time and again, they were delivered free to his door. These days he even felt established enough to give starving friends like Alfred Cohn (Jula Cohn's brother) a helping hand to get them into the editorial offices—but warning them all along about the indisputable harshness of that way of life: "Even earning only three hundred marks a month with literature is impossible before you've endured several years of waiting, and even then it's never a guaranteed minimum."[17]

Benjamin knew what he was talking about. But at last, everything seemed to be going his way. Rowohlt wanted to collect the best of his reviews and publish them as a single volume. And there was the essay about *Elective Affinities*. Kracauer would soon become Berlin correspondent for the *Frankfurter Zeitung*. Adorno and Bloch also spent more and more time in the capital, where Benjamin had been welcomed into the exclusive circle around Bertolt Brecht and Helene Weigel.

Brecht's dialectical theater finally enjoyed its breakthrough with the premiere of *The Threepenny Opera* at the Berlin Ensemble in the autumn of 1928. Enormous hopes in Germany rested on the shoulders of this brilliant thirty-one-year-old dramatist, not least social-revolutionary ones. Left-wing parties had performed very strongly in the Reichstag elections of May 1928, while the National Socialist Party had dropped to a 2.59 percent share of the vote. Something was under way here, as the communist camp—essentially living in a state of revolutionary eschatological expectation—clearly thought it discerned.

During those months Benjamin increasingly felt that he was part of the movement. Something was stirring in him; his creative demon was guiding him increasingly toward the idea of class struggle. His work on the Paris arcades, originally conceived as a small study, had acquired a life of its own, and dominated the whole of his literary output: "Work on the Paris Arcades has assumed an increasingly enigmatic, urgent face, and is wailing through my nights like a small beast, if I haven't watered it from the remotest springs during the day. God knows what it will do if I let it off the leash one day," he established as early as May 1928.[18] A year later nothing had changed. Extensive research on the Arcades Project in the Berlin State Library took up almost all of his time. All other articles and commissioned pieces of writing were subordinated to it, and at best fell under the category of quasi-original side projects.

This remained true in March 1929, when Benjamin was working on two major essays for *Literarische Welt*. One was devoted to Proust's oeuvre, and titled "On the Image of Proust,"[19] and the other to the development of contemporary French Surrealism since 1919, and titled "Surrealism: The Last Snapshot of the European Intelligentsia."[20] Every line of both indicates the consistency with which Benjamin's thought (and that of the authors he engages with) took as its point of departure the constantly accelerating experiences of the metropolis that a denizen of the countryside simply cannot know or comprehend.

That spring, both essays blossomed into classic Benjaminiana. That is, once again Benjamin interpreted the authors he chose by the light of his own current insights into life, and hence his own research interests.

And what question motivated those interests in 1929? The question of the nature of time and, in that context, a possible breakthrough from finitude into eternity. The question of bourgeois decadence and its fate at a time of crucial events and decisions. The question of freedom and, in parallel with that, the possibilities of true (self-)knowledge in the real conditions of contemporary urban existence.

THE DOORS

PRECISELY THE RANGE OF SUBJECTS discussed in Davos, then, but imbued with the texture, and through the medium, of French literature, which—according to Benjamin—granted a German critic particular insights precisely because of his cultural semi-detachment from it. Because where Proust and above all Surrealism were concerned, "the German observer is . . . not at the source. That is his good fortune. He is standing in the valley. He can gauge the energies of the movement. For him, long familiar with the crisis in the intelligentsia or, more precisely, the humanistic question of freedom, as a German who knows the frantic will that has awoken within it to emerge from the stage of eternal discussions and reach a decision at any price. And as someone who has had personal experience of his extremely exposed position between anarchist rebellion and revolutionary discipline, he would have no excuse if even at the most superficial examination he saw it as an 'artistic,' 'poetic' movement."

In this passage Benjamin is accusing primarily himself. This had been his view of both the Surrealists and the Dadaists in the early 1920s. In the shadow of the book on tragedy, he understood them as the degenerative artistic phenomena of a lost and decadent age. His age. But now his eyes were opened. In fact, Surrealism was a social revolutionary movement. The "writings of the circle no longer concern literature, but something else: manifestation, slogan, document, bluff, forgery." Surrealism was not "about theories" but about "experiences." And about everyday experiences that revealed that the reification *and* alienation of the capitalist city subject had advanced so far that the boundary between sense and nonsense, reality and dream, intoxication and sobriety, waking and sleeping, art and advertising, could no longer be clearly drawn.

In other words: The actually liberating, actually revolutionary *realism* of the 1920s could at first be only *Sur*realism! According to Benjamin, what Surrealism was searching for could be found when it succeeded, through the forms of the most immediate expression of this now all-too-everyday state of intoxication, in opening doors to what he called a *"profane illumination."*[21] Hashish and other drugs with which he himself had experimented since 1928, a feature of the Surrealist imagination since its ancestor Rimbaud, could provide the "preliminary training" for that illumination. But the genuinely liberating intoxication, the actual path toward the prerevolutionary event of "profane illumination," lay in nothing other than yielding to the experiences, which had themselves become a drug of the insanely accelerated life of the city. Benjamin, now himself writing in manifesto mode: "Gaining the powers of intoxication for the revolution—that is what Surrealism revolves around in all books and undertakings.... They bring the powerful forces of 'mood' which are ... concealed in things to an explosion. How do we imagine the configuration of a life that had at a crucial moment allowed itself to be defined by the latest popular song?"[22]

BREATHLESS

BUT BENJAMIN REFRAINED from using the exclamation mark actually required by the manifesto form. Just as, in "On the Image of Proust," he did not wish to go so far as to claim that Proust had ultimately endorsed the global communist revolution. But of course, as far as he was concerned, Proust's work was about nothing but, in the mode of perpetual recall, keeping watch for moments of "profane illumination":

> What was it that Proust sought so frenetically? What was at the bottom of those infinite efforts? Can we say that all lives, works, and deeds that matter were never anything but the undisturbed unfolding of the most banal, most fleeting, most sentimental, weakest hour in the life of the one to whom they pertain? . . . In Proust, too, we are guests who enter through a door underneath a suspended sign that sways in the breeze, a door behind which eternity and rapture await us. . . . But Proust's eternity is by no means a platonic or a utopian one: it is rapturous. . . . The eternity which Proust opens to view is intertwined time, not boundless time. His true interest is in the passage of time in its most real—that is, intertwined—form, and this passage nowhere holds sway more openly than in remembrance within and aging without.[23]

And of course the whole Proustian universe, precisely because it remains permanently on the threshold between the deepest layers of meaning and perfect presence, appears as a world in which it is no longer always possible to distinguish clearly between dream and reality, fact and fiction, conscious and unconscious, given and wrought, complete distortion and the most unvarnished authenticity: even the moments of the truest emotion, and hence the most liberating instants, are still suspect and may be only the results reaching for meaning hidden in the depths of creation, the imposition of connections between signs external and internal. Day and night, waking and dreaming, being and seeming . . . the boundary is irremediably blurred.

GASLIGHT

WE MIGHT IMAGINE these extracts from Benjamin's metaphysical and revolutionary phase of work of March 1929 as direct verbal contributions to the Davos debate. In fact, they could have been inserted directly into the transcript of the Davos debate using the same collage technique that, it was becoming increasingly clear in the spring of 1929, formed the basic architectural principle of Benjamin's Arcades Project. The result would have been: Where Heidegger places his Dasein-redeeming confidence in primal anxiety, Benjamin places it in the rapture of different kinds of artificial paradise; the wild roar of rush-hour traffic replaces the experience of the storm high in the Black Forest; aimless flâneuring replaces the ski slope down to the abyss; absorption in outward things replaces the retreat into the interior; apparently random distraction occupies the space of contemplative concentration; the deracinated, disenfranchised masses of the international proletariat replace those people rooted in their homeland . . . Both Benjamin and Heidegger longed for revolutionary change, in everything that they were and had. Just to get out, out of the one-way street of the modern age! Back to the junction where they had taken the wrong turn. And the two agreed on the sources and traditions that were absolutely to be avoided in that endeavor: bourgeois culture, so-called liberal-democratic constitutional orders, worn-out moral principles, German idealism as a cult of the mind, academic philosophizing, Kant, Goethe, Humboldt . . .

In 1929, when Heidegger, the philosopher of origins, cast a diagnostic eye back, he saw the beginning of philosophizing itself as a sacred "place" of an awakening that remained possible. That place lies deep within Dasein, timelessly guaranteed by the essence of temporality itself. Benjamin's now materialistic concept of history lacked that option. His task was to point out the fatal origin, demonstrate the moment when falsehood made its appearance in history itself, and make it as available to concrete experience as possible.

In 1929, Benjamin once again believed that he could pinpoint when, where, and how the breakthrough into the unreal and universally falsifying spirit of his age occurred. In Paris, in fact, the capital of the nineteenth century. Not in the form of an individual or a book, but in a new form of construction, built from iron and steel: the Paris arcades, the cabinets of curiosity, bathed in a perpetual artificial twilight, of coming consumer capitalism. In their window displays the whole disparate world of commodities, forms, and symbols was placed side by side for the onlooker's gaze, and in the end offered for purchase. Neither entirely an internal space nor a part of the streetscape, the arcades were deliberately arranged as liminal places that leveled out every fundamental difference. Half cave, half house; half passageway and half room.

In the finite individuals who strolled aimlessly through them, with their always brimming, constantly redecorated vitrines, these arcades created the appearance of infinite availability, which would soon extend to the rest of the world—and anesthetize it. If the window to future salvation was left ajar, it meant penetrating this configuration of arcades. And thus with the question: What concrete material conditions made them possible in the first place?

> Most of the Paris arcades came into being in the decade and a half after 1822. The first condition for their emergence is the boom in the textile trade. *Magasins de nouveautés*, the first establishments to keep large stocks of merchandise on the premises, make their appearance. They are the forerunners of department stores. This was the period of which Balzac wrote: "The great poem of display chants its stanzas of color from the Church of the Madeleine to the Porte Saint Denis." The arcades are a center of commerce in luxury items. In fitting them out, art enters the service of the merchant. Contemporaries never tire of admiring them, and for a long time they remain a drawing point for foreigners. An *Illustrated Guide to Paris* says: "These arcades, a recent invention of industrial luxury, are glass-roofed, marble-paneled corridors extending through whole blocks of buildings, whose owners have joined together for such enterprises. Lining both sides of these corridors, which get their light from above, are the most elegant shops, so that the *passage* is a city, a world in miniature." The arcades are the scene of the first gas lighting.
>
> The second condition for the emergence of the arcades is the beginning of iron construction. The Empire saw in this technology a contribution to the revival of architecture in the classical Greek sense.[24]

This is from the first chapter of *The Arcades Project*, and it says a great deal about the collage technique that carries the work that Benjamin leaves it up to a seemingly random quotation from a seemingly random publication (in this case, a guidebook) to set out the crucial philosophical markers right at the beginning. Because even if the author of the article in the Paris guide that Benjamin cites did not see it, and in all likelihood did not deliberately intend it, it reflects the whole history of metaphysics. It is expounded in what we might call magazine-speak, and is granted a weird afterlife as if by a ghostly hand: just like the shadow plays in Plato's cave, the displays of commodities in the deep mirrored passageways of the arcades receive "their light from above," in the form of artificial fire (gaslight). As in Leibniz's *Monadology*, even the windowless arcades appear as "a world in miniature." And as Kant (and of course Marx) would have it, all that maintains these passages through whole buildings—which are themselves only superficially buildings—is the "speculative" will of their owners, "united" for this apparent purpose, if not for anything else.

A textual monad inside a textual monad, mounted with the sole intention of making visible for a brief bright moment the unfathomable ways in which time itself entwines things together. Benjamin's vision of reality. Remembrance as knowledge.

THE SELF-DESTRUCTIVE PERSONALITY

IN THE SPRING OF 1929, Benjamin reached the height of his powers as a thinker and a journalist. Which is not to say, of course, that he was not at this time involved in various tangles intertwined several times over, of almost metaphysical profundity. The first to have a clear vision of the calamity that was about to take its course, and how it would, was probably Gershom Scholem, on receiving the following letter from his friend in Berlin in early August 1928: "My trip to Palestine, as well as the strictest observance of the study plan prescribed by Your Hierosolymitan Excellency, has been decided upon. . . . Now to the details. First of all, the date of my arrival. This may be postponed to mid-December. That depends . . . on whether I can finish the Arcades Project before I leave Europe. Secondly when I will see my Russian friend in Berlin in the autumn. Both are still undecided."[25]

Of course the Arcades Project wasn't completed in autumn 1928. At that point it was only just getting going. In addition, it would not be until March 1929 that Benjamin made the slightest progress with his Hebrew. The date for his passage to Palestine hadn't been fixed, either. This may have been due chiefly to the fact that Asja Lacis had turned up in Berlin in September 1928. She had been sent officially, or rather "posted" there, to the film department of the Soviet trade delegation. And with the express mandate, as a member of the "Proletarian Theatre Group . . . of establishing contact with the League of Proletarian Writers."[26] Reich, too, was back in Germany, although for now he was professionally tied up in Munich.

When Benjamin learned that Asja was coming, he was already aware of another piece of welcome news. Despite lacking a second reference from Cassirer (or any other high-ranking literary figure), Dr. Magnes of the Hebrew University had authorized funding for Benjamin's one-year full-time language course, along with travel to and accommodation in Jerusalem. The funds, being dependent on his study quota, were to be paid out in monthly installments. Scholem himself had argued for that course of action. For not only did he know Benjamin all too well, he had also acted as his guarantor from the beginning. But to both Benjamin's and Scholem's great surprise, in October 1928—when Asja had been in the city for just three weeks—events took a new turn:

....

Dear Gerhard,

I can confirm with many thanks receipt of the dispatch of the check for 3,042 Marks (70/100) sent by Dr. Magnes. Please pass on my warmest thanks. He will hear from me directly later on. Everything else in a few days. Warm regards,

Yours, Walter[27]

....

Without consulting Scholem or even putting him in the picture, Magnes had paid the whole grant—a year's earnings for Benjamin—in one lump sum by check.

Only two weeks later Benjamin rented a spacious apartment for Lacis and himself on Düsseldorfer Strasse. Their cohabitation did not last for more than two months, but in spite of their frequent fights, which occurred on regular three-day cycles, they got on well enough, together enjoying a pleasantly extravagant lifestyle. Lacis kept the apartment and Benjamin moved back to Delbrückstrasse, to his wife, who had just become unemployed once again, his son, and his mother, who was in bed recovering from a stroke. At least now they had some money.

It was Lacis who encouraged Benjamin's contact with Brecht at this time. And it was Benjamin who gave Lacis new insights into Berlin's intellectual life, and hence its nightlife, too. It was Lacis who brought Benjamin closer to the life and work of a professional revolutionary operating in the field of culture. And it was Benjamin who made Lacis familiar with his own cultural circles, which included Erwin Piscator and Siegfried

Kracauer, Victor Klemperer and Leo Strauss, Brecht and Adorno. They met, spoke, debated, and planned new projects. Together, and shortly again with Dr. Reich, they moved through the nightlife of the city that was the real capital of the 1920s—Berlin.

HOT DOGS

EVERY EVENING WAS FILLED with things to take in and admire. Josephine Baker, for example, was producing epiphanies of a very special kind. "After midnight to Vollmoeller's on Pariser Platz to see Baker. He had a strange party once again, no one knowing what the other person was. . . . Women in all stages of nakedness, whose names you couldn't make out and couldn't tell whether they were 'girlfriends,' prostitutes, or ladies. . . . The gramophone was playing a steady stream of old songs, Baker sat on the sofa and, rather than dancing, ate one bockwurst after another ('hot dogs'), Princess Lichnowsky, Max Reinhardt, [Max] Harden were expected but didn't appear. It went on like that until three, when I took my leave."[28] At the end of October 1928, Erwin Piscator hosted a party at his place: "Pretty, light apartment, furnished by Gropius, 'sober' but attractive, and the people look good in it. Quite a big party, forty to fifty people, men and women joined by more and more until after midnight; apparently the event was being held in honor of the Russian-Jewish director Granowsky. . . . Met Brecht."[29] Are these lines from Benjamin? No. But they easily could be. These were extracts from the diary of the busy socialite Harry Graf Kessler. He was always in the midst of things.

Jazz was playing everywhere, now sung in German by the Comedian Harmonists. At the time Benjamin, Wiesengrund, and their gang couldn't agree on what to make of this musical hybrid between "jungle and skyscraper" (Kessler).[30] But they did agree on the subject of Russian cinema: without a doubt it was the measure of all things.

Benjamin put Lacis in touch with Kracauer. That, too, went down well with the higher-ups in the Communist Party. She would soon speak about Russian cinema in Frankfurt. But in Berlin first, about contemporary Soviet drama:

> I suggested repeating the lecture in a big hall for the unemployed. A huge hall, it was full. The unemployed listened attentively. But I was disturbed in the middle of the lecture. Opposite the podium, by the entrance, there was shouting: "Away with the red Moscow agitator!" The duty officers threw themselves on the intruders—SA men. A fight developed—knuckle-dusters clashed. All of a sudden Red Front boys ran over to me. They called: comrade, don't be afraid—but you must get out of here at once! Becher grabbed me by the arm and pulled me away from the stage. He led me—upstairs, downstairs, across a courtyard, down an alleyway and then another courtyard. We ended on a street corner and went into a pub. We sat down at a table and Becher ordered sausages and beer. He said it often happened. Wherever there are communist events, the SA was there at once. But Red Front smacks them in the face.[31]

Not exactly Benjamin's world. And certainly not his style. But "overall," Lacis immediately added in her memoirs, "Benjamin was now more concentrated, more strongly connected with practice, with the earth. . . . During this time he met Brecht more often. Benjamin almost always accompanied me to the public events of the League of Proletarian Writers in workers' halls."

Love worked genuine miracles and changed things around. At least for a few moments or certain phases. Barely worth mentioning: that's not how you learn Hebrew. And that was what the money, most of which had evaporated by mid-May, had actually been intended for.

On May 22, 1929, Benjamin proudly announced to Scholem that he was drawing his "first Hebrew cursive characters." He was really taking lessons, and also found the courage—more than six months had passed since he had received the check—to thank Dr. Magnes in person for the first time. Meanwhile his classes lasted a whole two weeks. The daily teacher he had taken so much trouble to find had to leave the country. His mother was seriously ill. What objections could Benjamin make to that? He was aware enough of that problem from his own experience.

Once again he found himself thrown back to Delbrückstrasse. On June 6, 1929, he wrote to Scholem, who was becoming seriously furious: "Unfortunately I have no answer to give to your accusations; they are absolutely justified, and with regard to this matter I am aware of a pathological feeling of hesitancy from time to time. My arrival in the autumn depends only on my financial situation. On nothing else."[32]

The grant was gone. So the financial situation was back to precarious normality. There was only one area that spring in which Benjamin managed to overcome his "pathological hesitancy." Asja had been "ordered" back to Moscow for the autumn. She would be able to go on living in Berlin only if she got married. It is unclear whether Benjamin actually consulted Asja on this matter or even put her in the picture, but in late spring 1929 he filed for divorce from Dora. The reason: anti-matrimonial conduct.

By August he had moved out of Delbrückstrasse, this time with everything he owned. He put his library in storage and moved in temporarily with his close friend and fellow translator Franz Hessel. It was now the middle of autumn. If everything had gone according to the promise he had given, he would have been able to spend at least eight months in Jerusalem. Time for another letter to Scholem: "I don't remember if I wrote to tell you that a friend, Frau Lazis [!], has been in Germany for about a year. She was about to go back to Moscow, when the day before yesterday, or so it seems, she suffered an acute attack of encephalitis, and yesterday, since her condition still allowed it, I put her on the train to Frankfurt, where Goldstein, who knows her and who has treated her in the past, expects her. I will also . . . soon travel over. . . . Recently I've been working unusually hard, just not in Hebrew."[33]

The neurologist Kurt Goldstein was, incidentally, one of Ernst Cassirer's closest friends. But that was no longer particularly interesting. Benjamin had other worries now. And he still had projects. He spent the autumn of 1929 commuting back and forth between Berlin and Frankfurt. He met up with Adorno and his wife, Gretel Karplus, and Max Horkheimer and Lacis several times in a vacation home at the spa resort of Königstein. There Benjamin read to the group from the current sketches for the Arcades Project. Those weekends devoted to discussion in Königstein are now seen as the actual founding events of the so-called Frankfurt School, which would dominate German intellectual life for fifty years after the war.

THE HIKER

WITH HIS SHORT FLANNEL TROUSERS, heavy peasant shoes, and hiker's rucksack, the young-looking man immediately stood out from the crowd of conference participants who had just traveled in. Presumably a student who had gone on the trail of Robin Hood in Nottingham and didn't know that this hotel was reserved for speakers. "I'm afraid there is a gathering of philosophers going on in here," John Mabbott, a professor from Oxford, said, attempting to sum up the situation in a single sentence. To which the stranger replied: "I too."[34]

Until the last second, Wittgenstein had hesitated about whether he should travel to that annual meeting of the Aristotelian Society—the most important association of British professional philosophers. But he would not deliver the talk on the subject he had announced ("Some Notes on Logical Form"). Admittedly, he had written an academic essay especially for it, the first in his life, but the questions relating to it remained more unclear than ever, in spite of nightlong conversations with Frank Ramsey. It was better to think freely about the "Concept of Infinity in Mathematics" and see what the moment revealed to him. Otherwise, the author of the *Tractatus*, even at this conference, precisely at this conference, had no hopes that the other participants would even begin to understand him. "I fear that whatever one says to them will either fall flat or arouse irrelevant troubles in their minds."[35]

That was what he had written a few weeks previously, in his old familiar tone, to Bertrand Russell, with whom he was now friends again, and who was officially his doctoral supervisor. And he had asked him to attend the conference. In vain, as it turned out.

A DAY OFF

IN FACT, WITTGENSTEIN'S LECTURE on July 14, 1929, would remain his sole appearance at an academic conference, just as the talk he wrote for it would be his only "academic publication." Like Heidegger, he had a low opinion of such gatherings and conference papers. He wanted nothing to do with manifestoes, self-styled movements, or even schools, not in thought or politics. In Vienna, a Festschrift in honor of Moritz Schlick was being drawn up under the guidance of Friedrich Waismann with the title *The Scientific Worldview: The Vienna Circle*. If at all possible, Wittgenstein was to contribute something. Waismann made the request carefully. Not a good idea: "Precisely because Schlick is not an ordinary person, he deserves to be spared from having himself and the school whose representative he is being made a mockery of through good intentions and boasting. When I say 'boasting,' I mean any kind of complacent self-reflection. 'Rejection of metaphysics!' As if *that* was anything new. The Vienna school must *show*, not say what it does. . . . The *work* must praise the master."[36]

Show, don't tell. Wittgenstein had based his own masterpiece on that principle in 1919. Admittedly the significance of the distinction still struck him as indisputable. Many of the other pillars of his *Tractatus* had become deeply questionable to him in the six months or so since his return to Cambridge, however. Clearly not all "problems had essentially been solved once and for all." Either by him or anyone else.

INTERNAL DIFFICULTIES

IN PARTICULAR, the hypothesis fundamental to the *Tractatus* that a meaningful proposition was a *picture of reality* now seemed to Wittgenstein increasingly dubious. Do all meaningful propositions without exception depict a possible state of the world? For example, what about a proposition like "The series of natural numbers is infinite"? Obviously meaningful, obviously not trivial, obviously true. But is there a conceivable state of the world that really shows the truth of this proposition? Indeed, can finite beings conceive of infinity as such? And if so, what might "conceive" mean in this context? Is the existence of an infinitely long series of natural numbers just as imaginable as the existence of an infinitely long piece of string? Or is it "conceivable" in a different way? Or might it perhaps be "infinite" in a different way? Such serious questions kept Wittgenstein awake at night during his first few months back in Cambridge. He was also troubled by a methodological question: How can we get a grip on the differences in the use of words such as "infinite" or "imaginable," on which, in terms of their meaningful use as concepts, simply everything depends? By exposing the logical, subject-predicate structure of elementary propositions? *No*, it's not quite as simple as that, as Wittgenstein was certainly coming to understand in the summer of 1929. During this phase he was thus abandoning the last lingering belief that really supported his depiction of the world in the *Tractatus*: faith in the language of logic as the primary language at the basis of our form of life.

BACK TO THE EVERYDAY

HE SOON SHARED this U-turn in his thinking, the major development of his first months in Cambridge in 1929, with Schlick and Waismann. It wasn't insignificant news for either of them, since as "logical empiricists" of the Vienna Circle, which now existed officially, they pinned their philosophical hopes much more consistently than Wittgenstein on an interplay of logic and experimentally verifiable experience, intended to exhaust all meaningful study. But Wittgenstein was traveling in another direction. And he let them know this very clearly:

> I used to believe that there was the everyday language in which we all speak normally and a primary language that expresses what we really know, namely phenomena. . . . Now I would like to explain why I no longer maintain that view. I believe that in essence we only have one language and that is ordinary language. We do not need to find a new language or construct a set of symbols, rather everyday language *is* already *the* language, provided that we can liberate it from the obscurities

that lie within it. Our language is already completely in order if only we are clear about what it symbolizes. Other languages than the ordinary ones are also valuable . . . for example artificial symbolism is useful in the depiction of the processes of deduction. . . . But as soon as one sets about considering real states of affairs, one sees that this symbolism is at a disadvantage compared to our real language. Of course it is quite wrong to talk about *a* subject-predicate form. In reality there is not *one*, but very many.[37]

Even Schlick was astonished by this. He asked Wittgenstein very directly whether, by bidding farewell to the notion of purely logical form as a foundation, he was not going straight back to that contradiction-riven hornets' nest of fundamental questions on which Immanuel Kant had toiled away in his *Critique of Pure Reason*.

A breakthrough into infinity and eternity—on what basis could it be grasped: through experience of form, decision, or law? What about the role of human language within that process? And is it really a matter of only one language? How can the structure of experience that underlies all meaning be described, and with what methods: physical and experimental, phenomenologically varied, descriptive in everyday terms? What criteria exist for the unambiguous separation of being and seeming, sense and nonsense? And what role does time play, either as something physically measurable, experienced, or even collected through remembrance? During 1929, as if in a state of intoxication, Wittgenstein filled several notebooks with thoughts that revolved around precisely these questions from Davos. They dominated his discussions with his sparring partners Ramsey and Moore, Schlick and Waismann. In conversation all grew increasingly irritated—and overwhelmed—by the extreme dynamism of Wittgenstein's development of his theses, which were by now changing daily.

NAPLES IN CAMBRIDGE

THE RETURN OF GOD caused deep social consternation not least with his appearances in the social circles of the Cambridge Apostles—and the loosely related Bloomsbury Group around Virginia and Leonard Woolf. Certainly, even in 1912 Ludwig was an esoteric presence. But in this milieu the Wittgenstein of 1929 assumed the domineering role of know-it-all, or perhaps the peevish sourpuss. He suffered from particularly intense awkwardness, if not physical pain, when engaging in conversation with women. As a dinner guest he proved incapable of contributing anything more than stale one-liners. Not so amusing.

Even though they met several times in Keynes's house, he never spoke properly with Virginia Woolf. A shame, for both of them. Particularly where communism and concrete social reality were concerned, however, a new and inspiring friend entered his life. This was the Italian economist Piero Sraffa. A convinced socialist and confidant of Antonio Gramsci, Sraffa fled Mussolini's Italy in 1927. Thanks to Keynes's intercession he found a new academic home in Cambridge. It was Sraffa whose robustly disputatious nature and quick-wittedness were a productive challenge to Wittgenstein during this period. When Wittgenstein insisted once again in conversation that a meaningful statement and what it described as a state of the world must have the same logical form, Sraffa responded with a gesture from his homeland. He rubbed his finger under his chin and asked: "And what is the logical form *of that*?"[38]

In terms of his philosophical impact, Sraffa was for Wittgenstein something like Benjamin's Naples and Brecht in one. He grounded his thoughts about the foundations of language, brought them nearer to concrete contexts, and opened up perspectives for the labyrinthine twists and turns of the way we operate with signs. In the preface to his second major work, *Philosophical Investigations*, Wittgenstein thanks Sraffa for "the most consequential ideas in this book."

USEFUL REMINDERS

STARTING FROM THE INSIGHT that we have only one true primary sign system—namely the natural language of the everyday—the importance of this work lies in its will to explore the inner diversity and the context-relatedness of that language. Because essentially, at least from a philosophical point of view, everything is in excellent order and hence unquestioned—assuming, of course, that one is in the position to make the clearest general impression of all the ways in which that language can symbolize.

From this point of view the assumption that something like genuinely philosophical problems exists is nothing other than the product of a confusion, of what Wittgenstein would call the *"bewitchment of our understanding by means of language."*[39] The philosophical process of clarification or healing must therefore assume the form of a constant, patient disentangling, revelation, and diagnosis of the confusions that have arisen. This main method consists in recalling the contexts in which one has used which words truly meaningfully. To philosophize is to issue reminders for a purpose.[40] And that purpose would be a liberatory clarification of the role that words play in our lives. But their true significance is found and shown only in concrete and correct usage, which therefore guarantees meaning: "The meaning of a word is its use in the language."[41]

THE CITY OF WORDS

FOR WITTGENSTEIN, this new program was also reflected in the formal shape of his philosophizing. He was no longer concerned with pouring his own thought into the rigid, hierarchically structured, and rigorously demonstrative form of a treatise. His philosophizing had much more in common with the genre of the commonplace book or the notes of a flâneur in equal measure astounded and fascinated by detail. Wittgenstein set off on this path in 1929. And by consistently following it, he completed his *Philosophical Investigations* in 1945. It is a collection, as he writes in the preface, of remarks "like a number of sketches of landscapes that were made in the course of these long and involved journeyings." Travel pictures, then, thought-pictures, produced in the course of an exploration of the diversity of human speech itself: "The same points or almost the same points," Wittgenstein goes on, almost in the spirit of Benjamin the flâneur, "were always being approached afresh from different directions, and new sketches made . . . so that you could get a picture of the landscape. Thus this book is really only an album."[42]

Because in the end, Wittgenstein says in his second major work, a philosophical problem is akin to the feeling "I have gotten lost, I can no longer find my way." Which is why he compares language itself to a labyrinthine city of narrow alleys, in which one can all too easily (and perhaps all too willingly) get lost. The task of philosophers, then, is to draw a map of that city so that it is clear to the lost people (the philosophers themselves) where they actually are, and hence which paths are available to them at this point, so they can continue walking with the greatest possible self-determination and clarity of direction. *Let the way praise the master!* The rest is advertising. Or fate.

In order to render an accurate picture of the city, we must of course thoroughly explore it for ourselves—starting from the spot where we find ourselves questioning. No one has their map in their head a priori, and in any case it would be of no use. In the end this city (of words) is understood through the comings and goings of those who live in and with it, who are themselves constantly in a state of motion and change. New passages, one-way streets, and cul-de-sacs constantly appear, including some features that are recognized as such only very late, indeed too late. For Wittgenstein—and at the same time for Heidegger, Benjamin, and Cassirer—the modern philosophy that began with Descartes was the textbook example of this massive transformation that had by now defined the whole "cityscape" from within and given it an all-too-artificial sheen. More or less as cars and electricity do in our cities even today. Progress assumes different appearances.

AGAINST THE WALL

PROGRESS—the keyword that, according to Wittgenstein, dazzles and misleads our culture more than any other. For that reason progress cannot exist in philosophy. For that to be so, philosophy would need to have genuine problems of its own, and its own methods for solving them. But according to Wittgenstein it lacks these. It has language, and the confusions it entails. And the possibility, always open, of freeing ourselves from them through the use of language and the exercise of memory. That is all. Nothing in this world is fundamentally hidden from us. That is the new direction that Wittgenstein's thought took in the summer of 1929, with the same apodictic rigor and poetic precision that characterized the *Tractatus*.

While the image that Wittgenstein had of language might have changed radically with his return to Cambridge, his vision of the goals and boundaries of philosophizing remained precisely the same as at the time of the *Tractatus*. In fact, there are no philosophical problems. The essential insights cannot be said, let alone decreed, but must show themselves and be shown through their own implementation. The whole sphere of ethics, of value, of religion and the true meaning of life is an illusory sphere of assertions that cannot be factually confirmed and that are hence meaningless, and about which, for that very reason, we must remain silent, because they concern the genuinely crucial ideas and emotions.

It was with these very messages that Wittgenstein directly approached the Cambridge student body in November 1929. At the invitation of the "Heretics"—as their name suggests, after the Apostles the second elite association at the university—he delivered a popular lecture to their Moral Sciences Club. In it he had the following to say:

> My tendency and I believe the tendency of all men who ever wanted to write or talk Ethics or Religion was to run against the boundaries of language. This running against the walls of our cage is perfectly, absolutely hopeless. Ethics so far as it springs from the desire to say something about the ultimate meaning of life, the absolute good, the absolute valuable, can be no science. What it says does not add to our knowledge in any sense. But it is a document of a tendency in the human mind, which I personally cannot help respecting deeply and I would not for my life ridicule it.[43]

He was already familiar with the experiences most likely to encourage this tendency, the treasures of his life:

> I will describe this experience in order, if possible, to make you recall the same or similar experiences, so that we may have a common ground for our investigation. I believe that the best way of describing it is to

say that when I have it *I wonder at the existence of the world*. And I am then inclined to use such phrases as "how extraordinary that anything should exist" or "how extraordinary that the world should exist." I will mention another experience straight away which I also know and which others of you might be acquainted with: it is, what one might call, the experience of feeling *absolutely* safe. I mean the state of mind in which one is inclined to say "I am safe, nothing can injure me whatever happens."[44]

At his best, Wittgenstein was able not only to inhabit this liberatory state of wondrous absorption himself but also to communicate it as a guiding model to others. Whatever else happened that evening, it was his true initiation as a philosophy teacher in Cambridge.

EPILOGUE

MARTIN HEIDEGGER DELIVERED his inaugural lecture as the new incumbent of Husserl's professorial chair on July 24, 1929. In it he described man as the "place-holder of nothingness." At the end of the year he wrote to Elisabeth Blochmann: "Compulsory schooling and misjudged academicism and everything that goes with it have fallen from me. Of course responsibility grows and often one feels very lonely with what I thought I had to do."

Three and a half years later, on May 1, 1933, Heidegger, newly appointed rector of Freiburg University, delivered a speech titled "The Self-Assertion of the German University." Now a member of the National Socialist Party, he addressed the German student body in a newspaper article accompanying his appointment: "Let not theoretical principles and 'ideas' be the rules of your Being. The Führer himself and he alone *is* the German reality and its law today and in the future."[1]

Ernst Cassirer was elected, by a large majority, rector of Hamburg University on July 6, 1929. He delivered an inaugural speech on November 7, titled "Forms and Form Transformations of the Philosophical Concept

of Truth." The ceremony was disturbed by nationalist student corpora-
tions. Aby Warburg did not live to see it. He died suddenly on October 26,
1929.

Effectively forced by Hitler's Law for the Restoration of the Professional Civil Service to abandon his teaching post, Ernst Cassirer, along
with his wife, left Hamburg for Switzerland on May 2, 1933. The couple
would never return to Germany. Cassirer wrote his last book in exile in the
United States as a guest professor at Yale University. It is titled *The Myth
of the State.*

Walter Benjamin, crippled by the predictably "cruel" financial outcome of
his divorce proceedings, suffered a severe nervous breakdown in mid-
October 1929. As the New York stock market crashed on October 24, he
was by Asja's side. He spent the next New Year's alone in a hotel in Paris.
He would never again have a fixed place of residence. He would never
complete the Arcades Project. He would never again see Asja Lacis. He
would never again take Hebrew classes. He spent most of the next ten
years in Paris. When Hitler came to power, Benjamin's opportunities for
publication were severely curtailed.

On the night of September 26, 1940, fleeing in fear of deportation by
the Nazis, Benjamin committed suicide with morphine in a hotel in the
Pyrenean town of Portbou, only a few hundred meters from the Spanish
border. The suitcase he had brought with him contained a watch, a pipe,
two shirts, an X-ray, and a handwritten manuscript titled "On the Concept
of History."

Ludwig Wittgenstein spent Christmas of 1929—as he did in subsequent
years until Austria was annexed by the Nazis—in the circle of his siblings

in Vienna. In January 1930 he was to begin teaching a course at Cambridge. Shortly before he set off for the holidays he was asked by one of his colleagues there what title his course should be given on the lecture list. Wittgenstein thought for a while.

Finally he replied: "'Philosophy.' What else?"[2]

ACKNOWLEDGMENTS

N O ONE SHOULD, no one can, write a book alone. Here my special thanks go to:

Michael Gaeb and Tom Kraushaar, who have accompanied the project from the beginning. Christoph Selzer, Yelenah Frahm, Dorothea Scholl, and Christiane Braun for their copyediting and corrections.

Michael Hampe and Fritz Breithaupt for conversations and vital tips.

Fabrice Gerschel and the whole team at *Philosophie Magazin* for space and forbearance.

To the organizers and participants of the Philosophy and Literature working group (ETH Zurich), in the context of which I was able to discuss parts of the manuscript.

To the Department of Germanic Studies at Indiana University, Bloomington, which gave me the best imaginable working conditions as Distinguished Max Kade Visiting Professor in the spring of 2017. And to the students in the GER-G 625 course there ("The Explosion of Thought") for their questions and insights.

To the great biographers of my four magicians: Rüdiger Safranski (*Martin Heidegger: Between Good and Evil*), Ray Monk (*Wittgenstein:*

ACKNOWLEDGMENTS

The Duty of Genius), Thomas Meyer (*Ernst Cassirer*), and Howard Eiland and Michael W. Jennings (*Walter Benjamin: A Critical Life*). Their works were constant companions and a perpetual inspiration while I was writing.

To Pia, Venla, and Kaisa, who not only endured all those years, but carried me through them.

LIST OF WORKS

WALTER BENJAMIN

Gesammelte Briefe (GB).

GB Vol. II (1919–1924). Edited by C. Gödde and H. Lonitz. Frankfurt: Suhrkamp, 1996.

GB Vol. III (1925–1930). Edited by C. Gödde and H. Lonitz. Frankfurt: Suhrkamp, 1997.

Gesammelte Schriften (GS), 7 vols. Edited by R. Tiedemann and H. Schweppenhäuser. Frankfurt: Suhrkamp, 1974–1989.

GS Vol. I-1. *Der Begriff der Kunstkritik in der deutschen Romantik. Goethes Wahlverwandtschaften / Ursprung des deutschen Trauerspiels.*

GS Vol. I-2. Includes *Über den Begriff der Geschichte.*

GS Vol. II-1. *Frühe Arbeiten zur Bildungs- und Kulturkritik. Metaphysisch-geschichtsphilosophische Studien. Literarische und ästhetische Essays.*

GS Vol. II-2. *Literarische und ästhetische Essays (Fortsetzung). Ästhetische Fragmente. Vorträge und Reden. Enzyklopädieartikel. Kulturpolitische Artikel und Aufsätze.*

GS Vol. III. *Kritiken und Rezensionen.*

GS Vol. IV-1. *Charles Baudelaire, Tableaux parisiens. Übertragungen aus anderen Teilen der "Fleurs du mal." Einbahnstraße. Deutsche Menschen. Berliner Kindheit um Neunzehnhundert. Denkbilder. Satiren, Polemiken, Glossen. Berichte.*

GS Vol. V. *Das Passagen-Werk.*

ENGLISH TRANSLATIONS

The Arcades Project. Translated by H. Eiland and K. McLaughlin. Cambridge, MA: Belknap Press of Harvard University Press, 1999.

The Correspondence of Walter Benjamin, 1910–1940. Edited and annotated by G. Scholem and T. W. Adorno. Translated by M. R. Jacobson and E. M. Jacobson. Chicago: University of Chicago Press, 1994.

Moscow Diary. Edited by G. Smith. Translated by R. Sieburth. Cambridge, MA: Harvard University Press, 1986.

One-Way Street and Other Writings. Translated by E. Jephcott and K. Shorter. New York: Harcourt Brace Jovanovich, 1978.

The Origin of German Tragic Drama. Translated by J. Osborne. London: New Left Books, 1977.

Selected Writings (SW). Cambridge, MA: Harvard University Press, 1999.

SW Vol. 1 (1913–1926). Edited by M. Bullock and M. W. Jennings. Translated by R. Livingstone et al. *Metaphysics of Youth*, 1913–1919; *Angelus Novus*, 1920–1926.

SW Vol. 2, Part 1 (1927–1930). Edited by M. Bullock, H. Eiland, and G. Smith. Translated by R. Livingstone et al. *Moscow*, 1927; *Image Imperatives*, 1928; *The Return of the Flâneur*, 1929; *Crisis and Critique*, 1930.

ERNST CASSIRER

Gesammelte Werke: Hamburger Ausgabe (ECW). Edited by B. Recki. Hamburg: Felix Meiner, 1998–2009.

ECW Vol. 6. *Substanzbegriff und Funktionsbegriff.* Edited by R. Schmücker. 2000.

ECW Vol. 7. *Freiheit und Form.* Edited by R. Schmücker. 2001.

ECW Vol. 10. *Zur Einsteinschen Relativitätstheorie: Erkenntnistheoretische Betrachtungen.* Edited by R. Schmücker. 2001.

ECW Vol. 11. *Philosophie der symbolischen Formen.* Part 1. *Die Sprache.* Edited by C. Rosenkranz. 2001.

ECW Vol. 12. *Philosophie der symbolischen Formen.* Part 2. *Das mythische Denken.* Edited by C. Rosenkranz. 2002.

ECW Vol. 13. *Philosophie der symbolischen Formen.* Part 3. *Phänomenologie der Erkenntnis.* Edited by J. Clemens. 2002.

ECW Vol. 14. *Individuum und Kosmos in der Philosophie der Renaissance. Die platonische Renaissance in England und die Schule von Cambridge.* Edited by F. Plaga and C. Rosenkranz. 2002.

ECW Vol. 16. *Aufsätze und kleine Schriften 1922–1926.* Edited by J. Clemens. 2003.

ECW Vol. 17. *Aufsätze und kleine Schriften 1927–1931.* Edited by T. Berben. 2004.

ECW Vol. 18. *Aufsätze und kleine Schriften 1932–1935.* Edited by R. Becker. 2004.

ECW Vol. 23. *An Essay on Man: An Introduction to a Philosophy of Human Culture.* Edited by M. Lukay. 2006.

Wesen und Wirkung des Symbolbegriffs (WWS). Darmstadt: Wissenschaftliche Buchgesellschaft, 1956.

UNPUBLISHED WRITINGS

Disposition of *Philosophie des Symbolischen Formen* (allg[emeine] Disposition), 1917. Ernst Cassirer Papers, GEN MSS 98, Box 24, Folders 440, 441. Beinecke Rare Book and Manuscript Library, Yale University.

Material for *Philosophie des Symbolischen Formen* (Blatt 1–241). Ernst Cassirer Papers, GEN MSS 98. Beinecke Rare Book and Manuscript Library, Yale University.

Untitled manuscript, 1919. Ernst Cassirer Papers, GEN MSS, Box 25, Folders 476–480. Beinecke Rare Book and Manuscript Library, Yale University.

ENGLISH TRANSLATIONS

The Individual and the Cosmos in Renaissance Philosophy. Translated by M. Domandi. New York: Dover, 1963.

The Philosophy of Symbolic Forms (PSF). Translated by R. Manheim. New Haven: Yale University Press, 1955. Vol. 1. *Language.* Vol. 2. *Mythical Thought.* Vol. 3. *The Phenomenology of Knowledge.* Vol. 4. *The Metaphysics of Symbolic Forms.*

....

MARTIN HEIDEGGER

Gesamtausgabe (GA), 102 vols. Frankfurt: Vittorio Klostermann (ongoing).

GA Vol. 1. *Frühe Schriften* (1912–1916).

GA Vol. 2. *Sein und Zeit* (1927). Text quotations from *Sein und Zeit* (SuZ). Tübingen: Max Niemeyer, 1993.

GA Vol. 3. *Kant und das Problem der Metaphysik* (1929). Includes "Davoser Disputation zwischen Ernst Cassirer und Martin Heidegger," 274–296.

GA Vol. 16. *Reden und andere Zeugnisse eines Lebensweges* (1910–1976).

GA Vol. 19. *Platon. Sophistes* (1924–1925).

GA Vol. 20. *Prolegomena zur Geschichte des Zeitbegriffs* (1925).

GA Vol. 26. *Metaphysische Anfangsgründe der Logik im Ausgang von Leibniz* (1928).

GA Vol. 29–30. *Die Grundbegriffe der Metapyhsik: Welt—Endlichkeit—Einsamkeit* (1929–1930).

GA Vol. 56–57. *Zur Bestimmung der Philosophie.* 1. *Die Idee der Philosophie und das Weltanschauungsproblem* (Kriegsnotsemester 1919). 2. *Phänomenologie und tranzendentale Wertphilosophie* (1919). 3. *Anhang: Über das Wesen der Universität und das akademische Studium.*

LIST OF WORKS

GA Vol. 62. *Phänomenologische Interpretationen ausgewählter Abhandlungen des Aristoteles zur Ontologie und Logik* (1922). *Anhang: Phänomenologische Interpretationen zu Aristoteles (Anzeige der hermeneutischen Situation).*

GA Vol. 94. *Überlegungen II–VI* (Schwarze Hefte 1931–1938).

ENGLISH TRANSLATIONS

Being and Time (BT). Translated by J. Macquarrie and E. Robinson. Oxford: Blackwell, 1962.

Kant and the Problem of Metaphysics. Translated by R. Taft. Bloomington: Indiana University Press, 1990.

LUDWIG WITTGENSTEIN

Vortrag über die Ethik und andere kleine Schriften. Edited by J. Schulte. Frankfurt: Suhrkamp, 1989.

Werkausgabe (WA). Frankfurt: Suhrkamp.

WA Vol. 1. *Tractatus logico-philosophicus. Tagebücher 1914–1916. Philosophische Untersuchungen* (PU). Frankfurt: Suhrkamp, 1984.

WA Vol. 2. *Philosophische Bemerkungen.* Edited by R. Rhees from unpublished material. Frankfurt: Suhrkamp, 1984.

WA Vol. 3. *Wittgenstein und der Wiener Kreis: Gespräche.* Recorded by F. Waismann. Frankfurt: Suhrkamp, 1984.

WA Vol. 4. *Philosophische Grammatik.* Frankfurt: Suhrkamp, 1984.

WA Vol. 5. *Das Blaue Buch: Eine philosophische Betrachtung (Das Braune Buch).* Frankfurt: Suhrkamp, 1984.

Wörterbuch für Volksschulen. Vienna: Österreichischer Bundesverlag, 1977.

ENGLISH TRANSLATIONS

Philosophical Investigations (PI). Translated by G. E. M. Anscombe. Oxford: Blackwell, 1953.

Tractatus Logico-Philosophicus. Translated by C. K. Ogden. London: Kegan Paul, 1922.

NOTES

Please refer to the List of Works (pages 369–372) for full citations of the following publications, which are indicated by abbreviations in these notes.

BT: Martin Heidegger, *Being and Time*

ECW: Ernst Cassirer, *Gesammelte Werke*

GA: Martin Heidegger, *Gesamtausgabe*

GB: Walter Benjamin, *Gesammelte Briefe*

GS: Walter Benjamin, *Gesammelte Schriften*

PI: Ludwig Wittgenstein, *Philosophical Investigations*

PSF: Ernst Cassirer, *The Philosophy of Symbolic Forms*

PU: Ludwig Wittgenstein, *Philosophische Untersuchungen*

SuZ: Martin Heidegger, *Sein und Zeit*

SW: Walter Benjamin, *Selected Writings*

WA: Ludwig Wittgenstein, *Werkausgabe*

WWS: Ernst Cassirer, *Wesen und Wirkung des Symbolbegriffs*

....

I. PROLOGUE: THE MAGICIANS

1. The account of the oral examination and its circumstances follows R. Monk, *Ludwig Wittgenstein: The Duty of Genius* (London: Vintage, 1991), 255ff.
2. A good impression of the atmosphere among the "Apostles" can be found in K. Hale, *Friends and Apostles: The Correspondence of Rupert Brooke and James Strachey, 1905–1914* (New Haven and London: Yale University Press, 1998).

3. B. McGuinness and G. H. von Wright, eds., *Ludwig Wittgenstein: Cambridge Letters—Correspondence with Russell, Keynes, Moore, Ramsey and Sraffa* (Oxford: Blackwell, 1995).

4. Quoted in Monk, 271.

5. Monk, 272.

6. For detailed descriptions of the dispute and its context, see D. Kaegi and E. Rudolph, eds., *Cassirer–Heidegger: 70 Jahre Davoser Disputation* (Hamburg: Felix Meiner, 2002).

7. T. Cassirer, *Mein Leben mit Ernst Cassirer* (Hamburg: Felix Meiner, 2003), 186ff.

8. M. Friedman, *A Parting of the Ways: Carnap, Cassirer, and Heidegger* (Chicago: Open Court, 2004).

9. G. Neske, ed., *Erinnerungen an Martin Heidegger* (Pfullingen: Neske 1977), 28.

10. Quoted in R. Safranski, *Martin Heidegger: Between Good and Evil*, trans. E. Osers (Cambridge, MA: Harvard University Press, 1999), 202.

11. GS, vol. IV-1, 237.

12. GS, vol. I-1, 227.

13. For a detailed description of this period of his life, see H. Eiland and W. Jennings, *Walter Benjamin: A Critical Life* (Cambridge, MA: Harvard University Press, 2014), 145ff.

14. Quoted in H. Puttnies and G. Smith, eds., *Benjaminiana* (Giessen: Anabas, 1991), 145ff.

II. LEAPS: 1919

1. GS, vol. II-1, 171; SW, 1, 201.

2. See O. Lubrich, "Benjamin in Bern," *UniPress* 167 (University of Bern, 2016), 29.

3. Cf. H. Eiland and W. Jennings, *Walter Benjamin: A Critical Life* (Cambridge, MA: Harvard University Press, 2014), 102.

4. GB, vol. II, 29.

5. GS, vol. I-I, 7–122; SW, 1, 116–201.

6. GS, vol. I-I, 78; SW, 1, 159.

7. GS, vol. I-I, 58; SW, 1, 146.

8. GS, vol. I-I, 65f; SW, 1, 151.

9. GB, vol. II, 51.

10. Quoted in R. Monk, *Ludwig Wittgenstein: The Duty of Genius* (London: Vintage, 1991), 171.

11. L. Wittgenstein, *Briefwechsel mit B. Russell, G. E. Moore, J. M. Keynes, F. P. Ramsey, W. Eccles, P. Engelmann und L. von Ficker*, ed. B. F. McGuinness and H. von Wright (Frankfurt: Suhrkamp, 1980), 96.

12. Cf. A. Waugh, *The House of Wittgenstein: A Family at War* (London: Bloomsbury, 2010), 38ff.

13. WA, vol. I, 169; L. Wittgenstein, *Notebooks 1914–1916*, ed. G. H. von Wright and G. E. M. Anscombe, trans. G. E. M. Anscombe (Oxford: Blackwell, 1961), 75.

14. WA, vol. I, 169; Wittgenstein, *Notebooks 1914–1916*, 79.

15. WA, vol. I, 174; Wittgenstein, *Notebooks 1914–1916*, 80.

16. Quoted in H. Ott, *Martin Heidegger: A Political Life*, trans. A. Blunden (London: HarperCollins, 1993), 107.

17. Quoted in Ott, 107.

18. Ott, 106ff.

19. Ott, 115.

20. The central significance of this lecture for the development of Heidegger's thought is particularly stressed in R. Safranski, *Martin Heidegger: Between Good and Evil*, trans. E. Osers (Cambridge, MA: Harvard University Press, 1999), 93ff. This account follows Safranski's interpretation in its essential features.

21. GA, vol. 56–57, 3–118.

22. GA, vol. 56–57, 63f.

23. GA, vol. 56–57, 67f.

24. GA, vol. 56–57, 220.

25. J. W. Storck, ed., *Martin Heidegger, Elisabeth Blochmann: Briefwechsel, 1918–1969* (Marbach: Deutsche Schillergesellschaft, 1990), 14.

26. T. Cassirer, *Mein Leben mit Ernst Cassirer* (Hamburg: Felix Meiner, 2003), 120f.

27. ECW, vol. 7, 389.

28. Cf. T. Meyer, *Ernst Cassirer* (Hamburg: Ellert & Richter, 2006), 81.

29. ECW, vol. 6.

30. For a biography of the family, see S. Bauschinger, *Die Cassirers—Unternehmer, Kunsthändler, Philosophen: Biographie einer Familie* (Munich: C. H. Beck, 2015).

31. This configuration is elaborated in exemplary fashion in P. Leo, *Der Wille zum Wesen: Weltanschauungskultur, charakterologisches Denken und Judenfeindschaft in Deutschland, 1890–1940* (Berlin: Matthias & Seitz, 2013).

32. T. Cassirer, *Mein Leben mit Ernst Cassirer*, 120.

33. This is confirmed for the first time in the outstanding study by A. Schubbach, *Die Genese des Symbolischen: Zu den Anfängen von Ernst Cassirers Kulturphilosophie* (Hamburg: Felix Meiner, 2016), 33ff.

34. ECW, vol. 18, 36.

III. LANGUAGES: 1919–1920

1. B. McGuinness, ed., *Wittgenstein in Cambridge: Letters and Documents 1911–1951*, 4th ed. (Oxford and Malden, MA: Wiley-Blackwell, 2012), 99.

2. H. Wittgenstein, *Familienerinnerungen*, ed. I. Somavilla (Innsbruck and Vienna: Haymon, 2015), 158.

3. M. Fitzgerald, "Did Ludwig Wittgenstein Have Asperger's Syndrome?," *European Child and Adolescent Psychiatry* 9, no. 1 (2000): 61–65.

4. R. Descartes, *Meditations on First Philosophy*, in *Philosophical Works*, vol. 1, trans. and ed. E. S. Haldane and G. R. T. Ross (New York: Dover), 155.

5. WA, vol. 1, PU, 378, §309; PI, 103, §309.

6. See particularly A. Janik and S. Toulmin, *Wittgenstein's Vienna* (London: Weidenfeld & Nicolson, 1973).

7. See particularly W. W. Bartley, *Wittgenstein* (Chicago: Open Court, 1983), 24f.

8. The description of the visit follows R. Monk, *Ludwig Wittgenstein: The Duty of Genius* (London: Vintage, 1991), 182ff.

9. Cf. Monk, 182.

10. G. Heidegger, ed., *Mein liebes Seelchen! Briefe Martin Heideggers an seine Frau Elfride 1915–1970* (Munich: Deutsche Verlags-Anstalt, 2005), 98.

11. G. Heidegger, 96ff.

12. G. Heidegger, 95.

13. G. Heidegger, 99.

14. G. Heidegger, 101.

15. GA, vol. 56–57, 91f.

16. G. Heidegger, 116.

17. G. Heidegger, 112.

18. GB, vol. II, 87ff.

19. GS, vol. II-1, 140–157.

20. GB, vol. II, 108.

21. GA, vol. 1.

22. GB, vol. II, 127.

23. GS, vol. IV-1, 7–65.

24. GS, vol. IV-1, 112f.

25. GS, vol. IV-1, 7; SW, 1, 253.

26. GS, vol. IV-1, 12; SW, 1, 56.

27. GS, vol. IV-1, 13f; SW, 1, 257.

28. GS, vol. IV-1, 1; SW, 1, 259.

29. GS, vol. II-1, 144.

30. M. Scheler, quoted in P. Witkop, ed., *Deutsches Leben der Gegenwart* (Berlin: Wegweiser, 1922), 164.

31. T. Cassirer, *Mein Leben mit Ernst Cassirer* (Hamburg: Felix Meiner, 2003), 111.

32. E. Cassirer, "Disposition" of "Philosophie des Symbolischen," 32, quoted in A. Schubbach, *Die Genese des Symbolischen: Zu den Anfängen von Ernst Cassirers Kulturphilosophie* (Hamburg: Felix Meiner, 2016), 433.

33. ECW, vol. 12, 231; PSF, vol. 2, 196.

34. WWS, 175f; E. Cassirer, "The Concept of Symbolic Form in the Construction of the Human Sciences" (1923), in *The Warburg Years (1919–1933): Essays on Language,*

Art, Myth and Technology, trans. S. G. Lofts with A. Calcagno (New Haven: Yale University Press, 2013), 76.]

35. WWS, 101; E. Cassirer, *Language and Myth*, trans. S. K. Langer (New York: Dover, 1953), 31.
36. ECW, vol. 11.
37. ECW, vol. 11, 48; PSF, vol. 1.
38. ECW, vol. 11, 49; PSF, vol. 1, 113.
39. ECW, vol. 11, x; PSF, vol. 1, 71.
40. Manuscript, 1919, 243, quoted in Schubbach, *Die Genese des Symbolischen*, 355f.

IV. CULTURE: 1922–1923

1. G. Heidegger, ed., *Mein liebes Seelchen! Briefe Martin Heideggers an seine Frau Elfride 1915–1970* (Munich: Deutsche Verlags-Anstalt, 2005), 124.
2. W. Biemel and H. Saner, eds., *Martin Heidegger / Karl Jaspers: Briefwechsel 1920–1963* (Munich: Piper, 1990), 33.
3. GA, vol. 62, 348.
4. GA, vol. 62, 354.
5. GA, vol. 62, 350.
6. GA, vol. 62, 358.
7. Biemel and Saner, *Martin Heidegger / Karl Jaspers*, 122.
8. G. Heidegger, *Mein liebes Seelchen!*, 127.
9. Quoted in T. Cassirer, *Mein Leben mit Ernst Cassirer* (Hamburg: Felix Meiner, 2003), 138.
10. Quoted in T. Cassirer, 132.
11. Quoted in T. Cassirer, 131.
12. Cf. T. Cassirer, 126.
13. See the Kulturwissenschaftliche Bibliothek Warburg website at http://www .warburg-haus.de/en/the-kulturwissenschaftliche-bibliothek-warburg/.
14. Quoted in T. Meyer, *Ernst Cassirer* (Hamburg: Ellert & Richter, 2006), 102.
15. See Meyer, 103.
16. WWS, 21.
17. WWS, 24.
18. T. Cassirer, *Mein Leben mit Ernst Cassirer*, 133.
19. WWS, 38.
20. T. Cassirer, *Mein Leben mit Ernst Cassirer*, 146.
21. GB, vol. II, 182.
22. GB, vol. II, 270.
23. GB, vol. II, 274.
24. GB, vol. II, 274.

25. GB, vol. II, 290.

26. GS, vol. I-1, 123–201; SW 1, 297–360.

27. GS, vol. I-1, 134; SW 1, 304.

28. GS, vol. I-1, 270; SW 1, 308.

29. GS, vol. I-1, 154; SW 1, 319.

30. GS, vol. I-1, 164f; SW 1, 327.

31. GS, vol. I-1, 185; SW 1, 343.

32. GS, vol. I-1, 169f; SW 1, 331.

33. GS, vol. I-1, 188; SW 1, 345.

34. GS, vol. I-1, 189; SW 1, 346.

35. K. Wünsche, *Der Volksschullehrer Ludwig Wittgenstein* (Frankfurt: Suhrkamp, 1985), 202.

36. Wünsche, 202.

37. Wünsche, 140.

38. Letter to Engelmann, January 2, 1921, quoted in I. Somavilla, ed., *Wittgenstein: Engelmann, Briefe, Begegnungen, Erinnerungen* (Innsbruck and Vienna: Haymon, 2006), 32.

39. B. Russell, *Why I Am Not a Christian* (London: Allen & Unwin, 1957).

40. L. Wittgenstein, *Briefwechsel mit B. Russell, G. E. Moore, J. M. Keynes, F. P. Ramsey, W. Eccles, P. Engelmann und L. von Ficker*, ed. B. F. McGuinness and H. von Wright (Frankfurt: Suhrkamp, 1980), 123.

V. YOU: 1923–1925

1. K. Wünsche, *Der Volksschullehrer Ludwig Wittgenstein* (Frankfurt: Suhrkamp, 1985), 180f.

2. B. McGuinness, ed., *Wittgenstein in Cambridge: Letters and Documents 1911–1951*, 4th ed. (Oxford and Malden, MA: Wiley-Blackwell, 2012), 116, 122.

3. McGuinness, 138.

4. McGuinness, 139.

5. McGuinness, 139.

6. McGuinness, 140.

7. G. H. von Wright, ed., *Ludwig Wittgenstein: Letters to C. K. Ogden* (Oxford: Oxford University Press, 1975), 69.

8. McGuinness, 143.

9. McGuinness, 139f.

10. McGuinness, 152f. The second paragraph reads: "So: First of all I would like to thank you for the books and your kind letter. Since I am very busy and my brain is entirely unable to absorb anything academic, I have read only *one* of the books ("The economic consequences [of the peace]"). I found it very interesting, even though of

course I know practically nothing about the subject. You write to ask if you could do anything to help me return to academic work: no, nothing can be done in this regard; because I myself no longer have a strong inner drive to engage in such an occupation. Everything I really have to say I have said and the spring has consequently dried up. That sounds strange, but it is so. I would like, I would *very* much like to see you again; and I know that you would be so kind as to find me money for a stay in England. But when I think that I am now really to exploit your kindness, I have all kinds of concerns: What would I do in England? Should I just come to see you and distract myself in all kinds of ways? I mean to say shall I just come to be nice? Now I don't think at all that it isn't worth while being nice—if only I could be REALLY nice—or having a nice time—if it were a VERY nice time indeed."

11. BT, 76, n. xi.
12. A. M. Warburg and W. F. Mainland, "A Lecture on Serpent Ritual," *Journal of the Warburg Institute* 2, no. 4 (April 1939): 277–292.
13. For the context and course of that encounter, see H. Bredekamp and C. Wedepohl, *Warburg, Cassirer und Einstein im Gespräch* (Berlin: Wagenbach, 2015). The passage that follows takes its bearings from this.
14. Quoted in T. Cassirer, *Mein Leben mit Ernst Cassirer* (Hamburg: Felix Meiner, 2003), 150.
15. See T. Cassirer, 150.
16. C. Marazia and D. Stimilli, eds., *Ludwig Binswanger, Aby Warburg—Unendliche Heilung—Aby Warburgs Krankengeschichte* (Zurich: Diaphanes, 2007), 112.
17. Marazia and Stimilli.
18. See R. Safranski, *Martin Heidegger: Between Good and Evil*, trans. E. Osers (Cambridge MA: Harvard University Press, 1999), 134ff.
19. An earlier version of this chapter was published as W. Eilenberger, "Das Dämonische hat mich getroffen," *Philosophie Magazin* 5, no. 17 (2017): 48–51.
20. H. Arendt and M. Heidegger, *Briefe 1925–1975*, ed. U. Ludz (Frankfurt: Vittorio Klostermann, 1998), 14.
21. Arendt and Heidegger, 11.
22. For a detailed description of the loving relationship between Arendt and Heidegger, see A. Grunenberg, *Hannah Arendt und Martin Heidegger: Geschichte einer Liebe* (Munich: Piper, 2016).
23. Arendt and Heidegger, *Briefe 1925–1975*, 31.
24. For more about the philosophical concepts of love in Heidegger and Arendt, see the brilliant study by T. N. Tömmel, *Wille und Passion: Der Liebesbegriff bei Heidegger und Arendt* (Frankfurt: Suhrkamp, 2013).
25. Safranski, *Martin Heidegger*, 140.
26. GB, vol. II, 351.

27. GB, vol. II, 370.
28. GB, vol. II, 406.
29. GB, vol. II, 445.
30. Cf. GS, vol. IV-1, 308.
31. GB, vol. II, 448.
32. A. Lacis, *Revolutionär im Beruf: Berichte über proletarisches Theater, über Meyerhold, Brecht, Benjamin und Piscator*, ed. H. Brenner (Munich: Rogner & Bernhard, 1976), 46.
33. GB, vol. II, 466ff.
34. GB, vol. II, 486.
35. W. Benjamin, *Moscow Diary*, ed. G. Smith, trans. R. Sieburth (Cambridge, MA: Harvard University Press, 1986), 108.
36. GS, vol. IV-1, 307–316.
37. See also the thoughtful study by M. Mittelmeier, *Adorno in Neapel: Wie sich eine Sehnsuchtslandschaft in Philosophie verwandelt* (Munich: Siedler, 2013).
38. GS, vol. IV-1, 309–310.
39. This is also the judgment of Mittelmeier, *Adorno in Neapel*, 44f.

....

VI. FREEDOM: 1925–1927

1. On this and what follows, see M. Mittelmeier, *Adorno in Neapel: Wie sich eine Sehnsuchtslandschaft in Philosophie verwandelt* (Munich: Siedler, 2013), 52ff.
2. J. Später, *Siegfried Kracauer: Eine Biographie* (Frankfurt: Suhrkamp, 2016), 177.
3. See Mittelmeier, *Adorno in Neapel*, 52.
4. The stubbornly held view that anti-Semitic prejudices played a part in the Schultz case is convincingly dismissed with a large amount of evidence by L. Jäger, *Walter Benjamin: Das Leben eines Unvollendeten* (Frankfurt: Rowohlt, 2017), 151.
5. Quoted in Jäger, 153.
6. W. Benjamin, *The Correspondence of Walter Benjamin, 1910–1940*, ed. G. Scholem and T. W. Adorno, trans. M. R. Jacobson and E. M. Jacobson (Chicago: University of Chicago Press, 1994), 251.
7. GS, vol. II-1, 140–157.
8. W. Benjamin, *The Origin of German Tragic Drama*, trans. J. Osborne (London: New Left Books, 1977), 37.
9. GS, vol. II-1, 142.
10. GS, vol. I-1, 226; Benjamin, *The Origin of German Tragic Drama*, 45.
11. Cf. M. Heidegger, "Der Ursprung des Kunstwerks," in GA, vol. 5, 1–74.
12. Benjamin, *The Origin of German Tragic Drama*, 36.
13. Benjamin, 44.

14. For an influential example of this, see J. Habermas, *Erläuterungen zur Diskursethik* (Frankfurt: Suhrkamp, 1991).

15. Benjamin, *The Origin of German Tragic Drama*, 234.

16. GS, vol. II-1, 155; SW, 1, 73.

17. GS, vol. IV-1, 9–21; SW, 1, 253–263.

18. Benjamin, *The Origin of German Tragic Drama*, 229.

19. GB, vol. III, 73.

20. Quoted in Mittelmeier, *Adorno in Neapel*, 365.

21. GS, vol. I-1, 350.

22. GB, vol. I, 382.

23. GB, vol. III, 102.

24. H. Arendt and M. Heidegger, *Letters 1925–1975*, ed. U. Ludz, trans. A. Shields (New York: Harcourt, 2004), 16.

25. G. Heidegger, ed., *Mein liebes Seelchen! Briefe Martin Heideggers an seine Frau Elfride 1915–1970* (Munich: Deutsche Verlags-Anstalt, 2005), 140.

26. SuZ, 12, §4; BT, 32.

27. Cf. WA, vol. 1, *Tractatus*, 6:4312.

28. SuZ, 66f, §15; BT, 95–96.

29. SuZ, 68, §15; BT, 97–98.

30. SuZ, 69, §15; BT, 98.

31. W. Biemel and H. Saner, eds., *Martin Heidegger / Karl Jaspers: Briefwechsel 1920–1963* (Munich: Piper, 1990), 71.

32. SuZ, 187f, §40; BT, 232.

33. SuZ, 187f, §40; BT, 234.

34. Biemel and Saner, *Martin Heidegger / Karl Jaspers*, 47.

35. SuZ, 251, §50; BT, 294.

36. Biemel and Saner, *Martin Heidegger / Karl Jaspers*, 24.

37. G. Heidegger, *Mein liebes Seelchen!*, 147.

38. P. Kipphoff, "Das Labor des Seelenarchivars," *Die Zeit*, April 21, 1995.

39. ECW, vol. 14.

40. Cassirer's understanding of the Renaissance is elaborated in, for example, O. Schwemmer, *Ernst Cassirer: Ein Philosoph der europäischen Moderne* (Berlin: Akademie, 1997), 221–242.

41. ECW, vol. 14, 3.

42. I take this concept from a conversation with Michael Hampe.

43. E. Cassirer, *The Individual and the Cosmos in Renaissance Philosophy*, trans. M. Domandi (New York: Dover, 1963), 114.

44. R. Koder and L. Wittgenstein, *Wittgenstein und die Musik: Briefwechsel Ludwig Wittgenstein Rudolf Koder*, ed. M. Alber with B. McGuinness and M. Seekircher (Innsbruck: Haymon, 2000), 12.

45. PI, 2, footnote.

46. PI, 2, footnote.
47. PI, 4.
48. PI, 243.
49. See particularly K. Wünsche, *Der Volksschullehrer Ludwig Wittgenstein* (Frankfurt: Suhrkamp, 1985), 92ff.
50. Wünsche, 106.
51. Wünsche, 100f.
52. This story is taken from Wünsche, 272ff.

VII. ARCADES: 1926–1928

1. L. Wittgenstein, *Briefwechsel mit B. Russell, G. E. Moore, J. M. Keynes, F. P. Ramsey, W. Eccles, P. Engelmann und L. von Ficker*, ed. B. F. McGuinness and H. von Wright (Frankfurt: Suhrkamp, 1980), 113.
2. Quoted in A. Sarnitz, *Die Architektur Ludwig Wittgensteins: Rekonstruktion einer Idee* (Vienna: Böhlau, 2011), 57.
3. H. Wittgenstein, *Familienerinnerungen*, ed. I. Somavilla (Innsbruck and Vienna: Haymon, 2015), 163.
4. See R. Monk, *Ludwig Wittgenstein: The Duty of Genius* (London: Vintage, 1991), 162.
5. See A. Janik and S. Toulmin, *Wittgenstein's Vienna* (London: Weidenfeld & Nicolson, 1973), 248.
6. Quoted in K. Sigmund, *Sie nannten sich der Wiener Kreis: Exaktes Denken am Rande des Untergangs* (Wiesbaden: Springer, 2015), 121.
7. From P. Schilpp, *The Philosophy of Rudolf Carnap* (La Salle, IL: Open Court, 1963), 25ff.
8. B. McGuinness, ed., *Wittgenstein and the Vienna Circle: Conversations*, recorded by F. Waismann, trans. J. Schulte and B. McGuinness (New York: Barnes & Noble, 1979), 68.
9. GB, vol. III, 188f.
10. GS, vol. IV-1, 83–148.
11. W. Benjamin, *One-Way Street and Other Writings*, trans. E. Jephcott and K. Shorter (New York: Harcourt Brace Jovanovich, 1978), 45.
12. GB, vol. III, 158.
13. GB, vol. III, 158f.
14. GB, vol. III, 195.
15. GS, vol. VI, 292–409 (*Moskauer Tagebuch*); W. Benjamin, *Moscow Diary*, ed. G. Smith, trans. R. Sieburth (Cambridge, MA: Harvard University Press, 1986).
16. Benjamin, *Moscow Diary*, 127.

17. Benjamin, 30.

18. Cf. Benjamin, 16.

19. Benjamin, 25.

20. Benjamin, 34.

21. Benjamin, 57.

22. Benjamin, 72.

23. Benjamin, 73.

24. See N. Green, "(Neither) Expatriates (n)or Immigrants," *Transatlantica* 1 (2014), for various estimates.

25. Quoted in GB, vol. III, 305. A complete account of the meeting from Scholem's perspective can be found in G. Scholem, *Walter Benjamin: Die Geschichte einer Freundschaft* (Frankfurt: Suhrkamp, 1975), 172–175.

26. GB, vol. III, 346.

27. E. Cassirer, *The Phenomenology of Knowledge*, vol. 3 of *The Philosophy of Symbolic Forms,* trans. R. Manheim (New Haven: Yale University Press, 1955), 1.

28. T. Cassirer, *Mein Leben mit Ernst Cassirer* (Hamburg: Felix Meiner, 2003), 163ff.

29. Quoted in H. Blumenberg, *Schiffbruch mit Zuschauer* (Frankfurt: Suhrkamp, 1979), 73.

30. See H. U. Gumbrecht, *1926: Ein Jahr am Rand der Zeit* (Frankfurt: Suhrkamp, 2001), 187.

31. T. Cassirer, *Mein Leben mit Ernst Cassirer,* 165.

32. Cf. T. Meyer, *Ernst Cassirer* (Hamburg: Ellert & Richter, 2006), 109.

33. Meyer, 109.

34. S. Bauschinger, *Die Cassirers—Unternehmer, Kunsthändler, Philosophen: Biographie einer Familie* (Munich: C. H. Beck, 2015), 159.

35. Bauschinger, 111.

36. ECW, vol. 17, 291.

37. ECW, vol. 17, 295f.

38. ECW, vol. 17, 302.

39. ECW, vol. 17, 307f.

40. See Meyer, *Ernst Cassirer,* 152.

41. T. Cassirer, *Mein Leben mit Ernst Cassirer,* 181.

42. G. Heidegger, ed., *Mein liebes Seelchen! Briefe Martin Heideggers an seine Frau Elfride 1915–1970* (Munich: Deutsche Verlags-Anstalt, 2005), 148f.

43. G. Heidegger, 153.

44. GA, vol. 26, 185.

45. J. W. Storck, ed., *Martin Heidegger, Elisabeth Blochmann: Briefwechsel, 1918–1969* (Marbach: Deutsche Schillergesellschaft, 1990), 25.

46. G. Heidegger, *Mein liebes Seelchen!,* 157.

47. Storck, *Martin Heidegger, Elisabeth Blochmann,* 25f.

VIII. TIME: 1929

1. G. Heidegger, ed., *Mein liebes Seelchen! Briefe Martin Heideggers an seine Frau Elfride 1915–1970* (Munich: Deutsche Verlags-Anstalt, 2005), 160f.
2. G. Heidegger, 161f.
3. Quoted in M. Friedman, *A Parting of the Ways: Carnap, Cassirer, and Heidegger* (Chicago: Open Court, 2004), 22.
4. G. Heidegger, *Mein liebes Seelchen!*, 161.
5. J. W. Storck, ed., *Martin Heidegger, Elisabeth Blochmann: Briefwechsel, 1918–1969* (Marbach: Deutsche Schillergesellschaft, 1990), 30.
6. T. Cassirer, *Mein Leben mit Ernst Cassirer* (Hamburg: Felix Meiner, 2003), 188.
7. Quoted in J. M. Krois, "Warum fand keine Davoser Disputation statt?," in *Cassirer–Heidegger: 70 Jahre Davoser Disputation*, ed. D. Kaegi and E. Rudolph (Hamburg: Felix Meiner, 2002), 239.
8. Quoted in Krois, 244.
9. Quoted in Krois, 239.
10. T. Cassirer, *Mein Leben mit Ernst Cassirer*, 188.
11. Quoted in D. Kaegi and E. Rudolph, eds., *Cassirer–Heidegger: 70 Jahre Davoser Disputation* (Hamburg: Felix Meiner, 2002), v.
12. All quotations from the Davos debate are taken from the transcript published in GA, vol. 3, 274–296.
13. G. Heidegger, *Mein liebes Seelchen!*, 162.
14. J. W. Storck, *Martin Heidegger, Elisabeth Blochmann*, 30.
15. Quoted in Krois, "Warum fand keine Davoser Disputation statt?," 234.
16. M. Heidegger, *Kant and the Problem of Metaphysics*, trans. R. Taft (Bloomington: Indiana University Press, 1990).
17. GB, vol. III, 449.
18. GB, vol. III, 378.
19. GS, vol. II-1, 310–324.
20. GS, vol. II-1, 295–310.
21. GS, vol. II-1, 298.
22. GS, vol. II-1, 307, 320.
23. GS, vol. II-1, 312, 319f.
24. GS, vol. V-1, 45; W. Benjamin, *The Arcades Project*, trans. H. Eiland and K. McLaughlin (Cambridge, MA: Belknap Press of Harvard University Press, 1999), 5.
25. GB, vol. III, 403f.
26. A. Lacis, *Revolutionär im Beruf: Berichte über proletarisches Theater, über Meyerhold, Brecht, Benjamin und Piscator*, ed. H. Brenner (Munich: Rogner & Bernhard, 1976), 62.
27. GB, vol. III, 417.

28. H. Kessler, *Tagebücher 1918–1937* (Frankfurt: Suhrkamp, 1961), 462.

29. Kessler, 267f.

30. Cf. P. Blom, *The Vertigo Years, 1918–1938* (Munich: Hanser, 2014), 286f.

31. Lacis, *Revolutionär im Beruf*, 59.

32. GB, vol. III, 463.

33. GB, vol. III, 483.

34. Quoted in R. Monk, *Ludwig Wittgenstein: The Duty of Genius* (London: Vintage, 1991), 275.

35. Quoted in Monk, 275.

36. WA, vol. 3, 18.

37. WA, vol. 3, 44f.

38. Quoted in Monk, *Ludwig Wittgenstein*, 261.

39. WA, vol. 1, PU, 299, §109; PI, 47, §109.

40. See WA, vol. 1, PU, 109, §127; PI, 50, §127.

41. WA, vol. 1, PU, 262, §43; PI, 20, §43.

42. WA, vol. 1, PU, Vorwort, 231f; PI, preface, vii.

43. L. Wittgenstein, *Vortrag über die Ethik und andere kleine Schriften*, ed. J. Schulte (Frankfurt: Suhrkamp, 1989), 18f; L. Wittgenstein, "A Lecture on Ethics," *Philosophical Review* 74, no. 1 (January 1965): 3–12.

44. L. Wittgenstein, *Vortrag über die Ethik*, 14f.

EPILOGUE

1. GA, vol. 16, 184.

2. R. Monk, *Ludwig Wittgenstein: The Duty of Genius* (London: Vintage, 1991), 289.

SELECTED BIBLIOGRAPHY

Adorno, T. W. (1924). *Die Transzendenz des Dinglichen und Noematischen in Husserls Phänomenologie: Thema der Doktorarbeit.* Frankfurt: Suhrkamp.

——— (1990). *Über Walter Benjamin: Aufsätze, Artikel, Briefe.* Frankfurt: Suhrkamp.

Adorno, T. W., and S. Kracauer (2008). *Briefwechsel 1923–1966.* Frankfurt: Suhrkamp.

Apel, K.-O. (1973). *Transformation der Philosophie.* Vols. 1 and 2. Frankfurt: Suhrkamp. Translated by G. Adey and D. Frisbey as *Towards a Transformation of Philosophy.* London: Routledge and Kegan Paul, 1980.

Arendt, H. (1971). *Benjamin, Brecht: Zwei Essays.* Munich: Piper.

——— (1996). *Ich will verstehen: Selbstauskünfte zu Leben und Werk.* Edited by U. Ludz. Munich: Piper.

——— (2003). *Der Liebesbegriff bei Augustin.* Hamburg: Felix Meiner. Translated as *Love and Saint Augustine.* Edited by J. V. Scott and J. C. Stark. Chicago: University of Chicago Press, 1996.

Arendt, H., and M. Heidegger (1998). *Briefe 1925–1975.* Edited by U. Ludz. Frankfurt: Vittorio Klostermann. Translated by A. Shields as *Letters 1925–1975.* Edited by U. Ludz. New York: Harcourt, 2004.

Arendt, H., and K. Jaspers (1985). *Briefwechsel 1926–1969.* Edited by L. Köhler and H. Sauer. Munich: Piper.

Bartley, W. W. (1983). *Wittgenstein.* Chicago: Open Court.

Baudelaire, C. (1983). *Les fleurs du mal* (Paris, 1857). Translated into English by R. Howard. Boston: David Godine.

Bauschinger, S. (2015). *Die Cassirers—Unternehmer, Kunsthändler, Philosophen: Biographie einer Familie.* Munich: C. H. Beck.

Benjamin, W. (1978). *One-Way Street and Other Writings.* Translated by E. Jephcott and K. Shorter. New York: Harcourt Brace Jovanovich.

————— (1986). *Moscow Diary*. Edited by G. Smith. Translated by R. Sieburth. Cambridge, MA: Harvard University Press.

————— (1999). *The Arcades Project*. Translated by H. Eiland and K. McLaughlin. Cambridge, MA: Belknap Press of Harvard University Press.

Biemel, W. (1973). *Martin Heidegger in Selbstzeugnissen und Bilddokumenten*. Reinbek: Rowohlt. Translated by J. L. Mehta as *Martin Heidegger: An Illustrated Study*. New York: Harcourt Brace Jovanovich, 1976.

Biemel, W., and H. Saner, eds. (1990). *Martin Heidegger / Karl Jaspers: Briefwechsel 1920–1963*. Munich: Piper.

Bloch, E. (1969). *Geist der Utopie*. Frankfurt: Suhrkamp.

Blom, P. (2014). *The Vertigo Years, 1918–1938*. Munich: Hanser.

Blumenberg, H. (1979). *Schiffbruch mit Zuschauer*. Frankfurt: Suhrkamp.

————— (2006). *Beschreibung des Menschen*. Frankfurt: Suhrkamp.

Bredekamp, H., and C. Wedepohl (2015). *Warburg, Cassirer und Einstein im Gespräch*. Berlin: Wagenbach.

Breithaupt, F. (2008). *Der Ich-Effekt des Geldes: Zur Geschichte einer Legitimationsfigur*. Frankfurt: Fischer.

Carnap, R. (1928). *Der logische Aufbau der Welt*. Hamburg: Felix Meiner. Translated by R. A. George as *The Logical Construction of the World / Pseudoproblems in Philosophy*. Berkeley: University of California Press, 1967.

————— (1928). *Scheinprobleme in der Philosophie*. Berlin: Weltkreis.

————— (1934). *Logische Syntax der Sprache*. Vienna: Springer. Translated by A. Smeaton as *The Logical Syntax of Language*. London: Routledge and Kegan Paul, 1947.

————— (1993). *Mein Weg in die Philosophie*. Ditzingen: Reclam.

Cassirer, E. (1953). *Language and Myth*. Translated by S. K. Langer. New York: Dover.

————— (1953–1996). *The Philosophy of Symbolic Forms*. Vol. 1, *Language*. Vol. 2, *Mythical Thought*. Vol. 3, *The Phenomenology of Knowledge*. Vol. 4, *The Metaphysics of Symbolic Forms*. Translated by R. Manheim. New Haven: Yale University Press.

————— (1963). *The Individual and the Cosmos in Renaissance Philosophy*. Translated by M. Domandi. New York: Dover.

————— (2013). *The Warburg Years (1919–1933): Essays on Language, Art, Myth and Technology*. Translated by S. G. Lofts with A. Calcagno. New Haven: Yale University Press.

Cassirer, T. (2003). *Mein Leben mit Ernst Cassirer*. Hamburg: Felix Meiner.

Cavell, S. (1979). *The Claim of Reason: Wittgenstein, Skepticism, Morality, and Tragedy*. New York: Oxford University Press.

———— (1994). *A Pitch of Philosophy: Autobiographical Exercises.* Cambridge, MA: Harvard University Press.

———— (2002). *Die Unheimlichkeit des Gewöhnlichen, und andere philosophische Essays.* Edited by D. Sparti and E. Hammer. Frankfurt: Fischer.

Clark, C. (2012). *The Sleepwalkers: How Europe Went to War in 1914.* Harmondsworth, UK: Penguin.

Cohen, H. (1871). *Kants Theorie der Erfahrung.* Berlin: Dümmler.

———— (1902). *Logik der reinen Erkenntnis.* Berlin: Cassirer.

Descartes, R. (1998). *Meditations and Other Metaphysical Writings.* Translated by D. M. Clarke. Harmondsworth, UK: Penguin.

Dilthey, W. (1992). *Der Aufbau der geschichtlichen Welt in den Geisteswissenschaften.* Vol. 7 of *Gesammelte Schriften.* Stuttgart and Göttingen: Vandenhoeck & Ruprecht. Translated as *The Formation of the Historical World in the Human Sciences.* Edited by R. A. Makkreel and F. Rodi. Princeton, NJ: Princeton University Press, 2002.

Eiland, H., and W. Jennings (2014). *Walter Benjamin: A Critical Life.* Cambridge, MA: Harvard University Press.

Eilenberger, W. (2006). "Die Befreiung des Alltäglichen: Gemeinsame Motive in den Sprachphilosophien von Stanley Cavell und Michail Bachtin." *Nach Feierabend: Zürcher Jahrbuch für Wissensgeschichte 2.*

———— (2009). *Das Werden des Menschen im Wort: Eine Studie zur Kulturphilosophie M. M. Bachtins.* Zurich: Chronos.

———— (2017). "Das Dämonische hat mich getroffen." *Philosophie Magazin 5,* no. 17, 48–51.

Farias, V. (1989). *Heidegger and Nazism.* Philadelphia: Temple University Press.

Felsch, P. (2015). *Der lange Sommer der Theorie: Geschichte einer Revolte (1960–1990).* Munich: Beck.

Ferrari, M. (2003). *Ernst Cassirer: Stationen einer philosophischen Biographie: Von der Marburger Schule zur Kulturphilosophie.* Hamburg: Felix Meiner.

Figal, G. (2016). *Heidegger zur Einführung.* Hamburg: Junius.

Fitzgerald, M. (2000). "Did Ludwig Wittgenstein Have Asperger's Syndrome?" *European Child and Adolescent Psychiatry 9,* no. 1, 61–65.

Förster, E. (2012). *Die 25 Jahre der Philosophie: Eine systematische Rekonstruktion.* Frankfurt: Vittorio Klostermann.

Frede, D. (2002). "Die Einheit des Seins: Heidegger in Davos—Kritische Überlegungen." In *Cassirer–Heidegger: 70 Jahre Davoser Disputation,* ed. D. Kaegi and E. Rudolph. Hamburg: Felix Meiner.

Frege, G. (1960). *Translations from the Philosophical Writings of Gottlob Frege.* Translated by P. Geach and M. Black. Oxford: Blackwell.

———— (1962). *Funktion, Begriff, Bedeutung.* Göttingen: Vandenhoeck & Ruprecht.

———— (1966). *Logische Untersuchungen.* Göttingen: Vandenhoeck & Ruprecht.

———— (1989). "Briefe an Ludwig Wittgenstein aus den Jahren 1914–1920," edited by A. Janik. *Grazer Philosophische Studien*, 33/34, 5–33.

Friedlander, E. (1995). *Walter Benjamin: A Philosophical Portrait.* Cambridge, MA: Harvard University Press.

Friedman, M. (2004). *A Parting of the Ways: Carnap, Cassirer, and Heidegger.* Chicago: Open Court.

Fuld, W. (1981). *Walter Benjamin zwischen den Stühlen.* Frankfurt: Hanser.

Gabriel, M. (2015). *Warum es die Welt nicht gibt.* Berlin: Ullstein.

Gadamer, H.-G. (1977). *Philosophische Lehrjahre: Eine Rückschau.* Frankfurt: Vittorio Klostermann.

Gebauer, G., F. Goppelsröder, and J. Volbers, eds. (2009). *Wittgenstein: Philosophie als "Arbeit an Einem selbst."* Munich: Fink.

Geier, M. (1999). *Der Wiener Kreis.* Reinbek: Rowohlt.

———— (2006). *Martin Heidegger.* Reinbek: Rowohlt.

Glock, H.-J. *A Wittgenstein Dictionary* (1996). Oxford and Malden, MA: Blackwell.

Gombrich, E. H. (1970). *Aby Warburg: An Intellectual Biography.* London: Phaidon.

Gordon, P. E. (2010). *Continental Divide: Heidegger, Cassirer, Davos.* Cambridge, MA: Harvard University Press.

Grunenberg, A. (2016). *Hannah Arendt und Martin Heidegger: Geschichte einer Liebe.* Munich: Piper.

Gumbrecht, H. U. (1993). "Everyday-World and Life-World as Philosophical Concepts: A Genealogical Approach." *New Literary History* 24, no. 4, 745–761.

———— (2001). *1926: Ein Jahr am Rand der Zeit.* Frankfurt: Suhrkamp.

Habermas, J. (1987). *Philosophisch-politische Profile.* Frankfurt: Suhrkamp.

———— (1991). *Erläuterungen zur Diskursethik.* Frankfurt: Suhrkamp.

———— (1997). "Die befreiende Kraft der symbolischen Formgebung: Ernst Cassirers humanistisches Erbe und die Bibliothek Warburg." In D. Frede and R. Schmücker, *Ernst Cassirers Werk und Wirkung: Kultur und Philosophie.* Darmstadt: Wissenschaftliche Buchgesellschaft.

———— (2012). *Nachmetaphysisches Denken II: Aufsätze und Repliken.* Frankfurt: Suhrkamp.

Hale, K. (1998). *Friends and Apostles: The Correspondence of Rupert Brooke and James Strachey, 1905–1914.* New Haven and London: Yale University Press.

Hampe, M. (1996). *Gesetz und Distanz: Studien über die Prinzipien der Gesetzmäßigkeiten in der theoretischen und praktischen Philosophie.* Heidelberg: Winter.

————— (2006). *Erkenntnis und Praxis: Zur Philosophie des Pragmatismus.* Frankfurt: Suhrkamp.

————— (2015). *Die Lehren der Philosophie.* Frankfurt: Suhrkamp.

Haverkampf, H.-E. (2016). *Benjamin in Frankfurt: Die zentralen Jahre 1922–1932.* Frankfurt: Suhrkamp.

Heidegger, G., ed. (2005). *Mein liebes Seelchen! Briefe Martin Heideggers an seine Frau Elfride 1915–1970.* Munich: Deutsche Verlags-Anstalt.

Henrich, D. (2011). *Werke im Werden: Über die Genesis philosophischer Einsichten.* Munich: Beck.

Hertzberg, L. (1994). *The Limits of Experience.* Helsinki: Philosophical Society of Finland.

Hitler, A. (2016). *Mein Kampf: Eine kritische Edition.* Munich and Berlin: Institut für Zeitgeschichte.

Hobsbawm, E. (1995). *The Age of Extremes: 1914–1991.* London: Michael Joseph.

Horkheimer, M., and T. W. Adorno (1991). *Dialektik der Aufklärung.* Frankfurt: Fischer. Translated by J. Cumming as *Dialectic of Enlightenment.* London: Allen Lane, 1973.

Humboldt, W. von (1995). *Schriften zur Sprache.* Stuttgart: Reclam.

Husserl, E. (1966). *Zur Phänomenologie des inneren Zeitbewußtseins (1893–1917).* In R. Boehm, *Husserliana X.* The Hague: Nijhoff.

————— (1990). *Die phänomenologische Methode: Ausgewählte Texte I.* Stuttgart: Reclam.

————— (1992). *Phänomenologie der Lebenswelt: Ausgewählte Texte II.* Stuttgart: Reclam.

Illies, F. (2012). *1913: Der Sommer des Jahrhunderts.* Frankfurt: Suhrkamp. Translated by S. Whiteside and J. L. Searle as *1913: The Year Before the Storm.* London: Clerkenwell Press, 2014.

Jäger, L. (2017). *Walter Benjamin: Das Leben eines Unvollendeten.* Frankfurt: Rowohlt.

Janik, A., and S. Toulmin (1973). *Wittgenstein's Vienna.* London: Weidenfeld & Nicolson.

Jaspers, K. (1960). *Psychologie der Weltanschauungen.* Berlin/Göttingen/Heidelberg: Springer.

————— (1978). *Philosophische Autobiographie.* Munich: Piper.

————— (1989). *Notizen zu Martin Heidegger.* Edited by H. Saner. Munich: Piper.

Jecht, D. (2003). *Die Aporie Wilhelm von Humboldts: Sein Studien- und Sprachprojekt zwischen Empirie und Reflexion.* Hildesheim: Olms.

Jonas, H. (1984). *Das Prinzip Verantwortung.* Frankfurt: Suhrkamp.

Kaegi, D. (1995). "Jenseits der symbolischen Formen: Zum Verhältnis von Anschauung und künstlicher Symbolik bei Ernst Cassirer." *Dialektik* 1, 73–84.

Kaegi, D., and E. Rudolph, eds. (2002). *Cassirer–Heidegger: 70 Jahre Davoser Disputation*. Hamburg: Felix Meiner.

Kershaw, I. (2015). *To Hell and Back*. London: Penguin.

Kessler, H. (1961). *Tagebücher 1918–1937*. Frankfurt: Suhrkamp.

Kipphoff, P. (1995). "Das Labor des Seelenarchivars." *Die Zeit* 17 (April 21).

Klages, L. (1972). *Der Geist als Widersacher der Seele*. Bonn: Bouvier.

Klagge, J. (2001). *Wittgenstein: Biography and Philosophy*. Cambridge: Cambridge University Press.

Koder, R., and L. Wittgenstein (2000). *Wittgenstein und die Musik: Briefwechsel Ludwig Wittgenstein Rudolf Koder*. Edited by M. Alber with B. McGuinness and M. Seekircher. Innsbruck: Haymon.

Kreis, G. (2010). *Cassirer und die Formen des Geistes*. Frankfurt: Suhrkamp.

Krois, J. M. (1987). *Cassirer: Symbolic Forms and History*. New Haven: Yale University Press.

————— (1995). "Semiotische Transformation der Philosophie: Verkörperung und Pluralismus bei Cassirer und Peirce." *Dialektik* 1, 61–71.

————— (2002). "Warum fand keine Davoser Disputation statt?" In *Cassirer–Heidegger: 70 Jahre Davoser Disputation*, ed. D. Kaegi and E. Rudolph. Hamburg: Felix Meiner.

Lacis, A. (1976). *Revolutionär im Beruf: Berichte über proletarisches Theater, über Meyerhold, Brecht, Benjamin und Piscator*. Edited by H. Brenner. Munich: Rogner & Bernhard.

Langer, S. K. (1957). *Philosophy in a New Key*. Cambridge, MA: Harvard University Press.

Leitner, B. (1995). *The Architecture of Ludwig Wittgenstein: A Documentation*. London: Academy Editions.

Lenin, V. I. (2007). *Materialism and Empirio-Criticism*. Honolulu: University Press of the Pacific.

Leo, P. (2013). *Der Wille zum Wesen: Weltanschauungskultur, charakterologisches Denken und Judenfeindschaft in Deutschland, 1890–1940*. Berlin: Matthias & Seitz.

Lewin, K. (1981). "Der Übergang von der aristotelischen zur galileischen Denkweise in Biologie und Psychologie." In K. Lewin, *Kurt-Lewin-Werkausgabe*, vol. 1, *Wissenschaftstheorie*, ed. A. Métraux, 233–271. Bern: Hans Huber; and Stuttgart: Klett-Cotta.

Lotter, M. S. (1996). *Die metaphysische Kritik des Subjekts: Eine Untersuchung von Whiteheads universalisierter Sozialontologie*. Hildesheim: Olms.

Löwith, K. (1960). *Heidegger: Denker in dürftiger Zeit*. Göttingen: Vandenhoeck & Ruprecht.

————— (1986). *Mein Leben in Deutschland vor und nach 1933*. Stuttgart: Metzler.

Lubrich, O. (2016). "Benjamin in Bern." *UniPress* (University of Bern) 167, 28–31.

Lukács, G. (1971). *History and Class Consciousness*. Translated by R. Livingstone. Cambridge, MA: MIT Press.

———— (1971). *The Theory of the Novel: A Historico-Philosophical Essay on the Forms of Great Epic Literature.* Translated by A. Bostock. Cambridge, MA: MIT Press.

Lyotard, J.-F. (1984). *The Postmodern Condition: A Report on Knowledge.* Translated by G. Bennington and B. Massumi. Manchester: Manchester University Press.

Malcolm, N. (1989). *Ludwig Wittgenstein: A Memoir.* London: Oxford University Press.

Marazia, C., and D. Stimilli, eds. (2007). *Ludwig Binswanger, Aby Warburg—Unendliche Heilung—Aby Warburgs Krankengeschichte.* Zurich: Diaphanes.

Mayer, H. (1992). *Der Zeitgenosse Walter Benjamin.* Frankfurt: Jüdischer Verlag.

McGuinness, B., ed. (1979). *Wittgenstein and the Vienna Circle: Conversations.* Recorded by F. Waismann. Translated by J. Schulte and B. McGuinness. New York: Barnes & Noble.

———— (1990). *Wittgenstein, 1889–1921: Young Ludwig: A Life.* London: Penguin.

————, ed. (2012). *Wittgenstein in Cambridge: Letters and Documents 1911–1951.* 4th ed. Oxford and Malden, MA: Wiley-Blackwell.

McGuinness, B., and G. H. von Wright, eds. (1995). *Ludwig Wittgenstein: Cambridge Letters—Correspondence with Russell, Keynes, Moore, Ramsey and Sraffa.* Oxford: Blackwell.

Meyer, T. (2006). *Ernst Cassirer.* Hamburg: Ellert & Richter.

Mittelmeier, M. (2013). *Adorno in Neapel: Wie sich eine Sehnsuchtslandschaft in Philosophie verwandelt.* Munich: Siedler.

Monk, R. (1991). *Ludwig Wittgenstein: The Duty of Genius.* London: Vintage.

Moore, G. E. (1959). *Philosophical Papers.* London: Routledge.

Müller-Doohm, S. (2003). *Theodor W. Adorno.* Translated by R. Livingstone. Stanford, CA: Stanford University Press.

Nedo, M., and M. Ranchetti (1983). *Ludwig Wittgenstein: Sein Leben in Texten und Bildern.* Frankfurt: Suhrkamp.

Neiman, S. (1994). *The Unity of Reason.* Oxford and New York: Oxford University Press.

Neske, G., ed. (1977). *Erinnerungen an Martin Heidegger.* Pfullingen: Neske.

Neurath, O. (1981). *Gesammelte philosophische und methodologische Schriften.* Vienna: Hölder-Pichler-Tempsky.

Ott, H. (1993). *Martin Heidegger: A Political Life.* Translated by A. Blunden. London: HarperCollins.

Paetzold, H. (1993). *Ernst Cassirer.* Hamburg: Junius.

Palmier, J.-M. (2006). *Walter Benjamin: Le chiffonnier, l'ange et le petit bossu.* Paris: Klincksieck.

Peirce, C. S. (1983). *Phänomen und Logik der Zeichen.* Frankfurt: Suhrkamp.

———— (1991). *Schriften zum Pragmatismus und Pragmatizismus.* Frankfurt: Suhrkamp.

Peukert, D. J. K. (2014). *The Weimar Republic.* Translated by R. Deveson. New York: Farrar, Straus and Giroux.

Pinsent, D. (1990). *A Portrait of Wittgenstein as a Young Man.* Edited by G. H. von Wright. Oxford: Oxford University Press.

Plato (2007). *The Republic.* Translated by D. Lee. London: Penguin.

Pöggeler, O. (1983). *Der Denkweg des Martin Heidegger.* Pfullingen: Neske.

Poole, B. (1998). "Bakhtin and Cassirer: The Philosophical Origins of Bakhtin's Carnival Messianism." *South Atlantic Quarterly* 97, no. 3/4, 537–578.

Puttnies, H., and G. Smith, eds. (1991). *Benjaminiana.* Giessen: Anabas.

Quine, W. V. O. (1980). *Word and Object.* Cambridge, MA: MIT Press.

Rang, F. C. (2013). *Deutsche Bauhütte: Ein Wort an uns Deutsche über mögliche Gerechtigkeit gegen Belgien und Frankreich und zur Philosophie der Politik.* Leipzig, 1924. Reprint Göttingen: Wallstein.

Recki, B., ed. (2012). *Philosophie der Kultur—Kultur des Philosophierens—Ernst Cassirer im 20. und 21. Jahrhundert.* Hamburg: Felix Meiner.

Rhees, R., ed. (1984). *Recollections of Wittgenstein.* Oxford: Oxford University Press.

Rickert, H. (1922). *Die Philosophie des Lebens: Darstellung und Kritik der philosophischen Moderströmungen unserer Zeit.* Tübingen: Mohr.

Rorty, R. (1989). *Contingency, Irony and Solidarity.* Cambridge: Cambridge University Press.

——— (1991). *Essays on Heidegger and Others.* Cambridge: Cambridge University Press.

——— (2017). *Philosophy and the Mirror of Nature.* Princeton, NJ: Princeton University Press.

Russell, B. (1903). *The Principles of Mathematics.* Cambridge: Cambridge University Press.

——— (1957). *Why I Am Not a Christian.* London: Allen & Unwin.

——— (1998). *Autobiography.* London: Routledge.

Safranski, R. (2001). *Ein Meister aus Deutschland: Heidegger und seine Zeit.* Frankfurt: Suhrkamp. Originally published 1995. Translated by E. Osers as *Martin Heidegger: Between Good and Evil.* Cambridge MA: Harvard University Press, 1999.

Sarnitz, A. (2011). *Die Architektur Ludwig Wittgensteins: Rekonstruktion einer Idee.* Vienna: Böhlau.

Saussure, F. de (2016). *Course in General Linguistics.* Translated by R. Harris. London: Bloomsbury.

Scheler, M. (1926). *Wesen und Formen der Sympathie.* Bonn: Bouvier.

——— (1986). "Ordo Amoris." In Scheler, *Schriften aus dem Nachlass*, vol. 1, *Zur Ethik und Erkenntnislehre* (*Gesammelte Werke*, vol. 10). Edited by Maria Scheler. Bonn: Bouvier.

Schilpp, P., ed. (1949). *The Philosophy of Ernst Cassirer.* La Salle, IL: Open Court.

——— (1963). *The Philosophy of Rudolf Carnap.* La Salle, IL: Open Court.

Scholem, G. (1975). *Walter Benjamin: Die Geschichte einer Freundschaft.* Frankfurt:

Suhrkamp. Translated by H. Zohn as *Walter Benjamin: The Story of a Friendship*. New York: New York Review of Books, 2003.

——— (1994–1999). *Briefe*. 3 vols. Edited by I. Schedletzky and T. Sparr. Munich: Beck.

Schubbach, A. (2016). *Die Genese des Symbolischen: Zu den Anfängen von Ernst Cassirers Kulturphilosophie*. Hamburg: Felix Meiner.

Schulte, M., ed. (1989). *Paris war unsere Geliebte*. Munich: Piper.

Schwemmer, O. (1997). *Ernst Cassirer: Ein Philosoph der europäischen Moderne*. Berlin: Akademie.

——— (1997). *Die kulturelle Existenz des Menschen*. Berlin: Akademie.

——— (2002). "Zwischen Ereignis und Form." *Cassirer–Heidegger: 70 Jahre Davoser Disputation*, ed. D. Kaegi and E. Rudolph. Hamburg: Felix Meiner.

Sigmund, K. (2015). *Sie nannten sich der Wiener Kreis: Exaktes Denken am Rande des Untergangs*. Wiesbaden: Springer.

Simmel, G. (1921). *Goethe*. Leipzig: Heptagon.

——— (1995). *Kant und Goethe*. In *Georg-Simmel Gesamtausgabe*, vol. 10, 119–166. Frankfurt: Suhrkamp.

Somavilla, I., ed. (2006). *Wittgenstein: Engelmann, Briefe, Begegnungen, Erinnerungen*. Innsbruck and Vienna: Haymon.

——— (2012). *Begegnungen mit Wittgenstein: Ludwig Hännsels Tagebücher 1918/1919 und 1921/1922*. Innsbruck and Vienna: Haymon.

Somavilla, I., A. Unterkirchner, and C. P. Berger, eds. (1994). *Ludwig Hänsel–Ludwig Wittgenstein: Eine Freundschaft: Briefwechsel, Aufsätze, Kommentare*. Innsbruck: Haymon.

Später, J. (2016). *Siegfried Kracauer: Eine Biographie*. Frankfurt: Suhrkamp.

Spengler, O. (1922). *Der Untergang des Abendlandes: Umrisse einer Morphologie der Weltgeschichte*. Vol. 2, *Welthistorische Perspektiven*. Munich: Beck.

Storck, J. W., ed. (1990). *Martin Heidegger, Elisabeth Blochmann: Briefwechsel, 1918–1969*. Marbach: Deutsche Schillergesellschaft.

Taylor, C. (1999). *The Sources of the Self*. Cambridge: Cambridge University Press.

Thomä, D., ed. (2005). *Heidegger Handbuch: Leben–Werk–Wirkung*. Stuttgart: Metzler.

Tihanov, G. (2000). *The Master and the Slave: Lukács, Bakhtin and the Ideas of Their Time*. Oxford: Oxford University Press.

Tömmel, T. N. (2013). *Wille und Passion: Der Liebesbegriff bei Heidegger und Arendt*. Frankfurt: Suhrkamp.

Trabant, J. (1990). *Traditionen Humboldts*. Frankfurt: Suhrkamp.

von Wright, G. H., ed. (1975). *Ludwig Wittgenstein: Letters to C. K. Ogden*. Oxford: Oxford University Press.

Vossenkuhl, W., ed. (2001). *Ludwig Wittgenstein: Tractatus logicophilosophicus: Klassiker auslegen*. Berlin: Akademie.

Vygotsky, L. S. (2016). "Thinking and Speech." In *The Collected Works of L. S. Vygotsky*. New York: Springer.

Warburg, A. M., and W. F. Mainland (1939). "A Lecture on Serpent Ritual." *Journal of the Warburg Institute* 2, no. 4 (April): 277–292.

Watson, P. (2010). *The German Genius: Europe's Third Renaissance, the Second Scientific Revolution and the Twentieth Century*. London: Simon & Schuster.

Waugh, A. (2010). *The House of Wittgenstein: A Family at War*. London: Bloomsbury.

Weininger, O. (1905). *Geschlecht und Charakter: Eine prinzipielle Untersuchung*. Leipzig and Vienna: Braumüller. Translated by L. Lob as *Sex and Character: An Investigation of Fundamental Principles*. Bloomington: Indiana University Press, 2005.

Whitehead, A. N. (1984). *The Function of Reason*. Princeton, NJ: Princeton University Press.

Whitehead, A. N., and B. Russell (1910–1913). *Principia Mathematica*, 3 vols. Cambridge: Cambridge University Press.

Witkop, P., ed. (1922). *Deutsches Leben der Gegenwart*. Berlin: Wegweiser.

Witte, B. (1985). *Walter Benjamin*. Reinbek: Rowohlt.

Wittgenstein, H. (2006). *Ludwig sagt . . .* Edited by M. Iven. Berlin: H-E Verlag.

————— (2015). *Familienerinnerungen*. Edited by I. Somavilla. Innsbruck and Vienna: Haymon.

Wittgenstein, L. (1961). *Notebooks 1914–1916*. Edited by G. H. von Wright and G. E. M. Anscombe. Translated by G. E. M. Anscombe. Oxford: Blackwell.

————— (1965). "A Lecture on Ethics." *Philosophical Review* 74, no. 1 (January): 3–12.

————— (1969). *Briefe an Ludwig von Ficker*. Salzburg: Müller.

————— (1980). *Briefwechsel mit B. Russell, G. E. Moore, J. M. Keynes, F. P. Ramsey, W. Eccles, P. Engelmann und L. von Ficker*. Edited by B. F. McGuinness and H. von Wright. Frankfurt: Suhrkamp.

————— (1989). *Vortrag über die Ethik und andere kleine Schriften*. Edited by J. Schulte. Frankfurt: Suhrkamp.

Wizisla, E. (2004). *Benjamin und Brecht*. Frankfurt: Suhrkamp.

————— (2015). *Begegnungen mit Benjamin*. Leipzig: Lehmstedt.

—————, ed. (2017). *Benjamin und Brecht: Denken in Extremen*. Frankfurt: Suhrkamp.

Wünsche, K. (1985). *Der Volksschullehrer Ludwig Wittgenstein*. Frankfurt: Suhrkamp.

Wundt, W. (1911). *Probleme der Völkerpsychologie*. Leipzig: Wiegandt.

————— (1916). *Die Nationen und ihre Philosophie: Ein Kapitel zum Weltkrieg*. Leipzig: Wiegandt.

Ziegler, P. (2016). *Between the Wars 1919–1939*. London: Quercus.

PHOTOGRAPH CREDITS

INDEX

"About Language in General and Human Language in Particular" (Benjamin), 92–95, 99, 210, 222

absolute objectivity, 50–51

abstract symbolism, 67–68

academic culture, 103–4

active dialogue, 112

Adorno, Theodor Wiesengrund
and Benjamin's Arcades Project, 351
and Benjamin's career, 298–99, 337–38
and Benjamin's time in Berlin, 348–49
and Benjamin's time in Naples, 207–8
friendship with Benjamin, 194
and Heidegger's "fading of significance," 86–87
and Lukács's *History and Class Consciousness*, 223

allegory
and Arendt's "Shadow," 191
and Benjamin's "Epistemo-Critical Prologue," 212, 216–17, 219–21
and Benjamin's relationship with Lacis, 201
and Cassirer's travels by sea, 294
and Lukács's *History and Class Consciousness*, 224
Wittgenstein's logical symbolism, 67–68

American Constitution, 303

American Declaration of Independence, 302

analogy, 64–66, 68, 94, 97, 270, 286

analytic philosophy, 14, 244, 273, 276

Angelus Novus, 138

Angst. See anxiety

animal symbolicum, 16

anthropology, 178, 180–81

anti-Semitism
and Benjamin's academic career, 20, 140
and Cassirer's academic career, 57
and Davos conference, 324–25
and Heidegger, 11
and postwar German culture, 84
and totemistic thinking, 135–36
and Weimar Germany, 125–28, 131

anxiety
and Benjamin's Arcades Project, 342
and Davos conference, 330–33
Heidegger on death and existential angst, 187–88
and Heidegger's analysis of Dasein, 231, 234–37
and Heidegger's *Being and Time*, 237–40
and Heidegger's philosophy, at mother's death, 240
and Heidegger's view of human metaphysics, 16–17
and metaphysical foundation of philosophy, 312
and Warburg's theory of culture, 180
and Wittgenstein's logical empiricism, 275

"Apostles" club, 4, 356, 360

Arcades Project, The (Benjamin), 26, 291, 338, 342–45, 346, 351, 364

INDEX

architecture, 266–70, 276

Arendt, Hannah
  doctoral work, 192
  evolution of philosophy of, 240
  Heidegger's feelings for, 188–89
  on Heidegger's influence, 9
  relationship with Heidegger, 190–93, 203,
    225–26, 306, 320

Aristotle, 120–22, 124, 133, 229, 310–11

art and art criticism
  Benjamin on German Romanticism, 34–36
  Cassirer's symbolic forms, 109–10
  and critical object-reference, 36–37
  and mythical thinking, 136–37
  and Warburg Library, 132

astrology, 183, 247

astronomy, 183, 247

Augustine, Saint, 253–54

authenticity, 17, 86–89, 239–40

autism, 64

avant-garde culture, 289

Baker, Josephine, 348

Ball, Hugo, 32

Balzac, Honoré de, 344

barber paradox, Russell's, 73–74

Baroque tragic drama, German, 21, 194–95,
  201, 211, 217, 219, 224, 238. *See also*
  Origin of German Tragic Drama, The
  (Benjamin)

Bauch, Bruno, 323

Baudelaire, Charles
  and Benjamin's "Epistemo-Critical
    Prologue," 23
  and Benjamin's "Task of the Translator,"
    95–96, 120
  Benjamin's translations of, 33, 102, 137–38,
    210, 222
  on transitory nature of modern age, 295

Bavaria, 184–85

Being and Time (Heidegger)
  and analysis of Dasein, 228–30, 306–7
  and anxiety, 234–36
  and Davos conference, 9, 16, 325, 327–30
  and death of Heidegger's parents, 239–40
  and existential anxiety, 234–36
  and Heidegger–Cassirer meeting, 179–80
  and Heidegger's appointment to Marburg
    chair, 304–5
  and metaphysical foundation of philosophy,
    309–10
  pressure to publish, 227, 306
  reception and influence of, 304
  and study of equipment, 231–34
  and time and temporality, 230–31, 307–8

Bellevue Sanatorium (Kreuzlingen,
  Switzerland), 179–80

Benjamin, Dora
  and Benjamin's avoidance of draft, 32
  and Benjamin's relationship with Lacis,
    26–27, 201, 204
  divorce, 18, 27, 350, 364
  and financial difficulties, 38, 141, 194–95,
    290, 347
  health problems, 33
  marriage difficulties, 18, 26–27, 88–89, 142
  travel to Paris, 291

Benjamin, Stefan, 18, 27, 33, 291

Benjamin, Walter
  and academic ambitions, 20–21, 138–39,
    151–52, 194–95, 221–22
  and academic detachment, 104
  and academic misfortunes, 20–23
  allegorical method of, 220–21
  Arcades Project, 26, 291, 338, 342–46,
    351, 364
  and Cassirer's address on Weimar
    Constitution, 304
  and Cassirer's career, 298
  and Cassirer's philosophy of symbolic
    forms, 113
  and challenges of postwar philosophy,
    53, 92
  and choice between Moscow and Palestine,
    222–25
  and cognitive method, 23–25
  and "criticism," 34–36
  and Davos conference, 18–21, 329
  divorce, 18, 27, 350, 364
  Duns Scotus work, 92–95
  emotional struggles of, 25–27, 37–38, 95,
    102, 277, 281, 286
  "Epistemo-Critical Prologue," 21, 209–12,
    215–18, 221

and financial difficulties, 25–27, 37–38,
    89–91, 137–42, 197, 198, 337,
    350–51
and Frankfurt School, 299
and "Goethe's *Elective Affinities*,"
    142–44, 146, 194, 222–25,
    281–82, 338
health problems, 198
and Heidegger rivalry, 92–95
and Heidegger's analysis of Dasein,
    229, 230
and Heidegger's *Being and Time*, 313
and Heidegger's existential leap, 152–53
height of career, 345–48
and Lacis, 198–204, 282–85
on language after the fall, 217–20
marriage difficulties, 18, 26–27, 88–89
metaphysical and revolutionary phase,
    342–45
military service evasion, 31–32
at Mon Repos pension, 33–35
and *Moscow Diary*, 284–85
and *One-Way Street*, 277–82
and origins of Frankfurt School, 348–51
and origins of Wittgenstein's *Tractatus*, 252
political theology, 153
postdoctoral thesis, 21, 22–23, 90, 92, 93,
    138, 139. 193–96. *See also Origin of
    German Tragic Drama, The* (Benjamin)
and problem of progress, 359
publication of works, 224–25, 336–39
rejection of thesis, 208, 220–21, 222
and self-reference/heteroreference, 36–37
suicide, 364
and Surrealism, 339–41
symbolic worldview, 23
translation work of, 22, 33, 95–96, 102, 120,
    137–38, 204, 210, 222, 225, 282, 290
on translator's task, 96–102
travel to Capri and Naples, 196–97,
    198–200, 208
travel to Paris, 289–93
wartime refuge in Zurich, 32–33
and Wittgenstein's linguistic philosophy, 255
and Wittgenstein's "leap into faith," 161
Berg, Alban, 207
Berlin, 348–51

Berlin Childhood around Nineteen Hundred
    (Benjamin), 23, 24
Bible, 217
Bing, Gertrud, 245
Binswanger, Ludwig, 179, 184
biological science, 110, 178
Black, Dora, 166
Black Forest
    and advancement of Heidegger's work, 123
    and Benjamin's Arcades Project, 342
    and Heidegger's homes, 117–18, 314
    and Heidegger's self-image, 87–88, 232,
        237, 239, 258
    and Heidegger's youth, 8
Blackstone, William, 302
Bloch, Ernst, 204, 281, 337, 338
Blochmann, Elisabeth, 53, 306, 309, 314–15,
    335, 363
Bloomsbury Group, 168, 356
Bohr, Niels, 279
Bollnow, Otto F., 11
Born, Max, 279
bourgeois culture
    and Benjamin's analysis of Goethe, 146–53
    and Benjamin's Arcades Project, 339
    and Benjamin's conflict with neighbors, 141
    and Benjamin's financial difficulties, 90
    and Benjamin's "Goethe's *Elective Affinities*,"
        146, 223
    and Benjamin's relationship with Lacis, 201
    and Benjamin's time on Capri and in
        Naples, 199, 207, 208
    and Benjamin's time in Moscow, 288
    and Benjamin's view of philosophers, 197
    and Capri, 198
    and Cassirer's lifestyle, 18–19, 128
    and construction of Heidegger house in
        Freiburg, 313–14
    and Heidegger's marriage difficulties, 82
    and Heidegger's self-image, 88, 236
    and marriage practices, 144–45, 148–50,
        151, 190, 226, 306
    and revolutionary sentiment, 343
Braumüller, Wilhelm, 69
Brecht, Bertolt, 22, 26, 338, 347–48
Bröcker, Walter, 186
Bultmann, Rudolf, 186–87

Cabaret Voltaire, 32

Caesar, Friedel, 79, 82, 88

Campaign in France (Goethe), 11

Capri, 196–200, 204, 277

Carnap, Rudolf, 14, 271, 273, 321

Cartesian philosophy, 249. *See also*
    Descartes, René

Cassirer, Anna, 105, 126

Cassirer, Ernst
  address on Weimar Constitution, 299,
    300–304
  and anti-Semitism in Weimar Germany,
    125–28
  arrival in Hamburg, 102
  Benjamin contrasted with, 25
  and Benjamin's critique of bourgeois
    marriage, 144
  contrasted with other key figures, 103–5
  daily life, 104–5
  on dangers of culture, 135
  and Davos conference, 8–13, 15–19, 319–36
  elected rector at Hamburg University,
    363–64
  and financial difficulties, 137
  Hamburg University posting, 59–60
  and Heidegger's Marburg position, 227
  impact of Warburg Library, 128–32
  and *The Individual and the Cosmos*,
    242–50
  and interdisciplinary research at Warburg,
    245–47
  invited to Frankfurt University, 297–99
  and "Kant and German Intellectual Life,"
    105–6
  and Marburg School, 186
  military service evasion, 58
  and political upheavals of 1920s, 252
  and primal language, 101
  and problem of progress, 359
  Renaissance philosophy lecture,
    241–42
  on role of philosophy, 243–45
  sexuality, 105
  status among German scholars, 56–57
  and subjectivity of "character," 54–56
  travel to England and Netherlands, 293–97
  and university culture, 103–4

and Warburg Library, 177–78, 179

and Warburg School, 21–22

and Warburg's theory of culture, 182–83

and wartime struggles, 54, 58–59

and Wittgenstein's linguistic philosophy, 255

Cassirer, Georg, 105

Cassirer, Heinz, 105

Cassirer, Toni
  and anti-Semitism in Germany, 127, 135
  and Cassirer's journey to England, 296
  and Cassirer's Weimar Constitution
    address, 299, 304
  and Davos conference, 10–11, 320, 322,
    324–25
  injury, 294
  marriage dynamics, 153
  and Warburg Library, 131

Catholicism, 45–47, 94, 154–56, 239–40

Chaplin, Charlie, 329

"Chok" (shock) events, 214

Chomsky, Noam, 112–13

Christianity, 39–40, 43–44, 186–88. *See also*
    Catholicism; Protestantism

class struggle and conflict, 223, 285, 323, 338

Cohen, Hermann, 33, 57, 186, 298, 321,
    324–25, 326

Cohn, Alfred, 337

Cohn, Jula, 143, 153, 201, 289, 337

collage technique, 342, 344–45

Cologne University, 227–28

Combat League for German Youth, 322–23

communism, 185, 201, 202, 223, 285, 287–88,
    338, 341, 349, 356

"Concept of Art Criticism in German
    Romanticism, The" (Benjamin), 20,
    34–36, 97

*Concept of Substance and the Concept of
    Function, The* (Cassirer), 57

"Conceptual Form of Mythical Thought, The"
    (Cassirer), 132–34

Confessions (Augustine), 253–54

consumer capitalism, 343–44

continental philosophy, 276

Copernican revolution of Kant, 108

Copernicus, Nicolaus, 247

Cornelius, Hans, 194, 208–9

critical object-reference, 36–37

INDEX

critical theory, 299

Critique of Pure Reason (Kant), 6, 14, 16, 211, 320, 325, 355

"Cultural Crisis of the Present Day, The" (Spann), 322–23

cultural environment
  and Benjamin on art criticism, 34–35
  and Benjamin's "Epistemo-Critical Prologue," 211, 218, 221
  and Benjamin's time in Berlin, 347–48
  Cassirer on contrasts in, 106
  and Cassirer's "Conceptual Form of Mythical Thought," 133, 134–35
  and Cassirer's *Individual and the Cosmos*, 242–43, 247, 249
  and Cassirer's philosophy, 104, 106, 107
  and Cassirer's symbolic forms, 109, 111–12
  and Cassirer's Weimar Constitution address, 299, 300
  and Davos conference, 15, 17–18, 322–23, 332–34, 335, 339, 343
  and Enlightenment ideals, 80–81
  and Frankfurt University, 298
  and German nationalism, 56–57
  and Heidegger's analysis of Dasein, 229, 309
  and Heidegger's *Being and Time*, 309, 311
  and Heidegger's "fading of significance," 86
  and Heidegger's view of human metaphysics, 16–17
  impact of World War I, 31–32
  and Moscow, 283–84
  and mythical thinking, 136–37
  and organization of Warburg Library, 129–30
  and postwar anti-Semitism, 84
  and problem of progress, 359
  and Vienna Circle, 271
  and Warburg Library, 130–31
  and Warburg's theory of culture, 180–81, 183
  and Wittgenstein's *Dictionary for Primary Schools*, 256
  and Wittgenstein's logical empiricism, 274–75
  and Wittgenstein's response to German cultural crisis, 251, 252
  and Wittgenstein's *Tractatus*, 6, 68

"Curious Tale of the Childhood Sweethearts, The" (in Goethe's *Elective Affinities*), 151

Dadaism, 32, 340

Dalí, Salvador, 329

Darwin, Charles, 14–15

Das Kapital (Marx), 208

Dasein
  and anxiety, 231, 234–37
  and Arendt's doctoral work, 192
  and challenges of postwar philosophy, 123
  and Davos conference, 321, 327–31, 333, 342–43
  and existential angst, 16–17, 187–88
  and Heidegger's *Being and Time*, 228–30, 230–32, 234–40, 307–13
  and Heidegger's existential leap, 152–53
  and Heidegger's focus on authenticity, 86
  and Heidegger's "Phenomenological Interpretations of Aristotle," 121–22
  and Heidegger's phenomenology, 178
  and Heidegger's philosophical evolution, 50–52
  and Heidegger's relationship with Arendt, 190–91
  and metaphysical foundation of philosophy, 307–13

Davos University Conferences
  and Benjamin, 18–21, 22
  Cassirer–Heidegger debate, 11–12, 16–18, 325–34
  Heidegger's preparations, 315, 319–22
  impact on Benjamin, 339, 342
  impact on Cassirer, 334–36
  impact on Wittgenstein, 355
  Kant's metaphysics as theme for, 12–16, 17–18
  overview of, 8–11
  and political climate of Germany, 322–24
  Toni Cassirer's role at, 322, 324–25

Decline of the West, The (Spengler), 48

democracy and democratization, 105, 150, 300–304, 343

Denkbilder (thought-pictures), 23

INDEX

Der Brenner, 69

Descartes, René
  and academic detachment, 103
  and Cartesian skepticism, 76–78, 80, 85
  and Cassirer's *Individual and the Cosmos*,
    243, 249
  and Heidegger's analysis of Dasein, 229
  and modern epistemology, 65

dialectical materialism, 280

Dictionary for Primary Schools (Wittgenstein),
    255–57

Dostoyevsky, Fyodor, 23

drug use, 340

dualisms, 106

Duma Revolution (1905), 200

Duns Scotus: Theory of Categories and Meaning
    (Heidegger), 92–93

Ebert, Friedrich, 251

ecological movement, 87

Economic Consequences of the Peace, The
    (Keynes), 167, 175

economic theory and conditions
  and Cassirer's symbolic forms, 110
  and challenges faced by Weimar
    Germany, 300
  and collapse of Weimar Germany, 184
  and Davos conference, 15
  and Elfride Heidegger's education,
    46, 119
  and philosophical challenges of the
    1920s, 295
  and postwar Keynesian theory, 167–68,
    174–75
  and pressures on Frankfurt University, 195

Ego, 82

Einstein, Albert, 8, 14, 112

Elias, Norbert, 321

ellipse (geometrical form), 183, 241–42

empiricism
  and architectural design of Wittgenstein
    house, 270
  and Heidegger's phenomenology, 178
  and Heidegger's worldview problem, 48
  logical empiricism, 271, 274–76,
    353–55

Engelmann, Paul, 66, 155, 265, 267

Enlightenment era and ideals
  and Benjamin's analysis of Goethe, 149
  and Benjamin's "Epistemo-Critical
    Prologue," 214
  and Cartesian skepticism, 81
  and Cassirer's address on Weimar
    Constitution, 302
  and Cassirer's "Conceptual Form of
    Mythical Thought," 134
  and Cassirer's *Individual and the Cosmos*,
    249–50
  and Davos conference, 15
  and Heidegger's "Phenomenological
    Interpretations of Aristotle," 135
  and Warburg's theory of culture, 181–82
  and Wittgenstein's *Tractatus*, 158, 252

Enquiry into Human Understanding, An
    (Hume), 6

"Epistemo-Critical Prologue" (Benjamin), 21,
    209–12, 215–18, 221

epistemology
  Benjamin's "Epistemo-Critical Prologue,"
    21, 209–12, 215–18, 220–21
  and Benjamin's *One-Way Street*, 280
  and Benjamin's "Task of the Translator," 102
  and Cartesian skepticism, 85–87
  and Cassirer's philosophy, 108
  and Cassirer's symbolic forms, 109
  and Heidegger's analysis of Dasein, 233
  and Heidegger's religious crisis, 46–47
  and metaphysical foundation of
    philosophy, 311
  and subjectivity of "character," 55–56

equipment (*Zeug*), 231–34

Eros, 54, 82, 226, 306

es gibt question, 48–52, 82, 84–85. *See also*
    Dasein

esotericism, 23, 221

ethics
  and Benjamin's analysis of Goethe, 150
  and Benjamin's "Epistemo-Critical
    Prologue," 217, 218
  and Cassirer's Weimar Constitution
    address, 301–2
  and Davos conference, 13, 326, 327
  and problem of progress, 360
  and Wittgenstein's "leap into faith," 160–62

and Wittgenstein's logical linguistic
analysis, 43
and Wittgenstein's *Tractatus*, 40, 157, 159
Ethics (Spinoza), 6
evolution, 14–15
existential questions, 52, 84–85. *See also*
anxiety; Dasein
"experience-of-the-question," 52, 84
Expressionism, 219

Fall, the (*Verfallen*), 121–22, 181, 217, 218,
219, 229, 244
Fascism, 185
fatalism, 284
fate, 31, 145–48
"Fate and Character" (Benjamin), 31–32
Faust (Goethe), 268
Feigl, Herbert, 271
Fichte, Johann Gottlieb, 24, 34
Ficker, Ludwig von, 40, 69–70, 76
Fischer, S., 90
flânerie, 342
flight, 248
"Forms and Form Transformations of the
Philosophical Concept of Truth"
(Cassirer), 363–64
Forster, E. M., 168
Franco, Francisco, 251
Frankfurt School, 299, 351
Frankfurt University
and Adorno's education, 207–8
and Benjamin's academic ambitions, 20–21,
194–95, 221–22
and Cassirer's academic career, 297–99
and Davos conference, 319
and Heidegger's academic career, 320
Frankfurter Zeitung, 19, 207, 290, 336–38
freedom, 145–48, 246, 249, 330–31
Freedom and Form (Cassirer), 55, 58
Frege, Gottlob, 39, 66, 97, 275
Freiburg University
and Benjamin–Heidegger rivalry, 92
and Heidegger's academic career, 9, 46–47,
49, 119, 305, 313–15, 319, 363
and Heidegger's move to Marburg,
186–87, 189
and Heidegger's philosophical evolution, 50

and postwar food crisis, 87
and refugees, 184
Rickert seminars, 22
and World War I and aftermath, 47, 184
Freikorps, 185
French National Assembly, 302
French Revolution, 303
Freud, Sigmund, 68, 82, 252
Freudian psychoanalysis, 69, 229–30
Friedman, Michael, 11
Friedrich-Wilhelm University, 54
"Fundamental Concepts of Metaphysics, The"
(Heidegger), 310

Gadamer, Hans-Georg, 186
Gelb, Adhémar, 209
generative grammar, 112
geometry, 241–42, 270
George, Stefan, 143
German Baroque tragic drama, 21, 194–95,
201, 211, 217, 219, 224, 238. *See also*
Origin of German Tragic Drama, The
(Benjamin)
German Communist Party, 287–88
German culture, 84, 87
German idealism, 343
German nationalism, 57, 322–24
German People's Party (DVP), 185
German Romanticism, 35
Gesamtkunstwerk, 136–37
Gestalt theory, 279
Goethe, Johann Wolfgang von
and architecture, 268
and Benjamin's approach to existential leap,
152–53
and Benjamin's *Moscow Diary*, 285
and Cassirer's academic status, 298
and Cassirer's address on Weimar
Constitution, 300, 303–4
and Cassirer's *Freedom and Form*, 55–56
and Davos conference, 11, 332
on influence of history, vii
and revolutionary sentiment, 343
"Goethe's *Elective Affinities*" (Benjamin),
142–44, 146–53, 194, 222–25,
281–82, 338
Goldstein, Kurt, 351

Gorky, Maxim, 198
Gramsci, Antonio, 356
grief, 219, 221
ground concept, 309–10
Gundolf, Friedrich, 143
Gutkind, Erich, 139–40, 196

Haas, Willy, 337
Habsburg Empire, 39
Hachmann (Cassirer's neighbor), 127–28, 131, 135–36
Haidbauer, Josef, 259–61
Hamburg, 128
Hamburg Senate, 299, 301
Hamburg University, 59, 105, 112, 131–32
Hamburger Fremdenblatt, 297
happiness as goal of philosophy, 67
Hartmann, Nicolai, 186, 227
Haus Wittgenstein (Kundmanngasse, Vienna), 266–70
Hebrew language, 223, 225, 292, 346, 350–51
Hebrew University, Jerusalem, 291, 346
Hegel, Georg Wilhelm Friedrich, 143
Heidegger, Elfride (Petri)
    birth of second son, 88
    construction of Black Forest cabin, 117–18
    and construction of Freiburg house, 313–14
    and Davos conference, 334
    and death of Heidegger's parents, 239
    economics studies, 119
    and financial struggles, 117–18, 124–25, 184
    and Heidegger's academic career, 305, 306, 319
    and Heidegger's philosophical breakthrough, 80–81
    and Heidegger's relationship with Arendt, 191
    marriage difficulties, 78–83, 225–26
Heidegger, Fritz, 87
Heidegger, Hermann, 88
Heidegger, Jörg, 47
Heidegger, Martin
    and academic detachment, 104
    on "academic philosophizing," 103
    and anti-Semitism, 11
    appointment to Marburg University chair, 304–5

    and Arendt, 188–93
    Benjamin contrasted with, 25
    and Benjamin's approach to existential leap, 152–53
    and Benjamin's Arcades Project, 342–43
    Benjamin's conflict with, 22
    and Benjamin's critique of bourgeois marriage, 144
    and Benjamin's "Epistemo-Critical Prologue," 218
    Benjamin's rivalry with, 92–95
    and Benjamin's "spiritual essence," 213
    breakthrough of authenticity, 87–89
    burst of creativity in 1919, 78–79
    and Cartesian skepticism, 77–78, 80–83, 85–87
    and Cassirer's address on Weimar Constitution, 304
    and Cassirer's "Conceptual Form of Mythical Thought," 133
    and Cassirer's *Individual and the Cosmos*, 244
    and Cassirer's philosophy of symbolic forms, 113
    and challenges of philosophy, 44, 53–54, 120–22, 123–24
    construction of house in Freiburg, 305–6, 313–14
    and Davos conference, 8–13, 15–18, 315, 321–30, 332–36
    on death and existential angst, 187–88, 234–40
    death of parents, 239–40, 305
    Duns Scotus work, 92–95
    financial difficulties, 46, 117–18, 124–25, 184–85
    first postwar lectures, 48–52
    health problems, 44–45
    inaugural lecture at Cambridge, 363
    Jaspers's relationship with, 119–20, 142
    on "liberation of philosophy," 314–15
    and Marburg School, 186–87
    marriage difficulties, 78–83, 225–26
    and metaphysical foundation of philosophy, 310–11

military service, 45
and National Socialism, 363
and nature of "character," 54
origins of Dasein concept, 51. *See also*
    Dasein
position offered at Marburg, 227–28, 240
positions at Freiburg, 9, 46–47, 49, 119, 305,
    313–15, 319, 363
and primal language, 99–101
"problem horizons," 78, 80, 81
and problem of progress, 359
religious conflicts, 45–47, 54
and study of equipment, 231–34
at Warburg Library, 177–79
and Wittgenstein's linguistic
    philosophy, 255
and Wittgenstein's "leap into faith," 161
and Wittgenstein's logical empiricism,
    274–76
and Wittgenstein's *Tractatus*, 252
See also Being and Time (Heidegger)
Heidelberg University, 142–43
Heisenberg, Werner, 250, 279–80
Hemingway, Ernest, 279
Herbertz, Richard, 20, 38
Herder, Johann Gottfried, 98
"Heretics" club, 360
Hesse, Hermann, 336
Hessel, Franz, 290
Hessischer Rundfunk, 337
heteroreference, 36–37
hieroglyphic writing, 72
Hindenburg, Paul von, 251, 301
Hirschfeld, Magnus, 42
History and Class Consciousness (Lukács), 223
"History of the Concept of Time"
    (Heidegger), 228
Hitler, Adolf, 185, 251, 323–24, 363–64
Hofmannsthal, Hugo von, 21, 68,
    292–93, 298
Hölderlin, Friedrich, 143
Horkheimer, Max, 209, 299, 351
Human Place in the Cosmos, The (Scheler), 15
human progress, 214
Humboldt, Wilhelm von, 98, 108, 335, 343
Hume, David, 6, 103
Husserl, Edmund
    and Benjamin's Duns Scotus work, 93
    and Benjamin's "Task of the Translator," 97
    and Davos conference, 329
    and Heidegger–Jaspers meeting, 119–20
    and Heidegger's academic career, 305
    and Heidegger's analysis of Dasein, 230, 234
    and Heidegger's first postwar lectures,
        48–49, 54
    and Heidegger's "problem horizons," 81
    influence on Heidegger in phenomenology,
        46–48
Hütte (Heidegger cabin in Black Forest), 118,
    120, 123, 231–34, 236, 306
hyperinflation, 167

Id, 82
"Idea for a Universal History with a
    Cosmopolitan Purpose" (Kant), 302–3
"Idea of Philosophy and the Worldview
    Problem, The" (Heidegger), 48
In Search of Lost Time (Proust), 225
indigenous cultures, 180–81
*Individual and the Cosmos in Renaissance
    Philosophy, The* (Cassirer), 242–50, 320
infinitude, 246, 311, 327–28, 330–32, 343–44,
    352–55
inflation, 138
Insel Verlag, 70
Institute of Social Research, 299
interdisciplinary research, 245

Jahoda, Ernst, 69
James, Henry, 329
James, William, 329
Jaspers, Karl
    and Arendt's doctoral work, 192
    and Benjamin's academic ambitions, 139,
        151–52
    and Benjamin's financial difficulties, 141–42
    and Bultmann, 186
    and Heidegger's *Being and Time*, 239–40
    Heidegger's correspondence with,
        123–25, 227
    Heidegger's friendship with, 118–19, 142, 186
    and Heidegger's study of equipment,
        231–34
    and status of Heidelberg University, 143

Jewish identity and theology, 24, 94, 210, 223, 291, 298–99
Jewish Messianism, 101–2
Jonas, Hans, 186
Joyce, James, 329

Kabbalah, 24, 94
Kafka, Franz, 251
Kahr, Gustav von, 185
Kant, Immanuel
  and Benjamin's method and worldview, 24–25
  and Cassirer's academic status, 298
  and Cassirer's Weimar Constitution address, 300, 302–3
  Copernican revolution of, 108
  and Davos conference, 12–16, 19–20, 320, 323–28, 330–32, 335–36
  epistemology, 211
  and evolution of Wittgenstein's philosophy, 355
  and metaphysical foundation of philosophy, 310–11
  and revolutionary sentiment, 343
  and subjectivity of "character," 56
  transcendental method of investigation, 15
  and Warburg Library, 129
  and Wittgenstein's doctoral thesis, 6
  and Wittgenstein's logical empiricism, 274
  and Wittgenstein's *Tractatus*, 252
"Kant and German Intellectual Life" (Cassirer), 105–6
Kant and the Problem of Metaphysics (Heidegger), 310, 335–36
Kant Society, 177–78, 323
Karplus, Gretel, 351
Kegan Paul (publisher), 156–57
Kepler, Johannes, 183, 241–42, 247
Kessler, Harry Graf, 348
Keynes, John Maynard
  and "Apostles" club, 4
  attempts to lure Wittgenstein to Cambridge, 166–77
  and Davos conference, 9

  and Ramsey, 172
  and Wittgenstein's return to Cambridge, 3
  and Wittgenstein's temper, 4
Kierkegaard, Søren
  and academic detachment, 103
  and Benjamin's analysis of Goethe, 152
  and Benjamin's "Epistemo-Critical Prologue," 217
  and Bultmann, 186
  and Heidegger's "leap," 51
  influence on Wittgenstein, 153
  and Wittgenstein's logical empiricism, 275
  and Wittgenstein's logical linguistic analysis, 43
King's College, Cambridge, 293
Klages, Ludwig, 55
Klee, Paul, 138
Klemperer, Victor, 348
Klibansky, Raymond, 325
Klimt, Gustav, 266
Koder, Rudolf, 161, 168, 251
Kracauer, Siegfried, 207–8, 223, 337–38, 347–49
Kraus, Karl, 68–69, 252, 265
Krebs, Engelbert, 44, 46
Krise und Kritik, 22
Krüger, Gerhard, 186
Kuki, Shūzō, Count, 125
Kulturwissenschaftliche Bibliothek Warburg (KBW), 241–42. *See also* Warburg Library
Kundmanngasse (teacher training institute; Wittgenstein house), 70, 267, 269–70, 271, 276
Kundt, Wilhelm, 261

Lacis, Asja
  and Benjamin's divorce, 364
  and Benjamin's *One-Way Street*, 278
  and Benjamin's time in Berlin, 18, 346–51
  and Benjamin's time on Capri, 198–200
  and Benjamin's time in Moscow, 225, 282–89
  breakdown, 282–85
  and conflicts in Benjamin's life, 26
  influence on Benjamin's thinking, 200–204

Lacis, Daga, 198, 200, 285
"ladder" of propositions (Wittgenstein), 6–7,
    74–76, 160, 221, 251
language and linguistic philosophy
    Benjamin on language after the fall, 217–20
    and Benjamin's Duns Scotus work, 93–95
    and Benjamin's "Epistemo-Critical
        Prologue," 210–12, 215–18, 221
    Benjamin's "pure language," 212–13
    and Benjamin's "Task of the Translator,"
        96–101
    and Cassirer's symbolic forms, 59, 112–14,
        293–94
    dilemmas of, 63–65
    and Freudian psychoanalysis, 69
    generative grammar, 112
    intended object of language, 98–99
    and logical empiricism, 354–55
    and mathematics, 97
    metaphorical language, 96, 270
    mode of meaning of language, 98–100
    natural language, 109, 114, 357
    and Ogden's *Meaning of Meaning*, 170–71
    and problem of progress, 359
    pure language, 99, 112
    true language, 99–100, 218
    and Wittgenstein's *Dictionary for Primary
        Schools*, 255–57
    and Wittgenstein's "ladder" of
        propositions, 76
    and Wittgenstein's "leap into faith," 160
    and Wittgenstein's logical empiricism, 276
    and Wittgenstein's logical symbolism, 63
    and Wittgenstein's *Philosophical
        Investigations*, 253–55, 357
    and Wittgenstein's *Tractatus*, 6, 67–68, 252
Law for the Restoration of the Professional
    Civil Service, 364
law of identity, 310
League of Nations, 303
League of Proletarian Writers, 346, 349
"Lecture on Serpent Ritual, A" (Warburg and
    Mainland), 180–81
Lederer, Emil, 139
Leibniz, Gottfried Wilhelm, 300, 301–2, 345
Lenin, Vladimir, 32, 167, 280
Leonardo da Vinci, 246, 248

Levinas, Emmanuel, 321, 335
liberal democracy, 343
Lindbergh, Charles, 244
Literarische Welt, 19, 290, 336–39
logic
    and Benjamin's "Task of the Translator,"
        97, 101–2
    logical empiricism, 271, 274, 354–55
    logical paradoxes, 73–74
    logical symbolism, 63
    and Wittgenstein's *Tractatus*, 158, 354
Logical Construction of the World, The
    (Carnap), 14
Loos, Adolf, 265
"Love and Saint Augustine" (Arendt), 192
Löwith, Karl, 186
Lukács, György, 143, 223
Luxemburg, Rosa, 59

Mabbott, John, 351–52
Mach, Ernst, 68, 252
magasins de nouveautés, 344
Magic Mountain, The (Mann), 12
Magnes, Judah Leon, 291–92, 336,
    346–47, 350
Mahler, Gustav, 68
Mann, Thomas, 12
manual labor, 231–34, 266
Marburg School, 57, 186–87
Marx, Karl, 203, 208, 280
Marxist politics, 24, 224. *See also* communism
materialism, 280
mathematics
    and Cassirer's *Individual and the
        Cosmos*, 247
    geometry, 241–42, 270
    and Kepler's ellipses, 183, 241–42
    mathematical philosophy of language, 97
    set theory, 73–74
    and Wittgenstein's logical empiricism, 276
    and Wittgenstein's *Tractatus*, 353
Mauthner, Fritz, 68
Maxims and Reflections (Goethe), vii
Meaning of Meaning, The (Ogden), 170
Meditations (Descartes), 65
Mein Kampf (Hitler), 251
Messianism, 101–2, 153, 223, 230

metaphorical language, 68, 96, 270

"Metaphysical Foundations of Logic, The"
(Heidegger), 310

metaphysics
and architectural design of Wittgenstein
house, 270
and Benjamin's Arcades Project, 292,
342, 345
and Benjamin's "Task of the Translator," 96
and Cassirer's philosophy, 106, 107
and Davos conference, 12–14, 16, 19,
323–24, 326–34, 335
and evolution of Wittgenstein's
philosophy, 353
and Heidegger's analysis of Dasein, 307
and Heidegger's Being and Time, 308–13
and revolutionary sentiment, 342
and subjectivity of "character," 55–56
and Vienna Circle, 271
and Wittgenstein's linguistic philosophy, 255
and Wittgenstein's logical empiricism,
274–75

Metropolis (film), 285

Mill, John Stuart, 103

Mnemosyne, 131

modernity, 203, 217, 242, 249, 270, 274

Monadology (Leibniz), 345

monetary reform, 174

Moore, G. E.
and evolution of Wittgenstein's
philosophy, 355
and Ramsey, 172
and Wittgenstein's doctoral examination,
3, 5, 7–8
and Wittgenstein's temper, 4
and Wittgenstein's Tractatus, 157

Moral Sciences Club, 360

morality, 41

mortality, 187–88. See also anxiety; existential
questions

Moscow, 282–88. See also Moscow Diary
(Benjamin)

Moscow Diary (Benjamin), 285–86

Münchhausen, Thankmar von, 290

Munich University, 322–23

"Muri" (invented educational institution), 32

Musil, Robert, 68

Mussolini, Benito, 185

mysticism, 166

Myth of the State, The (Cassirer), 364

myths and mythology
Benjamin's critique of bourgeois marriage,
144, 146–48, 150
and Cassirer's "Conceptual Form of
Mythical Thought," 132–34
and Cassirer's Individual and the
Cosmos, 247
and Cassirer's symbolic forms,
109–10, 126
and Heidegger's phenomenology, 178
and totemistic thinking, 135–36
and Warburg's theory of culture, 181–83
and Wittgenstein's "leap into faith," 161

Naphta, Leo, 12

Naples, 207, 208

Naples (Benjamin and Lacis), 202–3, 222–23

national languages, 98

National Socialist Party (Germany), 323,
338, 363

nationalism, 185

Natorp, Paul, 186, 227, 305

natural laws and science
and Cassirer's Individual and the Cosmos,
247, 249
and Cassirer's symbolic forms, 110
and Davos conference, 13, 14
and Heidegger's philosophical evolution,
50–51
and Heidegger's time in the cabin, 123
and Kepler's ellipses, 183, 241–42
natural selection, 14–15
and Wittgenstein's Tractatus, 158–59
See also Enlightenment era and ideals;
scientific worldview

nautical metaphors, 295

Nazism, 11, 323, 363

near-death experiences, 118–19

neo-Kantian philosophy, 10, 57, 186,
325–26

Neue Zürcher Zeitung, 335

Neurath, Otto, 271, 295

New York (ship), 294

Newtonian physics, 108

Nietzsche, Friedrich, 14–15, 103, 295
Novalis, 34

objectivity, 49–50, 56, 83
Ogden, Charles Kay, 168–70
Old Testament, 99
"On the Concept of History" (Benjamin), 364
"On the Essence of the Ground"
    (Heidegger), 310
"On European Reactions to German Culture"
    (Cassirer), 58
"On the Image of Proust" (Benjamin), 339
One Hundred Years of Solitude (García
    Márquez), 219
One-Way Street (Benjamin), 23, 225, 277–82,
    291, 336–37
ontology
    and Benjamin's One-Way Street, 280
    and Davos conference, 325–27
    and Heidegger's Being and Time, 228, 307–9
    and Heidegger's leap, 52
    and metaphysical foundation of philosophy,
        311–12
Origin of German Tragic Drama, The
    (Benjamin), 21, 24, 208, 214,
    225, 298
Orthodox Judaism, 136

Palais Wittgenstein, 68,
    266, 269
Palestine, 127, 135–36, 195, 199, 223, 225,
    345–46
Panofsky, Erwin, 21–22, 245, 298
Paris, 289–93
Paris Arcades. See Arcades Project, The
    (Benjamin)
Peace of Versailles, 167
peasant idiom, 231–33
Petri, Elfride, 46. See also Heidegger, Elfride
    (Petri)
"Phenomenological Interpretations of
    Aristotle—Indication of the
    Hermeneutic Situation" (Heidegger),
    120–22, 135, 144, 147, 227
phenomenology
    and Benjamin's "Task of the Translator," 97
    and Cartesian skepticism, 81

and Heidegger's analysis of Dasein, 233–34
and Heidegger's first postwar lectures, 48,
    49–51
and Husserl, 46
Philosophical Investigations (Wittgenstein),
    252–55, 357, 358
Philosophy of Symbolic Forms, The (Cassirer)
    and Cassirer's commute in Berlin, 59
    and Cassirer's Individual and the Cosmos,
        243, 249–50
    and Cassirer's travels by sea, 294–95
    completion of first volume, 126
    and Davos conference, 10, 16, 320,
        326, 332
    epistemological issues of, 111–12
    and free will, 246
    and natural languages, 108–10
    on "pure form of language," 112–14
physics, 14, 108, 110, 279
Pinsent, David, 166
Piscator, Erwin, 347, 348
Planck, Max, 279
Plato, 65, 242
poetry, 67–68, 101–2
Poetry and Truth (Goethe), 147
porosity concept, 202–4
Position of Man in the Cosmos, The (Scheler),
    319–20
positivism, 41
poverty, 42
practical influence of philosophy, 103
primitivism, 180–81
Principia Mathematica (Russell), 7
progress, 244–45
Proletarian Theatre Group, 346
Protestantism, 45, 186–87, 272
Proust, Marcel
    Benjamin's essays on, 338–39
    and Benjamin's method and worldview,
        22–23
    Benjamin's "On the Image of Proust,"
        339, 341
    and Benjamin's translation of works by, 204,
        225, 282, 284, 290
    and Davos conference, 329
    and Surrealism, 339
Pseudo-Problems in Philosophy (Carnap), 14

psychology, 69, 178, 229–30, 279
Psychology of Worldviews (Jaspers), 118–19
Puchberg, Austria, 165–66
Pueblo Indians, 181

quantum physics, 279

Radbruch, Gustav, 143
Ramsey, Frank, 168–69, 172–73,
　352, 355
Rang, Florens Christian, 193–96
rational marriage, 148
realism, 340
reality of the environment, 85–87
Red Front, 349
refugee crisis, 184
Reich, Bernhard, 200, 204, 282–89,
　346, 348
relativity, theory of, 14, 112
religion
　and Cassirer's symbolic forms, 109–10
　and Heidegger's existential leap, 152
　and problem of progress, 360
　Wittgenstein's Catholicism, 154–56
　and Wittgenstein's *Tractatus*, 159
　See also Catholicism; Christianity;
　　Protestantism
Renaissance, 183, 242–50
Rickert, Heinrich, 22, 93, 326
Riezler, Kurt, 298, 319
Rilke, Rainer Maria, 69–70
Rimbaud, Arthur, 340
Ritter, Joachim, 245, 321
Romanticism, 37, 53
Rosenberg, Alfred, 323
Rowohlt Verlag, 224–25, 281–82, 292,
　336–38
Russell, Bertrand
　barber paradox, 73–74
　and mathematical and poetic
　　language, 68
　and publication of Wittgenstein's *Tractatus*,
　　156–57
　and Ramsey, 172
　support for Wittgenstein, 39, 71–76
　and Wittgenstein's doctoral work, 3,
　　5–8, 352

and Wittgenstein's "ladder" of propositions,
　74–76
and Wittgenstein's logical empiricism, 275
and Wittgenstein's logical symbolism, 63
and Wittgenstein's misanthropy, 156, 166
and Wittgenstein's religious evolution, 155
and Wittgenstein's struggle with existential
　problems, 66
Russian cinema, 348–49
Russian Revolution, 32. *See also* Duma
　Revolution (1905)

Safranski, Rüdiger, 192–93
Salomon, Gottfried, 21, 193–95, 222
Saxl, Fritz, 128, 131–32, 180, 182, 245
Saxony, 185
Scheler, Max, 15, 103–4, 319–20
Schelling, Friedrich Wilhelm Joseph, 24, 35
Schiller, Friedrich, 332
schizophrenia, 179–80
Schlick, Moritz, 270–73, 275, 321,
　352–55
Schoenflies, Arthur Moritz, 193–94
scholasticism, 244
Scholem, Gershom (Gerhard)
　and Benjamin's Arcades Project, 291–92
　Benjamin's correspondence with, 33–34,
　　89–90, 92–94, 199–200, 209–10,
　　291–93, 336, 345–46, 350–51
　and Benjamin's military service evasion,
　　31–32
　and Benjamin's plans for journal, 138
　and Benjamin's relationship with Lacis,
　　26–27, 225
　emigration to Palestine, 195, 223
　and grant paid to Benjamin,
　　346–47
Schön, Erich, 143
Schopenhauer, Arthur, 275
Schultz, Franz, 194, 195, 209
scientific worldview
　and Cassirer's *Individual and the Cosmos*,
　　242–50
　and Heidegger's phenomenology, 178
　and influence of Wittgenstein's *Tractatus*,
　　171–72
　and Kepler's ellipses, 241–42

and logical analysis, 41
and mythical thinking, 136–37
and physics, 14, 108, 110, 279
and Wittgenstein's *Tractatus*,
    158, 159
See also Enlightenment era and ideals;
    natural laws and science
Scientific Worldview: The Vienna Circle, The,
    352–53
Sein questions, 52. *See also* Dasein
"Self-Assertion of the German University,
    The" (Heidegger), 363
senses and sensory experience, 59, 107, 109,
    123. *See also* empiricism
set theory, 73–74
Settembrini, Lodovico, 12
Sex and Character (Weininger), 69
"Shadow" (Arendt), 189
signs, making and using, 16. *See also* symbols
    and symbolic expressions
Silesian School, 194
skepticism, 103
Social Democrats, 251, 258
Socrates, 103
Sohn-Rethel, Alfred, 208, 223
"Some Notes on Logical Form"
    (Wittgenstein), 352
Sophist (Plato), 227
Soviet Union, 167. *See also* communism;
    Duma Revolution (1905); Moscow;
    Russian Revolution
Spann, Othmar, 322–23
Spartacist uprising, 59
speech
    and Benjamin's "Epistemo-Critical
        Prologue," 215
    and Benjamin's "Task of the Translator,"
        99–101
    and primal language, 99–101
    See also language and linguistic
        philosophy
"Speech and Logos" (Benjamin), 95
Spengler, Oswald, 48, 55
Spinoza, Baruch, 6, 103, 157
Sraffa, Piero, 356–57
Stalin, Joseph, 251, 284
Stein, Gertrude, 279

Stern, William, 60, 293
Sterne, Laurence, 281
Stonborough, Jerome, 266
Stonborough-Wittgenstein, Margarethe
    ("Gretl"), 266–67, 269, 271
Strachey, Lytton, 168
Strauss, Leo, 186, 348
Stresemann, Gustav, 185, 302
"Sturm und Drang," 149
Sturmabteilung (SA), 349
subject–object dualism, 82–84, 311
subjectivity, 41, 55–56, 66–67
suicide, 42–44, 65, 238, 265, 281, 364
Surrealism, 339–40
"Surrealism: The Last Snapshot of the
    European Intelligentsia"
    (Benjamin), 339
Switzerland, 92
symbols and symbolic expressions
    abstract symbolism, 67–68
    and Benjamin's analysis of Goethe, 147
    and Benjamin's "Epistemo-Critical
        Prologue," 215–16, 219
    and Benjamin's method and worldview,
        23, 25
    and Benjamin's "pure language," 213
    and Cassirer's "Conceptual Form of
        Mythical Thought," 137
    and Cassirer's *Individual and the Cosmos*,
        243–44, 246–47, 249–50
    and Cassirer's *Philosophy of Symbolic Forms*,
        293–94
    and Cassirer's symbolic forms, 10, 16,
        59, 107–13, 126, 129–30, 182,
        293–96, 320
    and Davos conference, 326, 332, 343
    and geometry in Warburg's philosophy, 241
    and Heidegger's analysis of Dasein, 309
    and Heidegger's phenomenology, 178
    and logical empiricism, 354–55
    and Neapolitan culture, 201
    and Warburg's theory of culture, 131–32,
        180–81
    and Wittgenstein's logical symbolism, 59,
        67–68
    and Wittgenstein's *Philosophical
        Investigations*, 357

Tableaux parisiens (Baudelaire), 95

Tagore, Rabindranath, 272–73

"Task of the Translator, The" (Benjamin), 95, 96, 138

"Tasks and Paths of Phenomenological Research" (Heidegger), 178

taxonomic systems, 130–31

technology, critique of, 87

teleology, 15

terminology, 97–98

theology, 99–102. *See also* religion; *specific religions*

Theory of Color (Goethe), 55

theory of relativity, 14, 112

thought-pictures, 222–23, 280, 283, 291, 358

Threepenny Opera, The (Brecht), 338

Thuringia, 185

Timaeus (Plato), 242

Tolstoy, Leo, 39–40, 43, 153, 275

Torah, 94

totems, 133–35

Tractatus logico-philosophicus (Wittgenstein)

  and architectural design of Wittgenstein house, 269–70

  and Benjamin's "spiritual essence," 213

  and Cassirer's *Individual and the Cosmos*, 250

  and "closed window" metaphor, 67

  and evolution of Wittgenstein's philosophy, 353–54

  foreword, 40

  and Heidegger's analysis of Dasein, 230

  influence at Cambridge, 4

  and Kant's metaphysics, 13

  "ladder" of propositions, 6–7, 74–76, 160, 221, 251

  and "leap into faith," 160–61

  philosophical origins of, 251–52

  and pictures/propositions, 72

  and problem of progress, 359–60

  publication of, 156–57

  and Wittgenstein's correspondence with Keynes, 168–72

  and Wittgenstein's *Dictionary for Primary Schools*, 259

  and Wittgenstein's doctoral examination, 5–8

Tractatus theologico-politicus (Spinoza), 157

transcendence, 152–53, 228, 280, 328

Transcendence of the Objective and the Noematic in Husserl's Phenomenology, The (Adorno), 208

translation

  by Benjamin, 22, 33, 95–96, 102, 120, 137–38, 204, 210, 222, 225, 282, 290

  and Benjamin's "Task of the Translator," 96–101

  and Cassirer's "Conceptual Form of Mythical Thought," 134

Trattenbach, Austria, 155–56

Trauerspiel, 212, 219. *See also Origin of German Tragic Drama, The* (Benjamin)

trauma, 119

Treaty of Versailles, 123, 167, 174, 301

trench warfare, 45

Trial, The (Kafka), 251

Tristram Shandy (Sterne), 281

Trotsky, Leon, 284

true names (true language), for Benjamin, 99

Tzara, Tristan, 32

Ulyanov, Vladimir Ilyich (Vladimir Lenin), 32, 167, 280

uncertainty principle, 250

United States, 57, 195

Vienna, 39, 68–71, 295

Vienna Circle, 171–72, 270–77, 313, 354

Vienna University, 270

vocation, 51

Vossische Zeitung, 336

Wagner, Richard, 136–37

Waismann, Friedrich, 271, 352–55

Wall Street crash of 1929, 27

Warburg, Abraham ("Aby")

  and Cassirer's address on Weimar Constitution, 304

  and Cassirer's career, 297–98

  and Cassirer's *Individual and the Cosmos*, 245

death, 364
and Kepler's ellipses, 241–42
and origins of Warburg Library, 128–29
psychiatric treatment, 179–80
return to library, 183–84
theory of culture, 180–84
Warburg, Mary (Hertz), 182
Warburg Library, 128–32, 177–79, 241–42, 245–47
Warburg School, 21–22
Weber, Alfred, 139, 142–43
Weber, Max, 142–43
Weigel, Helene, 338
Weimar Constitution, 299, 300–304
Weimar Republic, 105, 142–44, 146, 150, 153, 299
Weininger, Otto, 55, 69
Weissbach, Richard, 95, 137–38, 197
Western metaphysics, 311. *See also* metaphysics
Whitehead, Alfred North, 329
"Why Hamburg Must Not Lose the Philosopher Ernst Cassirer" (Warburg), 297
Why I Am Not a Christian (Russell), 155
Wilhelm II, Kaiser, 71
Wind, Edgar, 245
Winterhude district (Hamburg), 60, 104, 112
Wittgenstein, Helene, 39
Wittgenstein, Hermine ("Mining"), 39, 42, 63–64, 66, 162, 266, 268–69
Wittgenstein, Johannes, 42
Wittgenstein, Kurt, 42
Wittgenstein, Ludwig ("Luki")
abandonment of family fortune, 38–39, 40–42, 63
and academic detachment, 104
and architectural design, 266–71, 276
Aristotelian Society address, 352–53
and Benjamin's critique of bourgeois marriage, 144
and Benjamin's "Epistemo-Critical Prologue," 218
and Benjamin's "spiritual essence," 213
and Cartesian skepticism, 77–78, 85–86
and Cassirer's philosophy of symbolic forms, 113
and Catholicism, 153, 154–56
and challenges of postwar philosophy, 53, 64
and "closed window" metaphor, 64–67, 78–79, 80, 86, 162
correspondence with Keynes, 166–73
death of mother, 265–66
Dictionary for Primary Schools, 255–57, 258
and dilemmas of linguistic philosophy, 63–65
discussions with Russell, 71–76
doctoral examination, 3, 5–8
emotional struggles, 4, 64–65, 265–66
and epistemology problem, 66–67
and "Haidbauer incident," 259–61
and Heidegger's analysis of Dasein, 229–31
and Heidegger's *Being and Time,* 313
and Kant's metaphysics, 13
"ladder" of propositions, 6–7, 74–76, 160, 221, 251
and "leap into faith," 159–62
and mathematical and poetic language, 67–68
military service, 39–40, 43
misanthropy and isolation of, 156–57, 162, 165–66, 172
and nature of "character," 54
and *Philosophical Investigations,* 356–57, 358–59
and philosophy's relationship to natural sciences, 50–51
and political upheavals of 1920s, 250–51
and primal language, 99–101
and problem of progress, 359–61
return to Cambridge, 3–5, 364–65
and Russell's barber paradox, 73–74
sexuality, 70
teaching method, 257–59
Tractatus completion, 4
and *Tractatus* meaning, 40–41
and *Tractatus* objective, 157–59
Tractatus publication attempts, 69–70
and Vienna Circle, 270–77

Wittgenstein, Margarete. *See* Stonborough-Wittgenstein, Margarethe ("Gretl")
Wittgenstein, Paul, 39, 42–43
Wittgenstein, Rudolf, 42
Wolf, Christian, 302
woodworking, 231–33
Woolf, Leonard, 168, 356
Woolf, Virginia, 168, 329, 356
World War I
   and Benjamin's career, 31–32
   and Cassirer's view of "character," 55
   and Cassirer's Weimar Constitution address, 300

challenges of postwar philosophy, 53
as failure of metaphysics, 56
impact on Enlightenment ideals, 15
and Jaspers's *Psychology of Worldviews*, 119
"worlding" environment, 86
worldview philosophy (*Weltanschauungsphilosophie*), 48, 49–51, 309. *See also* empiricism; scientific worldview

Zeug (equipment), 231–34
Zum Kater Hiddigeigei (Tomcat Hiddigeigei café), 198–99